Beyond D&I

Kay Formanek

Beyond D&I

Leading Diversity with Purpose
and Inclusiveness

Kay Formanek
Diversity and Performance
Loosdrecht, Noord-Holland
The Netherlands

ISBN 978-3-030-75335-1   ISBN 978-3-030-75336-8   (eBook)
https://doi.org/10.1007/978-3-030-75336-8

Cover credit: @eStudioCalamar

This Palgrave Macmillan imprint is published by the registered company Springer Nature Switzerland AG
The registered company address is: Gewerbestrasse 11, 6330 Cham, Switzerland

Thanking my children

Isabel

Jayme   Joya

for their daily inspiration and their loving support

Foreword

Equity, diversity, and inclusion must move to the heart of business leadership. Business leaders of today are faced with ever more global, complex, and interrelated challenges such as climate change, digitalization, and increasing demands for transparency. The role of business and its leaders in society was already changing from observer to participant in realizing the United Nation's Agenda 2030. And now the COVID-19 pandemic and social justice movements including Black Lives Matter and #MeToo, have laid bare longstanding inequalities that demand to be addressed.

The vast majority of employees, customers, investors, and suppliers around the world want their voices to be heard and for business leaders to take their views into account. Not least, this includes the youngest generations. They are demanding that attention be paid to equity, diversity, and inclusion. To address the challenges ahead, leaders need to engage with the full 360-degree richness, power, and commitment of all their stakeholders across industry value chains and beyond.

If business leaders want to play their role in addressing these challenges, "Diversity & Inclusion" must move from a nice-to-have value to a core capability at the heart of their organization and purpose. Yet D&I is still approached by many business leaders as a side-pillar in their leadership tasks. At a minimum, it is there to ensure that their organization obeys the law and minimizes the risks of non-compliance. In some organizations, the Human Resources leadership has started to develop a more systematic approach to D&I by organizing events, training, and creating specific functions. A few leaders have gone further, convinced that D&I is a key leadership attribute and they are vocal about the importance it holds for them. But too often, these leaders observe how good intentions and promising initiatives become gradually but surely diluted and eventually lost in the web of their large and complex organizations.

Kay Formanek, the author of this book, has all the experience and insights required to change the D&I conversation and guide leaders on this journey of transformation. She experienced the power of diversity and inclusion from her youth, growing up in South Africa and witnessing its transformation firsthand. This experience grounded her in her conviction of the very special force that inclusive leaders such as Nelson Mandela exercise in transformation. Her understanding of the importance of robust operational mechanisms to support D&I was honed during her 20-year professional career in a global consulting organization, where she deepened her knowledge and passion for D&I, and was instrumental in developing D&I initiatives within that organization. Advising and helping business leaders transform their organizations during that period also ensures that she never loses sight of what constitutes a feasible and pragmatic change track.

Within the framework of her own company, Diversity and Performance, Kay has spent the last six years undertaking extensive study and research in the areas of equity, diversity, and inclusion, collaborating with multiple organizations to develop and test her thoughts. Kay and I have collaborated for over two decades as executive consulting colleagues and D&I practitioners since the creation of her company.

This book is the result of that journey and brings it all together: her passion, knowledge, experience, and skills are drivers for the innovative approach to D&I that it presents. In it, Kay provides the tools and insights to ensure that actions can be put in place that actually deliver the desired results. Her direct interaction with corporate business leaders has provided her with the right skills to assist them in the development of their inclusive leadership skills.

I believe this book delivers true innovation in the areas of diversity, inclusion, and purposeful leadership. It makes a very strong case for why embedding these concepts at the heart and gut of any organization is now crucial for business leaders. It provides an innovative, strategic framework that leaders can apply to develop a clear strategic narrative for diversity, inclusion, equity, leadership, and purpose in their organizations.

The models presented in the book have strong validity since they are built on numerous research findings in this area and have been tried and tested by industry. A number of practical diagnostic tools are also included for managing the diversity and inclusion journey in a purposeful way, accompanied by multiple examples from the field, that effectively illustrate the challenges ahead and the hurdles which may arise on the journey. Equipped with the Virtuous Circle and Integrated Diversity Models, leaders now have a holistic and proven approach for developing and steering their overall transformation program.

Last but not least, this book enables you, as leaders, to have robust conversations about diversity, inclusion, and equity with all your stakeholders: the Board, Executive Committee, external stakeholders, and first and foremost your key asset: your colleagues throughout the organization.

Brussels, Belgium   Dirk Luyten
                                                  INSEAD Women in Business Alumni Global Club
                                                                  Member of the Exco and Supporter
                                                                            INSEAD Gender Initiative

Preface

This book has been inspired by the rich diversity that has shaped my personal and professional journeys. It is a journey that started in South Africa in the 1960s leading me to work globally over the last 25 years with some 50 organizations as they transformed their business and their culture through diversity performance.

I have learned that our present approach to diversity must fundamentally change: it must be strategic, it needs to be anchored in organizational transformation and it needs to meld both the art and the science of diversity if we are to meet the challenges of the future. I have also learned that advancing diversity is dependent on the personal commitment and conviction of courageous leaders.

I sometimes say to the leaders of organizations I advise and the students I teach, that I did not choose a career in diversity—diversity chose me. Born in the late 1960s to parents who had emigrated from Austria to South Africa, I grew up in the shadow of apartheid during a watershed period in that country's struggle for equality and inclusion. Just before I was born, Black South African schoolchildren had taken to the streets to protest apartheid policies, only to meet violent government reprisals in the Sharpeville killings. Nelson Mandela, leader of the African National Congress (ANC) had been sentenced to life imprisonment, and the ANC banned. Then 1976 saw the Soweto Riots and a state of emergency declared by the government in 1984. But by 1990, the inexorable march of progress led to the ANC being unbanned and Mandela was released from prison. The first multiracial elections took place in 1994, and two years later, the Truth and Reconciliation Commission was formed.

Growing up in a country that had legalized discrimination shaped me and led me to reflect on the complex, interconnected issues of diversity, inclusiveness, and leadership at play within organizations and the broader societies of which they are a part. From my parents, I learned from an early age to question those assumptions. They regularly challenged me and my only sibling, my late sister Celine, in heated debates about the events that were taking place around us. Celine, a brilliant lawyer and poet, invariably won the debates and also taught me that the way society sees you defines your access to opportunities. Her premature birth had led to a walking impairment and her "disability" created a smaller world for her. She certainly did not want pity or special favors—all she wanted was a fair chance to exercise her talents.

The importance of inclusiveness was a key insight reinforced at the multiracial girls' boarding school I attended in Johannesburg. The school's motto, *Franc ha Leal*, free and loyal, was understood to mean *privilege* and *responsibility*, concepts that go hand-in-hand. Outside the school, stereotypes and enforced segregation on the basis of race permeated daily life, but inside the school grounds, the closely knit group of diverse students were your family. This meant moving beyond the differences in color or background or culture and finding those strands of humanity that connect us. In a place of learning and safety, it was easy to find those connections.

Commencing my working career in the years before Nelson Mandela was released from prison, I observed firsthand how a homogenous (mostly male and white) organization had to transform in step with the wider societal shift taking place as South Africa moved to a post-apartheid system of government. I realized that organizations must align their diversity approach with their environment and the growing stakeholder voices pressing for inclusion and leadership.

When I moved to the Netherlands some twenty years ago, I experienced for the first time what it feels like to be a stranger in a foreign culture and I felt an intense yearning to belong. As an outsider, I confronted this feeling on multiple levels—as a new resident speaking a different language, as a female senior executive in a mainly male-dominated work environment, and as a full-time working mother in a society where the caretaker role of women is deeply ingrained. I realized that belonging is a powerful survival need and that feeling excluded hurts to the core. I also learned how one's own authenticity can be compromised when trying too hard to belong.

As well as experiencing transformation on a personal level, it was a central focus of my day-to-day work. As a Partner and sponsor for many D&I initiatives at one of the largest management consulting organizations in the world, I was overseeing the transformation of many life science firms as they aspired to become patient-centric enterprises. I witnessed the validity and legitimacy of the leadership mantra that to transform an organization, you must transform the culture and to transform a culture you must transform the person—and that without leadership, all transformation is difficult to achieve.

That led me, after 25 years in management consulting, to make diversity the anchor point of my work. In 2014, I founded Diversity & Performance, an organization committed to realizing the benefits of diversity and creating the conditions for inclusiveness through strategic leadership. The first step was to design a strategic diversity leadership approach that would deliver performance outcomes, while recognizing the unique context and diversity maturity of each organization. The second step was to validate this approach through research and real-life application in organizations.

This vision led to a rich collaborative partnership with business schools, leaders of organizations, and diversity practitioners to develop a strategic approach to diversity performance leadership. A Diversity Leadership Certification was established and leaders from around the world were invited to learn about and challenge the approach and supporting models, and apply them in their organizations.

This process of ongoing dialogue and continuous improvement enriched the models, delivered many lasting diversity outcomes, and built deep friendships with key collaborators.

Beyond D&I has been written to share this strategic approach for leading diversity with a wider audience. This book sets out the critical future role diversity will play for all organizations, whether in Singapore, London, Johannesburg, Dubai, or any other place in the world. It makes the case for moving from diversity as a tick-box exercise to incorporating it into the very essence of the organizational transformation journey. It argues that courageous leaders who are personally vested in their organizations' diversity journeys are the most powerful catalysts for transformation. To help them, it sets out five key elements of diversity performance, underpinned by core capabilities that make diversity performance possible. Through a structured, evidence-based approach, the book equips these leaders to move forward with confidence, and a clear roadmap, to transform their organizations for the better.

Finally, this book was also written with an eye to the future generation, who are demanding a more just and equitable world. Beyond D&I gives voice to them and the issues they care about. It is a generation that is deeply aware of inequities and wants organizations to be part of the solution. As I wrote this book, as a mother of three teenage children amid COVID-19 lockdowns, I witnessed the resilience and adaptability of this younger generation. They are more vocal, more connected, more demanding of themselves and others and they hold high expectations of organizations and their leaders.

It is my hope that this book will support those leaders in meeting these expectations. With the guidance contained in these pages, they can progress diversity with courage and conviction to unleash the performance that is present in each organization, just waiting for the right conditions. My children and their peers will soon be the customers, employees, owners, suppliers, regulators, and partners of these organizations. Leaders should foster now the vibrant diversity these future stakeholders expect, not only to support performance but to create a more sustainable and inclusive world.

Loosdrecht, The Netherlands   Kay Formanek

Acknowledgments

I like to describe this book as my fourth child because writing it has been filled with the wonder of a parent-to-be. The journey began with a dream—to share my passion for advancing diversity in organizations and in society and to equip leaders with a proven and evidence-based approach to lead diversity strategically. Then came the writing of the book, the many months of seeing it grow and preparing for its arrival in the world. I gathered around me a team of "guardians" for the child, a group of diverse peer reviewers representing the rich diversity of culture, specialization, and viewpoints that are all so important to diversity. They are leaders and practitioners of diversity in both public and private organizations, researchers, academics, and clients. This team also included family members, my editorial production team, Palgrave Macmillan, and inspiring clients and supporters along the way.

This book would not have been possible without them.

Thank you to Dirk Luyten for his consistent and inspiring support of my work over the last 25 years, for the co-development of so many models in this book and for having walked together the journey of the book.

Thank you to all my peer reviewers, who so diligently read the manuscripts, over and over again and imbued their wisdom in the book: Carin Beumer, Clarissa Cortland, Edwin Smelt, Els Houtman, Emmely Pieternelle, Ernst Dekker, Fred Formanek, Grant Hazell, Hans Lagaaij, Jan van Nieuwenhuizen, Leslie Bergman, Lionel Frankfort, Michele Ozumba, Tina Eboka, and Titi van der Poel.

Thank you to two outstanding editors, Amy Brown and Andrea Spencer-Cooke, who brought their own diversity to the process of editing the book, with countless suggestions and ideas, allowing my voice to be heard. And to Liz Barlow, from Palgrave Macmillan who has been an exemplary guardian-editor to the book.

Thank you to Arnoud van den Heuvel, who has brought the writing to life with the colorful models and images that fill the pages of this book.

This team represents the diversity that I write about: a rainbow of cultures, nationalities, genders, and professional backgrounds. As I have many times in my career, I once again witnessed the power of a team of diverse and critical voices to translate a set of ideas and concepts into enriched insights.

This book would not have been possible if it was not for the leaders of organizations that I worked with. It was in their organizations where ideas turned into proven concepts and where their dialogue and debate crafted the principles underpinning this strategic roadmap for diversity.

With humbleness, I acknowledge with all my heart the role that my upbringing in South Africa had on my writing of this book. I have not come across a greater leader of diversity than Nelson Rolihlahla Mandela, Madiba to many. Not only is Mandela regarded as one of the greatest political leaders in the past century, personifying moral authority around the world, but he also represents to me every single quality of an inclusive leader: courage, collaboration, personal conviction, deep listening, driving inclusiveness forward personally, and inspiring support.

I thank my friends who have supported me each day and have embraced the complete me. I thank my sister Celine, for having inspired me to stretch my writing wings and translate ideas into words. I thank my mother Gigi Formanek for not only her steadfast support of my writing but also her critical eye and her valuable comments on the various scripts of the book. And I thank my father Harry Formanek for instilling a deep desire for knowledge and science in me at an early age.

Finally, I would like to thank my immediate family for their steady support of my work over these many years and for providing me the space to follow my heart and write this book. Having a home base was so very important and reassuring. Having a heads-down mother during COVID-19 required resilience and maturity from my children, Isabel, Jayme, and Joya. They remind me every day why there is a "Beyond the D&I" of today and why it is so important for leaders to stride forward with courage and conviction to create the conditions for inclusiveness and contribute to a more sustainable world.

Contents

About the Author

Kay Formanek is a global speaker on Diversity and Inclusion, visiting lecturer at leading business schools and Founder of Diversity and Performance, which is committed to unleashing the power of Diversity Performance within profit and not-for-profit organizations around the world. Within this role, Kay offers advisory and research services, including coaching for inclusive and strategic diversity leaders. She has also worked for leading global professional services organizations for over 25 years as Partner and Managing Director, actively supporting their D&I strategy realization. Her proven approach to leading diversity strategically draws on extensive research and advisory work with over 50 organizations.

About Diversity and Performance

Diversity and Performance is committed to unleashing the power of Diversity Performance within profit and not-for-profit organizations around the world. It offers advisory and research services, including coaching for inclusive and strategic diversity leaders.

A proven and validated methodology is leveraged to identify the Diversity and Performance gap of the organization (through the Virtuous Circle) and close the Capability Gap (through the Integrated Diversity Model).

Diversity and Performance also delivers "Leading Diversity Strategically for Performance" Certification for diversity leaders.

List of Figures

List of Tables

Book Overview

OVERVIEW

Chapter 1

Introduction

WHY

Chapter 2

Why do organizations need to pursue diversity?

WHAT

Chapter 3

What are the elements of diversity performance and how are they defined?

Chapter 4

What is my ambition level for diversity performance and how does my current diversity performance compare?

Chapter 5

What initiatives and capabilities do I need to deliver my desired level of diversity performance?

HOW

Chapter 6

How do I mitigate personal and systemic bias within my organization?

Chapter 7

How do I build the case for diversity and investment in diversity performance?

Chapter 8

How do I embed inclusiveness into the culture and daily behaviors of the organization?

Chapter 9

How do I select and apply policies that provide value and support daily practices?

Chapter 10

How do I measure diversity performance?

Chapter 11

How do I re-energize the diversity journey and keep it relevant?

SYNTHESIS

Chapter 12

Summarizing the WHY, the WHAT and the HOW

Introduction: A New Narrative for Diversity

1

The script on diversity and inclusion (D&I) is fundamentally changing. A collective shift is underway in what it means to create value in society and this is reframing how organizational success is defined and achieved. Against this backdrop, leaders of organizations must re-evaluate how they lead diversity—more courageously and inclusively.

The year 2020 will be remembered as the moment the diversity tide turned, catapulting it into a new role as a leading character on the stage of organizational transformation. George Floyd's murder in police custody sparked worldwide uproar over systemic racial bias. "There is a George Floyd in every country" and "I can't breathe" became a war cry against law enforcement-related brutality, fanned by social media from Minneapolis to Melbourne. In just a matter of weeks, the #BlackLivesMatter hashtag appeared 47.8 million times on Twitter.[1] Disgraced Hollywood mogul Harvey Weinstein was indicted, convicted and sentenced to prison for rape and sexual assault.[2] From Turkey to Tehran, global activists continued to call time on sexual harassment and abuse by sharing the viral #MeToo hashtag.

The rapidity with which these grassroots social justice movements gathered pace has caught many leaders off-guard. But it is a re-writing of the script that has been in the making for many years, as people increasingly shine a light on inequality and raise awareness of pronounced parity gaps in society along racial, gender and other lines.

2020 also marked some progress, with the Global Gender Gap Report concluding gender parity in education had been fully achieved in 40 of 153 countries

---

[1] Monica Anderson et al. (2020).

[2] "#MeToo: A Timeline of Events," February 4, 2021, https://www.chicagotribune.com/lifestyles/ct-me-too-timeline-20171208-htmlstory.html.

© Diversity and Performance BV 2021
K. Formanek, *Beyond D&I*, https://doi.org/10.1007/978-3-030-75336-8_1

ranked, predicting that full education parity could be achieved within 12 years.[3] But progress remains too slow: it will take 95 years to close the gender gap in political representation, with women holding only 25.2% of parliamentary (lower-house) seats and 21.2% of ministerial positions in 2019.[4] Progress for Black people, ethnic minorities, the LGBTQI+community and people with disabilities has been slower still. The persistent wealth gap attributed to racial discrimination and institutional racism is a global phenomenon, and persons with disabilities and LGBTQI+individuals alike continue to face pronounced disparities in the labor force.

Now the fallout of the COVID-19 pandemic risks undermining further the gains that have been made.[5] Minority groups across the board have been hardest hit by the effects of the pandemic and the ensuing economic downturn. Coronavirus has laid bare entrenched inequity in our world, from access to healthcare, to employment and opportunity. Minorities have been the most affected by job loss or furloughs and people of color have suffered more in terms of health and mortality. There are real fears that many of the diversity advances made over the last couple of decades have been washed away as a result of the pandemic.

The disruption of COVID-19 provides an important opportunity for a reset. The pandemic has peeled back the veneer on diversity progress, revealing parity gaps that continue to limit organizations' talent pools. In doing so, however, it presents a valuable opportunity for leaders to fundamentally re-shape their approach to diversity.

1   Inclusive Leadership: Understanding Stakeholder Expectations

Turning the tide on diversity requires a strategic response from leaders—not lip service, but a clear narrative for how their organization is responding and what their role will be on the diversity stage.

The rising calls for organizations to take a stand can sit uncomfortably with commercial entities who still see their role as existing solely to advance shareholder profit, but this mantra, first put forward by Nobel Prize-winning economist Milton Friedman in the 1970s, is now being retired.[6] Instead the role of commercial entities in advancing broader stakeholder value imperatives—described

---

[3] "Mind the 100 Year Gap, the 2020 World Economic Forum Global Gender Gap Report," 2020, December 16, 2019, https://www.weforum.org/reports/gender-gap-2020-report-100-years-pay-equality.

[4] "Mind the 100 Year Gap, the 2020 World Economic Forum Global Gender Gap Report," 2020.

[5] "Edelman Trust Barometer 2021," https://www.edelman.com/sites/g/files/aatuss191/files/2021-01/2021-edelman-trust-barometer.pdf.

[6] Friedman (1970).

as some by stakeholder capitalism—has been building for several years, first in Europe and then more widely. It reached a tipping point in 2019 when the influential Business Roundtable, representing 181 CEOs of major U.S. companies, released a new statement on the purpose of a corporation, stating that customers, employees, suppliers, communities, and shareholders should be prioritized equally.[7]

In this new era of stakeholder value, maximizing shareholder profit is no longer considered a corporation's sole responsibility. Instead, creating value for all stakeholders is the new organizational mandate. Stakeholders—customers, consumers, employees, citizens—expect institutions to step up and do their part to address the daunting global social and environmental challenges we face, not least growing inequity. And as #MeToo and #BLM show, they are making their voices heard loud and clear.[8]

This rallying cry for change is loudest among Generation Z (Gen Z), who will soon eclipse Millennials as the most populous generation on earth—more than one-third of the world's population.[9] Gen Zers are the most connected and ethnically and racially diverse generation,[10] and they are calling for a more equitable and sustainable world. This matters to the strategic leader, because it is Gen Z who will soon make up the majority of voters, citizens, consumers and the future global talent pool.

The priorities embraced by Gen Z are also being advanced on the global stage through the United Nations 2030 Agenda. This ambitious global roadmap sets out 17 Sustainable Development Goals (SDGs) with a cross-cutting commitment to "leave no one behind" and target support toward vulnerable populations first. Equity is a central theme throughout Agenda 2030, and it includes a standalone goal to achieve "Reduced Inequalities" both within and between countries. In spite of pockets of "progress," SDG10 is considered to be one of the goals most unlikely to be met and inequalities are actually growing in most countries, not shrinking.

Tackling complex challenges such as inequality isn't the responsibility of any single institution, whether public or private, global or local. All organizations have a role to play in driving progress on the SDGs. To ensure they are aligned with stakeholder expectations, leaders can use the blueprint of the 2030 Agenda as a roadmap not only for how they run their organizations, but how they create value for society going forward.

---

[7] "Business Roundtable Redefines the Purpose of a Corporation to Promote 'An Economy That Serves All Americans'," Business Roundtable, August 19, 2019, https://www.businessroundtable. org/business-roundtable-redefines-the-purpose-of-a-corporation-to-promote-an-economy-that-serves-all-americans.

[8] Crawford et al. (2019).

[9] Welcome to Generation Z, Deloitte, accessed February 3, 2020.

[10] Fry and Parker (2018).

2   Inclusive Organizations Perform Better

A growing number of leaders recognize the stakeholder imperative for greater diversity and deeper inclusion, and many have undertaken D&I initiatives to make their organizations more inclusive. There are many drivers for this: as well as satisfying and anticipating increasing D&I regulation and compliance requirements for diversity characteristics, diversity of thought and skillsets help to support performance objectives and create the conditions for the organization to respond with greater agility and creativity in a fast-changing environment.

When organizations get diversity right—and as explained below this is unfortunately not often the case—tangible value is created. Research by McKinsey found that over the past five years the likelihood of diverse companies out-earning their industry peers has grown. They identified a strong correlation between gender diversity and positive behavior relating to better organizational health, leading in turn to better business performance.[11] Other D&I research shows that organizations in the top quartile for diversity are more likely to demonstrate above average financial performance, such as Return on Equity (ROE) and Return on Investment (ROI).[12,13,14] As well as increased customer congruence, customer satisfaction, innovation,[15] employee engagement and loyalty,[16] these organizations also enjoy better decision-making, better risk management,[17] lower fraud[18] and enhanced access to the best talent pool.[19]

Of significance, organizations that increased investments in diversity and inclusion during the financial crises of 2008 have been seen to be more resilient during the COVID-19 pandemic.[20] They were better positioned to anticipate employee needs and respond with policies that were helpful in navigating significant change, extending flexibility, mental health assistance, and adapting their sponsorship and personal development processes.[21]

---

[11] "Diversity Still Matters," McKinsey & Company, May 19, 2020, https://www.mckinsey.com/featured-insights/diversity-and-inclusion/diversity-still-matters.

[12] "Rise of the SHEconomy," Morgan Stanley, September 23, 2019, https://www.morganstanley.com/ideas/womens-impact-on-the-economy.

[13] Kersley et al. (2019).

[14] Dixon-Fyle et al. (2020).

[15] Lorenzo et al. (2017).

[16] "Waiter, Is That Inclusion in My Soup? A New Recipe to Improve Business Performance," Deloitte, May 2013, https://www2.deloitte.com/content/dam/Deloitte/au/Documents/human-capital/deloitte-au-hc-diversity-inclusion-soup-0513.pdf.

[17] Shin et al. (2020).

[18] Wahid (2019).

[19] Madera et al. (2019).

[20] https://fortune.com/2019/12/20/diversity-inclusion-key-to-beating-next-recession/.

[21] "Diversity Still Matters," McKinsey & Company, May 19, 2020, https://www.mckinsey.com/featured-insights/diversity-and-inclusion/diversity-still-matters.

3   D&I Investment Missing the Mark

But despite this evidence of positive impacts from diversity, for many organizations the significant investments they are making and the multitude of diversity initiatives they are implementing are not translating into better business performance, greater parity or societal value. It is not for lack of trying: a study from MIT Sloan School of Management found that $8 billion is spent each year on diversity training alone in corporate America.[22] Postings for diversity and inclusion professionals jumped 35% between 2016 and 2018[23] and a 2019 study revealed that 63% of diversity professionals in S&P 500 companies had been appointed or promoted to their roles during the past three years.[24] Given the resources being invested in diversity, Diversity Performance should be flourishing, yet this influx of investment and diversity professionals has not had the desired result—it is not translating into Diversity Performance.

Ineffective or misdirected D&I investments can end up doing more harm than good. Some diversity tools, such as diversity training, hiring tests, performance ratings and grievance systems have actually been associated with a decrease in the proportion of women and minorities in management.[25] In particular, those initiatives that were found to be top-down, rule-based, and disempowering line managers, were observed to activate bias and encourage rebellion instead of stimulating the desired inclusive leadership of diversity.[26] When they are wasteful, badly implemented or fail to deliver results, people start to resent diversity initiatives, resulting in cynicism or pushback where people tire of even hearing the world "diversity." It has led to what The Economist called "diversity fatigue," quipping that 12 of the most terrifying words in the English language are "I'm from Human Resources, and I'm here to organize a diversity workshop."[27]

Why are these sizeable investments in diversity not delivering? The underlying problem is the way diversity is currently led by most organizations—as a project, side-pillar, nice-to-have but not as a strategic part of the business. Leaders are often unsure of the level of Diversity Performance that is required for their organization, and which diversity capabilities they need to support Diversity Performance. In addition to not treating diversity strategically, leaders have tended to focus on two primary elements of Diversity Performance—diversity and inclusion, often shortened to "D&I." However, as this book argues, achieving strong Diversity Performance requires a more holistic way of "doing" diversity—one that also addresses the interrelated elements of equity, leadership and purpose.

---

[22] Kochan et al. (2003).

[23] Newkirk (2019).

[24] Newkirk, "Diversity Has Become a Booming Business. So Where Are the Results?"

[25] Pedulla (2020).

[26] Dobbin and Kalev (2016).

[27] Schumpeter (2016).

4   The Five Elements: An Integrated Approach to Diversity

To achieve the kind of Diversity Performance leading organizations are looking for today and remain aligned with shifting stakeholder expectations, a sole focus on D&I alone is insufficient. Without appropriate equity measures to support diversity and inclusion (E), strong leadership commitment to diversity (L), and a clear organizational diversity purpose and rationale (P), initiatives will fail to deliver their full potential. Instead of D+I, today's diversity leaders need to be thinking also about +E+L+P (Fig. 1).

Why five elements? Extensive academic research indicates that simply recruiting more "diverse" people does not magically transform into increased Diversity Performance. If more diversity is added (either acquired or inherited diversity) but leaders suppress diversity of thought through exclusionary practices such as stereotyping, then Diversity Performance is substantially undermined. Indeed, all of the elements of diversity need to be maintained in good health.

A sports analogy is helpful to explain why this integrated approach is needed to maximize Diversity Performance:

- **Diversity** is about selecting players with the best skills, experience and talent to build a winning team.
- **Inclusion** is showing up for practice, being selected for the team *and* having the opportunity to play
- **Equity** is being coached to realize your full playing potential *and* receiving the extra training that your circumstances require.
- **Purpose** unifies the team, values each player and highlights playing together for optimum results.
- **Leadership** models right behaviors and creates a team where every talent can reach its full potential.

It is when all five elements are working together that the team can perform to its full potential.

From   **D + I**

To   **D + I + E + L + P**

Fig. 1 Moving from Two Elements to Five Elements of Diversity Performance
To move beyond today's Diversity & Inclusion requires embracing five elements of Diversity Performance.

5   The Virtuous Circle: Understanding Diversity Performance

When these elements function together, they create synergy to form what can be described as a "virtuous circle" of Diversity Performance (Fig. 2).

All five elements support each other to enable diversity outcomes. However, if one element is weak or missing, it undermines Diversity Performance as a whole, creating "entropy" or inefficiencies in the organization. For example:

- **If there is no diversity:** The organization will suffer from "groupthink" and customer disengagement. It will struggle to anticipate stakeholder requirements and solutions may lack the creativity that allows breakthrough thinking and innovation.
- **If there is diversity but no inclusion:** The organization invites individuals in, but their ideas are not listened to unless endorsed by the dominant group. Employees fail to thrive and reach their potential or leave because they do not feel valued.
- **If there is diversity and inclusion but no equity:** Within the organization, individuals are treated the same, with no recognition that minority groups have faced historical, systemic discrimination in their lives. As a result, the organization unwittingly reinforces entrenched inequalities.
- **If there is diversity, inclusion, and equity, but no leadership:** The organization is likely to have the basis for rich diversity outcomes, but lack of leadership—or even toxic leadership—undermines those benefits and makes people question the authenticity and integrity of the organization's diversity commitments.
- **If there is no diversity purpose:** The organization has the right elements in place but has not joined the dots between Diversity Performance and organizational strategy. Lack of integration means diversity loses relevance over time.

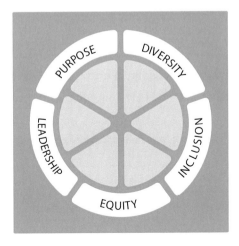

Fig. 2   The Virtuous Circle
The Virtuous Circle integrates the five reinforcing elements of diversity, inclusion, equity, leadership, and purpose.

The five elements of the Virtuous Circle enable the organization's Diversity Performance. They are also the Diversity Performance themes that matter most to stakeholders:

- **Diversity:** Stakeholders want organizations with diversity of representation that reflects their operating context and diversity of thinking that makes them resilient and adaptive to change.
- **Inclusion:** Stakeholders want organizations to be inclusive to their customers and employees and remove barriers that restrict some groups from participating socially and economically.
- **Equity:** Stakeholders want organizations to recognize that some people are negatively impacted by pervasive and persistent bias. They want organizations to mitigate this bias and provide access to resources and opportunities based on need.
- **Leadership:** Stakeholders want courageous and authentic leaders who are willing to challenge inequity and inspire inclusiveness.
- **Purpose:** Stakeholders want organizations to create stakeholder value, not only shareholder value.

The Virtuous Circle of Diversity Performance forms one of two key anchor models in the book. which, when applied together, with a clear understanding of the organization's diversity maturity and ambitions, enable a strategic, integrated and evidence-based approach to Diversity Performance. These models are the result of over 25 years of collaboration with clients, business organizations, researchers, academic institutions, and others. They merge validated research with lessons learned in the hands-on practice of Diversity Performance improvement in over 50 organizations to distil the essential elements and capabilities that underpin successful organizational diversity journeys.

The merit of these models is that they can be used by any organization at any stage of its diversity journey. Diversity and inclusion are not a one-size-fits-all exercise and cut-and-paste approaches do not generally deliver the desired outcome. Instead, leaders can apply these models to craft a unique and tailored diversity approach that is right for their organization, with the reassurance that every component in the models has been applied and validated to be effective.

6   The Five Stages: Understanding Diversity Maturity

Equipped with the five essential elements that make up the Virtuous Circle of Diversity Performance, the next step is for the leader to develop a clear understanding of the different stages of diversity maturity. There are five key stages, each characterized by a specific set of primary drivers and features that organizations at that stage typically exhibit, as follows:

Stage 1: Legal Compliance—diversity as mandated for regulatory compliance.

Stage 2: Stakeholder Requirements—diversity as required by, e.g., consumers and employees.

Stage 3: Organizational Performance—diversity to generate business outcomes such as shareholder profit, customer congruence, improved engagement, more innovation, and access to talent.

Stage 4: Reinvention—diversity to enable rapid innovation and transformation and to anticipate future required capabilities.

Stage 5: Societal Value—diversity to unlock complex values-based problem-solving to address global social challenges.

Stages 1–3 can be characterized as "push" stages, where the organization is impelled to improve Diversity Performance due to external factors such as legislation, customer demands or business performance imperatives. At Stages 4–5, in contrast, Diversity Performance becomes a "pull" factor, driven by the organization because diversity is recognized as an intrinsic strategic differentiator and means of value creation.

These five stages of maturity bring to the organization a deeper understanding of how the five elements of the Virtuous Circle evolve (Table 1), as described in Chapter 3. By viewing these elements through the lens of the stages, the organization can determine what its desired level of Diversity Performance is (its Future Diversity Narrative) and what its current level of Diversity Performance is (its Current Diversity Narrative). By comparing these, it can identify the gaps between its existing and desired levels. We call this Measuring the Diversity Performance Gap, and it is discussed in detail in Chapter 4 (Fig. 3).

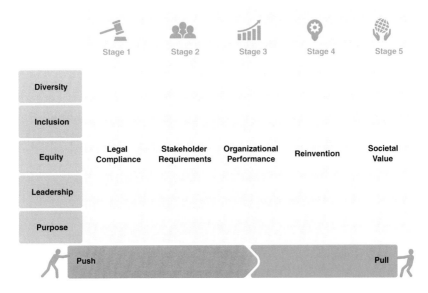

Fig. 3 Combining the Five Elements of Diversity Performance with the Five Stages
There are five key stages of Diversity Performance, each characterized by primary drivers and features that organizations at that stage typically exhibit.

7   The Integrated Diversity Model: Closing the Capability Gap

The second anchor model in the book is the Integrated Diversity Model (IDM). This builds on the Virtuous Circle to introduce six supporting organizational capabilities that enable the elements of diversity to flourish. Its function is to help organizations develop an integrated approach to diversity that combines all the necessary elements and capabilities for effective Diversity Performance. If the Virtuous Circle is about the essential elements of Diversity Performance—the "What"—the IDM is about the core competencies needed to operationalize performance—the "How" (Fig. 4).

The Integrated Diversity Model is founded on extensive primary scholarly research and applied learnings from guiding multiple organizations through their Inclusive Leadership Certification. This collaborative work has revealed six diversity capabilities that leaders need to cultivate within their organizations in order to close Diversity Performance gaps.

These capabilities are interdependent and work together: if one area of diversity competency is weak or missing, it undermines the impact and effectiveness of the other five, dampening the organization's overall Diversity Performance. These six capability areas are:

1. **Mitigate Bias**—The ability to mitigate personal and systemic bias so that stakeholders feel included, and equity is advanced.
2. **Build the Case**—The ability to translate the diversity purpose into a clear case for diversity, identify the appropriate performance level and invest in effective initiatives.

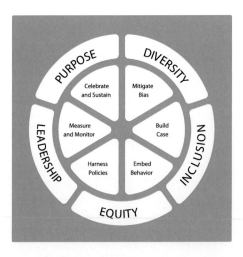

Fig. 4   The Integrated Diversity Model
The IDM introduces to the five core elements of Diversity Performance six supporting organizational capabilities that enable strong performance.

3. **Embed Behavior**—The ability to embed inclusive behaviors across the organization, supported by appropriate values, rituals, and daily practices.
4. **Harness Policies**—The ability to identify the right policies to guide, reward, and promote daily diversity practices.
5. **Measure and Monitor**—The ability to measure and monitor progress in closing the Diversity Performance gap.
6. **Celebrate and Sustain**—The ability to energize collective commitment to the diversity journey, stay aligned with stakeholder expectations and support the organization's transformation journey.

The rationale for these key diversity capabilities is presented in Chapter 5, where the leader is guided through a strategic capability gap analysis, using the IDM and the Five Stages Framework. We call this Closing the Capability Gap, and it repeats the process of comparing the organization's aspirational diversity capability level (its Future Diversity Capability needs) with its existing diversity capability level (its Current Diversity Capabilities), based on its desired level of Diversity Performance.

For each capability at each stage of maturity, there is a corresponding set of validated initiatives that organizations can implement to build that capability. These comprise only those measures that have been proven to be effective in raising diversity aptitude in organizations (Table 1).

In Table 1, for example, the organization has determined that its desired level of Diversity Performance (shown in green) is Stage 4 Reinvention. By mapping its existing initiatives, it can see that its current capability level (shown in orange) is actually between Stages 2 and 3. In this example, the gap analysis reveals that the organization has less capability in bias mitigation and inclusive leadership. To close the capability gap and reach its desired state, the organization will need to operationalize a combination of both Stage 4 and Stage 3 initiatives, with a priority focus on the areas where it is weaker.

Identifying the organization's capability gap enables the leader to develop a Strategic Roadmap for how to close it. The roadmap sets out the key initiatives that must be implemented in each capability area to ensure the organization develops the right competencies to reach its desired level of Diversity Performance. Each capability area, and the corresponding clusters of supporting initiatives that help to build that capability, is addressed in detail in Chapters 6–11.

Table 1 Combining the Six Diversity Capabilities with the Five Stages

Proven and effective initiatives for building diversity capability at each level of maturity.

Capabilities	Stage 1 Legal Compliance	Stage 2 Stakeholder Requirements	Stage 3 Organizational Performance	Stage 4 Reinvention	Stage 5 Societal Value
Mitigate Bias	Bias compliance training	Recruiting bias training; De-bias recruiting processes; Measure recruiter bias	Leadership bias training; De-bias all talent processes; Measure leadership bias; De-bias coaches	Personal bias training for all; De-bias all processes; Measure organization bias; Systemic bias training; Systemic bias audit; De-bias guardian roles	Systemic bias training value chain; De-bias value chain; Measure value chain Bias; Systemic value chain audit
Build Case	Legal case risk management role; Measure legal case; Budget assigned	+ Customer case marketing role; + Employee case HR role; + Measurement: client's case satisfied; Budget assigned	+ Business case CFO role; + Measurement business case objectives; Budget assigned; Resources assigned; Initiative effectiveness measured	+ Ethical case CEO role; + Measurement ethical case/equity advancement; Budget assigned; Resources assigned; Initiative effectiveness measured	+ Societal case CEO/board; + Measurement contribution to societal objectives; Value chain budget assigned; Value chain resources assigned; Value chain initiative Effectiveness measured
Embed Behaviour	Fit-in induction	Satisfaction survey	Inclusiveness index for leaders; Inclusive leadership training; Inclusive leadership evaluation	Inclusiveness index for organization; Inclusive leadership training organization; Inclusive leadership capability organization; Inclusive leadership language	Inclusiveness Index for value chain; Inclusive leadership training value chain; Inclusive leadership capability value chain; Inclusive leadership language value chain
Harness Policies	No discrimination policy	Zero tolerance discrimination	Zero tolerance discrimination; Performance policies	Zero tolerance discrimination; +Systemic bias policy; +Equity process and policy; Robust blueprint for organization	Zero tolerance discrimination value chain; Robust blueprint for organization
Measure and Monitor	Diversity demographic metrics; Compliance measurement	+ Measurement: Stakeholder requirements satisfied	Diversity of thought; Diversity contribution to business case levers	For organizations: Diversity gap closure; Diversity initiative effectiveness; Diversity contribution to business goals	For value chain: Diversity gap closure; Diversity initiative effectiveness; Diversity contribution to business goals
Celebrate and Sustain	No compliance issues celebration; New legal requirements review	Diversity client events; Stakeholder community events	Team celebration	Diversity celebration; Organizationwide events	Diversity celebration; Value chain events

8   The Six Key Diversity Capabilities

A short overview of each capability area and why it matters is presented below.

1.   **Mitigate Bias**

Personal bias and systemic bias must be mitigated together in an organization to advance equity, otherwise there is entropy. For example, once an organization has identified the diversity characteristics gaps within the organization, they must quickly identify the talent blind spots, unconscious bias or unwritten rules that combine daily to exclude the very people that they wish to attract to the organization.

Why is this important?

- Bias is the Achilles' heel of diversity in most organizations. It contributes to the gap between what leaders say and what they do in practice.
- Systemic bias refers to the inherent tendency of a system and its processes, policies, and protocols to support a particular outcome.
- Implicit Bias is held by individuals and is also referred to as unconscious, hidden, or personal cognitive bias.
- Implicit Bias is present in everyone. It is based in neuroscience and linked to evolutionary survival factors, information overload, energy conservation, and/or typical fight-freeze-flight responses.
- Biases lead to organizations favoring "in-group" profiles, yet by doing so the organization is prevented from delivering on its strategic narrative of Diversity Performance. As a result, the organization will fail to advance equity, will not be able to tap into diversity of thinking for breakthrough innovations and will fall short of its customer requirements. Instead, organizations end up penalizing the very minority candidates that they wish to attract.
- Depending on an organization's Diversity Performance maturity level, the Integrated Diversity Model sets out a range of evidence-based initiatives that can be implemented to build the necessary capabilities to overcome unconscious and systemic bias.
  - When bias runs unchecked, it undermines the diversity journey by favoring the hiring, promotion, and potential of certain people above others. This undermines engagement, performance outcomes, ability to transform, and long-term equity in society. Today's younger generations—Gen Z and Millennials—expect organizations to be proactive in raising awareness and mitigating bias. Tomorrow's diversity leaders are those who advocate publicly for change while putting in place the proven measures to deliver on their commitments.

Bias inhibits every element of Diversity Performance, so it is vital that organizations proactively address it. This is done by implementing the appropriate mitigation measures for their desired stage of Diversity Performance, as indicated in Fig. 5. The full range of measures for mitigating bias is presented and discussed in detail in Chapter 6.

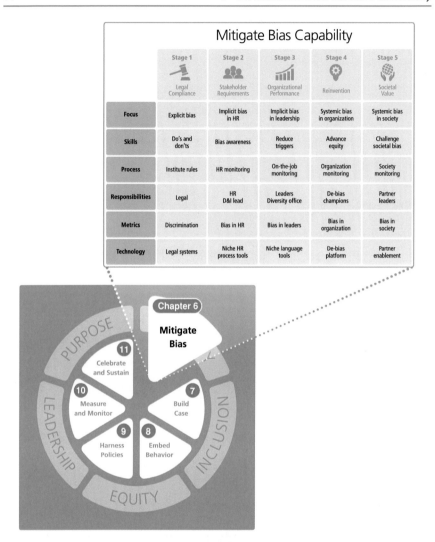

Fig. 5 Improvement Initiatives for Each Capability Area
Detailed bias mitigation measures for every stage of Diversity Performance are discussed in
Chapter 6.

For example, for an organization seeking to achieve legal compliance (Stage
1), bias mitigation is primarily about eliminating explicit bias arising from discriminatory practices. Building an anti-discrimination capability involves setting
out rules (e.g., Code of Conduct), revising policies and establishing clear "do's
and don'ts." The process is led by the Legal function with support from Human
Resources (HR). At Stage 2, the mitigation focus shifts to preventing implicit bias
in HR, with greater emphasis on building awareness and altering recruitment and

talent review processes. As the organization progresses through each stage, the bias mitigation effort moves from dealing with implicit bias to addressing more entrenched systemic bias.

2.   **Build Case**

There are various reasons why organizations seek to drive improved Diversity Performance. All are valid and provide the entity with a framing rationale that contextualizes diversity behaviors and actions by making the link between diversity inputs and performance outcomes. This is called the Diversity Case. Being able to develop and articulate a strong case for diversity within the organization is a crucial capability. There are four main cases:

- **Legal Case**—Satisfying legal diversity requirements, e.g., quotas, and avoiding sanction.
- **Business Case**—Satisfying performance requirements, e.g., increased access to talent, improved financial performance and decision-making.
- **Ethical Case**—Satisfying the moral responsibility to support the right of people to enjoy work and be fairly treated, without discrimination.
- **Societal Case**—Satisfying the role of organizations to support stakeholder value creation, social cohesion, and equality.

The Legal Case, for example, is primarily about avoiding penalties and reputational risk. This is a significant driver: a Harvard Business Review study found that since 2000, some $2 billion has been paid out in disclosed penalties by Fortune 500 companies to settle discrimination litigation cases.[28] Making sure the organization understands the legal landscape and has the right compliance capabilities is vital. However, there are also other imperatives for improving Diversity Performance.

To align with broader stakeholder expectations and responsible business principles, leaders are increasingly considering how the case for diversity can be framed beyond the legal and business case. While the most robust diversity case combines legal and business imperatives with ethical and societal imperatives for diversity, this is closely tied to the organization's diversity ambition—i.e., if the ambition is to achieve Stage 1 Compliance, then the focus will be on developing capabilities that support the Legal Case. If the ambition is to achieve Stage 5 Societal Value, all four imperatives and supporting capabilities will need to be in place to ensure balanced Diversity Performance.

Why is this important?

- Without a clear and compelling case for diversity, it is hard to build team ownership and understanding and initiatives and behaviors will fail to stick.

---

[28] Hirsh (2019).

- Developing the organization's diversity case contextualizes it by showing how diversity fits into and supports broader corporate objectives, making it easier to evaluate if progress is being achieved.
- Research on the business case has shown correlational evidence between greater diversity and:
  - Financial performance: profitability, higher cash flows, longer-term value creation.
  - Customer congruence and customer satisfaction: higher loyalty.
  - Innovation, more creativity.
  - Talent pool access, employee engagement, and loyalty of employees.
  - Good decision-making, effective risk-management practices.

- While there are business benefits to be gained from diversity, stakeholders increasingly expect organizations to pursue diversity for reasons beyond profit. Building the capability to develop a balanced diversity case for the organization supports optimum Diversity Performance.

It is worth underlining that even a Stage 5 organization needs to maintain the Legal Case capability. Legislation is continually evolving, and new affirmative action quotas are being introduced. All cases for diversity should be continually monitored and periodically reviewed and updated. The Build Case Capability is covered in Chapter 7.

3.   Embed Behavior

The role of the leader in embedding diversity behaviors cannot be underestimated. Leaders are role models and set the tone in the organization. Indeed, research has found that as much as 70% of feelings of inclusion are influenced by the daily micro-behaviors of senior leaders and line managers.[29] Adapting leadership behaviors to create an inclusive environment is therefore a crucial capability to ensure that the organization's diversity initiatives are not unintentionally undermined. To keep inclusive behaviors top of mind, leaders also need to be held accountable.

A core capability for the twenty-first century, inclusive leadership creates the conditions where all members of the organization are encouraged to behave in a way that creates safety, fosters respect and cultivates collaboration to magnify the benefits of diversity. Inclusive leadership is founded on self-reflection. When leaders engage in self-reflection and become aware of their own diversity and uniqueness, it makes them more open and amenable to creating the space and conditions for other individuals to do the same. Through self-reflection, inclusive practices can grow.

In fact, diversity must be embraced by the entire organization in their day-to-day behaviors. It is not enough to bring diversity into the organization and to ensure people understand why it is important.

---

[29] Dillon and Bourke (2016).

Why is this important?

- Leaders have an outsized impact on whether people feel included in the organization.
- Driving Diversity Performance demands an inclusive environment where people feel they are treated fairly and respectfully, their contributions are valued, they have a sense of belonging and can bring their whole selves to work and feel psychologically safe.
- Non-inclusive leadership can be costly to organizations, not only financially but in terms of employee wellbeing, according to recent business research: disengaged workers have been shown to display 37% more absenteeism and 60% more errors and defects.[30] In organizations where employee engagement scored low, productivity dropped by 18%, profitability by 16%, job growth by 37% and the share price declined 65% over time. In contrast, organizations where employees were highly engaged saw a 100% uptick in job applications.[31]

There are six main traits of inclusive leaders:

- **Personal commitment to diversity**—They take the time to think deeply about why diversity matters to them and how the quest for diversity connects to their personal values. They consider their personal journey in life and where diversity has been meaningful to them. They may have experienced what it is like to be excluded and as a result inclusion has become an important value for them. This makes them naturally motivated to support diversity because it is not an intellectual exercise but a personal and emotional process. Above all, it is authentic.
- **A conscious leader**—Inclusive leaders are humble; they are aware that they—like everybody else—have unconscious biases and blind spots or lack of cultural knowledge. They invite others to act as a mirror and play back to them what they, as a leader, says and does, to become more self-aware. This kind of leader is curious about people and knows that effective change is built on understanding. They can step back in the heat of the moment to observe the dynamics and possess the ability and willingness to adjust their behavior and inspire others to be more mindful too.
- **A deep listener**—They listen not to confirm what they want to hear, but with genuine curiosity to challenge and expand their knowledge and to learn from others. They listen with their heart, which means listening with empathy and compassion, and making other people feel seen, heard and valued. They are genuinely interested in what people have to say and in broadening their lens on the world. By listening deeply, they can arrive at deeper insights and better solutions.

---

[30] Seppälä and Cameron (2015).

[31] Seppälä and Cameron, "Proof that Positive Work Cultures Are More Productive."

- **A natural collaborator**—This leader has trust in the team and values the insights and experience they bring to a shared approach. They appreciate the dynamics of psychological safety and create the circumstances for team cohesion. Empowering others and enabling the team to be more than the sum of its parts is a key focus for them.
- **A courageous leader**—When team members are excluded or bias creeps in, equity is not advanced. This leader has the courage and the conviction to step up and say what needs to be said or addressed, even if it is uncomfortable. This leader is prepared to have frank discussions about what might be occurring in the organization and, where necessary, to acknowledge their own failings. They are not afraid to stand up, in a spirit of humility and service to the organization and be accountable.
- **An active driver of diversity**—The inclusive leader does the day-to-day heavy lifting to ensure team members are treated fairly. They strive for continuous improvement, through targeted actions and initiatives, and serve readily as sponsor and ally as required. This leader is not passive and takes ultimate accountability but expects others to be partners in diversity, too.

As Chapter 8 explains, the behavior of leaders exerts strong influence on the culture of an organization. They are exemplars and are emulated by the team. That is why cultivating the inclusive leadership capability is so important to embed desired behaviors and create a feeling of inclusiveness. At Stage 1, this is primarily focused on integrating members within the existing culture, for example through new hire orientation programs and established organizational rituals. At Stages 4 and 5, however, embedding behavior is so important that it is elevated to a core competency, with the aim of sponsoring and advancing equity both within the organization and throughout its wider value chain and partner ecosystem.

4.   **Harness Policies**

Chapter 9 addresses the importance of policies that support and add value to daily practices. Policies are the security net that ensures that statements, pledges and commitments to diversity are actually implemented in practice. They are one of the chief ways that the organization operationalizes its diversity objectives. Critical policies that affect every member of the organization—such as anti-discrimination policies—must be consistently applied and enforced in a zero-tolerance manner.

Ensuring that the organization has the right policy mix for its Diversity Performance level and that each policy is effective is an important capability. For example, policies need to be regularly assessed to ensure that they are leading to the intended benefits for their target beneficiaries and are valued and informed by minority groups. Top-down policies imposed without consulting beneficiaries risk being ineffective.

Why is this important?

Policies provide guidance, ensure consistency in how to interpret guidelines and use them in practice. They also establish accountability for actions and outcomes, deliver efficiency in operations, and give members clarity on how an organization operates. When members of the team understand that there are not only generally accepted rules of engagement, but recourse when the rules are broken, this provides a sense of safety and lowered stress for all members of the organization, but especially for minority group employees. For example, an organization with a zero-tolerance policy on discrimination will ideally address incidents of discrimination immediately and decisively, with clearly defined consequences. When applied consistently, such a policy gives minorities confidence that the organization takes diversity seriously and that there is remedy when policies are breached.

While diversity policies can bolster workplace equity and business performance, poorly developed policies can lead to pushback or resistance that perversely engender further difficulties for marginalized or underrepresented workers[32],[33]:

Issues arise with this capability when:

- **Policies are not pruned**—Many organizations have too many diversity policies which are not integrated or suitable for their performance stage, and therefore difficult to apply.
- **Policies are not applied consistently**—Uneven implementation or selective enforcement can cause confusion and undermine commitment.
- **Policies are mired in legalistic language that does not inspire**—To bring diversity practices to life, they need to motivate, and resonate with the team.
- **Gaps in perception**—There is a mismatch between leaders and target groups over the value of a policy. Diversity policies are not equally valued by all minority groups.
- **Insufficient consultation**—Minority employees are not sufficiently consulted and as a result policies are maladapted or not fit-for-purpose.
- **Failure to harness technology**—Technology can play a critical role in embedding policies and engaging the organization.

Policies are valuable when they are tailored and targeted to drive performance. The policy capability can be strengthened by asking beneficiary employees to rank which policies they consider most valuable. At Stage 2, for example, this might include a policy setting representation targets, whereas for Stage 4 organizations, policies become a differentiator and means of pioneering new diversity approaches.

---

[32] Dobbin et al. (2015).

[33] Lambouths III et al. (2019).

At all stages, policies should be supported by clear recourse and individuals should have confidence that they will not face retaliation. Well-designed policy is a critical tool in the diversity capability toolkit.

5.   **Measure and Monitor**

Just as there are vital signs to monitor good health, leaders need to monitor the vital signs of diversity. At its most basic, this includes tracking infractions or violations of diversity-related policies such as anti-discrimination or anti-sexual harassment. Many organizations measure basic diversity statistics such as gender percentages, but few measure all five elements of Diversity Performance. This is essential to manage diversity holistically and strategically and ensure that the organization is getting a return on investment from its diversity initiatives. This can be measured in a range of ways, including non-financial returns. Where diversity initiatives are not delivering or are only partially effective, they need to be evaluated and adjusted or discontinued.

Why is this important?

- **Measurement *is* performance**—If Diversity Performance is not measured, it is impossible to know whether diversity interventions are working, whether improvement is occurring and whether the organization is successfully closing the performance gap to achieve its desired level of performance.
- **Measurement enables correction**—Having the right combination of lead and lag indicators helps the organization to gauge if diversity is "healthy" or if it is losing momentum. This enables quick intervention and correction before performance gets off-track and valuable diversity investments are wasted.

Indications that organizational diversity health is dipping include the following:

- **A negative trend in employee engagement pulse surveys**—Decrease in overall engagement, satisfaction and inclusion figures, where possible, compared to engagement in minority groups.
- **Unstable rates of retention**—Lower retention rates for minorities relative to the overall population.
- **Job offer declines**—Fewer recruitment offers accepted, particularly by minorities.
- **Benefit gaps**—Bigger salary and benefits gaps for minorities versus the rest of the population.
- **Grievances**—Unconscious bias or systemic bias emerge more frequently in the organization's grievance channels.
- **Leadership rating decline**—Negative trend on inclusive leadership pulse surveys.
- **Shrinking minority representation**—Decreased or static level in percentages of minority representation per level, location, business units showing gaps.
- **Negative feedback from customers and suppliers**—Feedback on diversity issues in pulse surveys reveal a problem.

- **Promotion gaps**—Minorities not being promoted or advanced at same rate as overall population.
- **Distribution of line versus staff and specialized versus general roles**— Imbalance in minority representation in the positions holding more responsibility, authority, and higher compensation.

Organizations also frequently encounter barriers which need to be addressed in order to measure progress successfully. Among the most prominent are:

1. **Data privacy restrictions**—An inability to collect data about individuals based on minority status due to existing legislation in many countries.
2. **Incomplete measurement of all five elements of the Virtuous Circle**—If measurement focuses only on diversity demographic metrics to the exclusion of inclusion, equity, leadership, and how to realize the case for diversity, the organization gains only a partial measurement of performance.
3. **Lack of global diversity measurement standards**—The absence of global diversity measurement standards. Lack of global, universal standards that allow benchmarking and comparing apples-to-apples is a hindrance to measuring performance.
4. **Failure to contextualize metrics**—A reliance on copy-and-paste diversity metrics rather than taking context into account. Each organization is unique, with varying degrees of privacy laws, all of which must be taken into account for a full picture of Diversity Performance.
5. **Faulty interpretation of metrics**—When a single metric is viewed in isolation, it can be misleading and lead to erroneous conclusions that hinder progress.
6. **Lack of holistic measurement**—A holistic measurement system for diversity is needed to get a complete view of the organization's vital signs. Having a full picture enables early intervention.
7. **Unclear accountability and responsibilities**—Lack of clarity and communication around responsibility for delivering on metrics and tracking progress can present a serious obstacle.

To support the measurement capability, the Virtuous Circle and Integrated Diversity Model are underpinned by an integrated system of metrics that includes the following: closure of the Diversity Performance gap, progress of the Strategic Roadmap per milestone and outcome; achievement of business goals linked to the diversity case; and the health of the Virtuous Circle within the organization, given changes in the external environment and company mandate.

As part of this framework, Chapter 10 sets out a number of questions to help evaluate the organization's progress, with accompanying metrics, including: "Do we have the right diversity investments in place and are we optimizing the benefits?" Whereas at Stage 1, measurement primarily focuses on the degree of achievement of compliance—such as number of litigation cases or amount of fines paid—at Stage 3 focus shifts to measuring the relationship between increased diversity (e.g., inherent and acquired characteristics) and identified performance outcomes (e.g., increased innovation revenues, decreased employee sickness and increased employee engagement). Stage 5 measurement extends to capturing diversity-related impacts and outcomes in the wider value chain and linking diversity investments with societal objectives, such as the UN SDGs or the 10 Principles of the UN Global Compact.

6.   Celebrate and Sustain

Diversity is not easy. It requires constant renewal and reinforcement. To keep the flame alive, it is important to celebrate events, communicate progress and share achievements. Sustaining diversity is about ensuring it is well resourced and that it keeps in sync with the external environment to refresh the Strategic Narrative and consolidate diversity gains. This is the focus of Chapter 11.

Why is this important?

A diversity journey is an organizational change journey. It can be hard-going, especially when it is clouded by a history of discrimination, bias and polarization between teams. While no diversity journey is the same, there are common ways to sustain it—to create energy that the organization can draw from to keep diversity in a state of renewal. The diversity journey needs to be tended like a fire: it requires the right number of logs to be put on at the right time, and enough oxygen, so the fire can burn brightly but not go out, or get out of control.

Key ways that the leader can help to sustain the diversity journey in their organization include:

- **Celebrate and create communities**—Honor specific days or diversity milestones that are meaningful (e.g., International Women's Day, Juneteenth and key religious or cultural holidays).
- **Nurture grassroots support**—Appoint diversity champions to be the "face" of diversity in the organization, spread the passion, and share the load.
- **Make accountable and reward**—It should be clear who is formally responsible for delivery of diversity programs and connect this to rewards. Cascade ownership to everyone in the organization.
- **Pilot interventions and share best practice**—Test approaches and scale only what works. A Diversity Council can help to share experience across regions and business units.
- **Provide continuous feedback and endorsement**—Invite two-way feedback to discuss how the organization is progressing and how gaps are being closed. Diversity champions can be a valuable source of information.

Diversity is not a project; it is a journey. By definition, the Virtuous Circle of diversity, inclusion, equity, purpose and leadership is never static. It is a dynamic feedback loop and reflects the constantly evolving external environment.

Sustaining this journey is about injecting adequate energy and resources, reviewing whether the organization is at the right stage, whether its capabilities are up to scratch and adjusting as needed in response to stakeholder requirements.

9   The Diversity Performance and Capability Roadmap

Organizations have been lacking a strategic and integrated approach to diversity and inclusion. This book extends the concept, explains why existing approaches fail and equips the leader with a tried and tested framework for Diversity Performance success. The two anchor models support the leader to identify and articulate their desired level of diversity ambition, understand their current level of performance, and identify and build the necessary diversity capabilities and initiatives to close the performance gap.

This Diversity Performance and Capability methodology can be summarized in ten key steps:

1. Understand your stakeholder Diversity Performance requirements and expectations.
2. Determine your desired level of Diversity Performance across each of the Diversity Performance elements: diversity (characteristics), inclusion, equity, leadership, and purpose.
3. Determine your current level of Diversity Performance.
4. Map the gap between your future aspirational level of Diversity Performance and current Diversity Performance, according to the five elements of Diversity Performance.
5. Identify the required diversity capabilities needed to support your desired level of Diversity Performance.
6. Identify which initiatives you need to implement to build the right capabilities to achieve your desired level of Diversity Performance. Each package of initiatives includes strategic objectives, knowledge and skills, processes, responsibilities and enabling technologies validated for your given stage.
7. Identify your current portfolio of initiatives and capabilities.
8. Map your capability gap and prioritize the largest gaps.
9. Develop a Strategic Roadmap to close your prioritized capability gaps.
10. Monitor your Diversity Performance and evolving stakeholder requirements to sustain and revitalize your diversity journey.

This process is captured in the Performance and Capability Roadmap (Fig. 6).

When diversity is appreciated by the organization as a strategic enabler, this creates the opportunity to really unleash the power of Diversity Performance as an asset for the organization, its stakeholders and society as a whole.

Leaders understand that for business transformation to occur, there needs to be cultural transformation and for cultural transformation, personal transformation must occur. This is the case for diversity as well. A culture of inclusiveness, with

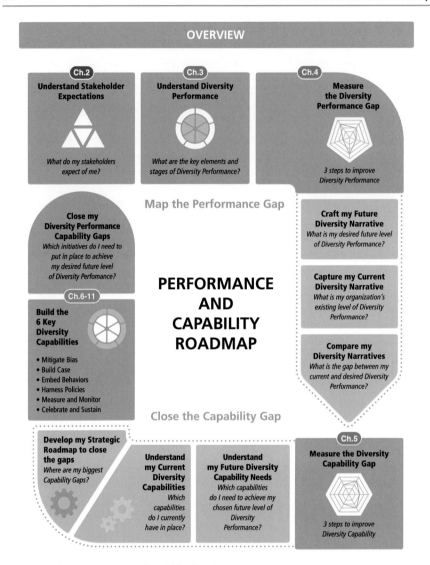

Fig. 6 The Performance and Capability Roadmap
There are ten key steps organizations can follow to map their performance gap and close their capability gap to achieve improved Diversity Performance.

all the hallmarks of equity and inclusion, flourishes when leaders—and indeed every member of the organization—display the right combination of values, behaviors and practices to foster diversity transformation.

This starts with inclusive leaders who embody the values required to drive Diversity Performance, deep personal conviction of the importance of diversity, the courage to create needed shifts in behavior and direct strategic engagement with the diversity journey.

For those leaders, and anyone embarking on their Diversity Performance journey, *Beyond D&I* offers an inclusive itinerary for the journey ahead.

References

Anderson, Monica, et al. "#BlackLivesMatter Surges on Twitter After George Floyd's Death." Pew Research Center, June 2020. https://www.pewresearch.org/fact-tank/2020/06/10/black-livesmatter-surges-on-twitter-after-george-floyds-death/.

Crawford, Bridget J., et al. "Talking About Black Lives Matter and #MeToo." *Wisconsin Journal of Law, Gender & Society*, 34, no. 2 (2019). https://digitalcommons.pace.edu/cgi/viewcontent.cgi?article=2152&context=lawfaculty.

Dillon, Bernadette and Juliet Bourke. "The Six Signature Traits of Inclusive Leadership." February 5, 2016. https://www2.deloitte.com/content/dam/Deloitte/au/Documents/human-capital/deloitte-au-hc-six-signature-traits-inclusive-leadership-020516.pdf.

Dixon-Fyle, Sundiatu, et al. "Diversity Wins: How Inclusion Matters." McKinsey and Company, May 19, 2020. https://www.mckinsey.com/featured-insights/diversity-and-inclusion/diversity-wins-how-inclusion-matters.

Dobbin, Frank and Alexandra Kalev. "Why Diversity Programs Fail." *Harvard Business Review*, July–August 2016. https://hbr.org/2016/07/why-diversity-programs-fail.

Dobbin, Frank, Daniel Schrage, and Alexandra Kalev. "Race Against the Iron Cage: The Varied Effects of Bureaucratic Personnel Reforms on Diversity." *American Sociological Review*, 80, no. 5 (2015): 1014–1044.

Friedman, Milton. "A Friedman Doctrine – The Social Responsibility of Business Is to Increase Its Profits." *The New York Times,* September 13, 1970. https://www.nytimes.com/1970/09/13/archives/a-friedman-doctrine-the-social-responsibility-of-business-is-to.Html.

Fry, Richard and Kim Parker. "Early Benchmarks Show 'Post-Millennials' on Track to be Most Diverse, Best-Educated Generation Yet." Pew Research Center, November 15, 2018. https://www.pewsocialtrends.org/2018/11/15/early-benchmarks-show-post-millennials-on-track-to-be-most-diverse-best-educated-generation-yet/.

Hirsh, Elizabeth. "Do Lawsuits Improve Gender and Racial Equality at Work?" *Harvard Business Review*, November 14, 2019. https://hbr.org/2019/11/do-lawsuits-improve-gender-and-racial-equality-at-work.

Kersley, Richard, et al. "The CS Gender 3000 in 2019: The Changing Face of Companies." Credit Suisse Research Institute, October 10, 2019. https://www.credit-suisse.com/about-us-news/en/articles/news-and-expertise/cs-gender-3000-report-2019-201910.html.

Kochan, T., et al. "The Effects of Diversity on Business Performance: Report of the Diversity Research Network." *Human Resource Management*, 42 (2003): 3–21.

Lambouths, Danny, III, William Scarborough, and Allyson Holbrook. "Who Supports Diversity Policies? It Depends on the Policy," October 4, 2019. https://hbr.org/2019/10/who-supports-diversity-policies-it-depends-on-the-policy.

Lorenzo, Rocío, et al. "The Mix That Matters: Innovation Through Diversity." The Boston Consulting Group, 2017. https://www.bcg.com/publications/2017/people-organization-leadership-talent-innovation-through-diversity-mix-that-matters.

Madera, Juan M., et al. "Top Management Gender Diversity and Organizational Attraction: When and Why It Matters." *Archives of Scientific Psychology*, 7, no. 1 (2019): 90–101. https://doi.org/10.1037/arc0000060.

Newkirk, Pamela. "Diversity Has Become a Booming Business. So Where Are the Results?" *Time*, October 10, 2019. https://time.com/5696943/diversity-business/.

Pedulla, David. "Diversity and Inclusion Efforts That Really Work." *Harvard Business Review*, May 12, 2020. https://hbr.org/2020/05/diversity-and-inclusion-efforts-that-really-work.

Schumpeter. "Diversity Fatigue." *The Economist*, February 11, 2016. https://www.economist.com/business/2016/02/11/diversity-fatigue.

Seppälä, Emma and Kim Cameron. "Proof that Positive Work Cultures Are More Productive." *Harvard Business Review*, December 1, 2015. https://hbr.org/2015/12/proof-that-positive-work-cultures-are-more-productive.

Shin, Y.Z., et al. "Female Directors on the Board and Investment Efficiency: Evidence from Korea." *Asian Bus Manage,* 19 (2020): 438–479 (2020). https://doi.org/10.1057/s41291-019-00066-2.

Wahid, A.S. "The Effects and the Mechanisms of Board Gender Diversity: Evidence from Financial Manipulation." *J Bus Ethics,* 159 (2019): 705–725. https://doi.org/10.1007/s10551-018-3785-6.

Part I
Why Do Organizations Need
to Pursue Diversity?

WHY do organizations need to pursue diversity?

Ch.2
Understand Stakeholder Expectations

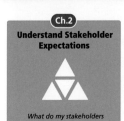

What do my stakeholders expect of me?

Understand Diversity Performance

What are the key elements and stages of Diversity Performance?

Measure the Diversity Performance Gap

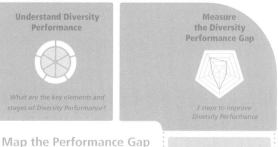

3 steps to improve Diversity Performance

Map the Performance Gap

Close my Diversity Performance Capability Gaps

Which initiatives do I need to put in place to achieve my desired future level of Diversity Performance?

Craft my Future Diversity Narrative

What is my desired future level of Diversity Performance?

Capture my Current Diversity Narrative

What is my organization's existing level of Diversity Performance?

Build the 6 Key Diversity Capabilities

* Mitigate Bias
* Build Case
* Embed Behaviors
* Harness Policies
* Measure and Monitor
* Celebrate and Sustain

PERFORMANCE AND CAPABILITY ROADMAP

Compare my Diversity Narratives

What is the gap between my current and desired Diversity Performance?

Close the Capability Gap

Develop my Strategic Roadmap to close the gaps

Where are my biggest Capability Gaps?

Understand my Current Diversity Capabilities

Which capabilities do I currently have in place?

Understand my Future Diversity Capability Needs

Which capabilities do I need to achieve my chosen future level of Diversity Performance?

Measure the Diversity Capability Gap

3 steps to improve Diversity Capability

A Call to Action for Courageous Leadership on Diversity

2

The courageous leadership exemplified by Nelson Mandela in the racial integration of South Africa, not least its national rugby team, the Springboks, offers a masterclass in diversity and inclusion. Such leadership is still in demand today. The COVID-19 pandemic has highlighted serious disparities in access to healthcare, education, and economic opportunity for minorities which existed long before the pandemic. Globally, gender parity is lagging in economic participation and opportunity. The Black Lives Matter movement has renewed focus on racial discrimination and systemic racism. LGBTQI+ individuals continue to face discrimination, and globally, people with disabilities face barriers to employment. All stakeholders want to change, but Generation Z, the most diverse and purpose-driven generation, is particularly committed to a fairer and more equitable future. This wider societal transformation is embodied in the UN Agenda 2030, with its mantra to leave no one behind. How organizations drive change through diversity, inclusiveness and purpose will be the new measure for success in a stakeholder-centered economy. In this chapter we explore why organizations need to pursue diversity and how their response to diversity is shaped by the rallying cry of stakeholders (Fig. 1).

1   The Story of Nelson Mandela and the Springboks

On June 24, 1995, spectators packing the sellout Ellis Park stadium in Johannesburg, South Africa waited nervously for the first kickoff to start the much-anticipated Rugby World Cup between the South African national team, the Springboks, and the New Zealand All Blacks.

The backdrop to this legendary match was more than the usual high stakes of a world sporting competition. For years, South Africa had been the object of international sports boycotts because of apartheid, starting with its stinging exclusion from the Olympic Games in 1964. But in 1992, as the country moved

© Diversity and Performance BV 2021
K. Formanek, *Beyond D&I*, https://doi.org/10.1007/978-3-030-75336-8_2

Fig. 1 **Understanding**
Stakeholder Expectations
Determining what is
important to stakeholders
and their expectations of
organizations.

toward democracy, rugby was admitted back into international competition. As an acknowledgment of that transition, and a gesture of international esteem for Nelson Mandela who had campaigned for it the 1995 Rugby World Cup venue was awarded to South Africa. It was the first major sporting event to take place in the country following the end of apartheid.

Sport has the power to unite, but it was not certain that the match would deliver this result. In 1995, South Africa was at the beginning of racial transformation in every sphere of life. Just a year earlier, apartheid had ended, with South Africans electing Mandela as the first Black South African president in the first multi-racial elections. Sport still lagged: rugby was predominantly white, the team jersey's Springbok insignia a symbol of that segregation, and on that symbolic day at Ellis Park, some 60,000 spectators at the stadium were overwhelmingly white with the Springboks counting only one Black South African player in their team.

The Springboks were the underdogs. They were rusty and ill-prepared for this big match. It takes years of training and competition at international level to achieve competitive peak condition and the team entered the competition seeded ninth. The top seed, the New Zealand All Blacks (for their rugby playing colors), had been the Springbok's traditional mortal enemy for close to a century. But in what is now recognized as one of the most transformative moments in sporting history, minutes before the final began, the stunned crowd at Ellis stadium went silent as Mandela strode onto the pitch with his signature slow stride, wearing the team jersey with the Springbok on his heart and the captain's number, to shake the players' hands. Slowly, the chants began, rising louder, *"Nelson, Nelson, Nelson..."* What this pioneering inclusive leader understood was the power of sport to unite a nation. It was a language spoken by all.

At the final whistle, the teams were level going into extra time when the winning drop goal was scored by the Springboks, propelling them to victory against all odds. In that moment, with Mandela at their side, the Springboks became the

Fig. 2 Nelson Mandela, Francois Pienaar, and the Springboks
Nelson Mandela shaking the hand of Francois Pienaar, the captain of the Springboks.

World Rugby Champions of *all* South Africans—despite being a mainly white team. In a post-match interview, Francois Pienaar, captain of the Springboks, commented on the support and cohesion the team experienced: "We didn't have 60,000 South Africans, we had 43 million South Africans."[1]

The courageous leadership exemplified by Nelson Mandela throughout South Africa's troubled transition to democracy offers a masterclass in how to lead diversity and inclusion. While the scourge of apartheid in that nation may be gone, inequality persists, and the world today faces many challenges that demand the same courageous, inclusive leadership. To illustrate this ongoing leadership journey, we will return to the story of the Springboks in Chapter 5 and in the Conclusion (Fig. 2).

2   Leading with Diversity in a Time of Disruption

The fallout from the global COVID-19 pandemic has plunged societies once again into a time of disruption, when courageous leadership is called for as organizations take stock of the impacts of the pandemic, not least on diversity. The novel coronavirus first appeared in late 2019, causing millions of deaths worldwide. It not only triggered an unprecedented global public health crisis but brought longstanding and pronounced inequalities out of the shadows. Around the world, the pandemic has highlighted serious disparities in access to healthcare, education, and economic opportunity. It has had a devastating impact on poverty levels, and women, people of color, LGBTQI+ individuals, and people with disabilities, alongside the poor, elderly, and migrant populations, have borne the brunt.[2] Pre-pandemic, the world was already struggling to achieve diversity and inclusion: COVID-19 has made this worse.

As leaders come to terms with the ongoing impact of the pandemic on their operating model, they also need to consider the wider impacts of COVID-19 on diversity within their organizations and the societies of which they are a part. The pandemic has created important changes in the workplace and leaders have had to respond rapidly in tackling a number of key challenges—how to secure the safety of their employees, how to enable and support virtual work, how to create engagement and community when workers are confined to their homes—all while being affected by the most serious economic downturn since the Great Depression. While vaccines for COVID-19 have been developing and rolling out at record

---

[1] Smith (2013).

[2] "Diverse Employees Are Struggling the Most During COVID-19—Here's How Companies Can Respond," McKinsey & Co, November 17, 2020, https://www.mckinsey.com/featured-insights/diversity-and-inclusion/diverse-employees-are-struggling-the-most-during-covid-19-heres-how-companies-can-respond.

speed, it is uncertain when many developing countries will receive them, and different regional outlooks will persist as we continue to experience the aftershocks of the pandemic.

This disruption provides an important opportunity for a reset. The pandemic has peeled back the veneer on diversity progress, revealing parity gaps that continue to limit organizations' talent pools. In doing so, however, it presents a valuable opportunity for leaders to fundamentally re-shape their approach to diversity.

3   Gender Parity Still Lagging

Before COVID-19, women globally already faced a lack of parity, economically, politically, and in many regions around access to education and healthcare and post-pandemic this has worsened. The World Economic Forum's 2020 Global Gender Gap Report revealed a 31.4% gap to achieve gender equality. This was the result of analyzing gender parity in 153 countries across four dimensions: Economic Participation and Opportunity, Educational Attainment, Health and Survival, and Political Empowerment, as well as gender gap prospects in professions considered critical to the future.[3]

The good news was that educational attainment (96.1%) and health and survival (95.7%) had improved. But economic participation and opportunity remained a concern. This was the only dimension where progress had backtracked, reaching only 57.8% parity. Women's participation in the broader labor market has been stagnating, with growing financial disparities. The trend is even more pronounced in emerging and developing economies, offsetting advances for women in OECD countries. The upshot: it will be a stunning 257 years before gender parity can be reached in economic participation and opportunity.[4]

Why this lack of progress for women in the workforce? The Global Gender Gap Report noted three main reasons: women are overrepresented in roles that are being automated; too few women are entering professions with the highest wage growth (e.g., the tech sector), and women face the ongoing problem of inadequate care infrastructure and access to capital. A major factor preventing the economic gender gap from closing is women's under-representation in roles that will be part of the future work landscape. Women comprise only 12% of professionals in cloud computing, 15% in engineering, and 26% of data and AI roles.[5]

Regional differences are notable. Achieving gender parity in North America is expected to take *three times as long* as Western Europe—a wake-up call for

---

[3] Mind the 100 Year Gap, the 2020 Worldsw Economic Forum Global Gender Gap Report 2020, December 16, 2019, https://www.weforum.org/reports/gender-gap-2020-report-100-years-pay-equality.

[4] Mind the 100 Year Gap, World Economic Forum.

[5] Mind the 100 Year Gap, World Economic Forum.

leaders. Some countries have bucked the trend, such as Iceland, the most gender-equal country in the world, along with the high-performing Nordic countries. Others ranked in the top 10 included Nicaragua, Ireland, Spain, Rwanda, Germany, and New Zealand.[6] Overall, though, no region can claim that they are where they need to be.

COVID-19 has further slowed progress in women's economic participation as they have been disproportionately affected by the economic downturn. In Europe, the crisis is expected to increase the number of economically deprived people, particularly under-educated youth and single-parent families headed by women.[7] Nearly four times more women have left or lost employment than men.[8,9] Globally, women are on the frontlines of the pandemic, comprising 70% of health and social-services staff (a 200-million workforce),[10] increasing their exposure to the virus.[11] They are also highly concentrated in less secure, part-time work and in sectors experiencing high rates of pandemic-related unemployment, including hospitality, food services, and retail.[12]

Other concerns arising from the pandemic for women include health and safety of onsite workplaces, mental health issues, and work-life balance. More than men, women have struggled to balance work with increased household responsibilities. The stress of this "double shift" is not new but was exacerbated by the pandemic in some regions. Women in emerging economies such as India and Brazil, for example, were two to three times more likely to report challenges around balancing work and household responsibilities as a result of COVID-19 than women in developed countries, showing the compounding effect of local context.[13] School closures also disproportionately impacted working mothers: in a concerning sign that recent gains in women's employment could be eroded, in the U.S. and Canada the double shift led to one in four women in corporate jobs considering downshifting their careers or leaving the workforce.

While these gender inequalities are challenges for society at large, there are many areas where leaders can take action to address gender parity within their

---

[6] Mind the 100 Year Gap, World Economic Forum.

[7] Efi Koutsokosta, "Helping Europe's Poor Cope with COVID," Euronews, last updated June 4, 2020, https://www.euronews.com/2020/06/03/helping-europe-s-poor-cope-with-covid.

[8] Alon et al. (2020).

[9] Washington (2020).

[10] Women in the Health Workforce, World Health Organisation, last update March 2, 2018, https://www.who.int/hrh/events/2018/women-in-health-workforce/en/.

[11] Linde and Laya (2020).

[12] "COVID-19 and Gender Equality: Countering the Regressive Effects," McKinsey & Co, July 15, 2020, https://www.mckinsey.com/featured-insights/future-of-work/covid-19-and-gender-equality-countering-the-regressive-effects.

[13] "Diverse Employees Are Struggling the Most During COVID-19—Here's How Companies Can Respond," McKinsey & Co, November 17, 2020, https://www.mckinsey.com/featured-insights/diversity-and-inclusion/diverse-employees-are-struggling-the-most-during-covid-19-heres-how-companies-can-respond.

organizations to make sure women are not left behind post-pandemic. Committing to 50:50% gender representation, for example, supporting flexibility at work, adapting performance review processes, and ensuring continuing personal development, are among the many ways that leaders can help to stem the outflow of women from their organizations. We can also learn from the example of a remarkable courageous and inclusive leader, Prime Minister Jacinda Ardern (see Profile).

Profile of a Courageous Leader: Jacinda Ardern

Jacinda Ardern, the Prime Minister of New Zealand, is considered to be a trailblazer in diversity, demonstrating authenticity and courage since she came into office in 2017, as the world's youngest female head of government at age 37.[14] She was also the second sitting head of government to give birth while in office and her then three-month-old daughter Neve was the youngest person ever to attend the UN General Assembly.[15] With these acts, Ardern has helped break through stereotypes of women not being able to combine career and motherhood. On November 6, 2020, sworn in for her second term, she announced the country's most diverse cabinet ever: 40% women, 25% Māori, 15% Pacific islander background, and 15% LGBTQI+. Asked about the basis of her cabinet selection, she said it was based on "merit, talent and diversity."[16]

What makes Ardern such a stand-out leader is that she is both inward-looking, as shown by the commitment to diversity within her own Cabinet, but also outward-looking. At every opportunity, she emphasizes inclusiveness, diversity, sustainability, and her values. To the UN General Assembly in 2018, in an address that began in the Māori native language, she said New Zealand strives to be "outward looking, engaged in global institutions," and implored the world's leaders to recommit to gender equality and take a collective global approach to global challenges like isolationism, protectionism, climate change, racism, and inequality.[17] Ardern is among women leaders globally who demonstrated strong leadership during the COVID-19 pandemic, successfully flattening the curve to only a couple of dozen deaths in a country of 5 million.[18] New Zealand was recently ranked in the top spot for its response to the pandemic.[19] Empathy in crisis is a signature of her leadership style, displayed in March 2019 when she led the country through the aftermath of the Christchurch mosque shootings.[20]

---

[14] Wallenfeldt (2020).

[15] Wilkinson (2018).

[16] Curtin (2020).

[17] Ardern (2018).

[18] Friedman (2020).

[19] "Covid Performance Index," Lowy Institute, January 9, 2021, https://interactives.lowyinstitute.org/features/covid-performance/.

[20] Wikipedia, Christchurch Mosque Shootings, https://en.wikipedia.org/wiki/Christchurch_mosque_shootings, accessed November 20, 2020.

New Zealand was the first nation to give women the vote, in 1893.[21] "As a girl I never grew up believing that my gender would stand in the way of me achieving whatever I wanted in life," she told the UN General Assembly, "I am, after all, not the first, but the third female Prime Minister of New Zealand."

Ardern recognizes many countries do not share that heritage of equal rights for women. So, she fights on, knowing that around the world so many other women and girls experience a lack of the most basic dignity and opportunities. As she told world leaders reflecting on the global #MeToo movement that had galvanized women to stand up against sexual violence: "Me Too must become We Too."[22]

4   Calling Time on Racial Inequality

The persistent wealth gap attributed to racial discrimination and institutional racism is a global phenomenon. Already before the pandemic, there was a growing racial wealth gap for Black families in the U.S: in 2019 the median white household held $188,200 in wealth—7.8 times that of the typical Black household ($24,000).[23,] This is attributed to the weighty legacy of discrimination, poverty, and shortage of social connections, including role models and mentors in the community, that has arisen from entrenched racial economic inequity and oppression.[24,25]

It is a similar situation around the world: Black African employees born in the UK are paid 7.7% less than UK-born white British employees with similar occupational and educational backgrounds.[26] Despite making up almost four-fifths of the economically active population, Black South Africans still account for only 15% of top management positions in the country.[27] A recent government report found that despite efforts to transform the labor market, there is a pervasive and persistent preference for appointing, promoting, and developing White South Africans and Indian South Africans over Black South Africans.[28]

---

[21] "New Zealand History, Women and the Vote," https://nzhistory.govt.nz/politics/womens-suffrage#:~:text=On%2019%20September%201893%20the,to%20vote%20in%20parliamentary%20elections, accessed November 20, 2020.

[22] Ardern, Jacinda. New Zealand National Statement.

[23] Moss et al. (2020).

[24] Rodrigue and Reeves (2015).

[25] Chetty et al. (2019).

[26] Romei (2019).

[27] South African Government, August 19, 2020, Employment and Labour on 20th Commission for Employment Equity (CEE) Annual Report 2019–20, Department of Employment and Labour. https://www.gov.za/speeches/employment-and-labur-20th-commission-employment-equity-cee-annual-report-2019%E2%80%9320-19-aug.

[28] South African Government, Employment and Labour.

Minority groups are confronted with discrimination and racism in different ways. In recent years several European countries have been criticized for intolerance of diverse populations as nationalist, anti-religious minority and anti-immigrant sentiment has flared.[29,30] The refugee crisis that emerged in 2015 has exposed challenges around integration, multiculturalism, identity, and a sense of belonging.[31] In the Netherlands, some 78% of non-white citizens believe institutional racism still exists, with 56% experiencing discrimination in shops and businesses and 40% in schools or universities.[32] Pushback and concern have also arisen over the country's *Sinterklass* (Saint Nicholas) tradition, in which white people paint their faces black to embody the fictional character Black Pete.[33]

With the impacts of COVID-19, the situation has worsened in many ways for people of color. The economic toll of the pandemic has had a disproportionate impact on communities of color: in September 2020, only 53% of the U.S. adult Black population was employed, compared with 57% of the corresponding white population.[34] As a result of COVID-19, 39% of jobs held by Black workers were identified as more vulnerable to loss versus 34% for white workers in vulnerable jobs, i.e., those subject to furloughs, layoffs, or being rendered unproductive (e.g., being kept on the payroll but not working) during periods of high physical distancing.[35] As many as 65% of U.S. Hispanics and Latinos work in the five sectors now suffering the largest drops in GDP, including leisure, hospitality, and retail trade.[36]

When it comes to health, Black and Latino people have been three times more likely to be infected and nearly twice as likely to die from COVID-19 as white people.[37] This is due to a number of reasons, including the large proportion of people of color working in frontline jobs that prevent them working from home or in essential professions such as nursing, where they are more likely to be exposed to the virus. Many also depend on public transportation, reside in cramped

---

[29] Diamant and Starr (2018).

[30] European Union Agency for Fundamental Rights, 2019. Being Black in the EU: Second European Union Minorities and Discrimination Survey, November 15, https://fra.europa.eu/sites/default/files/fra_uploads/fra-2019-being-black-in-the-eu-summary_en.pdf, p. 3.

[31] Diez (2019).

[32] Holligan (2020).

[33] Holligan (2020).

[34] "The employment situation,"—September 2020, US Department of Labor, Bureau of Labor Statistics, September 2020, BLS.gov.

[35] "COVID-19: Investing in Black Lives and Livelihoods," McKinsey & Co, April 4, 2020, https://www.mckinsey.com/industries/public-and-social-sector/our-insights/covid-19-investing-in-black-lives-and-livelihoods.

[36] "US Hispanic and Latino Lives and Livelihoods in the Recovery from COVID-19," September 2, 2020, https://www.mckinsey.com/industries/public-and-social-sector/our-insights/us-hispanic-and-latino-lives-and-livelihoods-in-the-recovery-from-covid-19.

[37] Oppel et al. (2020).

apartments or multigenerational homes where transmission of the virus is more likely to occur,[38] or experience gaps in access to healthcare.[39] Research has also shown that racial discrimination takes a toll on an individual's health and increases their risk of illness.[40] Given these disproportionate health impacts, it comes as no surprise that workplace health and safety during COVID-19 has been ranked as an acute concern by people of color.[41]

Against this backdrop of great personal and economic upheaval, a burgeoning global movement against systemic racism has been building, shown by the lightning speed at which Black Lives Matter (BLM) spread around the world as the rallying cry for those protesting against ongoing racial discrimination and systemic inequality.

Leaders need to acknowledge the real challenges that people of color face, not only through the pandemic but through the negative impacts that systemic racism exerts on job opportunities, promotion, and socio-economic equity. Supporting Black colleagues and employees, committing to invest in anti-racism training and actively mitigating implicit bias in their organizations are important steps leaders can take to address this.

5   Multiple Barriers Faced by the LGBTQI+ Community

A history of discrimination and inequality also characterizes the experience of LGBTQI+ individuals: people who identify as lesbian, gay, bisexual, transgender, queer, or gender nonbinary. LGBTQI+ communities have universally reported discrimination in the workplace, impacting individuals at every point of their career from the hiring stage and interview to everyday work culture. Nearly one in four LGBTQI+ Americans have reported being treated unfairly by an employer, and over half report being the target of slurs or jokes.[42]

A similar situation exists in Europe, where the EU Fundamental Rights Agency's annual survey reveals little, if any, progress between 2012 and 2019 with regard to how LGBTQI+ people in the EU experience fundamental human rights in daily life. While those who felt discriminated against during the hiring process fell slightly, from 13 to 11% between 2012–2019, 21% of LGBTQI+ individuals

---

[38] Oppel et al. (2020).

[39] Fitzhugh et al. (2020).

[40] Williams et al. (2003).

[41] "Diverse Employees Are Struggling the Most During COVID-19—Here's How Companies Can Respond," McKinsey & Co, November 17, 2020, https://www.mckinsey.com/featured-insights/diversity-and-inclusion/diverse-employees-are-struggling-the-most-during-covid-19-heres-how-companies-can-respond.

[42] "A Survey of LGBT Americans," Pew Research Center, June 13, 2013, https://www.pewsocialtrends.org/2013/06/13/a-survey-of-lgbt-americans/

reported feeling discriminated against once they were hired, up from 19% in 2012. The figures are even higher for trans respondents, where 36% reported feeling discriminated against at work in 2019, up from 22% in 2012.[43]

Globally, both the rights and experiences of LGBTQI+ individuals differ considerably based on country and geographic location. In the EU and U.S., sexual orientation is a legally protected diversity characteristic,[44] but that is far from the case in other parts of the world. Homosexuality, for instance, remains criminalized in at least 72 countries including Uganda, where Frank Mugisha, an advocate for LGBTQI+ is fighting for equal rights for his community (see Profile).[45]

Again, the COVID-19 crisis has disproportionately affected LGBTQI+ individuals. More than the general population, this community fears losing ground at work and feeling isolated during the pandemic. They are 1.4 times more likely to cite "acute" challenges in terms of fair performance reviews, heavier workload, and struggling to cope with loss of workplace connectivity and belonging.[46] Two out of three LGBTQI+ employees acknowledge experiencing acute or moderate challenges with mental health issues.[47] LGBTQI+ youth, in particular, face increased risk of anxiety and suicide and higher rates of unemployment and unstable housing, according to the US LGBT charity The Trevor Project.[48]

To counter these barriers, leaders can offer support and build more inclusive communities around their LGBTQI+ employees, including innovating in the way that mental health support and mentorship are provided.

Profile of a Courageous Leader: Frank Mugisha

Dr. Frank Mugisha is a prominent advocate for the rights of sexual minorities in Uganda, a respected champion of human rights, and an anti-violence advocate. He was born in 1979 in a suburb of Kampala, Uganda, raised in a strict Catholic family.[49] As he wrote in *The New York Times* in 2011, Mugisha came out to his brother at age 14; while some relatives accepted him, others became estranged.[50] He went on

---

[43] "European Union Agency for Fundamental Rights," 2020, A long way to go for LGBTI equality, https://fra.europa.eu/sites/default/files/fra_uploads/fra-2020-lgbti-equality-1_en.pdf.

[44] Poushter and Kent (2020).

[45] Erasing 76 Crimes. 72 Countries Where Homosexuality Is Illegal. Last modified July 2020, https://76crimes.com/76-countries-where-homosexuality-is-illegal/, accessed December 17, 2020.

[46] "Diverse Employees Are Struggling the Most During COVID-19—Here's How Companies Can Respond," McKinsey & Co, November 17, 2020, https://www.mckinsey.com/featured-insights/diversity-and-inclusion/diverse-employees-are-struggling-the-most-during-covid-19-heres-how-companies-can-respond.

[47] "Diverse Employees Are Struggling the Most During COVID-19," McKinsey & Co.

[48] Wareham (2020).

[49] The Ubuntu Biography Project, Dr. Frank Mugisha, https://ubuntubiographyproject.com/2017/06/17/dr-frank-mugisha, accessed November 20, 2020.

[50] "Gay and Vilified in Uganda," *The New York Times*, December 22, 2011, https://www.nytimes.com/2011/12/23/opinion/gay-and-vilified-in-uganda.html, accessed November 20, 2020.

to become an activist, and is now Executive Director of Sexual Minorities Uganda (SMUG), a coalition of the country's leading lesbian, gay, bisexual, transgender, and intersex (LGBTI) rights organizations. While at university in 2004 he founded Icebreakers Uganda, a support network for LGBTI Ugandans that now forms part of SMUG.[51]

Mugisha leads his community at great personal risk. Uganda is one of at least 72 countries around the world where homosexuality is criminalized.[52] In 2014, new legislation in Uganda that would have raised the penalty for homosexuality from life in prison to death was struck down in the country's Mugisha and other activists in fighting against it.[53] But the government has continued to threaten to revive the bill as part of its ongoing pressure on the LGBTQI+ population. In a country where the majority of people reject homosexuality, to be openly gay in Uganda is to risk bullying and beatings and to fear for your life. In 2010, Mugisha's close friend, fellow gay rights activist David Kato, was killed after a local tabloid exposed the names of gay people, picturing Kato and another man on the cover under the words "Hang them."[54]

"Still, I continue to hope," as Mugisha wrote. "Standing on David's shoulders, we are no longer alone. I call on other leaders … to stand with me and my fellow advocates, to help dispel harmful myths perpetuated by ignorance and hate. The lives of many are on the line."[55]

For his advocacy on behalf of LGBTQI+ people, Mugisha won the 2011 Robert F Kennedy Award for Human Rights, was a 2014 nominee for the Nobel Peace Prize, and in 2017, was included in Fortune magazine's list of the world's greatest leaders.[56]

6   An Uphill Road for Persons with Disabilities

Persons with disabilities make up 15% of the world population—over a billion people—and this is expected to double to two billion by 2030.[57] Women are more likely to experience disability than men and older people more than young.

---

[51] Dr Frank Mugisha. University of Glasgow Story, https://universitystory.gla.ac.uk/biography/?id=WH26895&type=P, accessed November 20, 2020.

[52] Erasing 76 Crimes. 72 Countries Where Homosexuality Is Illegal. Last modified July 2020, https://76crimes.com/76-countries-where-homosexuality-is-illegal/, accessed December 17, 2020.

[53] Amnesty International, 2014, Uganda: Anti-Homosexuality Act Struck Down in Step Towards Ending Discrimination, https://www.amnesty.org/en/latest/news/2014/08/uganda-anti-homosexuality-act-overturned/, accessed December 17, 2020.

[54] The Ubuntu Biography Project, Dr. Frank Mugisha.

[55] Mugisha, Gay and Vilified.

[56] The Ubuntu Biography Project, Dr. Frank Mugisha.

[57] World Health Organisation (2011), World Report on Disability.

Low- and middle-income countries have higher rates of disability than high-income countries, and the impact of disability on people in poorer areas is compounded by issues of accessibility and lack of healthcare services. Indigenous persons, internally displaced or stateless persons, refugees, migrants, and prisoners with disability also face particular challenges in accessing services.[58]

The disparity faced by persons with disabilities is particularly pronounced in the labor force. Globally, employment rates for people with disabilities are 53% lower for men and 20% lower for women with disabilities than for persons without disabilities.[59] In the 37 member countries of the Organisation for Economic Co-operation and Development (OECD), the employment rate of people with disability is 44%, compared to three-quarters of those without disability.[60] Starkly, in the U.S., just 19.3% of people with a disability were employed in 2019, compared to 66.3% for persons without disabilities[61] and of those who were employed, a third of workers with disabilities were employed part-time, compared with 17% of those with no disabilities.[62]

These gaps are perpetuated by stereotypes and incorrect assumptions that persons with disabilities are less productive than those with no disabilities.[63] Research shows that more than one in three people have an unconscious bias against those with a disability, higher than for either gender or race.[64] Those with hidden disability—i.e., disability that may not be immediately obvious—also face isolation and exclusion: a mere 16% of autistic adults are in full-time paid employment and 40% of autistic adults working part-time would like to work more hours.[65]

People with disabilities are not trying to claim 'special rights' or even 'disability rights'; for them it is important to see the person, not the disability. They claim the same fundamental human rights as everyone else. Yet despite legal protections that are part of national law in many countries and through the UN Convention on the Rights of Persons with Disabilities,[66] discrimination persists. One passionate

---

[58] World Health Organization, Disability.

[59] World Health Organization. Disability.

[60] World Health Organization, 2020, 10 Facts on disability. https://www.who.int/news-room/facts-in-pictures/detail/disabilities, accessed November 19, 2020.

[61] U.S. Bureau of Labor Statistics, Persons with a Disability: Labor Force Characteristics—2019, February 26, 2020, https://www.bls.gov/news.release/disabl.nr0.htm.

[62] U.S. Bureau of Labor Statistics, Persons with a Disability: Labor Force Characteristics Summary. https://www.bls.gov/news.release/disabl.nr0.htm.

[63] Bonaccio et al. (2020).

[64] ENEI, 2014, Disability: A Research Study on Unconscious Bias.

[65] "Government Pledges to Monitor Autism Employment Gap—For the First Time," July 4, 2019, https://www.learningdisabilitytoday.co.uk/government-pledges-to-monitor-autism-employment-gap-for-the-first-time.

[66] *Convention on the Rights of Persons with Disabilities (CRPD)*, New York, December 13, 2006, *United Nations Treaty Series*, vol. 2515, No. 44910, p. 3, available from https://treaties.un.org/doc/Publication/UNTS/No%20Volume/44910/Part/I-44910-080000028017bf87.pdf.

advocate for the rights of people with disabilities is Nujeen Mustafa, a Kurdish Syrian refugee, and activist (see Profile).

Governments have instituted different types of support to address employment challenges for people with disabilities, not always successfully. Some countries, like Japan, face criticism for inflating the number of persons with disabilities in order to meet quotas.[67] China put in place a quota for persons with disabilities in 2008, reserving 1.5% of jobs for people with disabilities, yet this has not translated into real integration, instead prompting the practice of *"guakao"*—employing disabled people without giving them actual work to complete.[68]

Against already challenging circumstances, COVID-19 has created new challenges for people with disabilities: approximately 1 million U.S. workers with disabilities lost their jobs—that is, 1 in 5 workers with disabilities compared with 1 in 7 in the general population.[69] The reasons for this are varied: when employers laid off or furloughed workers, it was the most recent hires—often people with disabilities—who were affected. People with disabilities were frequently employed in sectors facing the greatest job losses such as retail and hospitality. There has also been employer hesitancy to hire people with disabilities during the pandemic over whether allowing such new hires to work remotely could be considered a "reasonable accommodation" as required by the Americans with Disabilities Act—something employers are often concerned would be expensive, according to the National Organization on Disability.[70] Overall, people with disabilities more frequently report that coronavirus has affected their wellbeing and made their mental health worse,[71] notably when carers were required to self-isolate, leaving many vulnerable people without support services.

In meeting their organization's diversity goals, leaders need to make disability inclusion part of the company's broader diversity efforts and create workplaces that are more conducive to people with disabilities. Among the key barriers people with disabilities face is the implicit bias that results in more than 75% of people unconsciously favoring those with no disabilities over those with disabilities.[72]

---

[67] Reuters, "Japan Ministries May Have Fiddled Numbers of Disabled Employees: Media," August 17, 2018, https://br.reuters.com/article/idUSKBN1L20D5, accessed November 19, 2020.

[68] Increasing Employment of People With Disabilities in Asia.

[69] "New Employer Survey Portends Difficult Road Ahead for People with Disabilities Who Lost Their Jobs During COVID-19 Pandemic, National Organization on Disability," July 16, 2020, https://www.nod.org/new-employer-survey-portends-difficult-road-ahead-for-people-with-disabilities-who-lost-their-jobs-during-covid-19-pandemic/.

[70] New Employer Survey Portends Difficult Road Ahead, National Organization on Disability.

[71] "Coronavirus and the Social Impacts on Disabled People in Great Britain: September 2020," Office for National Statistics, https://www.ons.gov.uk/peoplepopulationandcommunity/healthandsocialcare/disability/datasets/coronavirusandthesocialimpactsondisabledpeoplein-greatbritainmay2020, accessed January 3, 2021.

[72] "Implicit Biases & People with Disabilities," ABA Commission on Disability Rights, January 7, 2019, https://www.americanbar.org/groups/diversity/disabilityrights/resources/implicit_bias/.

Profile of a Courageous Leader: Nujeen Mustafa

When she was just sixteen, Nujeen Mustafa, a Kurdish Syrian refugee, and activist with cerebral palsy, made the 3,500-mile journey from Syria to Germany in a steel wheelchair, fleeing conflict in the Syrian Civil War. As her family couldn't afford for all of them to make it safely to Germany, where Nujeen's brother lives, her parents remained in Turkey while Nujeen made the trip across the Mediterranean with her sister—facing insurmountable odds for the opportunity to live a normal life and get an education.[73]

Confined to her apartment in Aleppo, Nujeen had taught herself English by watching shows on TV. But she longed for so much more. As she told National Geographic, since her building had no elevator, she could only leave her apartment by having someone carry her down. She said it was like house arrest: "For me, it meant not being able to go to school, hang out with friends or go to the cinema…having a disability in Syria often means that you are hidden away. You confront shame, discrimination and physical barriers. You are someone who is pitied."[74]

With the same optimism and defiance that enabled her to flee Syria for a better life, Nujeen, now 21, has become a powerful advocate for refugee youth and for persons with disabilities. She speaks at high-profile events on behalf of the UN Refugee Agency and others. At the 2019 Global Refugee Forum, Nujeen stressed how important it was for people with disabilities to have active involvement and meaningful participation in every aspect of planning the refuges response. "We are not asking this as a favor," she said. "This is our right."[75]

7   An Accelerating Societal Trend Toward Greater Inclusiveness

Progress has often been painfully slow to address the myriad societal challenges that stand in the way of greater diversity, equity, and inclusion (Fig. 3). But the drive for greater progress has been accelerating—and will gather pace with pressure from Gen Z, as explored in the next section.

8   A Generation Battle-Hardened by COVID-19

Why is there such a focus on the pandemic in setting out the context for a book about diversity and inclusion? Because this once-in-a-generation event may prove to be an inflection point that alters the organizational landscape for good. Younger generations too have been disproportionately affected by COVID-19. In the UK,

---

[73] UNHCR, Nujeen Mustafa, https://www.unhcr.org/nujeen-mustafa.html, accessed November 21, 2020.

[74] Worrall (2016).

[75] UNHCR, Nujeen Mustafa.

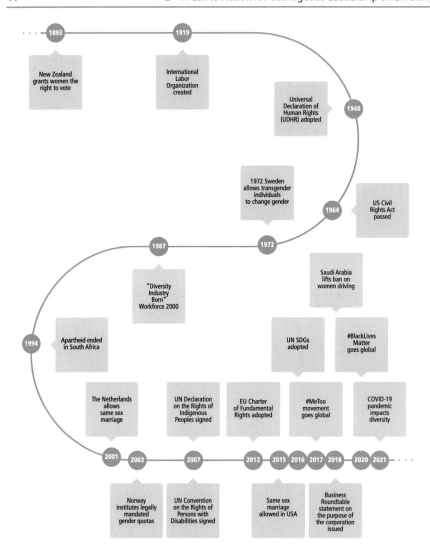

Fig. 3   Timeline of Select Diversity Developments
The frequency of significant diversity and inclusion milestones has been accelerating in recent years.

for instance, it was those aged 25 to 34 who faced the biggest risk of unemployment.[76] In the U.S., half of the oldest Gen Zers (aged 18 to 23) reported that they, or someone in their household, had lost a job or taken a pay cut because of the

---

[76]Labour Market Overview, UK: January 2021, https://www.ons.gov.uk/employmentandlabourmarket/peopleinwork/employmentandemployeetypes/bulletins/uklabourmarket/january2021.

outbreak, significantly higher than the share of Millennials (40%), Gen Xers (36%)or Baby Boomers (25%) (Table 1).

The long-term impacts of the pandemic on any generation remain to be seen but as the 2020 Deloitte Global Millennial Survey put it:

> When historians assess the effects of the 2020 COVID-19 pandemic on society, the response of millennials and Generation Z will be notable. Battle-hardened by the trying circumstances that have shaped their generations from the beginning, these younger generations are remaining steadfast, refusing to compromise their values—and that attitude may ultimately help change society.[77]

It is this group of individuals who make up the future employees, customers, and leaders of our organizations. They will bring into our organizations the causes that matter to them along with growing expectations on what constitutes good corporate conduct and courageous, inclusive leadership. These excerpts from the survey's findings show why this is relevant to the leader[78]:

1. "The pandemic has brought about an even stronger sense of individual responsibility. Nearly three-fourths said the pandemic has made them more sympathetic toward others' needs and that they intend to take actions to have a positive impact on their communities."
2. "Both generations said they'll make a special effort to more actively patronize and support businesses—especially smaller, local sellers—after the pandemic. But they won't hesitate to penalize companies whose stated and practiced values conflict with their own."
3. "A majority of respondents gave businesses and governments high marks for their pandemic responses. Actions taken during the crisis, however, did not translate into overall better opinions of business."
4. "Many are financially prudent and literate. While long-term finances are a top cause of stress, more than half of millennials, and nearly half of Gen Zs, are saving money and could cope if they unexpectedly received a large bill."
5. "Job loyalty rises as businesses address employee needs, from diversity and inclusion to sustainability and reskilling. In the primary survey, more millennials said they'd like to stay with their employers for at least five years than would prefer to leave within two years."

As millennials and Gen Zers join the different stakeholder groups that together form the operating ecosystem of organizations, they bring to the fore the themes that are important to them. To meet their needs and secure the future of an organization's chief asset—its people—it is crucial that leaders are prepared for this change.

---

[77] "The Deloitte Global Millennial Survey 2020: Resilient Generations Hold the Key to Creating a 'Better normal'," Deloitte, 2020, https://www2.deloitte.com/global/en/pages/about-deloitte/articles/millennialsurvey.html.

[78] "The Deloitte Global Millennial Survey 2020: Resilient Generations Hold the Key to Creating a 'Better Normal'," Deloitte, 2020, https://www2.deloitte.com/global/en/pages/about-deloitte/articles/millennialsurvey.html.

Table 1   Generational Views on Diversity
The six generations born between 1901 and 1997 hold different views on sustainability, diversity, equity, purpose, and inclusiveness.

Generational Group	Born (from)	Born (to)	Age in 2025	Other Names
Generation Z "Gen Z"	1997	No end point set	<=28	Post-Millennial iGen Homelanders
Millennials	1981	1996	29 - 44	Generation Y
Generation X "Gen X"	1965	1980	45 - 60	Sandwich Generation Latchkey Generation
Baby Boomers	1946	1964	61 - 79	Boomers
Silent Generation	1928	1945	80 - 97	Traditionalists
Greatest Generation	1901	1927	98 -	G.I. Generation WWII Generation

Adapted from Pew Research Center
"Defining generations: Where Millenials end and Generation Z begins", 2019

9   A Cohort Reshaping the Workplace

Millennials have been in the workforce for over 15 years and Gen Z is now knock-ing on the door. Worldwide, already 41% of the population is Gen Z.[79] In 2020, they represented five percent of the workforce[80] and they constitute the most diverse generation. In 2019, for the first time, over half of the U.S. population under age 16 identified as a racial or ethnic minority, with Latino, Hispanic or Black residents making up 40% of this group.[81] This is part of a trend which will see ethnic and racial minorities comprise the majority of the U.S. population by 2045.[82] These Gen Zers represent the future business leaders of tomorrow.

Both Millennials and Gen Z prioritize sustainability and working for, and buy-ing from, companies with "purpose." This new generation of citizens, consumers, and employees cares deeply about sustainability, diversity, inclusiveness, and pur-pose. Specifically Gen Z—the most racially and ethnically diverse of the generation groups—stands out as caring deeply about equity, equality, and the role of organ-izations in putting stakeholder value above shareholder profit.[83,84] The demands these groups place on society and business will have a lasting impact on the work-place of tomorrow, changing organizations and the context in which they operate.

Millennials and Gen Z, while distinct in several ways, are both mindful of the world they have inherited and the perils faced by the planet and many of its people (see Table 1). They have a strong sense that generations before them have colo-nized their future. They are worried about a number of global issues, including climate change, poverty, and hunger and they are supportive of the role of the United Nations to help solve world challenges.[85] But while Millennials are primar-ily invested in climate change and protecting the environment, Gen Z is concerned about income inequality, uneven distribution of wealth, diversity, and inclusive-ness. Both groups are deeply committed to equality and equity.[86]

---

[79] "World Population Prospects 2019," United Nations.

[80] Fry (2018).

[81] Frey (2020).

[82] Frey (2018).

[83] "Distribution of the Race and Ethnicity of the United States Population in 2018, by Genera-tion," Statista, 2019, https://www.statista.com/statistics/206969/race-and-ethnicity-in-the-us-by-generation/, accessed November 20, 2020.

[84] "Resident Population in the United States in 2019, by Generation," Statista, 2020, https://www.statista.com/statistics/797321/us-population-by-generation/, accessed November 20, 2020.

[85] "New Survey Reveals Strong Support of United Nations from Millennials and Gen Z but Have Little Understanding of the Sustainable Development Goals," Edelman, Cision PR Newswire, September 23, 2019, https://www.prnewswire.com/news-releases/new-survey-reveals-strong-sup-port-of-united-nations-from-millennials-and-gen-z-but-have-little-understanding-of-the-sustaina-ble-development-goals-300922991.html.

[86] Volini et al. (2020).

Both cohorts are deeply distrustful of organizations and their leaders, and they have little faith in the economy, politics, and the press. Some 81% of Millennials believe that the private sector has a very important role to play in achieving the UN Sustainable Development Goals—but less than 30% actually believe that businesses will put sustainability first.[87] Consequently, they feel a personal responsibility to act as agents of change in the world. A GlobeScan survey of 27,000 people across 27 countries, carried out in June 2020, found that: "We are increasingly moving into an age of activism, where younger generations are more likely to use their voices to affect change."[88] One in seven Gen Z respondents had protested publicly in the past 12 months "to make a difference on an economic, environmental, social or political issue that they care about."[89] These generations naturally tend to support organizations that align to their values and purpose.[90,91]

10   The Growing Influence of Gen Z

As Gen Z increasingly becomes part of every key stakeholder group, it will exert growing influence on the way organizations behave. A generation with incredible power to augment its messaging through a natural command of technology and social media, Gen Z will progressively transform the conversation around diversity through its determination to shape a fairer and more equitable future.

Thanks to the lightning pace of the digital revolution, information and news are disseminated faster than ever before around the globe, giving stakeholders a level of transparency unparalleled in history. Gen Z, who are digital natives—born in the digital era—are particularly adept at using technology to amplify their voice on the issues they care about.[92] They are intrepid users of social collaboration systems and mobile platforms that characterize this new era. They know how to tap into the rich information sources at their fingertips, which have made them savvy, self-reliant, resourceful, and able to thrive in agile environments where they are not afraid to challenge the status quo. With fiercely held, liberal views on diversity and inclusion, equality is non-negotiable.[93]

---

[87] "Millennials Want True Commitment to SDGs. Companies Can Start by Listening," Citibeats, May 2018, https://citibeats.com/millennials-sdgs-csr/.

[88] "GlobeScan Radar: The Latest Trends That Will Shape 2020 and Beyond," January 2020, https://globescan.com/wp-content/uploads/2021/03/GlobeScan-Insight-of-the-Week-Protested-Publicly-Mar2021.png.

[89] GlobeScan Radar: The Latest Trends That will Shape 2020 and Beyond.

[90] Volini et al. (2020).

[91] Daniela Flores, "Reaching Millennials and Generation Z with Purpose," PRCA, https://www.prca.org.uk/Reaching-Millennials-and-Generation-Z-with-Purpose.

[92] Parker and Igielnik (2020).

[93] Vander Linde and Weatherly, "Engaging Gen Z on Social."

While technology is certainly not a silver bullet, it does have transformative potential if harnessed to raise awareness of societal needs and challenges. For many of the grassroots movements campaigning for equality, it has been a gamechanger in rallying support, shining a light on persistent diversity gaps in society, and shifting the conversation.

11 Changing Stakeholder Expectations

Although research has primarily focused on the influence of younger generations in calling for a more equitable and sustainable world, these themes also resonate with older people and are increasingly being demanded by a wide range of organizational stakeholders. Organizations and their leaders exist as part of a global community, and each stakeholder group within that community has their own specific wants and needs (Fig. 4).

Across these stakeholder groups, when it comes to social or societal sustainability expectations, certain key themes or focus areas are converging (Fig. 5). These five common stakeholder themes center around diversity of people, inclusion, equity, leadership, and purpose.

The re-occurring Diversity Performance themes are:

1. **Diversity**: Stakeholders expect organizations to have diversity of representation and diversity of thinking to reflect their operating context and be resilient and adaptive to change.
2. **Inclusion**: Stakeholders expect organizations to be inclusive to their employees and customers and want the barriers restricting some groups from participating socially and economically to be removed.
3. **Equity**: Stakeholders expect organizations to recognize that many members of society are negatively impacted by pervasive bias. There is an expectation that organizations will mitigate bias and support access to resources and opportunities based on need.
4. **Leadership**: Stakeholders are looking for courageous and authentic leaders who are willing to challenge inequity and inspire inclusiveness in their organizations.
5. **Purpose**: Stakeholders are looking to organizations to create holistic stakeholder value, not only shareholder value.

Here we take a look at five stakeholder groups exerting a growing influence on organizations' pursuit of Diversity Performance.

Purpose increasingly important to consumers—A number of surveys confirm that a growing segment of consumers are rallying around key global themes, with

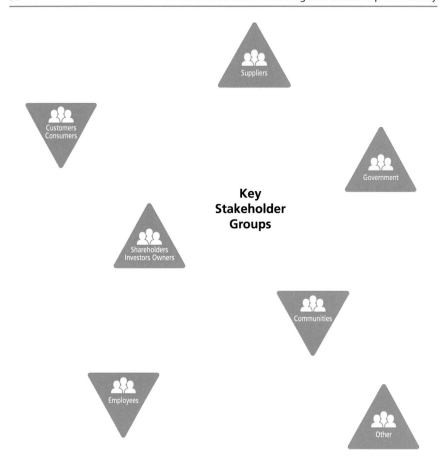

Fig. 4   Stakeholders are Shaping the Environment
Organizations face growing expectations and requirements from their key stakeholder groups, which primarily consist of employees, customers and consumers, suppliers, shareholders and investors or owners, communities and society at large.

sustainability and equality at the forefront. Two-thirds of global consumers say they are willing to pay more for sustainable brands[94] and over 90% of millennials would switch brands to one associated with a cause.[95] These consumers expect organizations to lead with purpose and demonstrate their core values in their customer interactions.

[94] "Nielson Global Corporate Sustainability Report," Nielsen, 2015, https://www.nielsen.com/us/en/insights/report/2015/the-sustainability-imperative-2/, accessed November 15, 2020.

[95] "2015 Cone Communications Millennial CSR Study," Cone, 2015, https://www.conecomm.com/research-blog/2015-cone-communications-millennial-csr-study, accessed November 15, 2020.

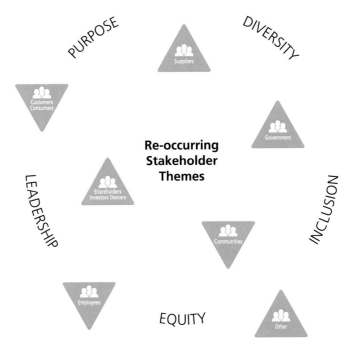

Fig. 5 **Re-occurring Stakeholder Themes**
There are five common stakeholder themes emerging around diversity of people, inclusion, equity, leadership, and purpose.

It is leading them to ask probing questions of the companies they buy from: Does this organization understand me? Does it speak to me in a diverse and inclusive way, or does it perpetuate stereotypes through its branding? Consumers see themselves as change agents and they are increasingly choosing to support with their wallets those organizations whose purpose and values mirror their own.[96]

Consumers are a powerful force for transformation because they start campaigns around causes that they care about and boycott businesses for practices they consider unfair or unsustainable. Their power is enhanced by social media, which allows small-scale activism to grow into large social movements around shared values. Millennial consumers in particular show an affiliation for these values and want corporations and institutions to act as forces for good.[97]

Employees rapidly changing the talent landscape—The expectation that employers show leadership on diversity is not only coming from younger generations in the global North. In Asia for example, 71% of women said they take into

---

[96] Porter et al. (2015).

[97] Chong (2017).

account whether an employer publicly shares progress on diversity when deciding to take a job with the company.[98] Two-thirds of early career Asian women (versus 58% globally) say it is important that employers publicly disclose diversity demographics of their workforce and leadership team. Leadership team diversity also mattered to 76% of Asian women when evaluating if they would take a position with their most recent employer, (compared to 61% globally).

Diversity is also a key driver of happiness at work. Before COVID-19, the following factors were named most often by employees as important to their happiness: employee trust in their company's leadership; employers' commitment to employees and their success; a culture where employees are encouraged to share ideas and individual opinions; a workplace where coworkers feel like family or friends; and benefits customized to meet employee needs. Post-pandemic, it is those employees who feel supported by their employers who report feeling more successful, valued, engaged, productive, and respected. If employees are unsupported, those feelings drop significantly.[99]

The rise of responsible investing—Investors and shareholders are also demanding that organizations demonstrate commitment to diversity, equity, and inclusiveness. Shareholder interest in social issues has grown significantly in recent years as part of a wider push to address Environment, Social and Governance (ESG) factors and is driving companies to demonstrate stronger action on diversity. Investor groups expect to see evidence that companies are recruiting, retaining, and promoting diverse talent across the organization.

Investor coalitions like Racial Justice Investing Coalition are amplifying Black voices in investor spaces and company engagements.[100] In the U.S., the market's first racial equity product, the Impact Shares NAACP Minority Empowerment ETF from the NAACP, the country's leading civil rights organization, is giving investors a lens for evaluating companies with strong racial and ethnic diversity policies.[101]

Shareholder activism is also on the rise, notably in the U.S., Europe, and Asia, as a means of pressuring organizations to demonstrate progress on issues such as diversity on boards and sustainability commitments.[102] Instead of divesting, these investors advocate vocally for change by making strategic use of resolutions and the proxy card at Annual General Meetings, for example.

Embracing diversity in the supply chain—In addition to calls for transparency and sustainability, there is growing demand for more diversity within supply chains.[103] In 2019, women accounted for 39% of the total supply chain workforce

---

[98] Loon (2020).

[99] Derks (2020).

[100] "Investor Statement of Solidarity to Address Systemic Racism and Call to Action, Racial Justice Investing," https://www.racialjusticeinvesting.org/our-statement, accessed February 7, 2020.

[101] Brown (2020).

[102] Grossman and Berg (2019).

[103] Maurelli and Mussomeli (2020).

but only 11% of executive supply chain leadership positions.[104] In recognition of this, some leading organizations are committing to inclusive procurement through supplier diversity programs. A "diverse supplier" is a business that "is at least 51% owned and operated by an individual or group that is part of a traditionally under-represented or underserved group."[105] This commonly includes small, woman- and minority-owned business enterprises, but also other minority-owned or operated businesses such as LGBTQI+, veterans, and proprietors with disabilities.

Inclusive procurement is being pursued not only for ethical reasons but for the commercial benefits of widening the pool of potential suppliers, enhancing competition, supporting an organization's brand proposition as a responsible employer and as a means to support positive societal impact in the value chain by obliging suppliers to uphold human rights, equal opportunities, and greater inclusion.

Government policy to accelerate diversity—Diversity and inclusion are enshrined global norms under many United Nations (UN) conventions and treaties. The Discrimination (Employment and Occupation) Convention 1958 (No. 111) of the International Labor Organization, for example, establishes equality of opportunity and treatment at work as a fundamental right in member states, with the aim of eliminating discrimination.[106] But in spite of longstanding legal protections, inequalities persist.

As a result, amidst growing pressure from consumers and citizens, regulators have passed a number of laws targeting board diversity and wage equity in recent years, marking a new era of diversity enforcement, characterized by pay equity protections, board diversity targets, and penalties. Under the motto "United in Diversity," for example, the EU has attempted to advance gender diversity by passing a set of anti-discrimination Directives in 2000. The Employment Equality Directives provide everyone in the EU (citizens and third-country nationals) with a common minimum level of legal protection against discrimination.[107] In 2010, it launched the EU Platform of Diversity Charters to support companies, public institutions, and nonprofit organizations in putting diversity, inclusion, and solidarity at the core of their activities[108] and in 2012, the EU set a goal for 40% female representation on the boards of directors of 5,000 large corporations listed in the

---

[104] Stiffler and Chumakov (2019).

[105] Bateman (2020).

[106] C111—Discrimination (Employment and Occupation) Convention, 1958, (No. 111), https://www.ilo.org/dyn/normlex/en/f?p=NORMLEXPUB:12100:0::NO::P12100_ILO_CODE:C111, accessed March 13, 2021.

[107] "The Employment Equality Directive, European Commission," January 31, 2008, https://ec.europa.eu/commission/presscorner/detail/en/MEMO_08_69.

[108] "EU Platform of Diversity Charters, European Commission," https://ec.europa.eu/info/policies/justice-and-fundamental-rights/combatting-discrimination/tackling-discrimination/diversity-management/eu-platform-diversity-charters_en.

EU.[109] In 2018, EU diversity reforms were introduced compelling companies to provide the public with clarity on wage gaps and diversity on boards.[110]

This is replicated at national level in many countries: France intends to fine companies that fail to disclose pay equity gaps.[111] The UK is considering a mandate requiring companies with 250 or more employees to report their ethnicity and Black, Asian, and minority ethnic pay gaps.[112] In 2018, Iceland became the first country in the world to mandate companies to pay men and women equally.[113] Canada's Bill C-86 includes pay equity protections[114] and in South Africa, employers are required to report and explain salary differentials for women and men of color.[115]

To promote diversity on boards, gender targets are being regulated worldwide. Norway pioneered corporate board quotas in 2003 and by the beginning of 2018, 10 European countries had followed suit. Many of the quotas impose sanctions for non-compliance. A common sanctioning mechanism implemented by France, Belgium, Germany, Portugal, and Austria is the "open seat" approach: vacant board positions can be filled only by the underrepresented sex. France and Belgium additionally place sanctions on organizations by withholding fees to the remaining board members while a board seat remains open.[116]

Regulatory resolve is also evident in the U.S. at state and federal levels. In October 2018 California passed Senate Bill 826, which imposes Corporate Board Quotas (CBQ) requirements for any public or foreign company with executive offices in California. In addition, by the end of 2021, companies with five directors were required to include at least two women on the board, and those with six directors must include at least three women. Failure to comply entails a penalty of USD$100,000.[117]

Whether it is consumers, employees, suppliers, investors, or regulators, each stakeholder group is reinforcing the need for greater diversity, inclusiveness,

---

[109] "Women on Boards: Commission Proposes 40% Objective," European Commission, November 14, 2012, https://ec-europa-eu.ezp.sub.su.se/commission/presscorner/detail/en/qanda_20_24.

[110] "2019 Report on Equality Between Women and Men in the EU," European Commission, 2019, https://ec.europa.eu/info/sites/info/files/aid_development_cooperation_fundamental_rights/annual_report_ge_2019_en_1.pdf.

[111] "France to Fine Companies If Gender Pay Gaps Not Erased," Reuters, March 7, 2018, https://www.reuters.com/article/us-france-women/france-to-fine-companies-if-gender-pay-gaps-not-erased-idUSKCN1GJ31U.

[112] Batha (2020).

[113] "Iceland Now the First Country to Enforce Equal Pay for Women and Men," BBC News, January 3, 2018, https://www.bbc.co.uk/bbcthree/article/253d8b3e-1891-43ab-8848-4a5110bda171.

[114] Dobson (2019).

[115] Salt (2018).

[116] Mensi-Klarbach and Seierstad (2020).

[117] Kennedy (2019).

equity, purpose, and leadership in organizations. It is all part of a wider societal transformation that is embodied in Agenda 2030.

12   Agenda 2030: A Blueprint for a More Inclusive and Equitable Future

"Leave no one behind" is the mantra of the United Nations 2030 Agenda for Sustainable Development' (Agenda 2030). In 2015, the 193 countries of the UN General Assembly adopted this Agenda, which sets out a bold vision for "the world we want" and a shared blueprint for a more equal and sustainable future.

Diversity, inclusiveness, and purpose are at the heart of Agenda 2030. It includes ambitious commitments to combat inequalities within and among countries; to build peaceful, just, and inclusive societies; to protect human rights; and promote gender equality and the empowerment of women and girls. The Agenda states:

> As we embark on this great collective journey, we pledge that no one will be left behind. Recognizing that the dignity of the human person is fundamental, we wish to see the Goals and targets met for all nations and peoples and for all segments of society. And we will endeavor to reach the furthest behind first.[118]

Business was among the many stakeholder groups which contributed to the development of this transformational agenda and all stakeholders need to contribute if its vision is to be realized by 2030. It represents a new leadership paradigm that organizations will need to align with if they wish to successfully navigate an increasingly complex world.

Agenda 2030 is underpinned by the Sustainable Development Goals (SDGs), a set of 17 goals and 169 targets designed to transform our world (Fig. 6). While tackling inequality is a particular focus of SDG 5 Gender Equality, SDG 8 Decent Work and Economic Growth, and SDG 10 Reduced Inequalities, it is also a cross-cutting principle that underlies every goal.

Agenda 2030 has been adopted by many organizations as a strategic roadmap, not only for their corporate responsibility initiatives, but for the core business itself. It is a valuable lens for understanding the biggest challenges facing society, the greatest unmet societal needs and the areas where organizations can contribute the most societal value.

Through this shared agenda, nations, not-for-profits, and businesses are united in tackling a range of societal challenges—and Millennials and Gen Z, the dominant consumers in 2030, see this agenda as particularly critical. Expectations are

---

[118]"Transforming Our World, The 2030 Agenda for Sustainable Development," United Nations, 2015, https://sustainabledevelopment.un.org/content/documents/21252030%20Agenda%20for%20Sustainable%20Development%20web.pdf.

The Member States of the United Nations adopted the Sustainable Development Goals (SDGs) by General Assembly resolution A/RES/70/1 of 25 Sep. 2015
The content of this publication has not been approved by the United Nations and does not reflect the views of the United Nations or its officials or Member States

Fig. 6   The UN Sustainable Development Goals
Diversity, inclusiveness and purpose are at the heart of Agenda 2030s vision to "leave no one behind."

growing that organizations will align their purpose with it and become active partners in championing diversity and inclusiveness to ensure that no one is left behind. Doing so not only helps the organization anticipate future required capabilities by aligning with stakeholder expectations, it helps to build a better future for all.

13   The Virtuous Circle: Understanding Stakeholder Expectations

COVID-19 has been a system shock, disrupting business-as-usual and bringing persistent parity gaps and vulnerabilities into sight. In doing so it gives leaders a rare opportunity for a reset—to reimagine their organizations not as they were pre-pandemic, but as they could be.

It has occurred against a backdrop of rising stakeholder expectations for organizations to do more to address inequality and promote equity, and these escalating calls for action are unlikely to go away. There is a rising consciousness in the world, especially among millennials and digital natives, that is recalibrating definitions of value creation and success in favor of inclusiveness, equity, and sustainability.

To make the most of the COVID-19 recovery opportunity, today's courageous leaders have an opportunity to double down on their diversity and inclusion efforts, spearhead real change within their organizations and use the power of their revitalized organizations to effect real change in the world. This will be the new measure for success in a stakeholder-centered economy.

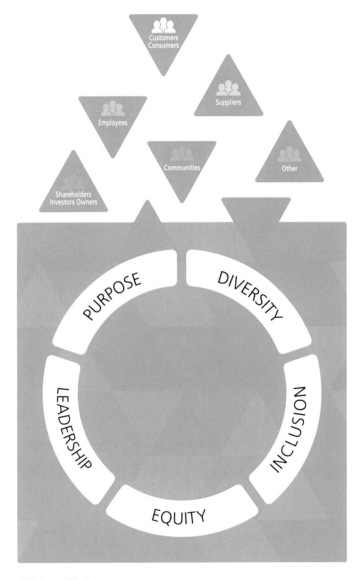

Fig. 7   The Virtuous Circle
Together the five societal themes that matter to stakeholders—Diversity, Inclusion, Equity, Purpose, and Leadership—constitute a Virtuous Circle for Diversity Performance.

Diversity, Inclusion, Equity, Purpose, and Leadership are key themes that stakeholders care about and key attributes that organizations need to foster to play their part in the 2030 Agenda. Together, these five elements form a virtuous circle (Fig. 7) that leaders can leverage to transform their organizations and the world.

The next chapter explores the new approach to diversity represented by the Virtuous Circle and how this can drive strong Diversity Performance.

References

Alon, Titan et al. "This Time It's Different: The Role of Women's Employment in a Pandemic Recession." *National Bureau of Economic Research*, August 2020. https://www.nber.org/system/files/working_papers/w27660/w27660.pdf.

Ardern, Jacinda. "New Zealand National Statement to United Nations General Assembly." Speech, 73 Session of the General Assembly of the United Nations, New York, September 27, 2018.

Bateman, Alexis, Ashley Barrington, and Katie Date. "Why You Need a Supplier-Diversity Program." *Harvard Business Review*, August 17, 2020. http://hbr.org/2020/08/why-you-need-a-supplier-diversity-program.

Batha, Emma. "Britain Urged to Force Companies to Publish Ethnicity Pay Gaps." *Reuters*, October 20, 2020. https://www.reuters.com/article/us-britain-race-pay-trfn/britain-urged-to-force-companies-to-publish-ethnicity-pay-gaps-idUSKBN2751HB.

Bonaccio, Silvia et al. "The Participation of People with Disabilities in the Workplace Across the Employment Cycle: Employer Concerns and Research Evidence." *Journal of Business and Psychology*, 35, no. 2 (2020): 135–158. https://doi.org/10.1007/s10869-018-9602-5.

Brown, Amy. "Racial Equity Fund Backed by NAACP Bridges Capital to Cause." TriplePundit, July 27, 2020. https://www.triplepundit.com/story/2020/racial-equity-fund-naacp/121016.

Chetty, Raj et al. "Race and Economic Opportunity in the United States: An Intergenerational Perspective." *Quarterly Journal of Economics*, 2019. https://www.brookings.edu/blog/social-mobility-memos/2015/01/15/five-bleak-facts-on-black-opportunity/. Accessed August 28, 2020.

Chong, Kelsey. "Millennials and the Rising Demand for Corporate Social Responsibility." *California Review Management*, January 20, 2017. https://cmr.berkeley.edu/2017/01/millennials-and-csr/.

Curtin, Jennifer. "Can New Zealand's Most Diverse Ever Cabinet Improve Representation of Women and Minorities in General?," 2020. https://theconversation.com/can-new-zealands-most-diverse-ever-cabinet-improve-representation-of-women-and-minorities-in-general-149273. Accessed November 20, 2020.

Derks, Mare. "Employee Happiness Before and During Covid: Figures from the (Remote) Workplace." July 13, 2020. 2daysmood.com/us/news/employee-happiness-before-and-during-covid-figures-from-the-remote-workplace/.

Diamant, Jeff, and Kelsey Jo Starr. "Western Europeans Vary in Their Nationalist, Anti-immigrant and Anti-Religious Minority Attitudes." Pew Research Center, June 19, 2018. https://www.pewresearch.org/fact-tank/2018/06/19/western-europeans-vary-in-their-nationalist-anti-immigrant-and-anti-religious-minority-attitudes/.

Diez, George. "The Migration Crisis and the Future of Europe." *The American Prospect*, 2019. https://prospect.org/world/migration-crisis-future-europe/. Accessed November 15, 2020.

Dobson, Sarah. "Bill C-86 Brings Major Changes." Canadian HRReporter, January 1, 2019. https://www.hrreporter.com/employment-law/news/bill-c-86-brings-major-changes/299373.

Fitzhugh, Earl, et al. "COVID-19: Investing in Black Lives and Livelihoods." McKinsey & Company, April 4, 2020. Report available at https://www.mckinsey.com/industries/public-and-social-sector/our-insights/covid-19-investing-in-black-lives-and-livelihoods.

Friedman, Uri. "New Zealand's Prime Minister May Be the Most Effective Leader on the Planet." *The Atlantic*, April 19, 2020. https://www.theatlantic.com/politics/archive/2020/04/jacinda-ardern-new-zealand-leadership-coronavirus/610237/.

Frey, William H. "The US Will Become 'Minority White' in 2045, Census Projects," Brookings Institution, March 14, 2018, https://www.brookings.edu/blog/the-avenue/2018/03/14/the-us-will-become-minority-white-in-2045-census-projects/.

Frey, William H. "The Nation Is Diversifying Even Faster Than Predictged, According to New Census Data." July 2020. https://www.brookings.edu/research/new-census-data-shows-the-nation-is-diversifying-even-faster-than-predicted/.

Fry, Richard. "Millennials Are the Largest Generation in the U.S. Labor Force." *Pew Research Center Fact Tank*, April 11, 2018. https://www.pewresearch.org/fact-tank/2018/04/11/millennials-largest-generation-us-labor-force/.

Grossman, Richard J., and Alexander J. Berg. "Recent Trends in Shareholder Activism, Harvard Law School Forum on Corporate Governance." October 11, 2019. https://corpgov.law.harvard.edu/2019/10/11/recent-trends-in-shareholder-activism/.

Holligan, Anna. "Wounds of Dutch History Expose Deep Racial Divide." *BBC News*, July 12, 2020. https://www.bbc.com/news/world-europe-53261944. Accessed November 19, 2020.

Kennedy, Valerie. "Game Change: The New Age of Diversity Regulation." Legal Business World, June 14, 2019, https://www.legalbusinessworld.com/post/2019/06/14/game-change-the-new-age-of-diversity-regulation.

Linde, Ann, and Arancha Gonzalez Laya. "What the COVID-19 Pandemic Tells Us About Gender Inequality." World Economic Forum, May 9, 2020. https://www.weforum.org/agenda/2020/05/what-the-covid-19-pandemic-tells-us-about-gender-equality/.

Loon, Karen. "Why 'Walking the Diversity Talk' Is Key," 2016. https://www.pwc.com/gx/en/about/diversity/internationalwomensday/blogs/winning-the-fight-for-female-talent-in-asia.html. Accessed November 20, 2020.

Maurelli, Mona, and Adam Mussomeli. "Inclusion as the Competitive Advantage: The Case for Women in Supply Chain." Deloitte, 2020. https://www2.deloitte.com/content/dam/insights/us/articles/5054_deloitte-women-in-supply-chain/DI_Deloitte%20Women%20in%20supply%20chain.pdf.

Mensi-Klarbach, Heike, and Cathrine Seierstad. "Gender Quotas on Corporate Boards: Similarities and Differences in Quota Scenarios," *European Management Review* 17, no. 3 (Fall 2020): 615–631. https://doi.org/10.1111/emre.12374.

Moss, Emily, et al. "The Black-White Wealth Gap Left Black Households More Vulnerable." Brookings Institution, December 8, 2020. https://www.brookings.edu/blog/up-front/2020/12/08/the-black-white-wealth-gap-left-black-households-more-vulnerable/.

Oppel, Richard A. Jr., et al. "The Fullest Look Yet at the Racial Inequality of Coronavirus," *The New York Times*, July 5, 2020. https://www.nytimes.com/interactive/2020/07/05/us/coronavirus-latinos-african-americans-cdc-data.html.

Parker, Kim, and Ruth Igielnik. "On the Cusp of Adulthood and Facing an Uncertain Future: What We Know About Gen Z So Far." Pew Research Center, May 14, 2020. https://www.pewsocialtrends.org/essay/on-the-cusp-of-adulthood-and-facing-an-uncertain-future-what-we-know-about-gen-z-so-far/.

Porter, Kim, Rich Nanda, Barb Renner, and Anupam Narula. "Consumer Product Trends." Deloitte, 2015.

Poushter, Jacob, and Nicholas Kent. *The Global Divide on Homosexuality Persists* (Pew Research Center, 2020).

Rodrigue, Edward, and Richard V. Reeves *Five Bleak Facts on Black Opportunity* (Brookings Institution, 2015).

Romei, Valentina. "Ethnic Minority Pay Gap in UK Still Stubbornly Wide." *Financial Times*, July 9, 2019. https://www.ft.com/content/fd47bc10-a238-11e9-974c-ad1c6ab5efd1.

Salt, Lauren. "South Africa: Regulation on Gender Pay Gap Equity Is Emerging." SHRM, August 10, 2018. https://www.shrm.org/resourcesandtools/legal-and-compliance/employment-law/pages/global-south-africa-gender-pay-equity.aspx.

Smith, David. "Francois Pienaar: 'When the Whistle Blew, South Africa Changed Forever'." *The Guardian*, December 8, 2013. ww.theguardian.com/world/2013/dec/08/nelson-mandela-francois-pienaar-rugby-world-cup.

Stiffler, Dana, and Caroline Chumakov. "2019 Women in Supply Chain Research." Awesome and Gartner, April 2019.

Volini, Erica, Jeff Schwartz, and Brad Denny. *2020 Global Human Capital Trends* (Deloitte, 2020).

Wallenfeldt, Jeff. Jacinda Ardern, in *Britannica*, 2020. https://www.britannica.com/biography/Jacinda-Ardern. Accessed November 20, 2020.

Wareham, Jamie. "Unique Impact of Coronavirus on LGBT+ Community 'Will Disproportionately Affect Us'." Forbes, March 24, 2020. https://www.forbes.com/sites/jamiewareham/2020/03/24/the-unique-impact-of-coronavirus-on-uk-lgbt-community-will-disproportionally-affect-them/?sh=20c9c37ab401.

Washington, Kemberley. "COVID-19 Is Forcing Women from the Workplace in Record Numbers—And We Don't Know When They'll Be Back." Forbes, October 19, 2020. https://www.forbes.com/sites/advisor/2020/10/19/women-are-leaving-the-workplace-in-record-numbers-and-we-dont-know-when-theyll-be-back/?sh=7319442c6ab5.

Wilkinson, Bard. "New Zealand PM Jaacinda Ardern Makes History with Baby at UN Assembly." CNN, September 25, 2018. https://edition.cnn.com/2018/09/24/asia/new-zealand-ardern-baby-un-intl/index.html.

Williams, David R., Harold W. Neighbors, and James S. Jackson. "Racial/Ethnic Discrimination and Health: Findings from Community Studies." *American Journal of Public Health* 93, no. 2 (2003): 200–208.

Worrall, Simon. "This Girl Escaped From a Syrian War Zone in a Wheelchair." *National Geographic*, November 6, 2016.

Part II
What Are the Diversity Performance Gaps?

WHAT are the Diversity Performance Gaps?

Understand Stakeholder Expectations

What do my stakeholders expect of me?

Ch.3

Understand Diversity Performance

What are the key elements and stages of Diversity Performance?

Ch.4

Measure the Diversity Performance Gap

3 steps to improve Diversity Performance

Map the Performance Gap

Close my Diversity Performance Capability Gaps
Which initiatives do I need to put in place to achieve my desired future level of Diversity Perfomance?

Build the 6 Key Diversity Capabilities

- Mitigate Bias
- Build Case
- Embed Behaviors
- Harness Policies
- Measure and Monitor
- Celebrate and Sustain

PERFORMANCE AND CAPABILITY ROADMAP

Craft my Future Diversity Narrative
What is my desired future level of Diversity Performance?

Capture my Current Diversity Narrative
What is my organization's existing level of Diversity Performance?

Compare my Diversity Narratives
What is the gap between my current and desired Diversity Performance?

Close the Capability Gap

Develop my Strategic Roadmap to close the gaps
Where are my biggest Capability Gaps?

Understand my Current Diversity Capabilities
Which capabilities do I currently have in place?

Understand my Future Diversity Capability Needs
Which capabilities do I need to achieve my chosen future level of Diversity Performance?

Ch.5

Measure the Diversity Capability Gap

3 steps to improve Diversity Capability

The Virtuous Circle: Defining the Five Elements of Diversity Performance

3

As discussed in Chapter 2, organizations today face a clarion call to do more to address diversity, inclusion, and equity through renewed purpose and leadership—and these are the same elements that combine to form a Virtuous Circle that drives strong diversity performance within the organization.

This chapter takes a look at the five elements that make up the Virtuous Circle of diversity performance (Fig. 1).

As well as being the very things stakeholders are asking of organizations, these elements of performance must all be present for an organization to achieve and sustain a successful diversity journey; if one element is weak or missing, diversity performance will suffer.

But what exactly is intended by the terms diversity, inclusion, equity, leadership, and purpose? Before launching a diversity and inclusion journey, it is important that leaders clearly define each element so they can develop a shared understanding within their organization. Definitions set the parameters, and what you define, you lead. Leaders are expected to co-craft the organization's purpose, describe what success looks like, build a team that can deliver the strategic outcome and develop specific and measurable goals against which performance can be evaluated.

Leaders are usually keenly aware of the importance of definitions. When they define a business strategy such as customer value creation, they spend time with their teams to define "customer" and "value creation" and to couple the values, behaviors, and actions needed to support the strategy. That same level of scrutiny needs to be applied to the diversity and inclusion journey. To measure and manage diversity in all its complexity demands a clear understanding of what concepts such as diversity, inclusion, equity, and inclusive leadership actually mean. Clear definitions are a good place to start to devise a common vocabulary.

© Diversity and Performance BV 2021
K. Formanek, *Beyond D&I*, https://doi.org/10.1007/978-3-030-75336-8_3

**Fig. 1   Identifying the
Five Elements of Diversity
Performance**
The outer ring comprises the
elements that are required for
Diversity Performance.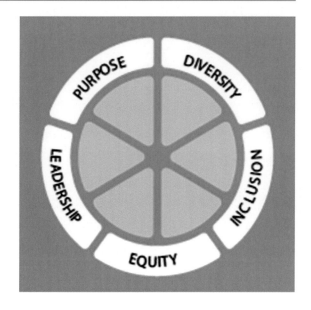

The five elements of the Virtuous Circle are defined below.

1.   Diversity—Selecting players with the best skills, experience, and talent to build a winning team

Human beings are naturally diverse and diversity in its broadest sense encompasses the many ways in which people differ. This includes gender, race, age, ethnicity, sexual orientation, physical ability as well as religion, culture, education, diversity of thought, style, preferences, functional expertise, and a wide array of other traits and characteristics. Some of these are inherent and some are acquired (sometimes described as visible and invisible characteristics). Inherent diversity refers to traits a person is born with or differences that can immediately be observed when looking at someone, such as gender, age, ethnicity, sexual orientation, physical disabilities, and sometimes religion (such as a woman wearing a head covering). Acquired diversity involves the traits a person gains from experience, for example, appreciation of cultural differences or language skills from working in another country.

The word "diversity" originates from the Latin word *dīversitās* and is translated as the fact or quality of being different. In the most literal translation, "diversity" simply means the presence of differences within a particular setting.[1]

Diversity is relative and refers specifically to a group; for example: "I am unique, and I have an array of experiences and specializations. But I am not

---

[1] Bolger (2020).

singularly diverse. I am diverse when I am part of a team where I inject differences—cognitively, demographically and culturally—in relation to the group and to the other team members." For example, a team comprised of four people who all have the same type of academic degree from the same university and with a similar cultural background, could be said to be "homogenous." A team made up of people from different cultural settings with different academic backgrounds would be regarded as being diverse—or "heterogeneous."

There are many thoughtfully considered and inspiring definitions of diversity that we can learn from, such as this example from Queensborough Community College in New York: "The concept of diversity encompasses acceptance and respect. It means understanding that each individual is unique, and recognizing our individual differences. These can be along the dimensions of race, ethnicity, gender, sexual orientation, socio-economic status, age, physical abilities, religious beliefs, political beliefs, or other ideologies. It is the exploration of these differences in a safe, positive, and nurturing environment. It is about understanding each other and moving beyond simple tolerance to embracing and celebrating the rich dimensions of diversity contained within each individual."[2] Ultimately, each organization must craft its own definition that is authentic and reflective of its needs and those of its stakeholders.

Leaders need to be mindful of how they talk about diversity. For example, the expression "I am hiring a diversity candidate" may increase the feeling of the candidate being different. Firstly, the candidate is not singularly "diverse" but only diverse in relation to the homogeneity of the group. Each member is a unique individual with an array of characteristics that they are born with, such as their gender, skin tone, and age, as well as characteristics that they have acquired during the course of their life. The label "diversity candidate" may lead to the candidate feeling offended because they perceive they are made to feel different relative to the group. Alternatively, the leader can simply stress that the aim is to recruit unique individuals who together create rich diversity that delivers better performance and engagement. In creating the vocabulary for diversity, there is an opportunity to create inclusive language. This is covered in Chapter 6.

2. Inclusion—Showing up for practice, being selected for the team, and having the opportunity to play

Inclusion refers to the behaviors and social norms that make people feel welcome and valued. The word "inclusion" originates from the Latin *inclusionem* and is translated as the "act of making a part of." Inclusion does not occur of itself, it requires the act of including.

---

[2] Definition of Diversity, Queensborough Community College, accessed March 13, 2021, https://www.qcc.cuny.edu/diversity/definition.html#:~:text=The%20concept%20of%20diversity%20encompasses,and%20recognizing%20our%20individual%20differences.&text=Practicing%20mutual%20respect%20for%20qualities,are%20different%20from%20our%20own.

The UN stresses this active process in its definition of inclusion in society: "Social inclusion is the process by which efforts are made to ensure equal opportunities—that everyone, regardless of their background, can achieve their full potential in life."[3] For many organizations, inclusion is used interchangeably with culture and depicts a state where a mix of people can optimally leverage their talents and skills through cultivation of respect for each person and positive recognition of differences.

The best way to make sense of inclusion is to understand how individuals describe their own sense of being included. This is addressed in Chapter 8, but often a sense of inclusion comes down to someone feeling that they are part of a team, that what they say matters, that they can bring their "whole self" to work, that they trust their leaders and that they feel safe to disagree. It is possible to have a diverse team that is not inclusive; however, this will not create the conditions for diversity performance success.

As with diversity, inclusion is defined differently depending on the organization's unique context and environment. The more ambitious the organization is about diversity and the higher their diversity performance aspirations, the richer their definition of inclusion will need to be.

3. **Equity—Being coached to realize your full playing potential and receiving the extra training that your circumstances require**

In its broadest sense, equity is fairness, sometimes known as a "level playing field." Indeed, equity is derived from Old French *equité*, a word whose Latin root means "even," "just," and "equal."

Equity is often used interchangeably with equality but in the field of diversity they are connected but different. Equality in an organization is usually evidenced by giving all employees the same support and access to resources, regardless of their needs. Equity is evidenced when the advancement of all employees is supported by recognizing that their unique circumstances may call for differentiated treatment and providing access to the specific resources they require to advance within the organization.

Unlike equality, equity recognizes that not all people come to the organization with the same opportunities or the same historic access to resources, whether this is access to personal and professional networks or having been afforded the financial support to attend a leading academic institution. When an organization brings in diverse people but offers the same opportunities without regard to equity, those who have experienced advantage and access to benefits will receive more benefit than those who do not—and the gap is not diminished.

---

[3] Social Inclusion, UN Department of Economic and Social Affairs, accessed March 13, 2021, https://www.un.org/development/desa/socialperspectiveondevelopment/issues/social-integration.html.

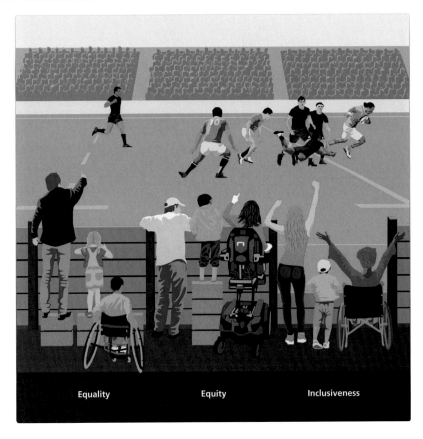

Fig. 2   **Equality vs Equity vs Inclusiveness**

The difference between equality and equity is shown in Fig. 2. In the first scenario, each spectator receives equal treatment. They are provided with an identical box to observe the rugby game. The result is that the tall spectator obtains an even a better view, the second spectator can barely see and the third spectator can neither make use of the resource nor see the game because they are wheelchair-bound. In the second scenario, the resource is customized to the needs of each spectator. The tall spectator is tall enough and thus does not need a box to stand on, a box is given to the second spectator who can now see well, and the third spectator has an adapted wheelchair that enables them to participate fully. The third and final scenario depicts an optimum state of diversity performance that we term societal or organizational inclusiveness. "Inclusiveness" is the practice or policy of including people. Within society and in organizations, inclusiveness refers to a desired culture and philosophy that encompasses the hallmarks of equity and the practice of inclusion.

In Fig. 2, spectators with varying circumstances come to the match and despite their differences, they are all able to observe the game and cheer. Equitable treatment delivers more equal outcomes—but removing barriers is always the better alternative. This is inclusiveness.

Every organization needs to carefully assess the needs of every member of their organization to determine whether certain groups of employees or individuals require specific resources and support optimum diversity performance.

4. Purpose—The team has a unifying purpose that values each player and highlights playing together for optimum results

Purpose is the reason something is done or created. The word "purpose" originates from the twelfth-century Old French word *propos*, meaning aim or intention, and from the Latin *proposer*, or "to put forth."[4] The American Heritage Dictionary describes purpose as "the object toward which one strives or for which something exists; an aim or goal." It is a synonym of "intention."[5]

Here purpose refers not to the purpose of the organization, but the rationale, or reason, for diversity within the organization. A diversity purpose can range from limited and reactive to expansive and proactive: for example, it can be as basic as stating that the organization will pursue diversity as prescribed by law, with the intention to avoid compliance issues and legal costs. Or, at the other end of the purpose spectrum, it can be intrinsically linked to the mandate of the organization, its ability to satisfy stakeholder expectations, to be agile in responding to a changing environment, and delivering on one or more of the UN Sustainable Development Goals (SDGs).

Each organization needs to be clear about the reasons why they are pursuing diversity and which performance outcomes they are looking to achieve, and this rationale for diversity needs to be communicated clearly within the organization.

5. Leadership—Creating a team where every talent can reach its full potential

Leadership is often described as the art of motivating a group of people to achieve a common goal. The word leader comes from the Old English word "*lædan*" meaning "to go before as a guide." And this is especially true for a diversity journey.

Leaders of diversity set out a clear narrative that explains the role diversity plays in achieving the key strategic objectives of the organization. Their role is more than simply articulating their authentic commitment to diversity, it is to make diversity a priority not only for the organization but also for themselves. They challenge the status quo, hold others accountable and they are obsessed

---

[4] Purpose, definition, Online Etymology Dictionary, accessed December 20, 2020, https://www.etymonline.com/word/purpose.

[5] Purpose, The American Heritage Dictionary of the English Language, accessed December 20, 2020, https://www.ahdictionary.com/word/search.html?q=purpose.

Table 1   Defining the Five Elements of Diversity Performance
Clear definitions are important for creating shared understanding. Diversity performance is made up of five key elements and this is how we define them in this book. Each organization must seek the definition that is right for its context and stakeholders.

Term	Definition	Analogy
Diversity	The sum of the traits and characteristics, inherent and acquired, that make a person unique relative to others.	Selecting players with diverse skills and talents who, together, form a winning team.
Inclusion	The actions, norms, practices and behaviors that create an environment where each unique individual is able to contribute fully to the organization's purpose, through the presence of a safe environment where people are treated fairly and respectfully, with recognition of their specific needs.	Showing up for practice, being selected for the team, and having the opportunity to play.
Equity	The recognition that individuals have had unequal access to resources through societal, institutional and personal bias practices that have limited their full participation. Equity enables their full access to resources by acknowledging the specific needs of historically prejudiced groups and individuals.	Being coached to realize your full playing potential and receiving the extra training that your circumstances require.
Leadership	The values, behaviors, practices and actions that gather the diversity characteristics required to deliver on purpose and goals of the organisation and create a safe and inclusive and equitable environment where all people are engaged to support the purpose.	Creating a team where every talent can reach its full potential.
Purpose	The motivating force that inspires and connects stakeholders to deliver a shared vision for diversity. How diversity intersects with the organization's reason for being and why it exists.	Unifying the team through a purpose that values each player and highlights playing together for optimum results.

about creating the psychological safety that is key to advancing a sense of inclusion and engagement. They are also focused on the metrics of diversity—because what gets measured gets done.

Leadership of diversity performance is not only the domain of senior leaders and each organization needs to define the team members who are together responsible for diversity outcomes. Ultimately, everyone has a role to play.

To recap, these key definitions are summarized in Table 1.

1   Strong Diversity Performance Requires All Five Elements

When it comes to diversity, leaders have tended to focus their attention on two elements from the Virtuous Circle in particular: diversity and inclusion. But D&I alone will not deliver the kind of diversity performance leading organizations are looking for today. Without leadership commitment, a clear organizational purpose

Fig. 3 **Beyond D&I to the Five Elements of Diversity Performance**
In the second of the two formulae, equity, leadership, and purpose are integrated with diversity and inclusion This holistic approach is the key to an organization reaching its full Diversity Performance potential.

and rationale, and appropriate equity measures, diversity initiatives will fail to deliver their full potential. Instead of D+I, today's diversity leaders need to be thinking about+E+P+L, too. Organizations need to pivot in their understanding of diversity from the first formula shown in Fig. 3 to the second.

The rationale for the second formula is described below.

If there is no diversity: The organization will likely be characterized by group-think. With groupthink, the perspectives that are brought into the organization are not sufficient to navigate complexity. The organization may not have the capacity to anticipate stakeholder requirements and solutions may lack the creativity to allow break-through thinking and innovation.

If there is diversity but no inclusion: In this scenario, individuals are invited into the organization, but their ideas are not listened to unless they are advocated by the dominant group. Employees fail to thrive and reach their potential or leave because they do not feel truly valued.

If there is diversity and inclusion but no equity: Within the organization, individuals are treated the same and there is no recognition that individuals from minority groups have faced historical, systemic discrimination in their lives. As a result, the organization unwittingly reinforces entrenched inequalities. The presence of societal and institutional bias continues to hamper individuals' ability to perform equally, and these individuals get left behind. Often, others look at those left behind and conclude that they must simply not be "good enough." The result is that diversity is invited in but does not flourish. There is no focus on mitigating systemic privileges, dismantling biases, and supporting the varying needs of a diverse employee population to advance full access to benefits for all and create an even playing field.[6]

If there is diversity, inclusion, and equity, but no leadership: The organization is likely to have the basis for rich diversity outcomes, but lack of leadership—or in some cases, toxic leadership—undermines those benefits and makes people question the authenticity and integrity of the organization's diversity focus. This can be seen in Fig. 4 showing the impact of leadership on team performance, adapted from the work of researchers Joseph Distefano and Martha Maznevski.[7]

---

[6]Burnette (2019).

[7]Distefano and Maznevski (2010).

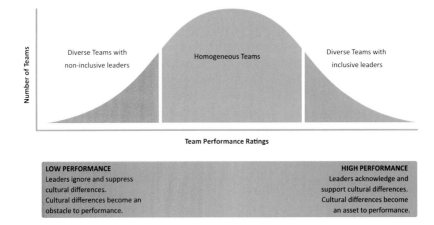

Fig. 4 **Impact of Leadership on Team Diversity Performance**
Diverse teams can outperform homogeneous Diversity Performance teams but require inclusive leaders to fulfill their potential. Without this, their performance lags that of homogeneous teams.

In situations where teams were culturally diverse, but leaders suppressed this, they found that these teams performed less well than a homogeneous team. However diverse cultural teams with leaders who supported diversity and where team members could display their diversity, outperformed homogeneous teams.

If there is diversity, inclusion, equity, and leadership but no purpose: Diversity is present, people feel included, and equity allows everybody access based on historic need. However, these ingredients are not anchored through a uniting purpose that creates alignment in the organization. In this case, the organization may scope their diversity activities as a side-pillar thereby missing out on the transformational benefits of diversity for the organization and its stakeholders. These range from happier and more engaged employees and closer alignment with customers, to greater innovation, better decision-making, and—as a number of prominent business research studies show—a correlation with higher profitability and return on investment.[8,9]

These diversity-related business performance benefits are explored further in Chapter 7. At a minimum, leaders need to set out the strategic narrative for why diversity, inclusion, and equity are fundamental to support the organization's mandate and transformation journey. When members of an organization understand why diversity, inclusion, and equity are critical to continued success, and what their role is in advancing these, the sense of energy and action in moving toward a common goal is reinforced.

---

[8] Delivering Through Diversity, McKinsey & Company, January 2018. https://www.mckinsey.com/~/media/mckinsey/business%20functions/organization/our%20insights/delivering%.20through%20diversity/delivering-through-diversity_full-report.ashx.

[9] Rocio Lorenzo et al. (2018).

2   The Virtuous Circle: A New Diversity Leadership Model

Against the backdrop of a complex, fast-changing, and increasingly inequitable world, organizations and their leaders are in need of a new diversity model—one that has all the necessary ingredients for longevity and sustainability.

The Virtuous Circle (Fig. 5) addresses this challenge. It is one of two core anchor models presented in this book which, together, can help organizations chart a successful and transformative diversity journey. The five elements of the Virtuous Circle meet two needs: as described in Chapter 1, they are the diversity-related themes that matter most to stakeholders, where organizations can create societal value; they are also the variables that, when combined, enable the organization to improve its diversity performance. By activating the Virtuous Circle, an organization can achieve two things: satisfy stakeholder expectations and grow its Diversity Performance. The circle is virtuous because it creates a positive feedback loop of improved diversity and enduring stakeholder satisfaction.

In charting a diversity roadmap for their organization, leaders face a number of questions. What is the right level of Diversity Performance? How do they assess their current state of diversity, inclusion, equity, leadership, and purpose? What narrative is needed to actively engage their team to achieve the desired level of Diversity Performance? The Virtuous Circle helps leaders to answer these questions.

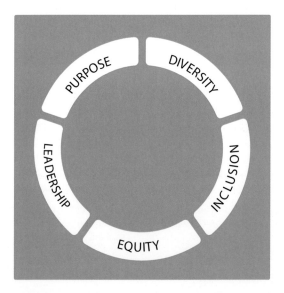

Fig. 5   The Virtuous Circle
The five elements that make up the Virtuous Circle—diversity, inclusion, equity, purpose, and leadership—are where organizations can both create stakeholder value and drive improved organizational diversity performance.

Underpinned by global research and extensive applied experience in organizational diversity journey design, the Virtuous Circle Model enables organizations to be responsive to stakeholders by identifying and setting the right level of organizational ambition for each of its five elements. Through the model, a Virtuous Circle is put in motion whereby the required diversity is invited in, diversity of thought is liberated by inclusion, diversity is channeled through a clear purpose, and inclusive leadership serves to pace the journey while supporting the advancement of equity.

3   Why a Virtuous Circle?

The term "virtuous" has been chosen deliberately in this anchor model. Virtuous means generally "excellence" and is also associated with the word "virtue." Virtue, c. 1200, *vertu*, means "moral life and conduct; a particular moral excellence," from Anglo-French and Old French *vertu* it expresses "force, strength, vigor; moral strength; qualities, abilities" (Old French), and from Latin *virtutem* (nominative *virtus*) it is defined as "moral strength, high character, goodness; valor, bravery, courage (in war); excellence, worth."[10]

The secret sauce of successful diversity journeys comprises excellence and moral strength. These ventures also call for ingredients such as courage, leadership, conviction, and a strong ethical compass. These qualities are all reflected in the Virtuous Circle of Diversity Performance. The concept of the Virtuous Circle is well-known in the leadership lexicon, having been used in a number of leadership books. The terms virtuous circle and vicious circle, also known, respectively, as virtuous cycle and vicious cycle, describe complex chains of events that reinforce themselves through a feedback loop. A virtuous circle has favorable results, while a vicious circle has detrimental results.[11]

A virtuous circle is comprised of a chain of events, with no tendency to equilibrium, where each iteration of the circle (or feedback loop) reinforces the previous one, namely, it is self-sustaining. When individual elements of diversity within the circle increase, momentum builds and performance grows. However, when the elements of diversity, inclusion, equity, leadership, and purpose are absent or one of the elements is negative (as in a toxic environment with leaders that suppress diversity of expression), the circle is no longer "excellent" and does not support performance. Rather, diversity efforts and performance will be undermined. It is this lack of a virtuous, self-sustaining, and reinforcing cycle that explains why the majority of diversity and inclusion initiatives fail to deliver effective organizational transformation.

---

[10] https://www.etymonline.com/word/virtue.

[11] Webel and Galtung (2012).

4   Why Five Elements?

The five elements that make up the Virtuous Circle—diversity characteristics, inclusion, equity, leadership and purpose—have emerged during the course of over 25 years of working with dozens of organizations around the world. They are supported by leading primary and secondary academic research in the field of diversity, including Joseph J. DiStefano and Martha L. Maznevski's work on diversity and team performance, in particular "Creating value with diverse teams in global management" (2000).[12] The model also draws on the thinking of Kathryn Williams Phillips and her research on the benefits that demographic diversity brings to teams and organizations,[13] including her 2014 article "How Diversity Works."[14] Other key academic sources consulted in developing the model include the work of Corinne A. Moss-Racusin, a leading researcher on bias[15] and Alexis Nicole Smith's research into gender dynamics, social identity, bias, and workplace diversity.[16]

While its five elements are universal to all organizations, application of the Virtuous Circle will not be exactly the same for any two organizations. This is because their context is different, their stakeholders are distinct and their current diversity capability varies, so every organization has to define for itself the right stage or ambition level for each element of the Circle. This is where the five stages of diversity performance come in.

5   Introducing the Five Stages of Diversity Performance

In addition to the five elements of the Virtuous Circle, there are five stages of Diversity Performance that characterize different maturity phases of an organization's diversity and inclusion journey (Fig. 6). Understanding where the organization is on its journey for each element is vital for developing a strategic and holistic approach to Diversity Performance. These five stages comprise:

1. **Legal Compliance**

   - *Key driver*: Satisfy regulatory and legal compliance requirements (i.e., quotas, equitable treatment of all and avoid sanctions attached to these requirements).

---

[12] DiStefano and Maznevski (2000).

[13] Phillips and O'Reilly (1998).

[14] Phillips (2014).

[15] Moss-Racusin et al. (2012).

[16] Smith et al. (2017).

2. **Stakeholder Requirements**

- *Key driver*: Satisfy stakeholder requirements for diversity (i.e., customers may wish to be serviced by an organization with employees that reflect their own diversity, investors may be seeking specific ESG outcomes, or employees may desire communities that advance their feeling of belonging e.g., employee resource group).

3. **Organizational Performance**

- *Key driver*: Turn diversity investments into performance returns for the organization (i.e., access to talent, improved engagement, more innovation).

4. **Reinvention**

- *Key driver*: Turn diversity investments into break-through thinking that allows continuous response and adjustment to developments in the environment and which enables the organization to reinvent its capabilities, products, and services. Reinvention is often linked to organizational attributes such as agility and resilience.

5. **Societal Value**

- *Key driver*: Turn diversity investments into capabilities and outcomes that support broader societal transformation to leave no one behind (i.e., Agenda 2030).

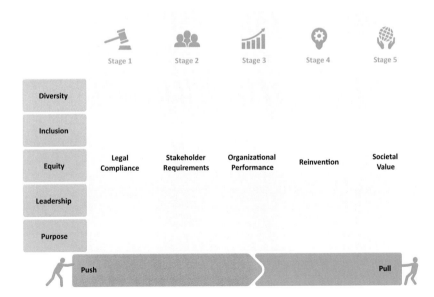

Fig. 6   The Five Stages of Diversity Performance
There are five evolutionary stages for each element of the Virtual Circle. Leaders can use this matrix to map current performance and set strategic Diversity Performance improvement goals.

These five maturity stages can be seen as evolutionary phases leading to progressively greater Diversity Performance. The state of diversity in an organization is the result of many variables, including its industry, geographic location, business focus, culture, and unique history. This staged approach honors the differences between organizations who are at different phases of the journey. There is no inherent judgment about which stage of Diversity Performance maturity an organization may be at—Diversity Performance is unique and specific to organizational context.

The five stages can be used to map the current state of diversity, inclusion, equity, leadership, and diversity purpose within the organization. They can also be used to depict where the organization would like to be—its aspirational or desired level of Diversity Performance (see Chapter 4). Each stage is "additive" meaning that organizations cannot leap from Stage 2 to Stage 4 without going through Stage 3. This is because Diversity Performance depends on certain diversity "capabilities" being in place (explored in depth in Chapter 5 through the Integrated Diversity Model). To advance from one stage to the next, the organization builds on its existing capability foundations by putting in place the corresponding diversity initiatives recommended for its desired stage.

6   Combining the Virtuous Circle with the Five Stages

With so many elements at play in an integrated diversity journey, a key challenge for the leader is to develop a clear understanding of the organization's current status and where its strengths and weaknesses lie. Armed with this insight, the leader can take a more strategic approach to Diversity Performance.

By combining the five elements of the Virtuous Circle with the five maturity stages of Diversity Performance, a "5 × 5" matrix is created. This matrix enables the leader to see at a glance each distinct evolutionary phase for each element of the Virtuous Circle. As an organization progresses from Stage 1 toward Stage 5, it evolves from being "pushed" into greater diversity by external drivers (reactive) to have a genuine appreciation of diversity as a business benefit (proactive). Beyond Stage 3, diversity increasingly becomes a pull factor for the organization, driving positive transformation across the business, its value chain, and broader society.

Below we explore in more depth what each element of the Virtuous Circle looks like at each of the five maturity stages.

7   The Five Stages of Diversity

The five evolutionary stages of diversity (inherent and acquired diversity characteristics) are represented in Fig. 7. The evolutionary stages are described as: Legal Compliance (Stage 1), Stakeholder Requirements (Stage 2), Organizational Performance (Stage 3), Reinvention (Stage 4), and Societal Value (Stage 5). These

Diversity

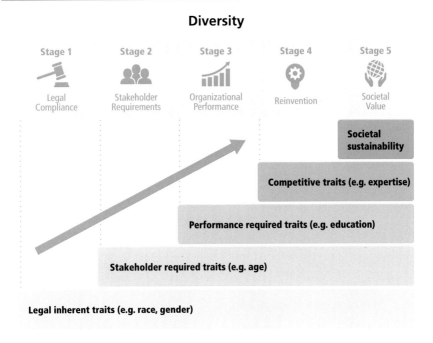

Fig. 7   The Five Stages of Diversity
At each stage there is a range of inherent and acquired diversity characteristics that relate to the type of Diversity Performance outcome being sought.

terms correspond to the key focus when congregating the right diversity character-istics within the organization, in an additive manner.

Stage 1—Legal Inherent Traits

Organizations at this stage equate diversity to the personal protected characteris-tics established in legislation or quotas. Leaders are concerned that they will be prosecuted and face lawsuits if they are seen to discriminate on the basis of these characteristics. Organizations respond by defining diversity according to legal requirements and protected characteristics such as gender, race, or nationality:

> Diversity means the required representation of minorities is satisfied as mandated by law.

Stage 2—Stakeholder Required Traits

At this stage, focus centers on what is required to avoid incurring penalties from stakeholders in the form of lost business, lost revenue through product boycotts, or unwanted news headlines due to lack of diversity. This is a reactionary stage in which organizations are defensive and driven by risk and reputation. At this stage, organizations expand their definition from regulation-driven demographic differ-ences to include other characteristics that are important to stakeholders within the organization and its extended community:

We reflect the diversity that is important to our customers and to our employees. Both stakeholders groups require our organization to reflect a multicultural talent pool that is able to anticipate and support cultural differences of our clients and our employees.

Stage 3—Performance Required Traits
Diversity characteristics are valued as a way to support organizational performance objectives to deliver business results. The focus here is on diversity as a way to generate organizational outcomes such as shareholder profit, customer congruence, improved engagement, more innovation, and access to talent. Organizations may supplement both their inherent and acquired diversity portfolio to drive additional performance. For example, an organization may recruit younger members to support a more social media savvy approach and may also recruit lifestyle diversity, different leadership styles, and multiple specializations to drive more growth, better risk management, or increased customer satisfaction. Stage 3 organizations expand their definition of diversity to stress specific characteristics that yield better business performance, for example:

Diversity means more to us than bringing together people with different backgrounds. It is a belief that our differences enable us to be a better team—one that makes better decisions, drives innovation and delivers better business results.[17]

Stage 4—Competitive Traits
Diversity characteristics begin to be seen as important for supporting organizational transformation. Coinciding with the technological revolution and the need to "adapt or die," organizations at this stage look to diversity to enable rapid innovation, to pivot or build future-proof capabilities. At this stage, diversity stresses the characteristics leading to greater diversity of thought, boosting creativity and agility. This example from the Australian Department of Defense demonstrates a key focus on agility in their diversity definition:

Diversity at Defence means respect for individual difference. It means valuing and utilizing the unique knowledge, skills and attributes that our people bring to their work. Diversity reflects the variety of personal experience that arises from differences of culture and circumstance. We maximize our capability by drawing on the diversity of our people.[18]

Stage 5—Societal Sustainability
Diversity is defined here as the characteristics that give the organization a unique vantage point for problem-solving to address global challenges. It is viewed as a way to support the societal case and contribute to Agenda 2030 and the SDGs. The understanding of diversity at this stage acknowledges rising stakeholder concerns

---

[17] "In solidarity: Standing against racism and advancing equal opportunity for all," Mastercard Newsroom, June 25, 2020, https://www.mastercard.com/news/perspectives/2020/in-solidarity-standing-against-racism-and-advancing-equal-opportunity-for-all/.

[18] https://www.defence.gov.au/diversity/strategy/default.asp.

about sustainability, equality, and purpose, as well as growing demand for organizations to act as a force of good in the world. Johnson & Johnson exemplifies the societal case in their diversity definition:

> Diversity at Johnson & Johnson is about your unique perspective. It's about you, your colleagues and the world we care for—all backgrounds, beliefs and the entire range of human experience—coming together. You view the world from a unique vantage point; a perspective that gives you problem-solving potential ideas, solutions and strategies that, when mobilized, can bring health to billions.[19]

Unilever is another good example of Stage 5 commitment:

> We're a diverse company and are determined to build a strongly inclusive culture which respects every employee for who they are—regardless of gender, age, race, disability or sexual orientation. We believe that our employees' contributions are richer because of their diversity, and we want to help them feel free to bring their authentic self to work every day. And we want to accelerate progress in equality of opportunity and women's empowerment, because as two of our most material issues, they're central to our business growth and our social impact.[20]

Initiatives to support greater diversity characteristics are explored in more detail in Chapter 6.

8   The Five Stages of Inclusion

The five evolutionary stages of inclusion are represented in Fig. 8. The evolutionary stages are described as: Admit (Stage 1), Welcome (Stage 2), Value (Stage 3), Embrace (Stage 4) and Societal Inclusiveness (Stage 5). These terms correspond to the key focus when admitting and including members who bring unique diversity into the organization, in an additive manner.

Stage 1—Admit
Here the inclusion focus is to find minority candidates—as required by law—admit them into the organization and make them "fit into" the organization. The primary intent is to "find" diversity candidates, "put" diversity candidates in a group and "impress" the culture of the most homogeneous group upon the diversity candidates. Active verbs are intentionally used to create a sense that diversity is "incorporated" unilaterally into the organization. Here minority groups are

---

[19] "Diversity, Equity & Inclusion," Johnson & Johnson, accessed August 28, 2020, https://www.jnj.com/about-jnj/diversity.

[20] Equity, diversity and inclusion, Unilever, accessed March 13, 2021, https://www.unilever.com/sustainable-living/enhancing-livelihoods/opportunities-for-women/advancing-diversity-and-inclusion/.

required to adapt to the dominant culture by absorbing the practices and behaviors of the dominant group. The organization offers limited to no form of integration or equal voice to group members, and the rank and privilege of the dominant group remains intact.

Leaders may say:

> We are committed to supporting minority groups and incorporating them into our organization. We are committed to ensure team processes and teamwork by ensuring adoption of our values, behaviors, and practices. A way we achieve this is through rigorous orientation processes where the culture of our organization is impressed on all new people.

Employees may say:

> I have been invited in, but I do not feel that I belong. I feel that to belong I am required to reflect the culture and also the perspectives of the dominant group in the organization. I feel that I am seen as a demographic—Black and/or a person with disability.

Stage 2—Welcome

At this stage, inclusion occurs in response—or in reaction—to what competitors and customers are doing and what employees are demanding. Organizations place more emphasis on welcoming the employees into the organization. They may start organizing and celebrating certain diversity events, creating a peer-to-peer buddy system, publishing their diversity focus on their corporate website, or participating in initiatives being developed in their sectors and by their clients. This is not in response to a clear inclusion blueprint but more in reaction to ad hoc inclusion initiatives that are regarded as the norm within an industry or sector.

Stage 3—Value

Inclusion is becoming more deliberate, with a focus on using it to liberate diversity performance from diversity of talent. For example, if the type of Diversity Performance required is customer congruence—i.e., a richer in-house understanding of the client achieved by having employees of that customer demographic—than the organization will not only recruit this customer demographic onto the talent bench, but also create an environment where their differences can be expressed. Organizations place more focus on making employees feel welcomed into the organization. Inclusionary practices focus on creating a safe environment, where different opinions are exchanged and where respectful interaction and dialogue is encouraged.

Stage 4—Embrace

At this performance level, inclusion is geared at stimulating optimum collaboration, mitigating bias, and advancing equity so that all talent has the opportunity to support transformation of the organization. At this stage employees feel truly embraced by the organization and have a sense of belonging.

Leaders will tend to use these type of statements when describing their inclusion focus at this stage:

Inclusion

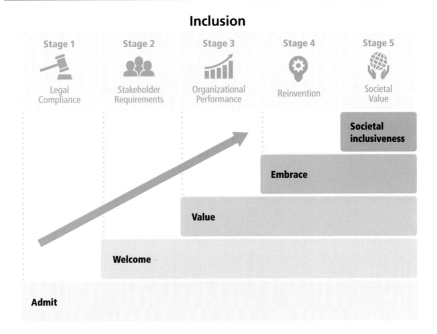

Fig. 8 The Five Stages of Inclusion
The focus and manifestation of inclusion change as organizations progress through the five stages of Diversity Performance.

> We want to invite all the participants at our meetings to contribute, and so we encourage certain *behaviors*, such as the practice of piggy-backing ideas, where we use the word "and" instead of "but" and where interruption is replaced by listening, acknowledging and enriching ideas.

And employees may report their feeling of inclusiveness as:

> I feel *valued* because I am appreciated and respected for my perspectives, and my talents are seen.
>   I feel *trusted* because I am solicited to make contributions, and I feel that my ideas really count in the decision-making.
>   I feel *comfortable* in hold a differing view and am invited to share these views. There is piggy-backing on these different perspectives.

Stage 5—Societal Inclusiveness

Inclusion has evolved to include actions that embrace stakeholders more broadly, across a wider ecosystem. Organizations at this stage wish to create an environment that is not only inclusive for their own employees, but for their partners, customers, and workers across their entire value chain. These organizations collaborate with partners to shape an inclusive environment that encompasses the hallmarks of equity and collaboration. Within such organizations, diversity in society is celebrated, and people are made to feel welcome and part of a diverse team. Leaders are committed to removing systemic biases and discrimination throughout the value chain, with the ultimate aim of creating safe and equitable environments for all.

From a societal perspective, the practice of inclusion entails broadening access to power and resources and improving the way society views marginalized groups. As noted by the Haas Institute for a Fair and Inclusive Society,[21] inclusion is realized when historically or currently marginalized groups feel valued, when differences are respected, and when fundamental needs and rights—relative to the dominant group—are met and recognized.

Organizations at this stage are active players in challenging and removing systemic societal bias and discrimination, advancing equity and supporting Agenda 2030s call for inclusivity and "leaving no-one behind."

Leaders may say:

> We believe that by creating an environment of inclusion we contribute directly to society, and to solving the broader problem of social exclusion. By advocating equity within our organization and in our value chain, by promoting equality of opportunity, by challenging systemic and personal bias, we not only transform our organization but drive transformation of society.

Employees may say:

> The commitment to inclusion is strategic to the organization and deeply rooted in their quest to contribute to greater inclusion in society. I feel that I am part of a movement and that the way my diversity is embraced is authentic and motivated by a societal value of inclusion.

We will explore the characteristics of an inclusive environment in Chapter 8.

9   The Five Stages of Equity

The five evolutionary stages of equity are represented in Fig. 9. The evolutionary stages are described as: Basic Support (Stage 1), Equality (Stage 2), Group Equity (Stage 3), Individualized Equity (Stage 4) and Societal Equity (Stage 5). These terms correspond to the key focus when attempting to create a fairer work environment within the organization and throughout its sphere of influence, in an additive manner. Equity relates to the configuration of access to resources in order to meet the requirements of the individual or the group (Fig. 9).

Stage 1—Basic Support
Resources are applied to find the person and support them entering the organization, following which very little extra support is provided to the person given that the priority is simply to have numerical representation at specified levels in the organization.

---

[21] Menendian et al. (2018).

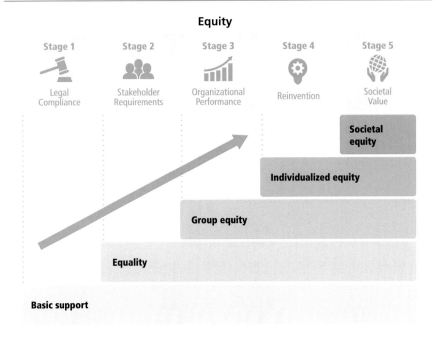

Fig. 9   The Five Stages of Equity
The five stages of equity focus on promoting increasing access to resources for key target groups at each level of Diversity Performance.

Stage 2—Equality
With the organization attempting to respond to customer requirements and also facing employee scrutiny, the organization tends to provide support, but in equal quantities to all employees, regardless of background and need.

Stage 3—Group Equity
At Stage 3, there is for the first time a conscious attempt to provide more sponsorship to those groups that lack access to the typical networks within the organization that are so important for advancement and retention. Instead of simply providing the same resources to all employees, there is a conscious attempt to identify groups of employees that may have faced barriers within society and to adapt support and access to resources to various group profiles to support their contribution and engagement.

Stage 4—Individualized Equity
Where support and access to resources at Stage 3 were done on the basis of the group, at Stage 4 there is more individualized support, with earmarking of resources based on individual need. For example, this could include offering of personal coaching, reverse mentoring, and personal development initiatives to create enhanced access.

Stage 5—Societal Equity
At this performance level, the focus on equity is significant as organizations directly connect their Diversity Performance goals to one or more of the SDGs and underlying targets—such as SDG 5.5: "Ensure women's full and effective participation and equal opportunities for leadership at all levels of decision-making in political, economic and public life." As a result the focus is on extending equity beyond the organization into society at large and the organization's wider sphere of influence.

We will explore how to advance equity by minimizing implicit and systemic bias in Chapter 6.

10   The Five Stages of Leadership

The importance of leadership in diversity performance cannot be underestimated. Leadership that is perceived to suppress diversity can have a negative impact on the organization's performance. Leader behavior has a direct link to an employee's experience of inclusion—in fact, almost 45% of employee experiences of inclusion are explained by their manager's inclusive leadership behavior.[22] Leadership therefore acts as a multiplier—positive or negative—for diversity, inclusion, equity, and purpose within the organization.

As for all other elements of Diversity Performance, leadership of diversity has five stages of evolution and reflects the shifting focus of responsibility for diversity outcomes (Fig. 10).

Stage 1—Legal/Risk Manager
In Stage 1 organizations, where diversity is driven to minimize legal sanction and seen as a risk to be mitigated, diversity oversight sits with the legal and/or risk management officer.

Stage 2—Human Resources
For organizations responding to customer requirements and facing employee scrutiny, the functions closest to these stakeholders will tend to be involved in monitoring Diversity Performance. Oversight of diversity at Stage 2 therefore primarily involves the Human Resources (HR) and Customer Relationship Management (Marketing) Functions.

Stage 3—Senior Leadership
At Stage 3, where there is a focus on realizing performance outcomes, diversity responsibility tends to sit with senior figures involved in supervisory and operational leadership. Within a commercial entity, this would be the CEO, CFO, and Business Unit Leaders. Within a University, it would be the Dean and Directors, and within an NGO, it would be the Advisory Board.

---

[22] Travis et al. (2019).

Leadership

Fig. 10   The Five Stages of Leadership
Responsibility for diversity leadership evolves through the five stages from legal professionals toward whole-of-organization accountability.

Stage 4—Whole Organization

At Stage 4, where there is a key focus on transformation and agility, organizations will assign responsibility for supporting this transformation to every member of the organization. This is because leaders understand that groupthink is a tendency in homogeneous teams, and that each person needs to encourage diverse opinions to be heard and reflected in transformational solutions.

Stage 5—Societal Partnership

At this performance level, leadership oversight and responsibility for Diversity Performance extends beyond the organization's boundary to partners within its value chain (e.g., supplier base) and the broader societies in which it operates. With leadership being so critical to realizing and embedding an organization's strategic diversity narrative, diversity responsibility allocation is key. Where in the earlier stages diversity responsibility is confined to an expert or specialist role, at the more advanced level leadership for diversity is cascaded throughout the organization. We will explore the practices and behaviors of the diversity leader and how they feed the Virtuous Circle of Diversity Performance more extensively in Chapter 8.

11   The Five Stages of Purpose

Just as leadership is a multiplier of diversity performance, so is diversity purpose. At the heart of this is the fact that human beings are social animals who desire to be part of a group, connected to each other by way of common reference points and shared values. Especially in diverse organizations—where default group connections like having similar cultural backgrounds, academic qualifications, specializations, and demographics are no longer in place—the organization's unifying purpose and strategic narrative for diversity function as the critical connector.

There has been a great deal of research focused on whether purpose-led organizations deliver higher performance than those where the purpose is either not known or not formulated in a manner that creates aspirational connections. For example, the U.S. research and polling organization Gallup has found that a primary reason for employees not feeling engaged is their lack of connection to the organization's purpose. This analysis showed that 87% of employees state that purpose is very important to them. When employees strongly agree that they know what their company stands for and what makes it different from competitors, nearly eight in 10 (77%) strongly agree that they plan to be with the company for at least one year.[23]

Done right, purpose can act as a multiplier and help to fuel the Virtuous Circle of Diversity Performance. A study of strategies that drive high growth in companies underscores the importance of purpose to organizational success and longevity, concluding: "Many high-growth companies use purpose to stay relevant in a fast-changing world."[24] However, if the purpose is disjointed or fails to unify the diverse people within the organization, it can also negatively impact diversity outcomes. Without unifying purpose, the diversity within the organization is not channeled toward shared outcomes. The result is that the rich diversity is dispersed across multiple initiatives, which can lead to frustration and ultimately undermine Diversity Performance.

Once again, there are five stages of diversity purpose and they are developed to create a call to action for the organization (Fig. 11).

Stage 1—Comply
At this level, the diversity purpose is quite simple, namely, to ensure that the organization satisfies the diversity characteristics required by law so as to minimize legal consequences.

Stage 2—Meet Expectations
Here diversity purpose is to reflect diversity in the organization as required by key stakeholders, usually customers and employees. This is not a legal requirement, but contributes to the organization's license to operate.

---

[23] Dvorak and Nelson (2016).

[24] Malnight et al. (2019).

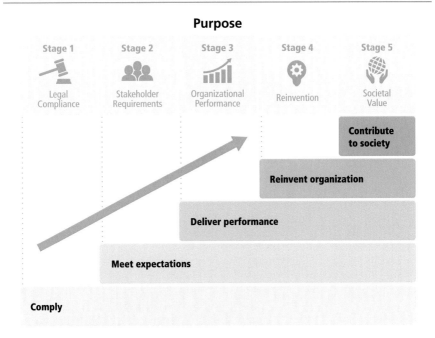

Fig. 11   The Five Stages of Purpose
Diversity purpose is the organization's rationale for pursuing Diversity Performance and evolves as they progress through the stages.

Stage 3—Deliver Performance

Diversity purpose at this stage is to deliver performance outcomes to the organization, including increased growth, more satisfied customers, more engaged and loyal employees, increased innovation, better decision-making, risk management, and increased access to talent.

Stage 4—Reinvent Organization

At Stage 4, the diversity purpose is to ensure the survival of the organization, usually in a complex environment, by creating diversity of thinking that allows for break-through ideas, agility, and continuous transformation.

Stage 5—Contribute to Society

Diversity purpose has evolved into wanting to be an exemplar of diversity, inclusion, equity, leadership, and purpose, and inspiring change in other organizations throughout the value chain or wider industry ecosystem.

As purpose is so critical to realizing Diversity Performance, we will explore this further in Chapters 4 and 5.

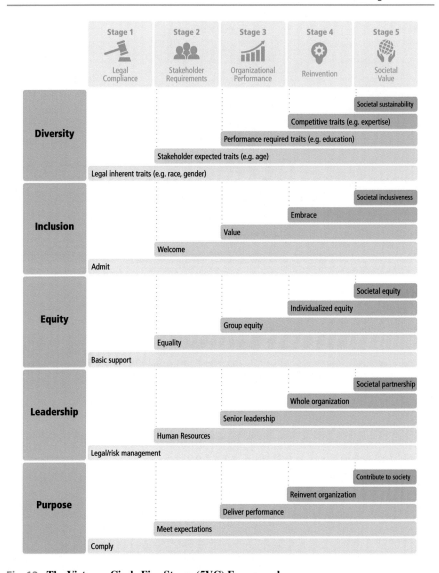

Fig. 12   The Virtuous Circle Five Stages (5VC) Framework
Figure 12 presents an overview of the elements of Diversity Performance at every maturity stage.

12   Concluding Remarks

Diversity and inclusion alone do not translate into Diversity Performance. This is driven when organizations focus on five diversity elements—namely, inherent and acquired diversity traits, inclusion of talent, the advancement of equity, leadership, and a clear diversity purpose to unite action. Together, these five elements create a Virtuous Circle that not only sustains diversity within the organization but creates broader stakeholder and societal value as well.

Diversity Performance is an evolutionary journey consisting of five distinct stages, and each element of the Virtuous Circle evolves as it matures. Combining the five stages with the five elements creates a useful strategic planning framework for the organization's diversity journey. As summarized in Fig. 12, the vertical axis shows the five elements of performance, and the horizontal axis shows the five stages of maturity, indicating at a glance the evolving and cumulative character of each of the key elements of Diversity Performance.

In Chapter 4 we will explore how leaders can apply this framework to craft a strategic diversity narrative for their organization, identify their desired future level of Diversity Performance and measure the gap between where they are today and where they want to be.

References

Bolger, Meg. "What's the Difference Between Diversity, Inclusion, and Equity?" *General Assembly*, May 24, 2020. https://generalassemb.ly/blog/diversity-inclusion-equity-differences-in-meaning/.

Burnette, Krys. "Belonging: A Conversation About Equity, Diversity, and Inclusion." *Medium*, January 22, 2019. https://medium.com/@krysburnette/its-2019-and-we-are-still-talking-about-equity-diversity-and-inclusion-dd00c9a66113.

Distefano, Joseph J., and Martha L. Maznevski. "Creating Value with Diverse Teams in Global Management." *Organizational Dynamics* 29: 45–63, September 2000. https://doi.org/10.1016/S0090-2616(00)00012-7.

Dvorak, Nate, and Bailey Nelson. "Company Missions: Not Resonating With Employees." *Gallup*, August 16, 2016. https://news.gallup.com/businessjournal/194642/company-missions-not-resonating-employees.aspx.

Lorenzo, Rocio, et al. "How Diverse Leadership Teams Boost Innovation." BCG, January 23, 2018. https://www.bcg.com/en-us/publications/2018/how-diverse-leadership-teams-boost-innovation.

Malnight, Thomas W., Ivy Buche, and Charles Dhanaraj. "Put Purpose at the Core Your Strategy." *Harvard Business Review*, September–October 2019. https://hbr.org/2019/09/put-purpose-at-the-core-of-your-strategy.

Menendian, Stephen, Elsadig Elsheikh, and Samir Gambhir. "2018 Inclusiveness Index: Measuring Global Inclusion and Marginality." *Haas Institute*, 2018. https://belonging.berkeley.edu/sites/default/files/haasinstitute_2018inclusivenessindex_publish.pdf.

Moss-Racusin, Corinne A., et al. "Science Faculty's Subtle Gender Biases Favor Male Students." *PNAS*, October 9, 2012.

Phillips, Kathryn W. "How Diversity Works." *Scientific American*, October 2014.

Phillips, Kathryn W., and Charles A. O'Reilly, "Demography and Diversity in Organizations: A Review of 40 Years of Research." *Organizational Behavior*, January 1998.

Smith, Alexis Nicole, et al. "'Making the Invisible Visible: Paradoxical Effects of Intersectionality on the Career Experience of Executive Black Women." *Academy of Management Journal*, 2017.

Travis, Dnika J., Emily Shaffer, and Jennifer Thorpe-Moscon. "Getting Real About Inclusive Leadership: Why Change Starts With You." *Catalyst*, 2019. https://www.catalyst.org/research/inclusive-leadership-report/.

Webel, Charles, and Johan Galtung. *Handbook of Peace and Conflict Studies*. Routledge, March 19, 2012. ISBN: 9780203089163.

Developing a Strategic Diversity Narrative to Close the Performance Gap

4

There is power in storytelling, and the most effective way to get your team onboard in delivering your desired level of Diversity Performance is to formulate a strategic narrative. This is your organization's unique diversity story, and it provides the connecting thread between your diversity purpose or intention and your desired diversity outcome. It serves as the North Star for the organization's diversity journey—and acts as a unifying call for transformation and shared mandate for the organization and its stakeholders.

In this chapter, we examine how to craft a strategic diversity narrative for an organization in a way that takes account of its current state and prepares it for the future. Equipped with a clear narrative, the leader is able to measure the Diversity Performance Gap (Fig. 1).

1   What Is a Strategic Narrative?

The strategic narrative for diversity sets out a vision and rationale for where diversity fits within the organization's transformation and value creation journey. It reminds all stakeholders why the desired state of diversity is so critical to the longevity and sustainability of the organization. It crystallizes the kind of diversity characteristics, inclusion, equity, leadership, and purpose that are the right fit for the organization within its context. And it serves as an anchor for the organization's diversity mandate, unifying the organization around a shared statement of intent for Diversity Performance.

Like all good narratives, it requires a compelling plot, characters, story arc, and conclusion. Through a good diversity story, employees can understand their role within the larger narrative and how they can be an active part of shaping the future of the organization. As described in Chapter 2, one key foundation for this story is to understand stakeholder expectations. Another is to have a solid grasp of what constitutes Diversity Performance—namely the reinforcing elements that make up

© Diversity and Performance BV 2021
K. Formanek, *Beyond D&I*, https://doi.org/10.1007/978-3-030-75336-8_4

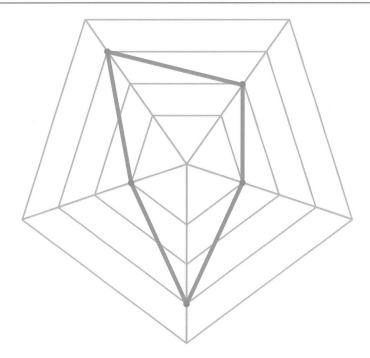

Fig.1 Evaluating the Diversity Performance Gap
Leaders require a strategic manner to measure their current and target Diversity Performance.

the Virtuous Circle, as described in Chapter 3. The process of developing a strategic narrative can then build on these foundations to reflect where the organization is on its diversity journey, and where it wants to go.

Achieving a state of diversity that results in transformative change demands leadership attention, stamina, and conviction. In some organizations, leaders begin the journey to expand diversity of thought but run out of steam. They lose sight of the drivers and bigger diversity picture. Or they may face so much pushback or resistance the diversity journey gets demoted from a strategic lever for organizational success to a side project with a shelf-life. This is where a good strategic narrative can help.

Developing an effective strategic narrative for diversity is not easy, however. Without the right guidance, few leaders are able to set out a narrative that is crisp, compelling, and authentic at first try. Copying and pasting another organization's strategic narrative is unlikely to work because it will not be a perfect fit for the organization's unique context: each strategic narrative needs to reflect the context, history, and aspirations of the specific organization. Ideally, it is an inclusive process that engages employees and other stakeholders as key actors in shaping and realizing the imagined diversity future of the organization. Done properly, the strategic diversity narrative builds a bridge from where the organization is today to where it wants to be, enabling everyone on the team to pull together to close the gap.

2   Three Key Steps

As set out in the Performance and Capability Roadmap presented in Chapter 1, measuring the organization's Diversity Performance gap is crucial for understanding where the organization is currently on its diversity journey and identifying key areas for improvement. There are three main steps required to map the gap beteen an organization's current Diversity Performance and where it would like to be.

These three steps are:

1. **Craft the future diversity narrative**—To articulate the organization's desired future level of diversity, the leader uses the Virtuous Circle 5 Stages Framework (5VC) from Chapter 3 to set the organization's aspirational level of Diversity Performance.
2. **Capture the current diversity narrative**—To understand the organization's existing level of Diversity Performance, the leader maps current performance against the 5VC.
3. **Compare the current and future diversity narratives**—By mapping both the current and desired future level of performance to the 5VC, key gaps can be pinpointed and used to identify priority areas for improvement.

About 60% of the time, leaders will start this strategic narrative process by defining where they need to go—in other words their desired level of diversity maturity. Others start by outlining their current state—for example where they have embarked on a general performance assessment or have already conducted structured reviews—then use the strategic planning process to look to the future. It is neither right nor wrong to start with the current or future state first; what matters is to capture both in order to identify the gap between them.

Once the leader can clearly perceive the gap between these two states, they can identify what to change and where to target attention. Below, these steps are explained in more detail, followed by a case study that demonstrates how one organization developed its narrative.

1.   **Craft the future diversity narrative**

The first step requires the leader to cast forward to anticipate the role that diversity will play in the organization in the future, the level of Diversity Performance that they hope to attain and a description of each element of the Virtuous Circle (described in Chapter 3, Fig. 4) as it will be once the organization's desired state of Diversity Performance is achieved.

A number of reflection questions help to steer this process. The aim is to stimulate richer reflection by the leader on their future strategic narrative through contextual questions and closer consideration of each element of the Virtuous Circle.

Tools

Reflection questions for strategic narrative

Context Setting

- What is the reason for being (raison d'être) of my organization?
- What is the transformation agenda for my organization (2–3 years)?
- What are my indirect and direct stakeholders requiring from my organization in the future?

Diversity

- What is the role of diversity in the transformational agenda of my organization?
- What is the role of diversity in supporting the needs and expectations of my stakeholders?
- What would happen to my organization if as a strategic leader I neither cared about diversity nor advanced it?
- What are the greatest diversity characteristic gaps (inherited and acquired) for meeting the future required Diversity Performance?
- How do I need to define diversity for my organization for the future?

Inclusion

- What is the role of inclusion in the transformational agenda of my organization?
- What level of inclusion is needed to liberate the diversity characteristics required for my organizational transformation?
- What level of inclusion do I need to respond to stakeholders' expectations?
- How should I define inclusion for my organization in the future?

Equity

- Why is it important to go beyond equality and focus on equity within my organization?
- How is Diversity Performance compromised in the organization if equity is not advanced?
- What is the expectation of my stakeholders with regards to the advancement of equity within my organization?

Leadership

- How engaged are leaders and people within the organization to steer the diversity journey?
- How do I empower others in the organization and hold them accountable for their support of the diversity journey and Diversity Performance?

> **Purpose**
>
> - How do I incorporate Diversity Performance into organizational purpose?
>   How can Diversity Performance aims be extended more broadly throughout our value chain and partnerships?

Answering these questions candidly allows the leader to develop a refined strategic narrative that is often aspirational and serves to unite the organization in realizing its diversity vision. It is an approach that can be applied by the strategic leader of any type of organization.

2. **Capture the current diversity narrative**

Using no more than 400 words, the leader answers the question "What is the current motivation for diversity in the organization and how is this evidenced?".

Here it is not necessary for the leader to conduct an elaborate "as is" analysis—what matters is that they reply briefly to the question themselves and do not outsource this to someone else. The value of this exercise is to capture the true nature of the leader's knowledge of the organization's current Diversity Performance and their ability to convert this into a narrative that accurately reflects the current situation within their organization.

Whether they lead small, medium-sized, or large organizations, the responses of leaders tend to fall into five different types of narrative (Table 1) that can be mapped to the five stages of Diversity Performance.

3. **Compare the current and future diversity narratives**

Equipped with these dual narratives for diversity in their organization, the leader is able to match these narratives to their corresponding stages of maturity using the Five Stages framework introduced in Chapter 3. As a reminder, this framework sets out five distinct maturity levels for the five elements of Diversity Performance, evolving from legal compliance to societal value. By reviewing the way that diversity, inclusion, equity, leadership, and performance are defined in each narrative, and comparing this to how these elements are defined in the five stages of the framework, it is possible to determine which stage best represents the desired level of Diversity Performance (through the future narrative) and what stage the existing level of Diversity Performance most closely corresponds to (through the current narrative).

For example, a leader may map their current and future narratives to the Five Stages framework and discover that their existing Diversity Performance level (shown in orange) is Stage 2: Stakeholder Requirements and their aspirational Diversity Performance (shown in green) is Stage 4: Reinvention, as shown in Fig. 2.

Table 1 Typical Current Diversity Narrative Responses

Most current diversity narratives typically use common words and phrases that can be mapped to the five stages of Diversity Performance.

Stage	Organizational Diversity Focus	Typical statement
Stage 1 Legal Compliance	To satisfy legal requirements and minimize risk. Words or phrases often used: – Risk management – Compliance management – Sanction avoidance – Quota risk/pressure	Our organization is committed to fully support diversity as legislated in the countries in which we operate. By ensuring that we are fully compliant, we minimize penalties that could occur if we were sanctioned for discriminatory offenses and/or not delivering on diversity quotas.
Stage 2 Stakeholder Requirements	To satisfy customer and employee requirements. Words or phrases often used: – Our customers expect us to be … – Industry requirements/rankings	Diversity is of growing importance for our stakeholders and within our sector. There is increasing scrutiny of diversity and we need to be seen to respond appropriately. Our stakeholders want to see more women and greater cultural diversity on our sales teams. If we do not want to lose our customers, we need to show that we have the required diversity in our teams and we take it seriously as an organization.
Stage 3 Organizational Performance	To reap business benefits. Words or phrases often used: – Business case – Organizational performance e.g. revenue growth, more profitable clients, talent supply	We are convinced that there is a strong business case for diversity. Diversity allows us to better anticipate the needs and wants of our customers. We also believe that diversity is important for driving more growth and profitability in our organization.
Stage 4 Reinvention	To support innovation, diversity of thinking and being agile in a complex world. Words or phrases often used: – Innovative capability – Survival – Continuity – Diversity is critical – Supply chain/value chain	We live in a complex environment and diversity is key to our ability to transform. Without diversity of thought, we are unable to respond to our external environment and will be blindsided by groupthink. Diversity is so important to us that we have elevated it as a key value of our organization. We recognize that without inclusion the benefits of diversity will not occur.
Stage 5 Societal Value	To support value creation, tackle societal challenges and harness diversity to be a force for good in the world. Words or phrases often used: – Societal case – Equality – Equity – Leave no one behind – Inclusiveness	We are committed to diversity because we are convinced that it allows us to deliver on our business mandate and anticipate changes occurring in our wider environment. Our commitment to diversity supports our greater purpose of being a force for good in society. We are proud that through our diversity and inclusion and equity efforts we directly contribute to the UN SDGs, including improving gender equality, providing decent work opportunities to more people in our value chain and supporting greater access and empowerment for our customers and consumers.

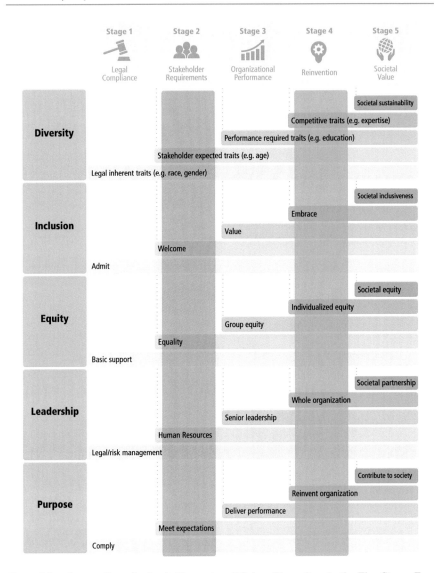

Fig. 2 Mapping an Organization's Current and Future Narratives to the Five Stages Framework

By mapping its current and future narratives to the Five Stages framework, this hypothetical organization discovers that its existing Diversity Performance level is Stage 2: Stakeholder Requirements and its desired Diversity Performance level is Stage 4: Reinvention.

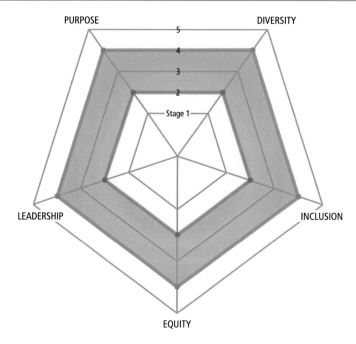

Fig. 3 Performance Gap Radar Chart
The gap between the orange and green lines in the diagram depicts the performance gap between the organization's existing and aspirational Diversity Performance levels.

The Diversity Performance gap for this hypothetical organization becomes visible by plotting its desired and actual performance levels for each element in a radar chart (Fig. 3).

The five concentric circles of the radar chart represent the Five Stages, starting at the center with Stage 1 (Legal Compliance), followed by Stage 2 (Stakeholder Requirements), Stage 3 (Organizational Performance), Stage 4 (Reinvention) and finally, represented by the outer circle of the radar chart, Stage 5 (Societal Value). Each point on the radar chart represents one of the five elements of Diversity Performance from the Virtuous Circle. Starting clockwise from the top righthand point, Diversity is followed by Inclusion, Equity, Leadership, and Purpose. The green line shows that the desired level of performance for each of these elements is Stage 4. The orange line shows that the organization's existing performance level for each element satisfies Stage 2. The radar chart reveals there is a two-stage Diversity Performance gap—in other words the organization needs to build its capabilities not only to move to Stage 3, but to progress beyond Stage 3 to Stage 4.

With a clearer understanding of their Diversity Performance gap, the leader can then set about closing this by implementing performance improvement initiatives to build the organization's core diversity capabilities. These are discussed in detail in Chapter 5.

To show how this three-step performance gap measurement process can catalyze effective organizational change, the following case study shares the experience of a software industry CEO who wanted to design and lead a diversity journey. As well as developing a strategic narrative for Diversity Performance, this leader leveraged the Virtuous Circle and Five Stages of Diversity Performance to highlight gaps and identify the actions required to align their organization with their diversity vision.

Case Study: How the CEO of a Software Firm Identified Their Diversity Performance Gap

A CEO of a European software company was navigating an organization experiencing a great deal of change. The company comprised four different business entities that had been acquired over several years. The organization was in the midst of a transformation to integrate these entities, expand geographically and transition from an Enterprise Resource Planning (ERP)-in-a-box provider solution to an iCloud solution for start-ups. The CEO was newly appointed, young, dynamic, and keen to drive a diversity agenda within the new organization.

Original strategic narrative

The CEO began by addressing the first assessment question: "What is the current motivation for diversity in the organization?".

To date we have not focused on the diversity agenda. This is because we are already quite diverse, by way of the merger of four different national entities. This brings us already national and cultural diversity and clearly, we have diversity in work experience, given that each entity has had a different history. However, we observe a great deal of focus being placed on gender diversity, by our customers and also by industry and sector organizations, and we have some gaps in gender diversity in our leadership team. To date, we have not specifically focused on inclusion activities, because we have a program in place to integrate our entities. Part of the integration is to develop an overarching purpose and with consistent values between the legal entities. Our purpose is to deliver software via the cloud to small, start-up businesses, offering them flexibility. While I have latitude in the investment and projects that I launch, the focus on shareholder return is top of mind. In my mind, our key focus should be to recruit more women to be part of our organization.

Analysis of the current strategic narrative

An evaluation of the CEO's response yielded the following insights:

- Organizational diversity is present through the acquisition of four national businesses which now have to be integrated.
- Gender diversity is the primary focus, in response to the stakeholder-driven gender focus in the technology sector.
- Diversity is not referenced within their business imperatives.
- Inclusion is (thought to be) supported through the merger activities.

Developing a future strategic narrative

In answer to the reflection questions, the CEO defined the organization's mandate, stakeholder needs, and transformation agenda for the next two to three years as follows:

Our organization's mandate is to deliver software in-a-box for start-up businesses. We are required to deploy our solutions via the cloud and serve our clients globally. Our stakeholders are predominantly young entrepreneurs who expect rapid deployment of new software solutions to allow them to be more agile and responsive to the changing world.

Within this clear business context, the CEO explored how diversity could support the organization's transformation agenda and meet the needs and expectations of their stakeholders. They also asked themselves a soul-searching question: What would happen to the organization if they did not care about diversity or work to advance it? Here is the CEO's response:

We currently do not have the diversity to meet our stakeholder needs, nor to assist us to deliver on the transformation. Our clients are on average 28 years old, while the average age of people in our organization is around 48 years old. We find that we are not having the relationship connection with our clients, and they do not trust us to understand them and transform with them. Also, when we look at our current specialization, we note that we have traditional ERP software skills, but we do not have iCloud skills. We are starting up operations in Asia, and we are currently leveraging our head office staff to facilitate this process. We realize that it would be far better to have local staff and more cultural diversity for this new territory. We also find that an increasing share of our clients are women. However, our sales team and technicians are predominantly men, and we are not seen as gender-rich to many of our clients. More than that, we find that in our decision-making, we tend to have a groupthink mentality when we look at different solution paths. We are absolutely convinced that having a better mix of men and women of different ages would assist us being able to adapt and innovate faster on behalf of our clients. So, in summary, we require a wide array of diversity: gender, iCloud skills, Asia-cultural diversity and age diversity.

The CEO then turned their attention to the level of inclusiveness that would be required, within and outside the organization, to realize this future narrative:

We have much work to be done on two fronts. Firstly, we are comprised of four separate legal entities, and now need to work together as one organization. Clearly, there are concerns for power and influence from each entity, with the jostling for having influence. Secondly, we see that we have a dominant in-group culture across all entities. Most of our people are drawn from the same larger players that dominate the software industry. We have started to conclude that we are not able to beat the bigger players at their own game. We prefer to create a differentiated culture and group that is well placed to serve the start-up entrepreneurs. This requires us to be inclusive to our target clients and also very inclusive to our internal people. We are convinced that we in fact have much of the diversity already, but the group dynamics are so powerful that our people often do not feel comfortable to speak up and share their perspectives. As a result, we wish to stress collaboration, respect, innovation, client value, and fun as our new overarching values.

Finally, the CEO was asked to reflect on the company's purpose, and how diversity and inclusiveness could be woven into this. Did that purpose live in the hearts and minds of the organization's employees and stakeholders? The CEO was also challenged to think about how the diversity and inclusiveness narrative could be aligned to the 2030 Agenda. Again, the response revealed important insights:

Currently, we do not refer to our talent, or the diversity of our talent, with respect to our purpose of delivering in-the-box agile solutions at speed to our clients. However, this discussion has confirmed to me that our differentiator will be our connection to our clients and the diversity of talent that we bring to our clients to make sense of their challenges and the opportunities they face as start-up entrepreneurs. We can translate these insights into software-at-speed. As a result, we will modify our purpose to better capture the role of our diverse talent as an accelerator for our clients. We realize now that while clearly our mandates to our owners and shareholders are critical, our goal is more than serving our shareholders alone. We recognize that our focus on start-ups and offering agility to young entrepreneurs globally allows us to support the Agenda 2030 SDG Goal 8, namely, Decent Work and Economic Growth.

Analyzing the future strategic narrative

The software company CEO's reflections on the future strategic narrative of the organization led to three crucial realizations:

– Their approach to diversity had been ad hoc and was not embedded into their strategic agenda.
– Their strategic agenda—their transformation—was highly dependent on their ability to leverage diversity and inclusion effectively to satisfy their clients' needs. This required more age and gender (inherited diversity characteristics) and cultural/natural diversity (Asia) and iCloud specialization.
– Diversity of talent was not only beneficial to their organization, but also the key to their differentiated offering and positioning in the market.

Equipped with these insights, the CEO developed a new strategic narrative for diversity. Here is an extract:

Our organization's purpose is to optimally support our clients, young entrepreneurs, in building out their start-up business by delivering in-the-box software solutions at speed and supporting the changing environment that faces our clients. Diversity of talent allows us to connect to our clients, develop long-term relationships with them as they scale their business, and innovate on their behalf. Client understanding and engagement is at the heart of our common purpose. We recognize that we have a rich history, comprising different legal entities being merged and now flexed for our clients. We recognize our unique history, and we aspire to collaborate seamlessly, so that the rich diversity of our organization is able to be truly leveraged for breakthrough innovations. We are united not only in our passion for our clients, but also in our conviction that the fruits of our work support the global aspiration of creating decent work and economic growth.

Compare the current and future diversity narratives

The CEO then moved to the critical third step in the process—mapping current and future strategic narratives to the Five Stages of Diversity Performance, presented in Chapter 3, to identify gaps and key actions. Through this comparison, the CEO was able to determine the following:

• The software organization was currently predominantly at Stage 1 and Stage 2 given that the organization focused on diversity in mostly a reactive manner (in response to stakeholder requirements), had limited initiatives to build inclusion and engagement, did not have a clear strategic purpose attached to its diversity focus, and did not advance equity proactively.
• The organization needed to have its Diversity Performance at Stage 4 given its focus on being adaptive and agile in a fast-changing digital world where their customers expected innovation at scale (Fig. 4).

Mapping the organization's current and desired performance on a radar chart (Fig. 5) revealed a visible performance gap that would need to be closed to reach Stage 4 (the green line). While the company's performance on diversity, equity, and leadership was at Stage 2, purpose and inclusion were still

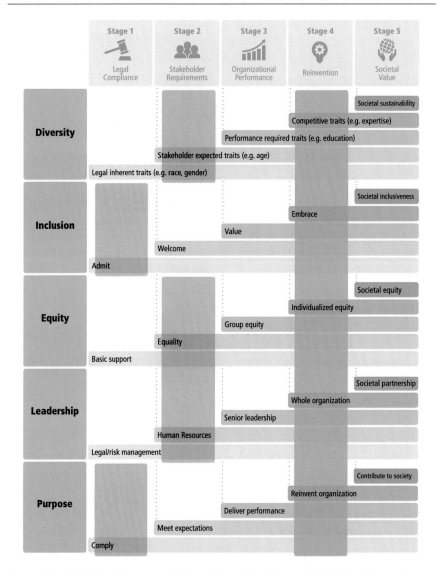

Fig. 4 Organization's Current and Future Narratives Mapped to the Five Stages Framework

By mapping its current and future narratives to the Five Stages framework, the Software Company discovered that its existing Diversity Performance level is at Stage 1 (Inclusion and Purpose) and Stage 2 (Diversity, Equity, Leadership), yet wishes to have its Diversity Performance at Stage 4: Reinvention.

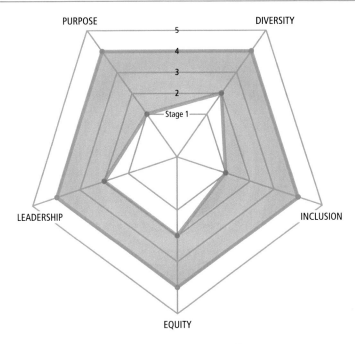

Fig. 5 Radar Chart Showing the Diversity Performance Gap
The green line indicates the desired, or required, level of Diversity Performance and the orange line shows the actual state of Diversity Performance. The area between the orange and green lines represents the Diversity Performance gap.

at Stage 1 (the orange line). Focusing on these two performance elements was therefore a priority.

Analyze the performance gap
Through this gap analysis, the CEO was also able to identify key roadblocks in their Diversity Performance approach. These became priority issues to overcome in the organization's plan to close the diversity gaps. Among these roadblocks were that:

- Diversity had been managed in a vacuum, in which a copy-and-paste approach of incorporating others' best practices had been adopted. This was a response to what the organization believed others were doing, rather than what was needed for the organization to survive and deliver on its mandate.
- There was a very limited connection between diversity and inclusion, the organization's mandate and its transformation agenda.
- Diversity and inclusion had been relegated as a side project and to a team that did not have the clout or oversight to steer it forward ambitiously, with the support of the whole organization.
- Without the strategic narrative and rationale for diversity, people within the organization had become deeply divided and cynical around the topic

of diversity. There was a widely held view that the new CEO was looking at diversity to tick boxes rather than because there was a real imperative that would be helpful to the organization.

The CEO was excited by the insights from the Virtuous Circle Assessment. The process was cascaded throughout the organization and a series of dialogues launched around the topic of diversity. Specifically, a challenge was created to develop a rich tapestry of quotes and assertions on why diversity was critical for the business to survive and deliver value to its stakeholders. As often happens, the leader felt liberated by "holding the space" of the subject of diversity and speaking about diversity strategically.

▶   **Key takeaway** This case study demonstrates that it is important for leaders to lead diversity as they would lead their business or organization. What appears second nature to leaders when leading a business seems to dissipate when leading diversity. Every new leader taking over the reins of a business will assess its strengths and weaknesses and what is required to deliver on its mandate now and in the future, based on changing context and stakeholders needs. The same approach is true for diversity. When the CEO of the software firm applied the same rigor to evaluating Diversity Performance as for other strategic initiatives, the next steps in their journey quickly became apparent.

The next case study illustrates how a methodical and strategic approach to diversity and inclusion can help an organization weather even the toughest storms.

Case Study: How Lack of Diversity Put the Central Bank of Ireland at Risk

Too often, it takes a crisis before the strategic necessity for diversity, and its role in making an organization more resilient, is truly appreciated. The role of the Central Bank of Ireland in the collapse of the Irish financial system, and how it created a strategic narrative for diversity, provides a powerful case study that other organizations can learn from.

Like most organizations, the Central Bank of Ireland, the country's main financial regulatory body, operates in an increasingly complex environment. This became painfully apparent with the global financial crisis (GFC) of 2007–2008. It was a crisis of historic proportions that shook confidence in the global monetary system. For Ireland, it was characterized as a "tsunami,"[1] as it brought the rapid growth of the Celtic Tiger era to a halt, becoming the first euro economy to slide into a recession,[2] the effects of which were still being felt in 2020.

---

[1] Taylor (2018).

[2] "Ireland officially in recession," *The New York Times*, September 25, 2008, https://www. nytimes.com/2008/09/25/business/worldbusiness/25iht-25ireland.16482373.html.

The GFC unveiled a widespread crisis of culture that characterized many financial institutions at the time. Banks had become detached from their stakeholders, in particular the interests of their customers, and lack of purpose, diversity, and inclusion played a key role in this. Indeed, an examination of the state of diversity and inclusion at the Irish Central Bank at the time of the financial collapse reveals a broken Virtuous Circle, in which diversity of thinking, inclusiveness, and a unifying purpose were lacking. As a result, the Irish Central Bank was unable to make sense of its external environment—just the day before the collapse, the Bank president expressed confidence, stating in November 2007: "The Irish banking system continues to be well-placed to withstand adverse economic and sectoral developments in the short to medium term."[3]

A complex external environment
Since 2000, the financial services system had been in flux. There was a massive increase in the complexity of the financial services industry worldwide, along with deregulation. Deregulation enabled banks to engage in hedge-fund trading with derivatives, which in turn created a bigger appetite for mortgages to support the profitable sale of these derivatives. This resulted in the creation of interest-only loans, which became affordable to subprime borrowers. A perfect storm was brewing, and it would strike at the time that the precarious balance was disrupted.

This happened in 2004, when the Federal Reserve raised interest rates. This event triggered a vicious circle whereby homeowners were unable to service their mortgage payments, housing prices fell as the supply of houses outpaced the demand, the derivative market was no longer profitable, and banks stopped lending to each other. Banks failed, which led to the government bailout of financial systems, the crash of multiple stock markets, and the near collapse of the entire financial system.[4,5] Ireland faced additional complexity because it was part of the new EU monetary system, but its primary and largest trading partner was the UK, with the pound currency.

This environment required the Central Bank of Ireland to be diligent in its duties and to ensure that it had the optimum talent composition and divergent perspectives to manage risk. This was not the case, as revealed in the 2011 report of the Statutory Commission of Investigation into the Irish Banking Sector. By studying the Commission's report, it is possible to assess the health of each element of the Irish Central Bank's Virtuous Circle for Diversity, Inclusiveness, and Purpose, as follows.

State of Diversity
At the Central Bank, lack of diversity and the presence of a homogenous team had resulted in groupthink. Gender balance is seen to moderate and enrich the risk management capability of banks, but as with many boards of major companies in Ireland,

---

[3] "Central Bank of Ireland," Wikipedia, last modified December 16, 2020, https://en.wikipedia.org/wiki/Central_Bank_of_Ireland#cite_note-15.

[4] Karp (2018).

[5] Amadeo (2020).

there was a significant gender imbalance.[6] This homogeneous group was defined by predominantly male leaders, with similar backgrounds, from similar educational experiences and operating in an impenetrable "old boys' club."[7] This stifled diversity and a 360-degree view on the external environment, generating significant risk. Christine Lagarde, now president of the European Central Bank, dubbed this period a "a sobering lesson in groupthink."[8]

State of Inclusion and Equity
The Commission found that groupthink was a significant contributing factor to the financial crisis in Ireland and that it was pervasive throughout the financial sector as a whole.

The Commission sought to find those who had a contrarian view, and it was clear that these contrarians dimmed their criticism, fearing that they would lose their jobs, face sanctions or take a hit to their reputation. This suppressed critical debate and dialogue and created a culture of submissiveness to superiors, with strong pressure for consensus. Some economists and individuals who had formed a critical evaluation of the monetary policy and the role of the Central Bank were silenced and sidelined. The result: The Central Bank did not have an environment of inclusiveness that allowed different voices to be heard and enriched decision-making to occur.[9]

State of Purpose and Leadership
On the surface, the purpose of the Central Bank was clear: "serve the public interest by safeguarding monetary and financial stability and by working to ensure that the financial system operates in the best interests of consumers and the wider economy."

Yet the mandate to protect the interests of consumers had not translated to a clear rationale and purpose for diversity within the bank, namely, to support diversity of talent that is in touch with consumers and has the diversity of thought to ensure that appropriate risk management is in pace to safeguard financial stability.

This failure to anticipate financial risk resulted in Ireland being one of the hardest hit nations in Europe and the period from 2007 to 2017 is often referred as the "lost decade" in Ireland. The financial crisis affected an entire generation, sparking personal insolvency, unemployment, a wave of emigration and heightened mortgage arrears.[10] The collapse of the banking system caused confidence in the Irish economy to plummet, and Ireland was forced to enter an EU–International Monetary Fund (IMF) loan program in November 2010.

---

[6] Ministers Donohoe and Stanton launch first report of the 'balance for better business' initiative, Department of Enterprise, Trade and Employment, Government of Ireland, May 29, 2019, https://enterprise.gov.ie/en/News-And-Events/Department-News/2019/May/29052019a.html.

[7] Ngu and Amran (2020).

[8] Lagarde (2018).

[9] McWilliams (2015).

[10] Brennan (2018).

A shift toward diversity

This experience drove a fundamental culture shift within Ireland and specifically in the Central Bank. The Central Bank Reform Act was enacted in 2010. A core aspect was changing the culture of the Central Bank and other players in the financial system from being reactive to being proactive and clear, from being homogeneous to heterogeneous, and from encouraging a culture of groupthink to encouraging a culture that allows for differences in thought and expression.

As the Deputy Governor of the Central Bank of Ireland noted in a speech in 2018 on the importance of diversity:

Having diverse teams can improve the quality of decision-making,[11,12] at all organizational levels, reduce groupthink,[13,14] and allow assumptions to be challenged more effectively.[15] Heterogeneous teams are, on average, better than homogeneous teams on creative and complex problems.[16] They increase the number of perspectives, provide better understanding of customer needs and flex management approaches. In a diverse and inclusive workplace, there is greater potential for internal crowd sourcing of ideas, innovation, challenging of ideas, and refining ideas in real time.[17]

Research based on mathematical models and social experiments, demonstrates how diversity can trump ability in group decision-making processes.[18] Diversity has been found to reduce the average error in decisions.[19] It has been found that the more variation in the pool, the better the selective process,[20] which is key to reducing groupthink. The more diverse a team, the more likely its predictive capability in the face of uncertainty.[21]

A new strategic narrative for diversity

In a speech on September 4, 2019 at the National Diversity & Inclusion Conference, the Central Bank of Ireland's Director of Financial Stability, Vasileios Madouros, laid out the bank's new vision and perspective on diversity and inclusion[22]—in essence, a new strategic narrative. The following elements of the speech capture this new strategic narrative, which is designed to help steer the bank through future crises.

---

[11] Padoa-Schioppa (2011).

[12] Kohn (2018).

[13] Bhawalkar (2019).

[14] Perez (2019).

[15] Farmer et al. (2014).

[16] Carney (2017).

[17] Gender pay gap report 2019, Central Bank of Ireland, 2019, https://www.centralbank.ie/docs/default-source/careers/policies/gender-pay-gap-report-2019.pdf.

[18] Gender pay gap report 2019, Central Bank of Ireland.

[19] Rowland and Sibley (2018).

[20] "Demographic Analysis – Applications for Pre-Approval Controlled Functions (PCF) roles in regulated firms – 2018," Central Bank of Ireland, 2018, https://www.centralbank.ie/docs/default-source/publications/demographic-reports/2018-demographics-of-the-financial-sector-report.pdf.

[21] "Behavior and Culture of the Irish Retail Banks," Central Bank of Ireland, 2018, https://www.centralbank.ie/docs/default-source/publications/corporate-reports/behaviour-and-culture-of-the-irish-retail-banks.pdf.

[22] Madouros (2019).

Diverse organizations are better equipped to tackle complex problems

There is no shortage of complex problems in the Central Bank. The functioning of the economy and the financial system depends on the behavior of large numbers of consumers and businesses. The factors that influence that behavior vary, both across different groups and over time. And the behavior of one group can affect the wellbeing of others.

The basis for better outcomes – especially in the face of particularly complex problems – is cognitive diversity [diversity of thought]. Cognitive diversity makes teams less susceptible to blind spots, biases and groupthink. As a result, diverse teams are better able to innovate, solve problems and make predictions.

The Central Bank is likely to be more effective if it represents the people we serve

"Listening to the public helps us understand the issues facing consumers and businesses. This, in turn, helps us design better policies. Explaining what we do—and in a way that people actually understand—helps strengthen the effectiveness of our policies. And it allows others to hold us to account. So, engaging with the public is important for the Central Bank. And we are more likely to do this better, if we genuinely represent the population that we serve."

Representing those we serve increases the likelihood we will engage effectively with the public

"The Central Bank's work often requires developing deep technical expertise. But we will not be effective in delivering our mandate if we are not trusted by the people we serve. So how can the public trust us—the technocrats? In part, I would hope, through the visible impact of our policies and by operating in an open, transparent and accountable manner. But familiarity also helps. Reflecting the diversity of the people that we serve can help build trust.[23] It can reduce misperceptions that central bankers are experts, sitting in their ivory towers, making decisions for someone else's benefit[24]… Representing those that we serve also increases the likelihood that we are trusted by the public."

A roadmap for diversity backed up by clear commitments

As a first step, the Central Bank set out inclusive diversity as a strategic priority for the organization. This vision was published in 2018 with a statement of intent: "Have a diverse workforce reflecting society in Ireland; harness difference to our benefit; be a thought leader on diversity and inclusion; and ensure our focus on diversity and inclusion has a positive impact on the behavior of the financial services industry."[25]

▶   **Key takeaway** Today, the Central Bank has made a long-term commitment to creating and continuously improving its culture of inclusion. Women make up almost 50% of the total workforce, 40% of its senior leadership team and

---

[23] Gender pay gap report 2019, Central Bank of Ireland.

[24] Rowland and Sibley, "Lack of diversity."

[25] Rowland (2020).

one-third of the board.[26] This is a fundamental transformation since 2008, when there was a clear lack of diversity. The Central Bank has made progress in closing the wage gap and has recorded increasing diversity and inclusion scores. Within the Central Bank Strategy 2019–2021, diversity and inclusion has been brought to the fore with statements of intent. However, the Central Bank recognizes that it is on a journey and will need to continually flex the cognitive diversity of the organization.[27] To close the gap, a coherent, integrated, and collaborative approach is needed.

3   Concluding Remarks

In this chapter we have seen how leaders can turn around Diversity Performance by taking a strategic approach. The first step is to craft a strategic narrative that can serve as the organization's North Star and provide direction to energize and sustain the diversity journey. This kind of unifying vision is fundamental to help the organization deliver on its diversity purpose and mandate. As we have seen, the Virtuous Circle and Five Stages of Diversity Performance are essential tools on this journey. By understanding the gap between the organization's current and future desired states of diversity, a leader can set priorities and devise a roadmap for closing the gap and achieving their diversity goals.

In Chapter 5, we introduce the Integrated Diversity Model as a proven means to make this happen.

References

Amadeo, Kimberly. "Causes of the 2008 Global Financial Crisis." *The Balance*, last modified May 28, 2020. https://www.thebalance.com/what-caused-2008-global-financial-crisis-3306176.

Brennan, Joe. "The Banking Crisis: Ireland's 'Lost Decade' in 10 Charts." *The Irish Times*, September 29, 2018. https://www.irishtimes.com/business/economy/the-banking-crisis-ireland-s-lost-decade-in-10-charts-1.3644680.

Bhawalkar, Gina. "The Inclusive Design Imperative: Win and Retain More Customers." Forrester, April 23, 2019. https://go.forrester.com/blogs/the-inclusive-design-imperative-win-and-retain-more-customers/.

Carney, Mark. "Reflecting Diversity, Choosing Inclusion." February 9, 2017. Available at https://www.bankofengland.co.uk/speech/2017/reflecting-diversity-choosing-inclusion.

---

[26] A lack of diversity at senior levels is a leading indicator of behaviour and culture risks in financial institutions – Director General Derville Rowland, Central Bank of Ireland, February 7, 2019, https://www.centralbank.ie/news-media/press-releases/dr--speechpr-7feb2019.

[27] Madouros, "Diversity and Inclusion: why it matters for the Central Bank."

Farmer, Harry, Ryan McKay, and Manos Tsaakiris, "Trust in Me: Trustworthy Others Are Seen as More Physically Similar to the Self." *Psychological Science*, 25, no. 1 (2014): 290–292. https://doi-org.ezp.sub.su.se/10.1177/0956797613494852.

Karp, Brad. "The Financial Crisis 10 Years Later: Lessons Learned." Harvard Law School Forum Corporate Governance, October 5, 2018. https://corpgov.law.harvard.edu/2018/10/05/the-financial-crisis-10-years-later-lessons-learned/.

Kohn, David. "From the Great Moderation to the Great Recession and Beyond—How Did We Get Here and What Lessons Have We Learned?" September 7, 2018.

Lagarde, Christine. "Ten Years After Lehman—Lessons Learned and Challenges Ahead." IMF Blog, September 5, 2018. https://blogs.imf.org/2018/09/05/ten-years-after-lehman-lessons-learned-and-challenges-ahead/.

Madouros, Vasileios. "Diversity and Inclusion: Why It Matters for the Central Bank." Central Bank of Ireland, September 4, 2019. Available at https://www.centralbank.ie/news/article/speech-vasileios-madouros-diversity-and-inclusion-04-sept-2019.

McWilliams, David. "Early Warnings, Divergent & Contrarian Views." Report of the Joint Committee of Inquiry into the Banking Crisis, Houses of the Oireachtas, February 26, 2015.

Padoa-Schioppa, Tommaso. "Markets and Government Before, During, and After the 2007–20xx Crisis." Per Jacobson Lecture, April 12, 2011.

Perez, Caroline Criado. *Invisible Women: Exposing Data Bias in a World Designed for Men* (Chatto & Windus, 2019).

Rowland, Derville. "The Importance of Diversity in the Financial Services Sector." February 17, 2020. Available at https://www.centralbank.ie/news-media/press-releases/speech-diversity-in-the-financial-services-sector-derville-rowland-11-feb-2020.

Rowland, Derville, and Ed Sibley. "Lack of Diversity Is Part of the Problem with Our Banking Culture." *The Irish Times*, October 26, 2018. https://www.irishtimes.com/opinion/lack-of-diversity-is-part-of-the-problem-with-our-banking-culture-1.3675900.

Sie Bing Ngu and Azlan Amran, "The Moderating Effect of Risk Management Committee On Corporate Governance and Financial Performance." 2020. https://doi.org/10.15405/epsbs.2020.10.10.

Taylor, Cliff. "The Crash—10 Years on: Scars Remain Amid the Recovery." *The Irish Times*, January 6, 2018. https://www.irishtimes.com/business/economy/the-crash-10-years-on-scars-remain-amid-the-recovery-1.3338508.

Closing the Performance Gap with the Integrated Diversity Model

5

Once the leader has envisioned and articulated their organization's future strategic narrative for diversity and identified the gaps between where they are today and where they want to be, the next step is to understand the actions, skills, and initiatives needed to close their Diversity Performance gap. We call this "Closing the Diversity Capability Gap" (Fig. 1).

The journey from crafting a strategic narrative and mapping the performance gap to closing the capability gap to deliver improved Diversity Performance is again vividly illustrated by the story of the South African national rugby team, the Springboks (introduced in Chapter 2).

1   The Springboks: The Road to Transformation

Nelson Mandela's aspiration for racial integration in the new landscape of a post-apartheid South Africa had provided a powerful strategic narrative for the nation's institutions—including the Springboks—to start the process of transformation. The foundations for change were laid in the months before the 1995 World Cup match, when Mandela invited Springboks captain Francois Pienaar to visit him in his offices. As Pienaar says, "We talked about all things—not just the World Cup. He wanted to know a lot about me." Even as high-powered people waited outside to see Mandela and his assistant came into the room to hurry him up, Mandela would say: "Mary, I am speaking to my captain."[1]

This early inclusive leadership helped spur the Springboks to victory and initiate the sport's subsequent journey toward diversity and inclusion. In the years ensuing that watershed World Cup victory, rugby in South Africa gradually became multi-racial as a direct result of deliberate packages of initiatives aimed

---

[1] Smith (2013).

© Diversity and Performance BV 2021   111
K. Formanek, *Beyond D&I*, https://doi.org/10.1007/978-3-030-75336-8_5

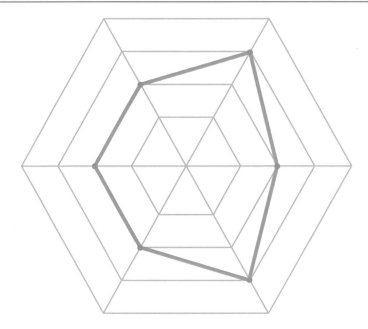

Fig. 1   Closing the Diversity Capability Gap
The Capability Gap is identified with reference to the Integrated Diversity Model that reflects the six diversity capabilities required to deliver Diversity Performance.

at supporting diversity. The setting of government quotas for racial composition of top-level teams, for example, was a deeply contested issue, both then and now, but it was a vital component in driving greater diversity in the nation's beloved sport.

Quotas were accompanied by a grassroots process to create a more diverse and inclusive player pipeline. In recognition that up-and-coming players needed to be nurtured and coached, starting at school level, the top rugby playing schools started to provide scholarships to young Black South African players, who were able to reside in school residential hostels to support the big changes in their lives. The most talented players would play school rugby at provincial and national levels, and from there move into the academies of the major professional provincial franchises which play in international leagues. Professional rugby at this level attracts not only crowds but television audiences, affording players the opportunity to earn income—a welcome benefit for many up-and-coming players. Change did not happen overnight, however. When South Africa again won the Rugby World Cup in Paris in 2007, the starting line-up included only two Black South African players in the entire match.

Although progress has been slow, thanks to these interventions, over the past 20 years professional rugby in South Africa has slowly become more integrated, with over a third of the national team constituting Black South African players in 2019—a solid increase but still falling short of the envisaged representation.

At the same time Black South African spectator participation has grown but remains in lockstep with representation. When in 2019, the Springboks were once again in the Rugby World Cup in Japan, for the first time in history the captain was a Black South African. A highly inspirational leader, Siya Kolisi had grown up in the impoverished township of Zwide. His mother died when he was 15, and he was raised by his grandmother and often went to bed hungry. When scouts detected his talent, at the age of 12, he was offered a scholarship to one of the elite South African rugby playing schools. His first night in the school hostel was the first time he had slept on a mattress. That was the beginning of a journey that brought him to the Springboks to ultimately serve as captain of the national team in the 2019 World Cup.[2]

Despite 12 to 1 betting odds against them, the Springboks once again surprised the pundits, claiming victory over the much-favored English team. The English had been so confident of victory that the route of their London victory parade had already been prepared to end with tea with the Queen at four o'clock the following Wednesday. But instead, 24 years after Mandela had steered South African rugby on its journey toward racial diversity and inclusion, it was Kolisi who carried the Cup aloft in his arms as his teammates surrounded him in jubilation. As Kolisi told *The Guardian*, "I don't think of myself in racial terms. When I walk out on the field, I want to be the best flanker in the world. If you think in racial terms, you are limiting yourself and your horizons."[3]

The lesson that emerges from the Springboks story is that improved Diversity Performance does not just happen by itself: it requires targeted initiatives to succeed as part of a deliberate and strategic approach.

2   A Strategic Approach to Diversity

It can be tempting to look for a quick diversity fix—or as one leader expressed it "find the golden goose that lays the diversity egg"—but while this sentiment is understandable, it is not that simple. As the Springboks story shows, there is no magic bullet for instant Diversity Performance—indeed in spite of dozens of diversity initiatives and reams of research on the topic, effort and investment to improve Diversity Performance often do not result in the desired state of diversity.

What is generally lacking is a strategic approach to identify the diversity capabilities that enable the desired performance. That is the function of the second anchor model in this book, the Integrated Diversity Model (IDM), and in this chapter we explain how the leader can use this model to answer three key questions:

---

[2] Ray (2018).

[3] Ray, "Siya Kolisi."

1. What kind of capabilities do we need to enable improved Diversity Performance?
2. How do we build these capabilities and what do we need to put in place to nurture them?
3. How do these capabilities evolve through each stage of Diversity Performance?

By combining the Virtuous Circle with the Five Stages framework, the leader has been able to determine the right level of ambition and develop a clear strategic narrative for their desired Diversity Performance (Chapter 4). The Integrated Diversity Model addresses the next step of the journey—namely helping the leader to determine which capabilities and initiatives are needed to close the gap between where they are today and where they want to be.

3   What is the Integrated Diversity Model?

The IDM comprises six key diversity capabilities that organizations need to develop to support greater inclusiveness and attain their chosen level of Diversity Performance (Fig. 2). These capabilities are interdependent and work together: if one diversity capability is weak or missing, it undermines the impact and effectiveness of the other five, dampening the organization's overall performance.

These six capability areas are defined as follows:

Fig. 2 The Integrated Diversity Model
The IDM comprises six key capabilities that work together to enable an organization to reach its desired level of Diversity Performance.

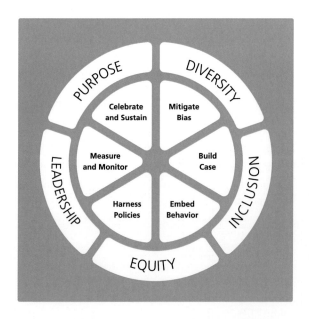

1. **Mitigate Bias**: the ability to mitigate personal and systemic bias so that stakeholders feel included and equity is advanced.
2. **Build Case**: the ability to translate the diversity purpose into a clear case for diversity, identify the appropriate performance level, and invest in effective initiatives.
3. **Embed Behavior**: the ability to embed inclusive behaviors across the organization, supported by appropriate values, rituals, and daily practices.
4. **Harness Policies**: the ability to identify and uphold the right policies to guide, reward, and promote daily diversity practices.
5. **Measure and Monitor**: the ability to measure and monitor progress in closing the Diversity Performance gap.
6. **Celebrate and Sustain**: the ability to energize collective commitment to the diversity journey, stay aligned with stakeholder expectations, and support the organization's transformation journey.

As explained below, each of these IDM capability areas comprises key initiatives and interventions that support improved Diversity Performance. The Model is the result of extensive review, critical analysis, and piloting of initiatives to gauge effectiveness in over 50 different organizations. By evaluating the impact of such initiatives on Diversity Performance, it has been possible to categorize them into six strategic capability areas, with distinct characteristics for each stage of Diversity Performance within the Five Stages framework. The Model has also been tested and refined through several generations of Inclusive Leadership and Mitigating Unconscious Bias Certification delivered to leaders around the world.

A strength of the IDM is that it has been developed to overcome typical obstacles that organizations encounter on the diversity journey. It provides leaders with a robust framework for selecting the right combination of initiatives that will build the necessary capabilities to achieve—and sustain—their desired level of Diversity Performance. Having a proven, evidence-based tool for planning diversity initiatives is extremely helpful to the leader. It enables them to identify which package of initiatives is required for—and has been proven to be effective in supporting the attainment of—their desired stage of performance. This helps them to avoid wasting valuable time and resources on trial-and-error, ad hoc initiatives that are neither efficient nor effective.

4   The IDM Helps to Avoid Common Roadblocks

The Integrated Diversity Model is designed to give the leader a clear line of sight on the short and long-term initiatives that, together, will deliver their required lift in Diversity Performance. The result is a strategic roadmap to guide the organization on a step-by-step, evidence-based journey of improvement and transformation achieved by enhancing the team's holistic diversity capability.

Taking a strategic approach to building diversity capability helps to overcome common roadblocks often encountered on the diversity journey. Chief among these are the duplication of diversity initiatives, the deployment of initiatives that are ineffective, or which are either too basic or too ambitious for the required performance stage, and lack of coordination and strategic integration of initiatives. Here we explore these typical barriers in more detail.

1. **Plethora of Initiatives**—An inventory of initiatives carried out in over 50 medium to large organizations and complemented by input received from leaders attending the Diversity and Performance Certification, reveals that organizations typically have 70 discrete diversity initiatives—and at times as many as 400 or more—underway at the same time to achieve diversity outcomes. Many are triggered by the ad hoc adoption of best practices and end up being initiated, or duplicated, by different organizational units in different geographical locations. In this situation, the leader finds it difficult to identify whether the right initiatives are in place, at the right level of ambition and whether they are actually delivering the right Diversity Performance outcomes. Moreover, duplicate initiatives inevitably lead to duplication of costs.

2. **Ineffective Initiatives**—Organizations often allocate significant budget, time, and resources to implement a host of diversity initiatives but are unable to identify whether these initiatives are actually effective in producing the desired or intended result. This comes down to both the efficacy of the intervention—namely its ability to produce the intended result—and the effectiveness of its implementation—namely the degree to which the desired result was achieved.[4] In healthcare, efficacy refers to the extent to which an intervention does more good than harm under *ideal* circumstances, whereas effectiveness assesses whether an intervention does more good than harm when provided under *usual* circumstances of healthcare practice.[5] Leaders need to be confident which packages of initiatives will deliver, and under what conditions.

   For example, unconscious bias training has been shown to be successful in changing behavior and attitudes if it is conducted with a number of key elements in place, such as explaining the origin of personal bias, creating empathy and compassion for groups that are the target of discriminatory practice and having the opportunity to dialogue and identify unconscious bias cues.[6] If these elements are not present, and unconscious bias training is mandated, rules-based, and delivered in a naming-and-shaming manner, then the unconscious bias training may have minimum impact on behavior and may even create pushback and reinforce stereotypes.[7]

3. **Non-integrated Initiatives**—Frequently, initiatives are launched in an isolated manner rather than connecting them up and ensuring that they reinforce

---

[4] Efficacy, Cambridge Dictionary, https://dictionary.cambridge.org/dictionary/english/efficacy, accessed December 21, 2020.

[5] Kim (2013).

[6] Moss-Racusin et al. (2016).

[7] Dobbin and Kalev (2016).

one another. Without an integrated approach, even if there is no duplication, there is a missed opportunity to create synergies. In this situation people tend to become weary of the constant project focus and are unable to see the link between initiatives and the business goals of the organization.

For example, many organizations initiate leadership training to promote inclusive leadership practices. The benefits of this would be enhanced by simultaneously instituting an inclusiveness index, establishing a baseline, and assessing uplift in the inclusiveness index after the training rollout. This would make the intervention more sustainable, promote feedback to leaders, and validate whether the intervention has delivered the expected Diversity Performance benefit. Too often, this is not done, and the inclusive leadership training investment does not translate into long-term benefits.

Any organization can use the Integrated Diversity Model to avoid these pitfalls. Like the Virtuous Circle, the IDM applies to all organizations and provides a universal capability architecture regardless of their stage of diversity. For example, the leader of a Stage 1 organization with a focus on achieving diversity compliance to minimize cost of penalties, can leverage the model just as effectively as a leader aiming for Stage 4 to realize agility and wider value chain benefits. Avoiding diversity journey pitfalls starts with all leaders reflecting on the same key questions regarding their organization's diversity capabilities, but their answers will differ in terms of the range, ambition, and degree of integration of initiatives to be undertaken. These core capability questions are:

1. Which systemic and talent biases and stereotypes undermine our diversity and how do we mitigate these to foster equity?
2. What investments are required to deliver our organizational case for diversity, and required Return on Investment?
3. What are the values and behaviors required from our team to be truly inclusive and how do we support these?
4. How do we select policies that are both valued by our employees and guide the inclusive behavior that we seek to support?
5. How do we measure our state of diversity holistically and reward those contributing to a diversity-rich and inclusive organization?
6. How do we create a culture of celebration around diversity and sustain diversity for organizational transformation?

The answers to these questions lie in applying the IDM to select the package of initiatives that is appropriate for the organization's particular diversity maturity stage.

5   Why Does Having the Right Diversity Capabilities Matter?

Without the right organizational capabilities, diversity journeys are unlikely to succeed over the long term. A key feature of the IDM is that it groups diversity initiatives together into "proven packages" that have been demonstrated to be effective in realizing the type of diversity capabilities needed at each stage of Diversity Performance. The six capabilities are what feed and sustain the Virtuous Circle of Diversity Performance.

A "package" of initiatives is an integrated suite of efforts, comprising multiple projects or actions, that work together to enhance the diversity capability of the organization. Within the IDM, capability initiatives are packaged because they have to be delivered together for that diversity capability to improve. They are also cumulative—in other words each new Diversity Performance stage builds on the package of initiatives from the previous stage. An organization cannot "jump ahead" to Stage 3, in other words, without having the foundational capabilities from Stages 1 and 2 in place first. In Chapters 6–11, a detailed description is provided of each IDM capability area across each of the five stages (Fig. 3).

Knowing which evidence-based initiatives to apply at any particular stage enables leaders to direct scarce resources toward those interventions that are going to be most appropriate and effective in achieving their level of diversity ambition. Implementing efficacious interventions together creates the right conditions for success: if part of a package is missing, the capability as a whole will be less effective.

Each capability area of the IDM comprises initiatives grouped under the following headings: focus, skills, process, responsibilities, metrics, and technology. Below we take a quick look at the packages of capability initiatives under each area of the IDM, which are covered in detail in Chapters 6–11.

6   Capability Area 1—Mitigate Bias

Why is this important? Every element of the Virtuous Circle is negatively impacted by bias: less diversity of thought, less inclusion, less equity, less leadership, and less unifying purpose. Bias is specifically detrimental to equity for it serves to either explicitly or unwittingly exclude members who are considered different to the homogeneous team. This leads to biased recruitment, promotion, succession planning, and advancement decisions and widens diversity gaps. Bias is often unconscious and the Mitigate Bias Capability is focused on building awareness of bias and why it occurs, cultivating the skills to intervene when bias does occur, de-biasing processes and removing triggers that are known to drive biased reactions, creating policies requiring systematic intervention when bias occurs, and ensuring that written and spoken language is reviewed so that biased and stereotyped language is removed.

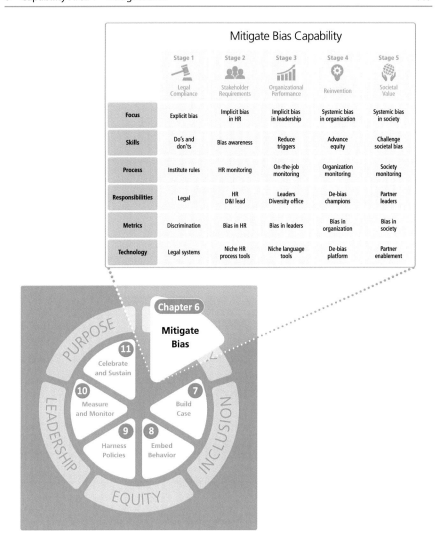

Fig. 3   Proven Initiatives Support Each IDM Capability Area
Each IDM capability area comprises proven "packages" of initiatives that apply at each stage of Diversity Performance. These are explored in detail in Chapters 6–11.

The Mitigate Bias Capability is comprised of "building blocks" of interventions to mitigate bias, depending on the organization's Diversity Performance maturity. These interventions are explored in greater detail in Chapter 6. A summary of initiatives for the Mitigate Bias Capability is shown in Table 1. As organizations evolve in their diversity maturity, there is an increasing richness in the objectives, scope, responsibilities, and enablement of this capability. For example, where the

Table 1 Initiatives that support the Mitigate Bias Capability
At each of the five stages, there are key initiatives that organizations need to take to support effective de-biasing. This is discussed in detail in Chapter 6.

	Stage 1 Legal Compliance	Stage 2 Stakeholder Requirements	Stage 3 Organizational Performance	Stage 4 Reinvention	Stage 5 Societal Value
Focus	Explicit bias	Implicit bias in HR	Implicit bias in leadership	Systemic bias in organization	Systemic bias in society
Skills	Do's and don'ts	Bias awareness	Reduce triggers	Advance equity	Challenge societal bias
Process	Institute rules	HR monitoring	On-the-job monitoring	Organization monitoring	Society monitoring
Responsibilities	Legal	HR D&I lead	Leaders diversity office	De-bias champions	Partner leaders
Metrics	Discrimination	Bias in HR	Bias in leaders	Bias in organization	Bias in society
Technology	Legal systems	Niche HR process tools	Niche language tools	De-bias platform	Partner enablement

focus of mitigating bias in Stage 1 is on reducing overt discrimination, in Stage 4 the capability shifts to removing systemic bias throughout the organization.

7   Capability Area 2—Build Case

Why is this important? The organization's ability to put forward a compelling case for diversity is critical to retain focus, attention, and support for the diversity journey. This especially impacts the leadership commitment to diversity and the allocation of resourcing and investments.

The Build Case capability is comprised of building blocks of interventions to establish and realize a compelling case for diversity across the organization. These interventions are described in more detail in Chapter 7. A summary of initiatives for the Build Case capability is shown in Table 2. As organizations evolve through the five stages, the diversity case not only grows in importance and scope but requires greater rigor in gauging the effectiveness of initiatives, targeting and identifying the return on diversity investments, and holding leaders accountable for the realization of the diversity case. As organizations mature, the diversity case becomes increasingly integrated with the strategic goals of the organization and its impact on society (e.g., through strategic alignment with the SDGs).

Table 2 Initiatives that support the Build Case Capability

At each of the five stages, there are key initiatives that organizations need to take to build a strong case for diversity. This is discussed in detail in Chapter 7.

	Stage 1 Legal Compliance	Stage 2 Stakeholder Requirements	Stage 3 Organizational Performance	Stage 4 Reinvention	Stage 5 Societal Value
Focus	Legal case	Business case Legal case	Business case Legal case	Ethical case Business case Legal case	Societal case Ethical case Business case Legal case
Skills	Developing legal case	Developing business case	Effectiveness of initiatives Maintain case	Investment review effectiveness	Societal impact SDG contribution
Process	Build case Review	Build case Monitor	Assess effectiveness	Review strategic contribution	Societal impact assessment
Responsibilities	Legal	HR and legal D&I lead	Senior leaders Diversity office	Top leadership	Partner leaders
Metrics	Legal incidents & costs	Stakeholder sanctions	Performance outcomes	Innovation competitiveness	SDG impact
Technology	Case management	HR	Enterprise	Enterprise & niche	Partner enablement

8   Capability Area 3—Embed Behavior

Why is this important? This capability focuses on embedding inclusive behaviors into the fabric of the organization. Diversity Performance is directly linked to the extent to which the work environment is considered safe, respectful, inclusive, and provides a sense of belonging and engagement. This capability is about much more than the conduct of senior leadership: it is the values and behaviors demonstrated by all people within the organization, supported by symbols, rituals, and beliefs reflecting how diversity is embraced.

This capability comprises building blocks of interventions to foster and reinforce inclusive behaviors that support the required stage of Diversity Performance. These interventions are described in more detail in Chapter 8. A summary of initiatives for the Embed Behavior capability is shown in Table 3, and these evolve as the organization matures in its approach. For example, in Stage 1, the focus is on incorporating greater diversity of people within the current culture, while at Stage 4, the ingredients of inclusiveness have become anchored within the culture of the organization. From Stage 4 onwards embedding inclusive behaviors becomes a

Table 3　Initiatives that support the Embed Behavior Capability

At each of the five stages, there are key initiatives that organizations need to take to embed inclusive behavior. This is discussed in detail in Chapter 8.

	Stage 1 Legal Compliance	Stage 2 Stakeholder Requirements	Stage 3 Organizational Performance	Stage 4 Reinvention	Stage 5 Societal Value
Focus	Incorporate in own culture; admitted	Create sense of community; welcomed	Support seamless collaboration; valued	Support break-through thinking; embraced	Contribute to societal inclusiveness
Skills	Own culture	ERGs; Networks; Communities	Team effectiveness; Equality & respect	Psychological safety; Equity; fairness	Leave no one behind
Process	Orientation	ERG Setup events	High-performance teams	Culture-wide values & behavior	Partner values & behavior
Responsibilities	Limited	HR; D&I lead	All leaders diversity office	All members	Partners & organization
Metrics	Hiring & retention	Satisfaction index	Inclusive leader Index	Inclusiveness index	Partner inclusion index
Technology	Training systems	ERG support tools	Collaboration tools	Idea tools pulse surveys networking tools	Partner sharing tools

key differentiating organizational capability for the twenty-first century.[8] With the increasing diversity in markets, employees, and customers, leaders need to create the conditions for seamless collaboration in order to achieve breakthrough thinking. Chapter 8 provides a number of tools to support this, including the Inclusive Leadership Capability Blueprint and Inclusive Leadership Index Measurement.

9　Capability Area 4—Harness Policies

Why is this important? This critical capability lends "teeth" to the various diversity initiatives, assigning clear lines of responsibility, setting out guidelines for implementation and consequences for non-adherence. This capability focuses on identifying the web of policies needed to support the organization's Diversity Performance objectives. It ensures that these policies create value for the various target beneficiaries, are consistently and fairly implemented (i.e., that people are rewarded for adhering or sanctioned for non-adherence), are continuously reviewed to reflect the intended stage of Diversity Performance, are

---

[8] "Six Signature Traits of Inclusive Leadership: Thriving in a Diverse New World," Deloitte, 2018, https://www2.deloitte.com/content/dam/Deloitte/us/Documents/about-deloitte/us-incl-six-signature-traits-inclusive-leadership.pdf.

Table 4   Initiatives that support the Harness Policies Capability
At each of the five stages, there are key initiatives that organizations need to take to ensure an effective policy framework. This is discussed in detail in Chapter 9.

	Stage 1 Legal Compliance	Stage 2 Stakeholder Requirements	Stage 3 Organizational Performance	Stage 4 Reinvention	Stage 5 Societal Value
Focus	Zero discrimination	Representation Talent processes	Team practices Rewarding Leadership role	Equity Needs-based Valued	Partners Value chain Reinforcement
Skills	Compliance training	HR requirements ERG interaction	Evidence in practice	Pre-requisite for advancement	Partner alignment
Process	Compliance rules	Develop Policies Best practices	Evaluate Apply	Co-craft with ERG Pioneer Prune	Reinforce with partners
Responsibilities	Legal	HR	Leaders diversity office	Leaders ERG	Partner diversity council
Metrics	Drive compliance	Incorporated by HR	Applied by teams	Valued by beneficiaries	Supporting partners
Technology	Compliance management	Policy management	Policy management	Policy management ERG platform	Partner policy enablement

well-communicated and instilled, and that clear lines of responsibility are established for policy oversight. For each of these aspects, digital support is increasingly available to assist in the implementation and monitoring of policy compliance.

This capability is comprised of building blocks of interventions that support sound policymaking and guidance. The initiatives for the Harness Policies capability are described in more detail in Chapter 9 and a summary is presented in Table 4. In this capability area, the focus at Stage 1 is on achieving "Zero Discrimination." As the organization moves into Stage 4 this evolves into more detailed guidelines on expected behaviors and key principles that support diversity, supplemented by inclusive leadership evaluation, measuring the inclusiveness of the environment, guidance on inclusive language, and direction on equity and access to resources, etc. Together, these norms and guidelines set out how diversity is "done" day-to-day within the organization and their design and application directly impact diversity outcomes.

10   Capability Area 5—Measure and Monitor

Why is this important? "What gets measured, gets done" is an adage used in many organizations. This capability ensures that diversity outcomes for each stage of performance are supported by meaningful targets and metrics, a process

Table 5   Initiatives that support the Measure and Monitor Capability
At each of the five stages, there are key initiatives that organizations need to take to ensure an effective measurement and monitoring. This is discussed in detail in Chapter 9.

	Stage 1 Legal Compliance	Stage 2 Stakeholder Requirements	Stage 3 Organizational Performance	Stage 4 Reinvention	Stage 5 Societal Value
Focus	Compliance outcomes	Representation Stakeholder satisfaction	Performance outcomes	Transformation outcomes	Societal impact
Skills	Definitions	Measurement protocol	Correlation diversity & performance	Correlation diversity & innovation	Applicability to partners SDGs
Process	Set targets Monitor	Evaluate satisfaction	Measure performance	Analyze contribution	Align with partners
Responsibilities	Legal	HR	CFO diversity office	CEO diversity office	Leaders diversity council
Metrics	Representation of inherent diversity traits	Representation of inherent & acquired diversity traits	Diversity & Inclusion Performance outcomes	Equity Strategic goals Roadmap Gap closures	Societal impact
Technology	Compliance	HR	Performance management system	Enterprise performance	Partner enablement

to measure and communicate performance, clear assignment of accountability and responsibility, and the right technology to ensure transparency over results achieved.

Just like the other capabilities, the Measure and Monitor capability is comprised of building blocks of interventions, this time with a focus on developing metrics and goals for diversity outcomes. This includes monitoring the health of each element in the Virtuous Circle, assessing the state of diversity capabilities, and evaluating progress in realizing the strategic diversity roadmap. The initiatives for the Measure and Monitor capability are summarized in Table 5 and described in detail in Chapter 10.

In this area of capability, the key focus for Stage 1 is measurement of diversity characteristics (often legislated inherent diversity characteristics). As the organization moves to Stage 4, goals are set and measured for all elements of the Virtuous Circle and a comprehensive and rigorous diversity measurement system is adopted to ensure that achievements are rewarded and lagging indicators acted upon. By Stage 5, diversity measurement is no longer a standalone set of metrics for the business but has been mainstreamed into the corporate strategic review process.

11   Capability Area 6—Celebrate and Sustain

Why is this important? This capability is critical to mobilize energy around the diversity journey and maintain momentum in closing Diversity Performance gaps. Diversity is not a project—it is a journey and it requires stamina, leadership attention, and ongoing organizational commitment. Celebration of accomplishments provides vital oxygen by creating moments to enjoy what has been achieved and rekindle the flame for the next step of the journey. It also makes progress visible to both the organization and its stakeholders. Sustaining activities are critical to ensure that diversity is not treated as static but as continuously evolving in step with the external environment, stakeholder requirements, and new developments within the organization itself.

Like all other diversity capabilities, the Celebrate and Sustain capability is comprised of building blocks of interventions that intensify as Diversity Performance matures. The initiatives for this capability are summarized in Table 6 and set out in full in Chapter 11. At Stage 1, celebration is limited and may simply amount to reporting on legal compliance internally and externally. By Stage 4, however, organizations celebrate diversity every day in small and big ways, D&I champions support all members in "living" diversity day-to-day, and the strength of their Virtuous Circle is evaluated frequently to identify new initiatives to sustain their diversity journey.

Table 6   Initiatives that support the Celebrate and Sustain Capability
At each of the five stages, there are key initiatives that organizations need to take to ensure that diversity is celebrated and commitment to inclusion sustained. This is discussed in detail in Chapter 11.

	Stage 1 Legal Compliance	Stage 2 Stakeholder Requirements	Stage 3 Organizational Performance	Stage 4 Reinvention	Stage 5 Societal Value
Focus	Meet legal obligations	Sharing with stakeholders Community building	Recognizing diversity accomplishments	Sustaining diversity journey Culture	Energizing further contribution to society
Skills	Legal reporting requirements	Stakeholder celebration events	Diversity events Cultural insights	Organization Celebrations	Partner gatherings
Process	Legal process	Stakeholder process	Performance process	Strategic process	Partner process
Responsibilities	Legal	HR Marketing	Diversity office D&I champions	All	Partner leaders Diversity council
Metrics	Legally reported	Stakeholder events Community events	Diversity celebrations	Culture celebrations Values days	Societal days of celebration
Technology	Compliance	HR CRM	Event management	ERG platforms	Partner enablement

12   Combining the IDM with the Five Stages to Map the Capability Gap

As the second anchor model in this book, the IDM is designed to be used in tandem with, and build on insights from, the Virtuous Circle. If the elements of the Virtuous Circle set out the "what" of Diversity Performance, the capabilities of the IDM build on this to pave the way for the "how."

Like the Virtuous Circle, this IDM combines with the Five Stages maturity framework to create a 5×6 matrix, setting out how each capability needs to evolve as an organization advances on its diversity journey. For every stage, specific initiatives are outlined that organizations need to implement to build the right type of capability to realize their desired Diversity Performance. These packages of initiatives comprise an evidence-based blend of performance objectives, skills and knowledge, processes, measurement, responsibilities, and technology enablement, as illustrated in Table 7.

As a reminder, in Chapter 3, the leader applied the Virtuous Circle Five Stages Framework (5VC) to establish their desired level of Diversity Performance and identify their performance gap. Now, using the IDM Five Stages Framework (5IDM), the leader is able to see what capabilities are required to achieve their desired level of performance and map the capability gap between where their organization is today and where it wants to be. Through this process, a comprehensive overview is obtained of the essential diversity capabilities and related evidence-based initiatives that the organization needs to have in place to satisfy each level of diversity maturity (Table 7).

There are five key steps involved in using the IDM to close the diversity capability gap:

1. Take stock of the organization's current diversity initiatives and map these against the IDM Capability Five Stages Framework.
2. Use the 5IDM to identify the specific initiatives that are required to meet the organization's desired level of Diversity Performance (as set out in its strategic narrative).
3. Map where the biggest gaps lie between its existing capabilities and initiatives and its desired performance level. These gaps indicate the priority initiatives for the organization to implement.
4. Develop a strategic roadmap to implement the organization's priority initiatives.
5. Implement the priority diversity initiatives to close the capability gap.

In Table 7, a hypothetical organization has set an ambition of reaching Stage 4 Diversity Performance, as depicted by the green shading. Taking stock of its existing diversity initiatives and mapping these against the framework reveals that its capability level is currently at Stage 2, depicted by the orange shading. This means there is a two-stage capability gap that the organization will need to close to attain

Table 7 The Integrated Diversity Model Five Stages Framework

The 5IDM framework shows which proven capability-building initiatives apply at each stage of Diversity Performance.

Capabilities	Stage 1 Legal Compliance	Stage 2 Stakeholder Requirements	Stage 3 Organizational Performance	Stage 4 Reinvention	Stage 5 Societal Value
Mitigate Bias	Bias compliance training	Recruiting bias training De-bias recruiting processes Measure recruiter bias	Leadership bias training De-bias all talent processes Measure leadership bias De-bias coaches	Personal bias training for all De-bias all processes Measure organization bias Systemic bias training Systemic bias audit De-bias guardian roles	Systemic bias training value chain De-bias value chain Measure value chain Bias Systemic value chain audit
Build Case	Legal case risk management role Measure legal case Budget assigned	+ Customer case marketing role + Employee case HR role + Measurement: client's case satisfied Budget assigned	+ Business case CFO role + Measurement business case objectives Budget assigned Resources assigned Initiative effectiveness measured	+ Ethical case CEO role + Measurement ethical case/equity advancement Budget assigned Resources assigned Initiative effectiveness measured	+ Societal case CEO/board + Measurement contribution to societal objectives Value chain budget assigned Value chain resources assigned Value chain initiative Effectiveness measured
Embed Behaviour	Fit-in induction	Satisfaction survey	Inclusiveness index for leaders Inclusive leadership training Inclusive leadership evaluation	Inclusiveness index for organization Inclusive leadership training organization Inclusive leadership capability organization Inclusive leadership language	Inclusiveness Index for value chain Inclusive leadership training value chain Inclusive leadership capability value chain Inclusive leadership language value chain
Harness Policies	No discrimination policy	Zero tolerance discrimination	Zero tolerance discrimination Performance policies	Zero tolerance discrimination +Systemic bias policy +Equity process and policy Robust blueprint for organization	Zero tolerance discrimination value chain Robust blueprint for organization
Measure and Monitor	Diversity demographic metrics Compliance measurement	+ Measurement: Stakeholder requirements satisfied	Diversity of thought Diversity contribution to business case levers	For organizations: Diversity gap closure Diversity initiative effectiveness Diversity contribution to business goals	For value chain: Diversity gap closure Diversity initiative effectiveness Diversity contribution to business goals
Celebrate and Sustain	No compliance issues celebration New legal requirements review	Diversity client events Stakeholder community events	Team celebration	Diversity celebration Organizationwide events	Diversity celebration Value chain events

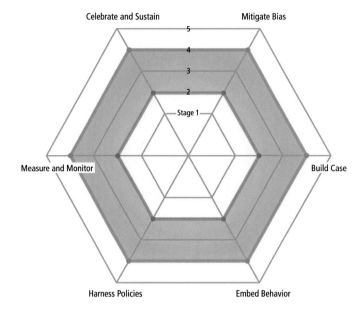

Fig. 4 Radar Chart Reflecting the IDM Diversity Capability Gap
The gap between the orange and green lines in the chart shows a two-stage gap between this organization's existing and required levels of diversity capability.

its desired level of performance. To close the gap, the organization will need to implement the Stage 3 and 4 packages of initiatives for each of the six capability areas.

This IDM capability gap can also be shown in a radar chart (or spider diagram), which is a graphical method of displaying current versus future performance (Fig. 4).

In Fig. 4, the hypothetical organization has identified that it needs to be at Stage 4 Diversity Performance (as represented by the green line). This means that each of the six diversity capabilities (listed on the axes) also needs to be at Stage 4, However, when looking at the current state of their initiatives they assess that these are at Stage 2 (represented by the orange line). The shaded area between the two lines depicts the performance gap that the organization will need to close in order to reach its desired level of performance.

13   Developing a Strategic Roadmap

The Performance and Capability Roadmap sets out the process by which leaders can identify how to help their organization reach its desired level of Diversity Performance. By following the steps in the roadmap, the leader can map the performance gap and identify which priority initiatives to implement to close the capability gap. The next step is to develop a strategic roadmap for closing the gap.

The general rule of thumb is that the strategic roadmap begins by addressing as a matter of priority those initiatives where the organization has the biggest diversity capability gaps, as these are most likely to be undermining performance. However the roadmap also needs to drive progress in other areas to ensure momentum is maintained.

Whatever the motivation and whichever the desired stage of Diversity Performance, the six capability areas need to be considered in an integrated manner when drawing up a strategic roadmap. Just as the Virtuous Circle requires all elements—diversity, inclusion, equity, leadership, and purpose—to be addressed, the Integrated Diversity Model requires all capabilities to be nurtured. If there is a capability gap, the whole system is weakened: the organization's diversity capability will only be as good as its weakest link. If, for example, an organization fails to focus on a core capability like mitigating bias, this will undermine the other five capability areas, leading the system to experience "entropy"—or in other words, lose momentum. This is when Diversity Performance plateaus or declines.

The following case study illustrates how an IDM capability evaluation works in practice. It shares lessons learned by an organization that aspired to have Stage 4 Diversity Performance but did not underpin this with the strategic initiatives and capabilities to deliver on their ambition.

Case Study: Evaluating the Integrated Diversity Model capability

A leader of a global hospitality organization wanted to develop a strategic diversity roadmap. The leader was personally committed to diversity and believed diversity was not only "good for business" but "the right thing to do." As a hospitality company, it was important to be in tune with the requirements and expectations of their clients, who had diverse cultures, religious backgrounds, and ethnicities. Discretion, respectful interaction with their customers, and professional service were all key hallmarks of their business proposition.

As a result, the company had followed a best-practice approach to initiating diversity within their organization. It was constantly on the lookout for new diversity initiatives being launched in their sector and was a fast adopter: at one point the organization was in the process of implementing, or had implemented, more than 150 different diversity initiatives. They allocated a significant budget spend to support these initiatives, yet they did not have a good sense of the actual return on these initiatives. Despite all of these efforts and investments, the company had been hit by public reports of racial slurs, demeaning behavior to employees of color and claims that some business units within the company instituted discriminatory practices. There were examples of salary gaps and overtime practices that negatively influenced career opportunities for people of color. The leader was shocked by these reports and determined to understand the current reality, which did not align with their efforts to integrate diversity or the company's public statements on diversity and the strategic narrative as described in their annual reports.

The CEO was concerned that given the diversity spend and focus that the company would be called out for hypocrisy. They were keen to identify where the organization had gaps in their diversity roadmap and what they needed to do to deliver on their promise of fair and respectful behavior to clients and employees alike. To solve their dilemma, the CEO adopted the following steps.

Steps 1 and 2—First, the CEO used the Virtuous Circle Five Stages Framework to establish that their desired state of diversity was Stage 4: Reinvention. Diversity was critical to their agility and being able to respond to their customer and stakeholder needs, so they were actively focusing on diversity of talent, inclusionary practices, leadership responsibility and had incorporated diversity into their purpose.

In practice, this means referring to the Integrated Diversity Model and identifying the initiatives required for each of the six diversity capabilities for the future required Diversity Performance stage. In this case this was the Stage 4 initiatives shaded in green (Table 8). The client then identified the initiatives that the organization currently had in place, shaded in orange. This mapping revealed a gap between the organization's current diversity capabilities and its required capability level, as captured in Table 8 and Fig. 5.

This analysis revealed that the required stage is Stage 4: Reinvention, that the Harness Policies and Measure and Monitor Capabilities were both at Stage 1 and the other capabilities were at Stage 2, as shown in the radar chart (Fig. 5).

Mitigating Bias
The first finding was that personal bias mitigation was confined to the recruitment process and not to the de-biasing of performance management or salary and benefits processes. There was no attention to mitigating systemic bias. Closer scrutiny revealed that the organization had an overtime policy wherein overtime was paid for specialist positions but not for administrative positions. This overtime principle had become global practice based on what was systemically done in some regions where the company operated, but this practice contributed to a significant wage gap between people of different races. Specialist roles were mostly held by white workers and the administrative jobs were held predominantly by people of color. The practice of overtime payment served not only to widen the salary gap but also career development opportunities. Employees who were being paid overtime tended to work more hours than those who were not compensated for overtime work. It was clear that the organization paid too little attention to mitigating both personal and systemic bias for their aspired stage of diversity, allowing racist practices to creep into the organization.

Building the Case for Diversity
A second finding was that while the company had adopted a best practice approach to implementing diversity initiatives, little systematic evaluation had been done to assess whether these initiatives contributed toward the organization's goals. Monitoring of the business case had been allotted to the Chief Financial Officer (CFO)

Table 8   Evaluation of Diversity Capabilities

The organization's current level of capability (Stages 1 and 2) was insufficient to deliver their desired level of Diversity Performance (Stage 4).

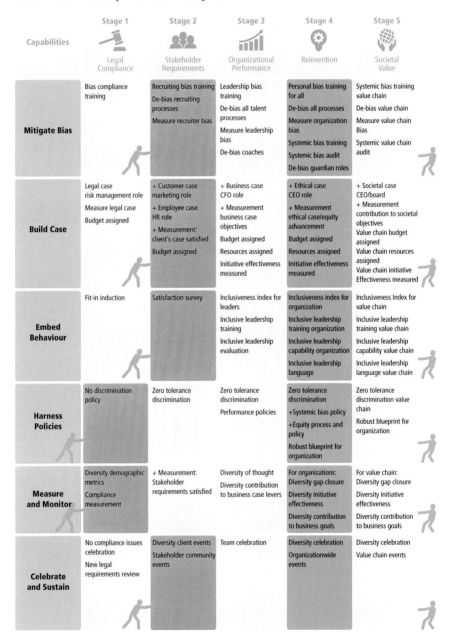

Capabilities	Stage 1 Legal Compliance	Stage 2 Stakeholder Requirements	Stage 3 Organizational Performance	Stage 4 Reinvention	Stage 5 Societal Value
Mitigate Bias	Bias compliance training	Recruiting bias training De-bias recruiting processes Measure recruiter bias	Leadership bias training De-bias all talent processes Measure leadership bias De-bias coaches	Personal bias training for all De-bias all processes Measure organization bias Systemic bias training Systemic bias audit De-bias guardian roles	Systemic bias training value chain De-bias value chain Measure value chain Bias Systemic value chain audit
Build Case	Legal case risk management role Measure legal case Budget assigned	+ Customer case marketing role + Employee case HR role + Measurement: client's case satisfied Budget assigned	+ Business case CFO role + Measurement business case objectives Budget assigned Resources assigned Initiative effectiveness measured	+ Ethical case CEO role + Measurement ethical case/equity advancement Budget assigned Resources assigned Initiative effectiveness measured	+ Societal case CEO/board + Measurement contribution to societal objectives Value chain budget assigned Value chain resources assigned Value chain initiative Effectiveness measured
Embed Behaviour	Fit-in induction	Satisfaction survey	Inclusiveness index for leaders Inclusive leadership training Inclusive leadership evaluation	Inclusiveness index for organization Inclusive leadership training organization Inclusive leadership capability organization Inclusive leadership language	Inclusiveness Index for value chain Inclusive leadership training value chain Inclusive leadership capability value chain Inclusive leadership language value chain
Harness Policies	No discrimination policy	Zero tolerance discrimination	Zero tolerance discrimination Performance policies	Zero tolerance discrimination +Systemic bias policy +Equity process and policy Robust blueprint for organization	Zero tolerance discrimination value chain Robust blueprint for organization
Measure and Monitor	Diversity demographic metrics Compliance measurement	+ Measurement: Stakeholder requirements satisfied	Diversity of thought Diversity contribution to business case levers	For organizations: Diversity gap closure Diversity initiative effectiveness Diversity contribution to business goals	For value chain: Diversity gap closure Diversity initiative effectiveness Diversity contribution to business goals
Celebrate and Sustain	No compliance issues celebration New legal requirements review	Diversity client events Stakeholder community events	Team celebration	Diversity celebration Organizationwide events	Diversity celebration Value chain events

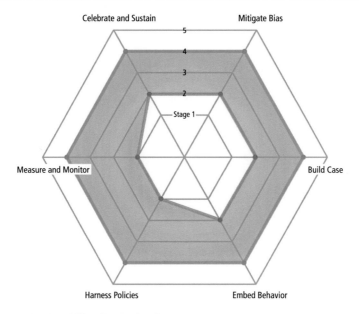

Fig. 5 **Diversity Capability Gap Radar Chart**
The organization's capability gap radar chart revealed a three-stage gap for two capabilities and a
two-stage gap for four capabilities.

and there had been no assessment of the effectiveness or return on investment of the
initiatives. The conclusion was that the company had not defined success in terms of
its strategic goals and the CEO was not involved in reviewing the benefits stemming
from diversity investments or evaluating whether the case was indeed being met.

Embedding Inclusive Behavior
A third finding was that despite the CEO acting as an "evangelist" for diversity and
setting out aspirations for diversity in their annual reports and public communications, the inclusive leadership capability was not robust enough for the aspired state
of diversity. The CEO communicated the importance of diversity but had delegated
leadership for diversity in a distributed manner so was removed from how the diversity narrative was being translated into initiatives. The organizational values focused
on customer alignment, which included the value of showing customers respect—yet
this value had not translated to employees showing one another respect and fairness.
Some inclusionary practices include employee training, but not as an integrated capability, spanning all talent-touching processes. The conclusion was that an inclusive
capability, cascaded throughout the organization, and deeply embedded into the values of respect for all, was not present, allowing a discriminatory and unsafe work
environment to develop for minorities.

Harnessing Policies
The fourth finding was that the organization had communicated an anti-discrimination policy, but not put policies in place to require zero salary gaps or inclusive

communication protocols and processes to identify systemic bias and facilitate the achievement of equity. Without these processes in place, the company would be open to discriminatory practices and could not rely on the bias and equity or inclusive leadership capability areas alone to create the conditions for an inclusive and respectful environment.

Measuring and Monitoring Diversity
The fifth finding showed an absence of measures to allow for the evaluation of inclusive leadership. An engagement survey was distributed but not analyzed separately for specialist and administration roles. Metrics were not at the level required for a company at Stage 4: diversity capabilities. While there was an engagement survey, it was not adequately analyzed or reported on. If this had been done, it would have given warning signals that there was poor engagement among administrative workers with a large representation of one ethnic group. Leadership could have done some analysis, sought feedback, and entered into dialogue with those members who were less engaged than the other groups.

Celebrating and Sustaining
The sixth and final finding showed that diversity celebrations focused mainly on the company's stakeholders, such as celebrating annual International Diversity Day, and International Women's Day. They were not focused on celebrating successes within the organization such as the achievement of diversity goals and ambitions.

▶   **Key takeaways** The organization aspired to be at Stage 4 but when looking at their current spread of initiatives and capabilities realized they were at levels 1 and 2. By identifying the gaps and highlighting the initiatives and capabilities they needed to put in place, they were able to create a strategic roadmap to improve their Diversity Performance.

This hospitality case study illustrates how helpful it can be for a leader to follow a robust methodology for their diversity journey. Leveraging the IDM allowed the CEO to work with their leadership team, line managers, and teams to define a strategic roadmap for delivering on their diversity objectives. As a result, there was a "spring cleaning" of their diversity initiatives whereby many of the current initiatives were halted and priorities reset according to the IDM gap analysis. Initial focus was placed on refining the diversity case and supporting processes, with a secondary focus on initiatives to mitigate personal and systemic bias and advance equity within the organization. Through this process, the organization was able to diagnose why its diversity initiatives were not delivering the desired results, correct its course, and put in place the right initiatives to close its Diversity Performance gaps.

14   Concluding Remarks

In this chapter, we have explored how the five essential elements of Diversity Performance that make up the Virtuous Circle (D+I+E+L+P) need to be supported at every stage by the six key organizational capabilities of the Integrated Diversity Model. We have also established that for each of the five Diversity Performance maturity stages, there is a relevant package of proven and effective initiatives which, when implemented together, create the conditions for success. By combining the IDM with the Five Stages framework, leaders at all stages of their diversity journeys can identify the key capability gaps in their current diversity approach and pinpoint which proven initiatives they need to implement to achieve their desired level of Diversity Performance.

In the next section of the book (Chapters 6–11), we address the How—namely, how to leverage each of the key IDM capability areas and their associated packages of initiatives to improve Diversity Performance.

References

Dobbin, Frank, and Alexandra Kalev. "Why Diversity Programs Fail." *Harvard Business Review*, July–August 2016. https://hbr.org/2016/07/why-diversity-programs-fail.

Kim, S.Y. "Efficacy Versus Effectiveness." *Korean Journal of Family Medicine*, 34, no. 4 (2013): 227. https://doi.org/10.4082/kjfm.2013.34.4.227.

Moss-Racusin, Corinne A., et al. "A 'Scientific Diversity' Intervention to Reduce Gender Bias in a Sample of Life Scientists." *CBE–Life Sciences Education*, 15, no. 3 (Fall 2016): 1–11. https://doi.org/10.1187/cbe.15-09-0187.

Ray, Craig. "Siya Kolisi: 'We Represent Something Much Bigger Than We Can Imagine'." *The Guardian*, June 6, 2018. https://www.theguardian.com/sport/2018/jun/06/siya-kolisi-interview-south-africa-first-black-test-captain-england.

Smith, David. "Francois Pienaar: 'When the Whistle Blew, South Africa Changed Forever'." *The Guardian*, December 8, 2013. www.theguardian.com/world/2013/dec/08/nelson-mandela-francois-pienaar-rugby-world-cup.

Part III
How to Close Diversity Performance Capability Gaps?

HOW to close Diversity Performance Capability Gaps?

Understand Stakeholder Expectations

What do my stakeholders expect of me?

Understand Diversity Performance

What are the key elements and stages of Diversity Performance?

Measure the Diversity Performance Gap

3 steps to improve Diversity Performance

Map the Performance Gap

Close my Diversity Performance Capability Gaps

Which initiatives do I need to put in place to achieve my desired future level of Diversity Perfomance?

Ch.6-11

Build the 6 Key Diversity Capabilities

- Mitigate Bias
- Build Case
- Embed Behaviors
- Harness Policies
- Measure and Monitor
- Celebrate and Sustain

PERFORMANCE AND CAPABILITY ROADMAP

Craft my Future Diversity Narrative

What is my desired future level of Diversity Performance?

Capture my Current Diversity Narrative

What is my organization's existing level of Diversity Performance?

Compare my Diversity Narratives

What is the gap between my current and desired Diversity Performance?

Close the Capability Gap

Develop my Strategic Roadmap to close the gaps

Where are my biggest Capability Gaps?

Understand my Current Diversity Capabilities

Which capabilities do I currently have in place?

Understand my Future Diversity Capability Needs

Which capabilities do I need to achieve my chosen future level of Diversity Performance?

Measure the Diversity Capability Gap

3 steps to improve Diversity Capability

Surfacing and Mitigating Bias

6

This chapter is one of six that explores in depth each of the key diversity capabilities that make up the Integrated Diversity Model. In this chapter and Chapters 7–11, we focus on the "How" of closing the Diversity Performance gap by presenting the initiatives organizations need to put in place to achieve their desired level of performance. The first diversity capability we will explore in depth is how to combat bias (Fig. 1).

Bias is the Achilles' heel of diversity in most organizations. It contributes to the gap between what leaders say and what they do in practice. Bias is a primary reason why, despite setting out the strategic narrative for diversity of thought in an organization, the same type of candidate is still selected, leading to the same type of team composition and team thinking. It explains why organizations that wish to advance equity, still sponsor and provide opportunities to those who already have excellent access to resources. Bias in daily behaviors and practices contributes to the often-heard statement "I do not feel that I belong, and I do not feel that I am really seen." And bias leads to even the most personally committed leaders of diversity unwittingly and unintentionally excluding some members of the organization while including others. Understanding how to identify and mitigate bias in an organization is fundamental to unlocking the huge amount of diversity potential that lies dormant.

Implicit bias differs from the explicit bias and deliberate discrimination that characterized apartheid South Africa and is still present in societies today, albeit largely penalized by law. The focus of this chapter is "hidden" bias—the bias that shapes mindsets and beliefs and whose inevitable consequence is less diversity, less inclusion, and less equity.

This chapter assists the leader in developing a common understanding of bias and why it occurs so that interventions can be implemented to mitigate it. Through case studies we illustrate how bias affects performance outcomes. Profiles of Courageous and Inclusive Leaders from the #MeToo and #BlackLivesMatter movements—both

© Diversity and Performance BV 2021
K. Formanek, *Beyond D&I*, https://doi.org/10.1007/978-3-030-75336-8_6

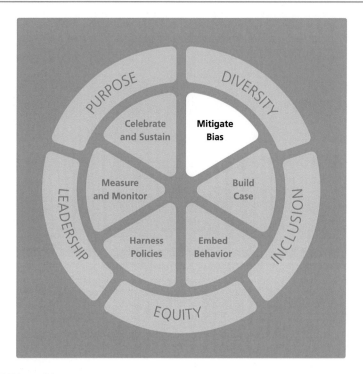

Fig. 1 Mitigate Bias
First Capability of the Integrated Diversity Model.

of which are tackling different forms of bias—are included to show how stakeholders are advancing these issues in the public conversation in powerful ways.

1   What Is Bias?

If diversity is inviting diverse members to play on a team, then bias is in part why
some players are not selected, get left on the bench, or are not asked to be part of
the starting team for big matches. Being part of a team is not only about being
included as a member, but actually getting the chance to play.

Leaders and employees unwittingly provide advantages to members whom they
identify with—their "in-group"—and perpetuate barriers for members whom they
do not identify with—their "out-group." This occurs even when leaders are ethically and intellectually committed to fostering diversity and inclusion.

This analogy sums it up well: bias is like wearing sunglasses where the lenses
have a specific filter—blue, red, or brown—which leads us to see the world
through those colors. The more people wear sunglasses with a red filter, the more
they will see the world with a reddish hue. In a perfect world, we would create
sunglasses with multiple filters, giving a kaleidoscope effect, but this does not

occur in practice. The second-best solution is to be aware that we have a specific lens on the world, recognize that there are other lenses and be curious in identifying what—and how—others see.

As the Black Lives Matter (BLM) movement has gone mainstream globally,[1] attention to bias and the vocabulary around it has also become mainstream. BLM has not only elevated the discussion on bias but has introduced the terms "systemic bias" and "implicit bias" into day-to-day conversation. These are now widely referred to by the media and by world figures: for example, asked during one of the 2020 US Presidential debates whether he believed in the presence of systemic racism in law enforcement, US President Joseph R. Biden responded:

> Absolutely. But it's not just in law enforcement, it's across the board. It's in housing, it's in education, and it's in everything we do. It's real. It's genuine. It's serious.[2]

In her 2020 State of the Union Address, Ursula von der Leyen, President of the European Commission, referred to the need and her commitment to "tackle unconscious bias that exists in people, institutions and even in algorithms."[3] And in June 2020, the UN Human Rights Council decided unanimously, without a vote, to have the UN's top human rights official, Michelle Bachelet, spearhead efforts to address systemic racism against people of African descent by law enforcement agencies.[4]

2   The Distinction Between Implicit and Systemic Bias

To put it simply, systemic bias is about barriers maintained by *institutions* while implicit biases are ones upheld by *individuals*.

Systemic Bias refers to the inherent tendency of a system and its processes, policies, and protocols to support a particular outcome. This can be in society or within organizations or institutions. In society, we see systemic bias when societal processes support an advantage for a specific group while disadvantaging another.

Implicit Bias is held by individuals and is also referred to as unconscious, hidden, or personal cognitive bias. We generally do not realize we have implicit biases as this bias occurs when our behavior toward individuals or groups is influenced by subconscious associations and judgments.[5] It affects our understanding, actions, and decisions in an *unconscious* way, making them difficult to control.

---

[1] Del Real (2020).

[2] Watson (2020).

[3] von der Leyen (2020).

[4] "Human Rights Council Calls on Top UN Rights Official to Take Action on Racist Violence," UN News, June 19, 2020, https://news.un.org/en/story/2020/06/1066722.

[5] Greenwald and Banaji (1995).

It is awareness of our beliefs and actions that determines the difference between implicit and explicit bias. Explicit bias refers to the attitudes and beliefs that we have about a person or group on a *conscious* level and is evidenced in deliberate discriminatory practices such as racial slurs, hate speech and intentionally treating people differently.

An example of systemic bias in the U.S. is "redlining," which refers to the practice of mortgage lenders drawing red lines around portions of a map to indicate areas or neighborhoods in which they do not want to make loans.[6] In this situation, banks redline mainly African American neighborhoods that they consider to be at high risk of loan default, with the result that white people receive housing loans while Black people in the redlined suburbs do not. It is a practice seen as contributing to the wealth gap in the USA and the deterioration of mainly African American neighborhoods. Redlining on a racial basis has been held by the courts to be an illegal practice.[7] Nonetheless, while the redlining maps are gone, researchers assert that the problem has not gone away.[8] A 2018 investigation by Reveal from The Center for Investigative Reporting found that Black, Latino, and Asian applicants were turned away for loans at a higher rate than whites in many US cities.[9]

Systemic bias can also occur within institutions and organizations in myriad ways. One example is when an organization's recruitment for roles is confined to networking events, on an invite-only basis. This practice immediately poses a barrier to entry for individuals who are not part of these networks. Another example is when criteria for shortlisting applicants requires that the candidate has held a leadership student role at their university. Many children of first-generation immigrants are excluded from the kind of networks and sponsorship that would enable them to be invited to be part of a student body.

Such systemic biases can compound to create an uneven and more challenging organizational environment across a number of desired diversity characteristics, such as age, race, gender, and social class. The parity gaps in wealth, education, political, and economic opportunity described in Chapter 2 are in part a result of these enduring systemic biases that shape people's access to resources and opportunities.

Organizations are composed of people who have biases (explicit and implicit) and operate in a society that has certain systemic biases, arising from its history, norms, and beliefs. Thus, every organization has a collection of mindsets, preferences, and biases that will tend to favor the dominant in-group, unintentionally

---

[6] Fair Housing Act, Federal Fair Lending Regulations and Statues, December 19, 2020, https:// www.federalreserve.gov/boarddocs/supmanual/cch/fair_lend_fhact.pdf.

[7] Fair Housing Act, Federal Fair Lending Regulations and Statues.

[8] Brooks (2020).

[9] Glantz and Martinez (2018).

creating barriers to others who belong in the out-group. In the case where diversity of thinking and representation is critical to the survival or continued success of an organization, it is essential to identify, acknowledge, and mitigate this bias—over and above the fundamental ethical principle that it is the right thing to do.

Profile of Courageous Leaders: Alicia Garza, Patrisse Cullors, and Opal Tometi

In 2013, three Black organizers—Alicia Garza, Patrisse Cullors, and Opal Tometi—created a Black-centered political will and movement building project called #Black-LivesMatter prompted by the acquittal in the killing of Trayvon Martin.[10] At the time, Garza was a special projects director of the National Domestic Workers Alliance in Oakland, California, Cullors was an artist, teacher, and prison reform activist in Los Angeles, and Tometi was executive director of the Black Alliance for Just Immigration in New York City. Garza's Facebook post after the acquittal, "Our lives matter" prompted Cullors to repost, adding the hashtag #blacklivesmatter. Tometi saw the hashtag online and called Garza and the three women met in person soon after. A movement was born.

Today, thanks to the vision of these three women, Black Lives Matter has become one of the most influential social justice groups in the world. It has more than a dozen chapters and affiliates in major cities and is a model for similar movements. All three women were named among the 100 Women of the Year by *Time Magazine* in 2020.[11]

Cullors, a performance artist, Fulbright scholar, popular public speaker, and an NAACP history maker, was named by *The Los Angeles Times* as a New Civil Rights Leader for the twenty-first century. She describes in *Esquire* magazine how she came out to her friends as queer in high school and in 2016 married her partner, Janaya Khan, a black transgender immigrant.[12] She wrote, "Our fight does not end with marriage. It is part of a larger conversation that pushes the LGBTQI+ community to think beyond the confines of the state; to understand the value of relationships, whether you have a license or not; to focus on vulnerable communities and demand that people, no matter their marital status, have access to healthcare and education."[13]

Garza, who is a self-described queer Black woman, reflected on what has made her successful as an activist and a leader in this interview in *National Geographic*: "My greatest strength is my ability to ignore it when I get *no* for an answer. When people tell me it cannot be done, it must not be done, it has never been done, there's something that goes off inside of me that says: Okay, watch me."[14]

---

[10] Black Lives Matter, "Herstory."

[11] Chan (2020).

[12] Cullors (2016).

[13] Cullors (2016).

[14] Garza (2020).

3   Why Should Organizations Care?

There are multiple reasons why organizations should care about bias. Those who mitigate bias will enjoy the immediate upside of better decision-making, more innovation, enhanced risk management, better customer congruence, and better application of the power of artificial intelligence (AI). Their efforts will also have the positive societal effects of advancing equity, being better aligned with stakeholder expectations, and supporting the #MeToo and #BLM Movements.

Equity in the organization—At the beginning of the book, we defined equity as a condition or state of fair, inclusive and respectful treatment of people. Bias undermines equity at the core as it results in unwittingly preferring members of the dominant group of an organization over minority members. This is a preference that affects all talent processes, from recruitment to promotion to sponsorship and to financial reward. As a result, those members of an organization who may already face critical barriers and difficulties in society, confront additional barriers within the organization.

Alignment to stakeholder concerns—Generation Z and Millennials care deeply about diversity, inclusion, and equity. With their increasing spending pool and their voice magnified by social media presence, these generations will require organizations to mitigate their biases. Not only are they less biased than previous generations,[15] but they are also unforgiving of those organizations who perpetuate biases. Gen Z are particularly uncomfortable with stereotyping and are ready to share examples of biased and stereotypical behavior on employer platforms like Glassdoor, the world's largest job and recruiting site. Biased corporate behavior becomes rapidly known and undermines the goodwill and branding of the organization.

A McKinsey study identified four core Gen Z behaviors, all anchored in one element: a search for truth.[16] Gen Zs "value individual expression and avoid labels." They object to the partial representation of individuals through stereotypes and mobilize for a variety of causes. With equity and diversity high on this list, bias is not condoned. They believe profoundly in the power of dialogue to solve conflicts and speaking out about bias is inherent in their behavior. This underscores the need for organizations to use every tool at their disposal to mitigate biases and rewire themselves to be future-fit.

Better results from artificial intelligence—Even our tools can be biased. Already, there is justifiable concern that artificial intelligence (AI) and machine learning algorithms used in the legal and judicial systems, advertisements, computer vision, and language models are exacerbating social and economic

---

[15] Wong (2019).

[16] Francis and Hoefel (2018).

disparities.[17] Addressing bias in this rapidly advancing field is critical to avoid further reinforcing entrenched disadvantage and inclusion.

In 2018, for example, Reuters reported that Amazon's recruiting system had been streamlined to more efficiently review resumés and select the best-qualified candidates through algorithms. However, the AI protocol was found to lead to gender discrimination because the programs had simply replicated existing hiring practices, perpetuating current biases against women in science. The algorithm was shown to be automating bias and the recruitment system was scrapped.[18]

In 2016, the independent investigative news organization ProPublica analyzed a tool called COMPAS (Correctional Offender Management Profiling for Alternative Sanctions), an algorithm used across the US in state court systems to predict the likelihood of a criminal reoffending.[19] ProPublica's analysis found that Black defendants were far more likely than white defendants to be incorrectly judged to be at a higher risk of reoffending, while white defendants were more likely to be incorrectly flagged as low risk.[20] Black defendants were almost twice as likely to be misclassified with a higher risk of reoffending (45%) in comparison to their white counterparts (23%).[21]

In 2019, Facebook was found to be allowing its advertisers to deliberately target ads based on gender, race, and religion (all protected classes under US law).[22] Job postings for preschool teachers and secretaries, for example, were shown to a higher fraction of women while postings for janitors and taxi drivers were shown to a higher proportion of minorities.[23] Further, ads about homes for sale were also shown to more white users while ads for rentals were shown to more minorities.[24] This case illustrates how machine learning forms patterns on the basis of data given. These patterns reflect existing societal inequalities and if machine learning is left unchecked, can end up propagating these biases and stereotypes further. In response to these findings, a spokesperson for Facebook said that they had "made important changes to our ad-targeting tools and know that this is only a first step," but the company was unable to avoid a lawsuit by the U.S. Department of Housing and Urban Development for violating the Fair Housing Act.[25] Fair housing groups

---

[17] "5 Examples of Biased Artificial Intelligence," Logically, July 30, 2019, https://www.logically.ai/articles/5-examples-of-biased-ai.

[18] "5 Examples of Biased Artificial Intelligence," Logically.

[19] Larson et al. (2016).

[20] Larson et al. (2016).

[21] Larson et al. (2016).

[22] Paul and Rana (2019).

[23] Hao (2019).

[24] Hao (2019).

[25] Hao (2019).

settled the historic lawsuit with Facebook in 2019 with an agreement that set a new industry standard in big data and tech concerning civil rights laws.[26]

In 2019, a team from the University of California Berkeley discovered a problem with an AI system that was being used to allocate care to 200 million patients in the US, which resulted in Black patients receiving a lower standard of care.[27] Across the board, Black people were assigned lower risk scores than white people, even though Black patients were statistically more likely to have comorbid conditions and thus in fact experience higher levels of risk.[28] The outcome meant that Black patients were less likely to have access to the necessary standard of care, and more likely to experience adverse effects through being denied proper care. The team worked with the company responsible for developing the tool to find variables other than cost through which to assign expected risk scores, reducing bias by 84%.[29]

AI is a powerful tool, but without efforts to design bias out, its built-in intelligence will merely replicate existing biases in organizations.

More support of global movements—Through the spotlight on racism that followed George Floyd's death in the U.S., Black Lives Matter has turned into a global movement for racial equality. At the same time, we have seen worldwide calls for gender equality through the #MeToo movement (see Profile of founder Tarana Burke). Both #MeToo and #BLM are fundamentally protesting against personal and systemic bias and entitlement, entrenched through many years of failing to address inbuilt bias. As a result, many leaders are now looking at their organizations afresh, questioning often long-held practices and assumptions and taking a stand in support of these movements by committing to unconscious bias training. This is not a silver bullet for advancing equity, as researchers have found.[30] Ultimately, equity is advanced by implementing widespread structural and institutional changes. But it is a process that begins with courageous and inclusive leadership.

Less bias, more business performance—Many of the business case benefits of diversity described in Chapter 7 are directly undermined by bias. Balanced decision-making, effective risk management, innovation, and selection of the best teams are all outcomes that are substantially compromised by biased thinking.

Without bias mitigation and training, teams will tend to favor information that confirms their preexisting beliefs (confirmation bias), they prefer to select options

---

[26] "Fair Housing Groups Settle Lawsuit with Facebook: Transforms Facebook's Ad Platform Impacting Millions of Users," National Fair Housing Alliance, March 28, 2019, https://nationalfairhousing.org/2019/03/18/national-fair-housing-alliance-settles-lawsuit-with-facebook-transforms-facebooks-ad-platform-impacting-millions-of-users/.

[27] Vartan (2019).

[28] Vartan (2019).

[29] Vartan (2019).

[30] Dobbin and Kalev (2018).

that are supported by a majority of members (conformity bias) or by the most senior leaders (authority bias) and lean toward options already adopted by others (bandwagon bias). The more homogeneous the team is, the more these biases will be re-enforced. It is precisely this sort of bias-in-operation that leads to the kind of groupthink described in the Bank of Ireland case study (Chapter 4) with far-reaching implications for risk management and business resilience.

In keeping with the principle of the Virtuous Circle, those organizations that are better able to mitigate bias will be better placed to secure the performance benefits of diversity.

Profile of a Courageous and Inclusive Leader: Tarana Burke

In 1997 activist Tarana Burke sat across from a 13-year-old girl who had been sexually abused. The girl's experience left Burke speechless, according to an interview in *The New York Times*, and it planted the seed for the nonprofit organization she founded in 2007, Just Be Inc., to support survivors of sexual violence, particularly young women of color from low wealth communities, find pathways to healing.[31] She gave her movement the name Me Too. Flash forward to 2017, when actress Alyssa Milano began using the hashtag #MeToo to encourage sexual abuse victims to come forward in the wake of sexual harassment and assault charges leveled against Hollywood producer Harvey Weinstein.[32] The hashtag went viral, with more than 12 million individuals coming forward in the first 24 hours and over 19 million in the first year. Today Burke has emerged on the global stage as a leader in giving voice to those most impacted by sexual violence.[33]

While Me Too has become a rallying cry for women of all races and backgrounds, Burke has persistently brought the focus back to girls and women of color who were the original inspiration for the movement. In 2018, her powerful TED-Women talk helped to educate future generations about the abuse of power and privilege[34] and since then she has visited 150 colleges to talk about preventing sexual violence.[35] She has joined heads of state and other leaders from over 165 countries to speak about the topic at the Women Deliver conference.[36] In November 2019, Burke accepted the 2019 Sydney Peace Prize for her work to change the way the world talks about sexual violence.[37] As she told *The Guardian* in 2018:

Inherently, having privilege isn't bad, but it's how you use it, and you have to use it in service of other people. Now that I have it, I'm trying to use it responsibly.[38]

---

[31] Garcia (2017).

[32] Garcia (2017).

[33] 'me too' Movement, "'me too.' Impact Report 2019."

[34] Burke (2018).

[35] 'me too' Movement, "'me too.' Impact Report 2019," p. 19.

[36] 'me too' Movement, "'me too.' Impact Report 2019," p. 19.

[37] 'me too' Movement, "'me too.' Impact Report 2019," p. 19.

[38] Brockes (2018).

4   Understanding the Phenomenon of Bias

One of the biggest barriers to dealing with unconscious bias is that people feel guilty and fearful about their biases and become defensive when unconscious bias programs are introduced. Fear is detrimental to building awareness and developing new skills. To help strengthen the Mitigate Bias capability, it first helps to understand the phenomenon of bias.

To combat this, at the outset of any program it is helpful to provide a scientific rationale for biased behavior—in effect a lesson in neuroscience. Mental shortcuts are built over our entire lifetime, as we make associations between people and outcomes. Usually, these associations are helpful to our survival as we navigate our way through huge streams of data. As soon as members of an organization realize that biases are mental shortcuts and that we all have them, the team can move beyond guilt and blame to discussion and development of effective interventions. To support this process, it is helpful for the leader to educate the organization on why bias is a reality and why it is important to mitigate. The phenomenon can be explained through concepts such as evolutionary survival factors, information overload, energy conservation, and/or typical fight-freeze-flight responses. Here we explore each of these in turn.

Evolutionary survival depended on "in-group" identification—Unconscious judgments or biases are essential for human survival and developed through evolution. The ability of our brains to pick up sensory cues (what we see, smell, feel, and hear) and categorize others according to these cues has allowed us to survive as a species. This was particularly important when one's life depended on having the protection of one's own group. As one researcher points out:

> From an evolutionary perspective, this tendency of bias makes good sense since we historically had to quickly assess who was a friend or foe, or a member of our tribe or another tribe, many centuries ago in order to survive. However, a particular survival tendency that might have made very good sense thousands of years ago when we were hunters and gatherers on the Savannah or living in caves can be deeply problematic for us today.[39]

This association with one's own group is still a phenomenon today. It is now defined as the social group or "in-group" to which one psychologically identifies as a member, while an "out-group" is a social group with which an individual does not identify. Even today our brain functioning picks up cues on how someone is dressed, the color of their skin, their name on a recruitment form, their accent, whether they are assertive or not, or by hobbies they list on their resumé, to name just a few examples. These cues trigger a categorization of whether the individual belongs to our in-group on the basis of mental rules and associations we have developed over time. Such mental shortcuts are also called heuristics or "rules

---

[39] Plante (2020).

of thumb" and are efficient mental processes that help humans solve problems and learn new concepts. These processes make problems less complex by ignoring some of the information coming into the brain, either consciously or unconsciously, but they can also lead us to make snap decisions about whether to hire, promote, develop, or invite an individual to have a seat at the table.

Bias protects against information overload—Bias also ensures that we don't face information overload. Our senses pick up about 11 million bits of information every second. However, our brain can only consciously process around 50 bits of information every second[40] and only seven pieces of information are processed by our working memory.[41] Why? Our brain can only sequentially process a limited information set so it filters out incoming information and orders it extremely quickly by using mental shortcuts. These mental shortcuts—called neural connections—are built rapidly in our first years of life by our direct environment but are continuously being built and pruned (albeit at a slowing rate) from early adulthood as we are exposed to social groups, media, and other environmental stimuli.

These shortcuts are extremely useful for our sanity and survival but when combined with sensory triggers, they may lead to unconsciously making talent decisions that can result in a homogeneous team.[42] That is because shortcut processing can create an incorrect mental perception that people who look and act like the dominant group within an organization are better. This works directly against the strategic narrative for diversity and undermines the organization's ability to recruit and retain the right mix of diversity required for diversity of thinking.

As an example, a leader in an organization is evaluating three candidates for an important strategic project. There is a great deal of information on each candidate's track record, specialization, and career at the company. The leader has not met two of the candidates but does know the third who is regarded for excellently leading another project, although it was quite different from the one the organization is currently recruiting for. Yet the leader selects the person they know. This is motivated by their past performance (even though it was not relevant to the strategic project for which they are being hired) and a feeling of safety ("I have worked with them before") and results in a great deal of relevant information being discarded in favor of what the leader "knows."

Bias conserves mental energy—Bias or unconscious processing is also related to conserving energy. The brain uses more energy than any other human organ, accounting for 20% of the body's energy usage. One third of this energy usage

---

[40] Physiology, Brittanica, https://www.britannica.com/science/information-theory/Physiology.

[41] McLeod (2009).

[42] Brain Architecture, Center on the Developing Child, Harvard University, December 19, 2020, https://developingchild.harvard.edu/science/key-concepts/brain-architecture/heur.

is for normal housekeeping such as cell maintenance but two thirds of this is expended on brain activity. We are configured to save energy for our survival and since certain brain tasks require more energy, we will default to passive or lazy thinking where possible. With functional magnetic resonance imaging (fMRI) it is now possible to see how our brain is activated differently when we are using a decision-making shortcut versus decisions made with mental effort.[43] More than 90% of our decisions are made using decision-making shortcuts.[44]

For example, a leader is provided with a thick file of resumes and reference letters of candidates who can fulfill an open role for the organization. The file contains no less than 100 pages of information and the leader is tired, stressed, and short on time. In this case they will not read, digest, or strategically reflect on the best candidate for the role. Instead, cognitive shortcuts will be taken, such as who has been successful in this role in the past, who is sure to fit into the current team, who has attended the best university, etc. In the case of an organization looking for enhanced diversity of their team, these mental shortcuts will probably not yield a choice for a different type of individual (Fig. 2).

Fight-freeze-flight responses—Our use of mental shortcuts is magnified in situations of stress, fear, and multi-tasking. When people make decisions in stressful situations, for example when the stakes are high and the potential consequences severe, or when a deadline is looming and the task demand is overwhelming, our bias is heightened. This runaway train of biological responses to stress has evolved to allow organisms to make a fight-or-flight response. When under stress, fast and effortless heuristics (problem-solving) may dominate over slow and demanding deliberation in making decisions under uncertainty. Situations that magnify fear and stress will usually be coupled with people resorting to intuitive, "gut feel" decision-making, and a preference for "safe decisions." Obviously, this point is absolutely critical for organizations to take into account: talent processes undertaken under stressful and high-stake situations will often magnify the degree of biased decisions.

A much-reported fight-free-flight triggered recruitment bias was found in the aftermath of the terrorist attacks on September 11, 2001 in the United States and on November 13, 2015 in Paris. Field tests showed that Arab Americans seeking employment in the USA and Muslim recruits seeking employment in France faced significantly more bias in the aftermath of these terrorist attacks when measured by callback rates. Research examining employer brain activity revealed activity in the amygdala, the zone involved in processing fear.[45]

---

[43] "Mental Shortcuts, Not Emotions, Guide Irrational Decisions," Neuroscience.news.com, March 31, 2017, https://neurosciencenews.com/irrational-decisions-mental-shortcuts-6319/.

[44] Brain Architecture, Center on the Developing Child, Harvard University, December 19, 2020, https://developingchild.harvard.edu/science/key-concepts/brain-architecture/heur.

[45] Valfort (2018).

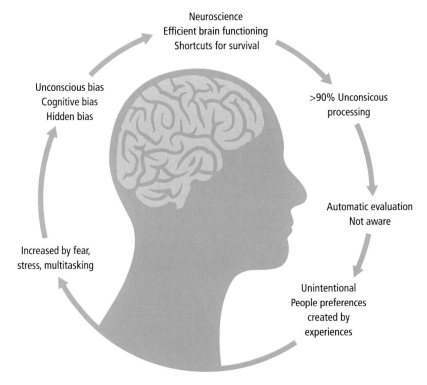

Neuroscience
Efficient brain functioning
Shortcuts for survival

Unconscious bias
Cognitive bias
Hidden bias

>90% Unconsicous
processing

Automatic evaluation
Not aware

Increased by fear,
stress, multitasking

Unintentional
People preferences
created by
experiences

Fig. 2   The Circle of Unconscious Bias
How brain function reinforces bias.

5   Bias Undermines Diversity Performance

As described above, there are sound biological explanations for why we harbor biases and many view bias as critical to survival, yet in a rapidly changing environment, the survival of an organization will depend on its ability to mitigate bias. Biases lead to organizations favoring in-group profiles, yet by doing so the organization is unable to deliver on its strategic narrative of Diversity Performance. As a result, the organization will fail to advance equity, will not be able to tap into diversity of thinking for breakthrough innovations, and will fall short of its customer requirements. Instead, organizations end up penalizing the very minority candidates that they wish to attract.

The following example illustrates how this bias translates into real barriers for minorities.[46] A legal memo was drafted for a hypothetical law student. The memo deliberately contained 22 errors, seven of which were minor spelling or grammar

---

[46] https://diversity.missouristate.edu/assets/diversityconference/14468226472014040114Written-inBlackandWhiteYPS.pdf.

errors and were distributed to 60 different partners of leading law firms, who had agreed to participate in a writing analysis study. All partners received the same memo, but half the partners received a memo that stated that the associate, Thomas Meyer, was African American while the other half received a memo that stated the associate was Caucasian.

Astonishingly, skin tone/race bias resulted in the same research memo being rated dramatically differently and resulting in the hypothetical Caucasian candidate being rated very highly at 4.1/5.0 while the hypothetical African American received a 3.2/5.0 rating. The lower rating was driven by bias, namely a bias about the expected quality of work of the Caucasian associate versus the African American associate. Only 2.9 out of 7 spelling errors were found for the Caucasian candidate and 5.8 of the 7 spelling errors were found for the African American candidate. Alarmingly, this process plays out every day in different situations within a variety of companies and institutions, with negative impacts on the hiring of minorities. As described in the boxes, it is a similar story with gender bias.

Case Study: Gender Bias in Orchestras

This case summarizes the findings from a pioneering study by researchers Claudia Goldin and Cecilia Rouse published in *The American Economic Review* in 2000, "Orchestrating Impartiality: The Impact of 'Blind' Auditions on Female Musicians."

In this study, the researchers found that the Boston Symphony Orchestra's use of a screen to conceal a candidate's identity from the jury increased the probability that a woman would be advanced and hired. In the 1970s, the top five orchestras in the U.S. counted fewer than five percent women. As audiences demanded more diversity, orchestras needed to adapt. Many suspected that part of the reason for the lack of women in orchestras was an unconscious bias that men players were more fit for orchestras and were thus able to advance from the preliminary to the final round of auditions. This led the Boston Orchestra, which only had five to 10% women musicians at the time, to begin blind auditions. This simple intervention did not create the benefits that they were hoping for, but when coupled with an instruction to candidates to remove their shoes, they saw a dramatic surge in the number of women advancing to the final round. When blind auditions were accompanied by candidates only wearing their socks so that high-heeled shoes were not audible, the percentage of women advancing from the preliminary to final round increased from 19.3% to 28.6% while for men this intervention diminished their advancement from 22.5% to 20.2%. This very simple intervention is still used today in orchestras (some for the entire audition process) and has been shown to increase the chance of women being selected by 50%. It increased the percentage of women in the Boston Symphony Orchestra from 10 to 35%s in the 1990. Today that figure is about 47% women, about the average for U.S. orchestras overall.

▶ **Key takeaway** Addressing unconscious bias through targeted interventions delivers significant diversity benefits.

These types of bias contribute to the ongoing lack of parity and representation of women and people of color and other minorities in a range of organizations, notably women in scientific professions, as demonstrated in the next case study.

Case Study: Gender-STEM Bias in Universities

Leading researcher in the field of bias, Corinne A. Moss-Racusin, led a famous experiment in 2012 to determine whether faculty in STEM (Science, Technology, Engineering, and Mathematics) expressed a bias against female students and to identify the process contributing to this bias.[47] In the study, a fictitious resumé was sent to 127 science lecturers from research-intensive STEM universities; the professors did not know they were participating in an experiment and were simply requested to rate the resume received. Half of the professors received a resumé with the name John Brown and the other half received the same fictitious resumé with the name Jennifer Brown. They were all asked to rate the resumé on a five-point scale across four evaluation criteria: an assessment of the student's competency, the salary they were prepared to offer if the candidate was hired, the readiness to hire the student, and their willingness to mentor the candidate.

The results sent a shock wave through the STEM community. Despite the resumés being identical, the respondents evaluated John Brown higher than Jennifer Brown in all criteria, and by a large margin (30%). Further investigation revealed a deep-seated unconscious bias that men are more proficient at science than women.

▶   **Key takeaway** Implicit and explicit gender bias in STEM has been shown to result in systemic discrimination against women candidates.

The subtle and not-so-subtle Gender-STEM bias reflected in the case of Jennifer-John Brown perpetuates the significant underrepresentation of women in the STEM workforce, eroding the potential for women to enter the field. At the 2015 World Conference of Science Journalists, biochemist and Nobel laureate Tim Hunt delivered controversial remarks suggesting that the inclusion of women in science labs may undermine scientific productivity.[48] While this led to a rush of critical remarks and the resignation of Hunt from his professorship at University College London,[49] it is testament to the widespread and often deep-seated assumptions consciously or unconsciously held in this sector.

As a result, across regions, women account on average for less than a third (29.3%) of those employed in scientific research and development (R&D).[50]

---

[47] Moss-Racusin et al. (2012).

[48] Ratcliffe (2015).

[49] Bever (2015).

[50] Women in Science, Fact Sheet No. 55, June 2019, UNESCO Institute for Statistics, http://uis.unesco.org/en/topic/women-science.

Globally, women account for only 16% of managers in the information technology industry[51] and represented only 17.9% of board members in that industry in 2019.[52] The situation is equally poor in the tech industry C-suite, where women comprise only three percent of CEOs and 20% of CFOs.[53]

6   How to Mitigate Bias in Practice

What can be done in practice to combat bias? Depending on an organization's Diversity Performance maturity level, the Integrated Diversity Model sets out a range of evidence-based initiatives that can be implemented to build the necessary capabilities to overcome unconscious and systemic bias (Table 1). The Mitigate Bias capability area is critical because if bias is allowed to persist within the organization, it will undermine Diversity Performance at every stage.

Below we take a more detailed look at these key bias mitigation initiatives.

Stage 1 Organizations: Legal Compliance
At Stage 1, the primary focus is on preventing discrimination lawsuits or legal fallout arising from discriminatory practices. Here the main purpose of the Mitigate Bias capability is to ensure legal compliance by ridding the organization of explicitly biased actions and communication.

A good place to start is by rolling out compliance training to all members of the organization. Often this takes the form of e-compliance modules to raise awareness of what constitutes explicitly biased behavior and could be construed as discrimination. Such training is essentially focused on "do's and don'ts": rules are set out and members are made aware of the consequence of explicitly biased behavior and the impact on the organization. Universal basic compliance training can be supplemented with specialized training, delivered by third party experts, setting out upcoming legal or quota requirements and good practice methods for ensuring compliance within the organization.

Stage 1 organizations can also undertake certain critical processes to ensure no evidence of explicit bias and discrimination. A key process review is to identify whether there are salary or benefit gaps between the majority and minority groups in the organization. Other talent processes such as recruitment announcements, employment contracts, and promotion criteria will also be assessed for non-compliance risk. Performance measurement at this stage involves use of metrics or proxies for explicit bias such as the number of discrimination accusations made,

---

[51] "Women in Science, Technology, Engineering and Mathematics (STEM): Quick Take," Catalyst, August 4, 2020, https://www.catalyst.org/research/women-in-science-technology-engineering-and-mathematics-stem/#easy-footnote-bottom-16-3713.

[52] Emelianova and Milhomem (2019, p. 15).

[53] Kersley et al. (2019, p. 15).

Table 1   Bias Mitigation Capability and Initiatives for the Five Stages
Overview of evidence-based initiatives to mitigate bias at each stage of diversity maturity.

	Stage 1 Legal Compliance	Stage 2 Stakeholder Requirements	Stage 3 Organizational Performance	Stage 4 Reinvention	Stage 5 Societal Value
Focus	Explicit bias	Implicit bias in HR	Implicit bias in leadership	Systemic bias in organization	Systemic bias in society
Skills	Do's and don'ts	Bias awareness	Reduce triggers	Advance equity	Challenge societal bias
Process	Institute rules	HR monitoring	On-the-job monitoring	Organization monitoring	Society monitoring
Responsibilities	Legal	HR D&I lead	Leaders diversity office	De-bias champions	Partner leaders
Metrics	Discrimination	Bias in HR	Bias in leaders	Bias in organization	Bias in society
Technology	Legal systems	Niche HR process tools	Niche language tools	De-bias platform	Partner enablement

the cost of legal discrimination actions, and negative publicity due to explicit bias, with data supplied by case management solutions or extracted from the enterprise system. In terms of policy, Stage 1 organizations commit publicly to having zero tolerance for discrimination, and responsibility for mitigating explicit bias and discrimination is allocated to the Risk Management Leader or senior leadership involved in Legal and Financial functions.

Stage 2 Organizations: Stakeholder Requirements
At Stage 2, organizations have achieved zero-discrimination compliance and now wish to avoid making unconsciously biased decisions within their talent recruitment and promotion processes.

As a first step toward building this capability, training is focused on creating awareness around implicit bias and specifically supporting the Human Resources function in recognizing typical biases and talent blind spots that occur during the employee lifecycle. Talent processes are reviewed to identify where bias is triggered and removing biased language (e.g., male-associated words like "chairman" or male-preferred phrases such as "driving the workforce"). The recruitment process is made more objective by eliminating opportunities to introduce own bias, for example removing sections on the interview form that ask for "other comments" or "do you think the candidate will fit into the culture of our organization?" The recruitment process will usually include multiple interviews and interviewers will provide independent feedback on their decisions and underlying rationale to avoid conformity bias, namely pressure to conform to a group decision.

Stage 2 metrics for evaluating the success of de-bias initiatives include independent audits of employee processes to identify biased language or bias triggers, as well as feedback from employees and customers on biased interactions. Some organizations at this stage will deploy tools like the Implicit Association Test to combat e.g., gender-career bias, gender-STEM bias, and skin tone bias, etc. Use of anonymized sharing tools that create a team profile for the HR team can help to avoid replication of default talent patterns, paired with reminders to slow down default, fast thinking. Bias identification tools such as word recognition can be used to detect and score bias in written documentation or spoken language. Usually, responsibility for de-biasing processes and language for employees and customers falls within the domain of the HR and Customer Relationship Management (CRM) functions and senior leadership responsible for Human Resources and/or marketing.

Stage 3 Organizations: Organizational Performance
At Stage 3 the focus shifts onto actions to mitigate implicit bias to create an environment where all talent collaborates effectively to drive performance outcomes. Whereas at Stage 2, organizations are attempting to mitigate bias in talent processes by raising awareness, here the focus is on ensuring that bias does not compromise leadership actions, teamwork, or on-the-job interactions.

Capacity-building at this Stage involves all leaders attending regular implicit bias sessions focused on the actions they can take to mitigate bias within their teams and wider organization. To help embed this, Stage 3 organizations may consider setting up an Implicit Bias Taskforce mandated to mitigate bias in all processes, rituals, and communication. Efforts are increased throughout the organization to remove biased and stereotypical language in all internal and external communication, supported by tools to identify biased written and spoken language. To measure performance, metrics may include the number of employee reports and findings from leadership bias audits.

Stage 4 Organizations: Reinvention
At Stage 4, the objective is for diversity to become a platform for organizational transformation and focus shifts from mitigating implicit bias in leadership and key functions to neutralizing systemic bias across the organization as a whole.

Systemic biases emerge in society through entrenched values and beliefs which impact mindsets and behaviors in the organization. For example, in societies that display a high gender-STEM bias in favor of men, this bias will usually be strongly evidenced in the organization. For example, STEM women report needing to prove themselves repeatedly. Women feel the need to appear masculine to appear competent in the job and to walk the tightrope of exhibiting too much masculine behavior and then being called "aggressive" and "too vocal."[54]

Given the importance of leadership in identifying bias, annual or interim bias training is replaced by ongoing coaching of leaders to reflect on their own bias and undertake courageous discussions or bold interventions when bias occurs. This

---

[54]Williams et al. (2014).

may be supplemented by the appointment of certified de-bias champions to embed diversity transformation. Performance metrics can be tied to organizational bias and systemic bias audit findings.

Stage 5 Organizations: Societal Value
At Stage 5, focus shifts from internal transformation of the organization to mitigating implicit and systemic bias within its wider value chain and partner ecosystem. Here the approach to bias mitigation is outward-facing. It requires the organization's leadership to be deeply committed to the societal case for diversity and act as an advocate or "evangelist" for diversity. Such proactive leaders will often be supported by a Bias Mitigation Council, along with certified de-biasing ambassadors or experts embedded in partner organizations within their broader value chain.

The full range of initiatives to develop the organization's bias mitigation capability at every stage of maturity is summarized in Fig. 1.

The following extended case study shows how one organization applied these tools to identify a key bias, then successfully mitigated it through a comprehensive multi-year program.

Case Study: "The Form Was Blank for Women"
Part 1—Situation: We Get That Diversity Is Important

Jane, the Vice President of a therapeutic business unit in a life sciences organization, initiated a comprehensive bias mitigation program in response to an event which convinced her that a serious approach was required.

In the five years since being appointed to her role, Jane had been personally committed to fostering diversity and actively involved in crafting a compelling strategic narrative for diversity in her business unit. Its central theme was that embracing diversity would allow her therapeutic unit to be more patient-centric and having a diverse and engaged team would lead to an accelerated path for registration of their drugs. Jane was convinced that having a gender-balanced team would result in a better mix of leadership styles and stimulate innovation. Some progress had been made, with women in senior leadership positions and research having increased from around 15 to almost 30%, but there was still a way to go. To support diversity, Jane had actively communicated the case for diversity and had instituted a leadership development program to support leaders advancing in the business unit.

As part of an annual personal development exercise to recognize leaders and invest in them, Jane would ask her direct reports to identify high-potential talent in their country units to attend a leadership development program. A multi-year program, it was highly acclaimed for being delivered by a leading business school and was viewed as critical to the further development and success of leaders within the organization as they assumed commercial and research responsibilities.

In previous years, Jane would send out the candidate selection form with a covering note stressing the importance of diversity to her business unit and emphasize her expectations for good gender distribution of candidates in the selection. Numerous leaders had provided feedback on this covering note, saying "Please, trust us. We get it that diversity is important. No need for you to send out this reminder communication each year." So, for the first time in the five years since the program began, she sent the candidate election form without her traditional covering note. The results were deeply disappointing. The list contained only men—not a single woman candidate was included on the selection form. This was despite the candidate population comprising an almost equal split between men and women, all with a track record of excellent performance.

Jane pondered the question: why after years of diversity focus, of individual coaching, of stressing that her unit needed a mixed and diverse group of candidates, would she still get a form featuring only male candidates when there was a population of high-performing women candidates available? "Is it that people are not individually motivated to support diversity?" or "Is it that my leaders are committed to diversity but still unwittingly choose men?".

As Vice President, Jane leveraged this disappointing outcome around the leadership development event to sponsor and design a multi-year program to mitigate bias.

Case Study: "The Form Was Blank for Women"
Part 2—Complication: The Silent Role of Triggers in Candidate Selection

Jane used this event to reach out to her leaders and hold a series of "courageous team discussions." In a facilitated and "safe" session, the leaders discussed their preferred candidate list and their rationale for selecting their candidates. They were given a simple sentence to conclude: "I chose X (male candidate) because ...." And "I did not choose Y (female candidate) because ..." These sessions were revealing. Leaders identified that there were certain triggers leading them to prioritize certain candidates above others, including that their preferred candidate was simply the one they knew best, a choice highly impacted by their previous work collaborations and supplemented by company social interactions.

They concluded that social interactions tended to skew participation to men candidates. Many of the leaders related that some candidates were prominently on their mind going into the selection process because these candidates had specifically reached out to them in the weeks preceding the nomination, advancing reasons for why they should be selected. This was done at a ratio of 80:20 male over female candidates. Finally, leaders concluded that they were also triggered to advance a candidate that "seemed to fit the profile" (affiliation bias), "reminded me of myself at that time" (mini-me bias) and were extrovert and present (extrovert bias). This discussion supported the leaders to reflect on the triggers that lead to candidate selection and allowed them to conclude that their selection process was largely unconscious and unwittingly biased.

Experience reinforces empathy—The Life Sciences organization had previously relied on the Implicit Association Test (IAT) as a manner to educate their employees on the phenomenon of unconscious bias. Introduced in 1998, the IAT is available on the Project Implicit website and more than 20 million people have taken the test.[55] While it has engendered some controversy in both the scientific literature[56] and

---

[55] Greenwald et al. (1998).

[56] Azar (2008, p. 44).

public sphere,[57] many organizations still leverage the IAT as part of their unconscious bias training initiatives. To help tackle and unearth hidden triggers, the Vice President now decided to introduce virtual reality so that leaders could experience workplace bias firsthand. Virtual reality (VR) is the term used to describe a three-dimensional, computer-generated environment which an individual can explore and interact with.[58] The person is immersed within an environment and while there, able to manipulate objects or perform a series of actions. VR-based training scenarios can support users to develop "lived" experience of workplace bias.[59]

In a virtual reality session, each leader had the opportunity to assume the role of a minority candidate—for this exercise, a researcher called Linda, the only woman of color in the research team. A typical research meeting was designed where participants shared their ideas on the design of a study. In this virtual reality session, Linda is systematically ignored despite attempting to contribute and raising her hand multiple times. In the virtual reality session Linda is an avatar and this simulation is used to provide leaders with an immersive experience of workplace bias. This session often ended with leaders removing their VR goggles feeling agitated and angry and complaining bitterly about how they were ignored in the meeting. Many concluded that this experience couldn't possibly happen in real life. The second part of the VR exercise was a "deep listening" session where leaders heard responses to the questions "Do I feel I am seen in the team?" and "What limits my contribution and what could support me contributing more?" This use of VR was extremely helpful in generating awareness and building empathy for those candidates who face bias every day. Whereas the IAT process was used to identify a strong, moderate, or slight association between gender and career and gender and STEM, the VR session allowed the leaders to experience bias firsthand. IAT is directed at the brain and the VR process is directed at the heart by conjuring strong emotions. By experiencing a biased situation, the leader has a better grasp of how it feels to be ignored, overlooked, or passed up for promotion.

De-biasing processes—Jane commissioned the Human Resources Group to work with an expert to de-bias their talent processes. A process-by-process review was conducted from the initial outreach to candidates (through job advertisements and university recruiting), to recruitment, to contracting, and to all the processes involved in the promotion of talent, succession planning, and even exit review. The design principle was to minimize moments where team members resort to "gut feel" and replace these with a process that required rational, conscious thinking. For example, to help reduce bias, the interview process was restructured to improve consistency, by providing a common set of questions with scoring parameters, asking every candidate the same questions, scoring the respondents' answers after each question; and each candidate being interviewed by three separate interviewers. Interview scores were gathered and where there were discrepancies, a recruitment coach would sit down with the interviewers to assess the underlying reason. This approach yielded

---

[57] Singal (2017).

[58] What Is Virtual Reality?, Virtual Reality Society, https://www.vrs.org.uk/virtual-reality/what-is-virtual-reality.html.

[59] Rabinowitz (2020).

Table 2   Examples of De-biased Language
The organization adapted its language to be more inclusive to people with disabilities.

Original	Adapted
Speak	Communicate
See	Identify, assess, discover
Carry	Move
Walk	Traverse
Type	Input data (e.g. by voice)

a more rigorous, fact-based review of candidates and kept all leaders accountable for an unbiased process.

Surfacing bias in language—Jane was delighted to find that these first two bias interventions resulted in leaders wishing to take further steps to mitigate bias and advance diversity of their team. The deep listening sessions suggested that the written and oral language was not helpful in promoting inclusion. For example many of the profiles for stereotypically male jobs used more masculine wording, leading women to think that more men worked there, or that they would not belong in that position, or that they would find the job less appealing. This feedback was consistent with ongoing research that found that "subtle language differences in how jobs are advertised may help explain the ongoing gender gap in historically male-dominated fields."[60] Jane commissioned a study of technology-enabled solutions that could unearth bias in both spoken and written language. An application was selected, much like a spelling and grammar checking tool, to flag typed words and phrases that are cliché, gender-biased, or otherwise off-putting. Such solutions can be hugely helpful given the fact that gender-biased job roles are a primary reason for many women not pursuing certain advertised jobs or courses.[61,62] At time of writing, the organization is evaluating a text analyzer software which can evaluate texts, whether in job descriptions, websites, or other external communication, and identify words that could contain a gender bias or be considered exclusionary, even providing a gender neutrality score for the text.[63] To become more inclusive to people with disabilities, a process was also put in place to replace active verbs in role descriptions with alternative terms (Table 2).

Other examples of word changes included replacing the technical term "master/slave" to "primary/replica."[64] in response to the BLM movement and the sensitivities that these words engender. In acknowledgment of their LGBTQI+ members, the organization paid specific attention to the use of pronouns using they/theirs and not he/his or she/hers. As a result, Jane received many emails from employees conveying

---

[60] Gaucher, Friesen, and Kay, "Gendered Wording".

[61] Silverberg, "Job adverts."

[62] Vervecken (2013).

[63] Stein (2020).

[64] McKenzie (2019).

their thanks and appreciation. One message stated: "I worked here but did not feel that I really was seen. Now I feel that I am starting to belong."

The program that Jane put in place was comprehensive and incorporated tangible and actionable measures. By investing in the team's realization of what it feels like to be excluded, she received the support and sponsorship to take steps such as removing biased language and de-biasing processes. The question was whether these actions would be sufficient to rewire how the organization responded to members who did not fit into the dominant profile.

Case Study: "The Form Was Blank for Women"
Part 3—Resolution: Re-Wiring the Organization for New Behaviors

Jane was aware that many organizations had already instituted implicit bias training, but she was justifiably concerned when reading that 66% of HR specialists report that diversity training has not had positive effects on attitudes or behaviors.[65] Benefits from implicit bias training tend to be short-lived and while awareness initially increases, the changed behavior is limited to a few days. Of concern to Jane was that implicit bias training can even reinforce stereotypes and biased behavior and breed resentment.[66]

Jane took time to meet with specialists and implicit bias practitioners to understand how implicit bias training can lead to long-term shifts of behavior under the right conditions. She wanted an implicit bias intervention aimed at women in STEM that would be effective and translate into less gender-STEM bias in her business unit. Drawing on the work of Corinne A. Moss-Racusin outlined in A "Scientific Diversity" Intervention to Reduce Gender Bias in a Sample of Life Scientists,[67] Jane obtained external support to develop a 120-minute implicit bias training workshop that satisfied Moss-Racusin's four key diversity intervention design elements:

(1)   Interventions based on theory and empirical evidence rather than intuition;
(2)   Approaches utilize active learning to foster participants' dynamic engagement with workshop content;
(3)   Diversity presented as a shared goal and responsibility rather than the "fault" of one group or individual; and.
(4)   Rigorous evaluation to assess efficacy, where outcomes being assessed are (i) increase in participants' awareness of diversity issues; (ii) reduction of participants' biases; and (iii) preparedness of participants to take action on diversity-related issues rather than avoid diversity.

This scientific workshop was rolled out to all leaders and cascaded to line managers with the intention that all people in the business unit would attend the training.

---

[65] Dobbin and Kalev (2018).

[66] Dobbin and Kalev (2016).

[67] Moss-Racusin et al. (2016).

Confronting Bias Through Rituals

Jane realized that a workshop would not be a silver bullet. Most of her leaders were genuinely committed to promoting diversity but were "unconsciously unskilled"—namely unaware of their biases. The organization would also need to put rituals and protocols in place to put a break on bias. One such ritual was that the promotion review process would commence with the chair saying: "Before we start evaluating the shortlist of candidates, let's acknowledge that we each bring our cognitive biases into the process. Let's be open about speaking about this to one another when we think bias is occurring or invite a third party in to observe our discussion and highlight when they see unconscious bias occurring." By repeating such practices over time, teams can become "consciously skilled" and avoid the trap of unconscious bias.

The organization's journey will never be over, however, as Jane concluded: "Bias mitigation is about developing compassion for those who bear the brunt of bias and, equipped with this empathy, setting a quest for oneself to move from 'unconsciously unskilled' to 'consciously excellent' in identifying and mitigating bias."

▶   **Key takeaway** As a result of concerted commitment, Jane's organization saw a dramatic return on its bias mitigation efforts. The pipeline of women increased, they broke through the 30% gender ceiling at the senior leadership level, there was an increase in employee engagement and they experienced an encouraging upward trend in productivity and business outcomes.

7   Concluding Remarks

For diversity to flourish, it is crucial to tackle both personal and systemic bias—within organizations and in society more broadly. Bias mitigation is a core diversity capability. Implicit bias is present in every person and systemic bias is intrinsic to the societies that organizations serve. When bias exists unchecked, it undermines the diversity journey by favoring the hiring, promotion, and potential of certain people above others. This undermines engagement, performance outcomes, ability to transform, and long-term equity in society. Today's younger generations—Gen Z and Millennials—expect organizations to be proactive in raising awareness and mitigating bias. Tomorrow's diversity leaders will be those who advocate publicly for change while putting in place the proven measures to deliver on their commitments.

In Chapter 7 we explore the next critical capability, building a strong case for diversity.

References

Azar, Beth. "IAT: Fad or Fabulous?" *Monitor on Psychology*, July/August 2008, p. 44. https://www.apa.org/monitor/2008/07-08/psychometric.

Bever, Lindsey. "Nobel Prize-Winning Scientist Tim Hunt Resigns After Commenting on the 'Trouble with Girls'." *The Washington Post*, June 11, 2015. https://www.washingtonpost.com/news/morning-mix/wp/2015/06/11/nobel-prize-winning-scientist-tim-hunt-resigns-position-after-commenting-on-the-trouble-with-girls/.

Brockes, Emma. "#MeToo Founder Tarana Burke: 'You Have to Use Your Privilege to Serve Other People'." *The Guardian*, January 15, 2018. https://www.theguardian.com/world/2018/jan/15/me-too-founder-tarana-burke-women-sexual-assault.

Brooks, Khristopher J. "Redlining's Legacy: Maps Are Gone, but the Problem Hasn't Disappeared." CBS News, June 12, 2020. https://www.cbsnews.com/news/redlining-what-is-history-mike-bloomberg-comments/.

Burke, Tarana. "Me Too Is a Movement, Not a Moment," TEDWomen 2018, TED. https://www.ted.com/talks/tarana_burke_me_too_is_a_movement_not_a_moment/?blog.

Chan, Melissa. "2013: Patrisse Cullors, Alicia Garza and Opal Tometi." *Time*, March 5, 2020. https://time.com/5793789/black-lives-matter-founders-100-women-of-the-year/.

Cullors, Patrisse. "A Black Lives Matter Leader Opens Up About Marrying Her Partner." *Esquire*, June 24, 2016. https://www.esquire.com/news-politics/a45823/patrisse-cullors-black-gay/.

Del Real, Jose A., Robert Samuels, and Tim Craig. "How the Black Lives Matter Movement Went Mainstream." *The Washington Post*, June 9, 2020. https://www.washingtonpost.com/national/how-the-black-lives-matter-movement-went-mainstream/2020/06/09/201bd6e6-a9c6-11ea-9063-e69bd6520940_story.html.

Dobbin, Frank, and Alexandra Kalev. "Why Diversity Programs Fail." *The Harvard Business Review*, July–August 2016. https://hbr.org/2016/07/why-diversity-programs-fail.

Dobbin, Frank, and Alexandra Kalev. "Why Diversity Training Doesn't Work: The Challenge for Industry and Academia." *Anthropology Now*, 10, no. 2 (2018): 48–55. https://scholar.harvard.edu/dobbin/publications/why-diversity-training-doesn%E2%80%99t-work-challenge-industry-and-academia.

Emelianova, Olga, and Christina Milhomem. *Women on Boards: 2019 Progress Report* (MSCI, December 2019), p. 15.

Francis, Tracy, and Fernanda Hoefel. "'True Gen': Generation Z and Its Implications for Companies." McKinsey & Company, November 12, 2018. https://www.mckinsey.com/industries/consumer-packaged-goods/our-insights/true-gen-generation-z-and-its-implications-for-companies.

Garcia, Sandra E. "The Woman Who Created #MeToo Long Before Hashtags." *The New York Times*, October 20, 2017. https://www.nytimes.com/2017/10/20/us/me-too-movement-tarana-burke.html#:~:text=In%201997,%20Tarana%20Burke%20sat,who%20had%20been%20sexually%20abused.&text=She%20sought%20out%20the%20resources,movement%20a%20name:%20Me%20Too.

Garza, Alicia. "From the Archives: Black Lives Matter Co-founder Reflects on a Life of Activism." Interview by Susan Goldberg, *National Geographic*, July 8, 2020. https://www.nationalgeographic.com/history/2020/07/archival-black-lives-matter-co-founder-reflects-life-activism/.

Glantz, Aaron, and Emmanuel Martinez. "For People of Color, Banks Are Shutting the Door to Homeownership." Reveal, The Center for Investigative Reporting, February 15, 2018. https://revealnews.org/article/for-people-of-color-banks-are-shutting-the-door-to-homeownership/.

Greenwald, A. G., and M. R. Banaji, "Implicit Social Cognition: Attitudes, Self-Esteem, and Stereotypes." *Psychological Review*, 102, no. 1 (1995): 4–27. http://doi.org/10.1037/0033-295x.102.1.4.

Greenwald, Anthony G., Debbie E. McGhee, and Jordan L. K. Schwartz. "Measuring Individual Differences in Implicit Cognition: The Implicit Association Test." *Journal of Personality and Social Psychology*, 74, no. 6 (1998): 1464–1480. https://doi.org/10.1037/0022-3514.74.6.1464.

Hao, Karen. "Facebook's Ad-serving Algorithm Discriminates by Gender and Race." *MIT Technology Review*, April 5, 2019. https://www.technologyreview.com/2019/04/05/1175/facebook-algorithm-discriminates-ai-bias/.

Kersley, Richard, et al. *The CS Gender 3000 in 2019: The Changing Face of Companies* (Credit Suisse Research Institute, October 10, 2019), p. 15.

Larson, Jeff, et al. "How We Analyzed the COMPAS Recidivism Algorithm." *ProPublica*, May 23, 2016. https://www.propublica.org/article/how-we-analyzed-the-compas-recidivism-algo-rithm.

McKenzie, Cameron. "Master-slave Terminology Alternatives You Can Use Right Now." *The ServerSide*, February 2, 2019. https://www.theserverside.com/opinion/Master-slave-terminol-ogy-alternatives-you-can-use-right-now.

McLeod, Saul. "Short Term Memory." *Simply Psychology*, 2009. https://www.simplypsychology.org/short-term-memory.html.

Moss-Racusin, Corrine A., et al. "Science Faculty's Subtle Gender Biases Favor Male Students." *Proceedings of the National Academy of Sciences*, 109, no. 41 (October 9, 2012): 16474–16479. https://www.pnas.org/content/109/41/16474.

Moss-Racusin, Corinne A., et al. "A 'Scientific Diversity' Intervention to Reduce Gender Bias in a Sample of Life Scientists." *CBE—Life Sciences Education*, 15, no. 3 (Fall 2016): ar29. http://doi.org/10.1187/cbe.15-09-0187. PMID: 27496360; PMCID: PMC5008876.

Paul, Katie, and Akanksha Rana. "U.S. Charges Facebook with Racial Discrimination in Targeted Housing Ads." *Reuters*, March 28, 2019. https://www.reuters.com/article/us-facebook-advertisers/u-s-charges-facebook-with-racial-discrimination-in-targeted-hous-ing-ads-idUSKCN1R91E8.

Plante, Thomas G. "Virtue Signaling, Implicit Bias and the Recent Black Lives Matter Move-ment." Markkula Center for Applied Ethics at Santa Clara University, July 15, 2020. https://www.scu.edu/ethics-spotlight/ethics-and-systemic-racism/virtue-signaling-implicit-bi-as-and-the-recent-black-lives-matter-movement/.

Rabinowitz, Howard. "Can VR Reduce Workplace Bias?" *Workflow*, February 4, 2020. https://workflow.servicenow.com/employee-engagement/virtual-reality-training-unconscious-bi-as-workplace/.

Ratcliffe, Rebecca. "Nobel Scientist Tim Hunt: Female Scientists Cause Trouble for Men in Labs." *The Guardian*, June 10, 2015. https://www.theguardian.com/uk-news/2015/jun/10/nobel-scientist-tim-hunt-female-scientists-cause-trouble-for-men-in-labs.

Singal, Jesse. "Psychology's Favorite Tool for Measuring Racism Isn't Up to the Job." *New York Magazine*, January 11, 2017. https://www.thecut.com/2017/01/psychologys-racism-measur-ing-tool-isnt-up-to-the-job.html.

Stein, Esther. "AI-Powered Tool Aims to Help Reduce Bias and Racially Charged Language on Websites." *TechRepublic*, July 30, 2020. https://www.techrepublic.com/article/ai-powered-tool-aims-to-help-reduce-bias-and-racially-charged-language-on-websites/.

Valfort, Marie-Anne. "Anti-Muslim Discrimination in France: Evidence from a Field Experi-ment." IZA Institute of Labor Economics, March 2018. http://ftp.iza.org/dp11417.pdf.

Vartan, Starre. "Racial Bias Found in a Major Health Care Risk Algorithm." *Scientific American*, October 24, 2019. https://www.scientificamerican.com/article/racial-bias-found-in-a-major-health-care-risk-algorithm/.

Vervecken, Dries, Bettina Hannover, and Ilka Wolter. "Changing (S)expectations: How Gender Fair Job Descriptions Impact Children's Perceptions and Interest Regarding Traditionally Male Occupations." *Journal of Vocational Behavior*, 82, no. 3 (June 2013): 208–220. https://doi.org/10.1016/j.jvb.2013.01.008.

von der Leyen, Ursula. "State of the Union Address by President von der Leyen at the European Parliament Plenary." European Commission, September 16, 2020. https://ec-europa-eu.ezp.sub.su.se/commission/presscorner/detail/en/SPEECH_20_1655.

Watson, Kathryn. "Biden Says There's 'Absolutely' Systemic Racism in Law Enforcement and Beyond." *CBS News*, June 10, 2020. https://www.cbsnews.com/news/joe-biden-systemic-rac-ism-exists-law-enforcement/.

Williams, Joan C., Katherine W. Phillips, and Erika V. Hall. Double Jeopardy? Gender Bias Against Women in Science." WorkLifeLaw, UC Hastings College of the Law, 2014. https://worklifelaw.org/publications/Double-Jeopardy-Report_v6_full_web-sm.pdf.

Wong, Cara. "How Generation Z, As the Multicultural Vanguard, Can Safeguard the Future of America." *Pacific Standard*, April 8, 2019. https://psmag.com/ideas/how-generation-z-as-the-multicultural-vanguard-can-safeguard-the-future-of-america.

Advancing the Four Cases for Diversity Performance

7

The second capability in the Integrated Diversity Model is building the "case" for Diversity Performance. This is the rationale or foundational argument for why the organization should pursue diversity. Building a strong case is important for winning support for diversity initiatives, securing resources and crafting the organization's strategic narrative (Fig. 1).

Today, the business case tends to be the dominant driving force for organizations to pursue diversity. It is often cited by leaders as the rationale for taking action. Certainly, it is a case that has merit: as will be corroborated later in this chapter, diversity has been shown to deliver clear performance benefits such as increased profitability, greater innovation, and better talent attraction and retention. Yet relying solely on the business case is insufficient to meet future challenges. As we argue in this chapter, there are in fact four cases for diversity and leaders are strongly advised to incorporate them all to develop the most compelling strategic diversity narrative.

The four most common cases for diversity in the organization are the legal case, the business case, the ethical case, and the societal case.

The Four Cases for Diversity

Legal Case—This case is built on satisfying legal diversity requirements, such as quotas, affirmative action, minimum representation, etc., such that there are no legal compliance issues and penalties that would result in financial sanction.

Business Case—This case is built on identifying and satisfying the diversity requirements (inherent and/or acquired characteristics) that are linked directly or indirectly to organizational performance such as enhanced financial performance, innovation, engagement, supply of scarce talent, customer satisfaction, etc.

Ethical Case—This case is built on satisfying moral considerations, such as the responsibility to support the universal rights of people to enjoy work and be fairly treated, without discrimination.

© Diversity and Performance BV 2021
K. Formanek, *Beyond D&I*, https://doi.org/10.1007/978-3-030-75336-8_7

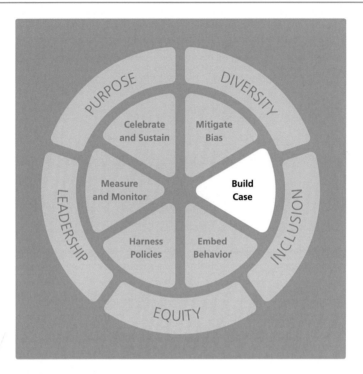

Fig. 1   Build Case
Second Capability of the Integrated Diversity Model.

Societal Case—This case is built on the responsibility of organizations to support social cohesion and equality. Closely linked to the ethical case, for many organizations this materializes in their commitment to Agenda 2030 and the role of inclusion in the SDGs.

Here we explore each of these in turn.

1.   The Legal Case for diversity

The legal case for diversity is built on satisfying legal diversity requirements, such as quotas, affirmative action, minimum representation, etc., such that there are no legal compliance issues and penalties that could result in financial sanction.

Penalties and sanctions—Since the 1960s there has been a steady march to both outlaw and penalize employers for discrimination. In the U.S., Title VII of the Civil Rights Act of 1964 was the first major development in anti-discrimination law, prohibiting discrimination based on race, sex, religion, or national origin, and similar legislation has been adopted by many other nations. This paved the way for employees to sue for employment discrimination if they can prove explicit discrimination, resulting in the obligation for organizations to financially settle back pay, compensatory damages, punitive damages, and/or reinstate the discriminated employee.

As a result of increasing anti-discrimination policy and regulation, organizations have experienced the rising cost of discriminatory practices and behaviors through financial sanctions. In the late 1990s and early 2000s, for example, the financial industry was hit by a number of high-profile lawsuits involving several financial and asset management companies, settling discrimination claims in the hundreds of millions of dollars.[1] Since 2000, 99% of Fortune 500 companies have paid settlements in at least one discrimination or sexual harassment lawsuit, not including the cases without a public record or incidents victims did not report.[2] Fortune 500 companies alone have paid out nearly $2 billion (in disclosed penalties) since 2000.[3] Discrimination suits attract bad publicity and media coverage, with a consequential impact on brand, goodwill, and customer and employee loyalty. In this regard, the legal and business cases are closely interrelated.

Quotas—In addition to the avoidance of lawsuits and financial sanctions, there are other legal drivers for diversity. Quotas have been used as an important means to encourage more diversity in organizations, in particular to advance gender diversity on boards. Quotas may be hard (leading to a sanction if quota not fulfilled) or soft (recommended percentage of women, but no sanction). Norway is an example of a hard quota, being the first nation in the world in 2003 to adopt a gender quota requiring a 40% female board representation in public limited and state-owned companies. The legislation was implemented in 2006, with full compliance required by 2008. There were more than 480 public limited companies affected by the quota who faced potential forced liquidation for non-compliance. The quota had its intended effect, resulting in a marked increase of women on boards from approximately six percent in 2002 to 40% in 2008.[4]

A number of European countries have since enacted law on board quotas, including Belgium, France, Germany, Iceland, Italy, the Netherlands, Spain, and Sweden, as well as Israel and India. France, for example, adopted in 2011 the French Gender Quota Law, the Copé Zimmermann, requiring all listed and non-listed companies with revenues or total assets of over EUR 50 million or employing over 500 persons for three consecutive years to reach a gender quota of 40% by 2017, with a first step of 20% by 2014. If there is non-compliance, the appointment of new directors is considered null and void.[5]

---

[1] Dobbin and Kalev (2016).

[2] Big Business Bias: Employment Discrimination and Sexual Harassment at Large Corporations, Good Jobs First.org, January 2019, https://www.goodjobsfirst.org/sites/default/files/docs/pdfs/BigBusinessBias.pdf.

[3] Hirsh (2019).

[4] Improving gender diversity in corporate boards, International Labour Organisation, 2019, https://www.ilo.org/wcmsp5/groups/public/---ed_dialogue/---act_emp/documents/briefingnote/wcms_754631.pdf.

[5] Improving gender diversity in corporate boards, International Labour Organisation

Whether a hard or soft quota, it has driven increased scrutiny of organizations regarding how they are delivering on the intended outcome of the quota, and this often impacts goodwill. Poor quota scores impact customer loyalty, reduce access to scarce talent, and undermine employee engagement. Organizations also need to satisfy laws where they are required to address underrepresentation or disadvantage.

Positive or affirmative action—this consists of targeted steps to address underrepresentation or disadvantage such as having a requirement to have the employee population reflect the national country population. It is utilized in countries such as South Africa, where historic laws (such as apartheid) led to deep socio-economic inequity.

Affirmative action in South Africa is defined in the Employment Equity Act No. 55 of 1998 ("the Act") as: "Measures designed to ensure that suitably qualified people from designated groups have equal employment opportunities and are equitably represented in all occupational categories and levels in the workforce of a designated employer." Designated groups refer to Black people, women, and people with disabilities. Section 6(2) of the Act also states that it is not unfair discrimination to take affirmative action measures consistent with the purposes of the Act.[6]

In conclusion, the legal case for diversity comprises the dual imperatives of anti-discrimination compliance and the desire to avoid significant financial risk of legal sanction on the one hand, and the proactive implementation of quotas and affirmative action to support diversity on the other. It is closely connected to the business case.

2. The Business Case for diversity

At a typical diversity award event, acceptance speeches reveal a common refrain about the importance of pursuing the business case for diversity: performance is top-of-mind for the business case-driven leader.

Extracts from Speeches Delivered at a Diversity Award Event, Regarding the Question "Why is Diversity Important to Your Organization?"

It is clear there is a business case for diversity in our organization. We believe that by increasing the share of women and other minorities in our organization, that we will deliver more performance to our shareholders and stakeholders.

We believe that diversity allows us to deliver the performance that our shareholders expect from us: more growth, more profit, more expansion. Without diversity we are unable to

---

[6] Affirmative Action and the Employment Equity Act, The South African Labour Guide, accessed March 4, 2021, https://www.labourguide.co.za/most-recent/2167-affirmative-action-and-.

deliver on our performance objectives. As a result, we have created a clear business case for diversity that serves to convince our people that diversity is important.

I will admit that I was originally a skeptic: how did diversity precisely fit into an organization that is focused on delivering outstanding performance? Yet, I am convinced now. We are able to identify key performance outcomes that can be attributed to us having a diverse workforce.

Yet, as exemplified in the "BOLD Initiative" case study discussed below, drawing on work done in the 1990s, one of the challenges facing diversity research when it comes to the business case is that it can be difficult to decipher if there is a causal link (causality) between diversity and performance outcomes or simply a relationship or pattern (correlation). Causation means that one event causes another event to occur, while correlation means there is a relationship or pattern between the values of two variables.

Case Study: The BOLD Initiative: Finding the case for diversity

The desire to definitively prove a link between diversity and improved business performance led to the launch in the mid-1990s of the Business Opportunities for Leadership Diversity (BOLD) Initiative. This was a group of industry chief executives and human resource professionals who came together to understand how to leverage their organizations' cultural diversity for competitive advantage.

An initial study by the group found that no organizations were collecting the necessary data to assess the effects of diversity practices on company performance. In 1997, therefore, the BOLD Initiative asked a group of researchers from a cross-section of universities to design a large-scale field research project to examine the relationships between gender and racial diversity and business performance in four large firms committed to building a diverse workforce and managing diversity effectively. The outcome of that five-year project was shared in a seminal academic research paper based on primary research: "The Effects of Diversity on Business Performance: Report of the Diversity Research Network."

One of the more notable parts of the research describes a meeting in which the CEO of Hewlett Packard stated that providing evidence to support claims of improved performance with increased diversity would accelerate the rate of progress employers would make in hiring and developing a more diverse workforce. It would also produce organizations that are more fully integrated across occupations and levels of hierarchy.[7]

The CEO summarized what he saw as the three main points to make the business case for diversity. This included a talent shortage that meant the company needed to seek out and use the full capabilities of its employees; a more diverse workforce that better reflected their customers' diversity, and thus an enhanced ability

---

[7] T. Kochan et al., "The Effects of Diversity on Business Performance: Report of the Diversity Research Network."

to communicate with customers and reflect their concerns, and finally, that diverse teams produce better results. As the CEO noted, "This last point is not as easy to sell as the first two—especially to engineers who want the data. What I need is the data, evidence that diverse groups do better."[8]

As the report concluded, best practices for demonstrating the business case for diversity included ensuring that formal policies supported and reinforced diversity objectives. Further, the research underscored the importance and value of organization-wide, diversity-sensitive managerial strategies, human resource policies, and organizational cultures.

But no matter the industry context, specific practices, or performance examined, quantitative results were "strikingly similar," the BOLD research found: "There were few direct effects of diversity on performance—either positive or negative. Our findings suggest that, as we expected, this is likely because context is crucial in determining the nature of diversity's impact on performance. Conditions that exacerbated racial diversity's negative effects on performance included a highly competitive context among teams. Finally, there was some promising evidence to suggest that, under certain conditions, racial diversity may even enhance performance, namely when organizations foster an environment that promotes learning from diversity."[9]

▶ **Key takeaway** While the BOLD Initiative failed to show a conclusive linkage between diversity and performance, it did offer guidance for leaders on the importance of taking an analytical and performance-based approach. It also provided a call to action for other scholarly researchers and business organizations to further their efforts to create a definitive business case for diversity.

1   What We Know About the Link Between Diversity and Business Performance

Research has identified a number of key performance outcomes related to an increased presence of diversity, mostly measured on inherent diversity characteristics such as gender, ethnicity and age, and/or on acquired diversity characteristics such as specialization and multicultural experience:

---

[8] T. Kochan et al., "The Effects of Diversity on Business Performance: Report of the Diversity Research Network."

[9] T. Kochan et al., "The Effects of Diversity on Business Performance: Report of the Diversity Research Network."

Business Case Diversity Outcomes

Financial performance—more diversity is linked to higher profitability and/or increased return on investment (ROI) and/or higher return on equity (ROE), and/or increased revenue growth.

Customer congruence—more diversity is linked to more satisfied customers and/or more loyal customers.

Innovation—more diversity is linked to higher innovation and creativity, as evidenced by higher revenue percentage coming from new/innovative products and services.

Employee engagement—more diversity is linked to happier employees, more engaged employees, more loyal employees, less sick employees, and the improved ability to tap into scarce resources.

Decision-making—more diversity is linked to better decision-making, such as risk management, lower occurrence of fraud, better functioning boards.

Link to financial performance—Research has shown correlational evidence for the link between greater diversity and higher financial performance:

- **Profitability**
    - Organizations with top quartile gender diversity on boards were 28% more likely to outperform on profitability.[10]
    - Organizations in the top quartile of diversity in terms of women in senior executive roles were 21% more likely to have above-average profitability than companies in the fourth quartile of gender diversity.[11]
    - Organizations in the top quartile of diversity in terms of ethnicity and culture in senior executive roles were 33% more likely to have above-average profitability than companies in the fourth quartile of ethnic and cultural diversity.[12]

- **Higher cashflows**
    - Organizations in which women held 20% or more management roles generated 2.04% higher cash flow returns on investment than companies with 15% or less women in management roles.[13]

---

[10] Diversity wins: How inclusion matters, McKiney & Company, May 2020, https://www.mckinsey.com/~/media/mckinsey/featured%20insights/diversity%20and%20inclusion/diversity%20wins%20how%20inclusion%20matters/diversity-wins-how-inclusion-matters-vf.ashx.

[11] Delivering Through Diversity, McKinsey & Company, January 2018, https://www.mckinsey.com/~/media/mckinsey/business%20functions/organization/our%20insights/delivering%20through%20diversity/delivering-through-diversity_full-report.ashx.

[12] Delivering Through Diversity, McKinsey & Company.

[13] CS Gender 3000 report shows one fifth of board positions globally now held by women, Credit Suisse, October 10, 2019, https://www.credit-suisse.com/about-us-news/en/articles/media-releases/cs-gender-3000-report-shows-one-fifth-of-board-positions-globall-201910.html.

- **Longer-term value creation**
  - Corporations that embraced gender diversity on their executive teams were more competitive and 21% more likely to experience above-average profitability. They also had a 27% likelihood of outperforming their peers on longer-term value creation.[14]

Link to customer congruence and customer satisfaction—There are compelling reasons why a diverse workforce better serves a diverse customer base. Organizations that succeed in creating inclusive and diverse environments lead to a 31% uplift in employees' responsiveness to customer needs. This responsiveness translates to more satisfied customers and more loyal customers, increasing the lifetime value.[15] Also organizations are increasingly recognizing customer affiliation and understanding requires diversity of talent. Sixty-two percent of all new cars sold in the U.S. are bought by women, according to research from Cars.com, which also found that women influence more than 85% of all car purchases.[16] Now automakers that may have once struggled to connect with female buyers are increasingly looking to tap into this market by appointing women engineers to be in charge of SUVs and pickup trucks. Dealerships are actively recruiting female sales associates.[17]

Link to innovation—Organizations experience higher levels of revenue from innovation with higher diversity. One important survey of 1,700 companies in eight countries (the U.S., France, Germany, China, Brazil, India, Switzerland, and Austria) found a correlation between organizations with diversity and innovation. It looked at different industries and company sizes, taking into account diversity in management positions, using the metrics of gender, age, national origin, career path, industry background, and education. The percentage of revenues arising from products launched in the previous three years was used as a proxy for innovation impact. Innovative companies were assumed to be those with fresher product portfolios, and these, too, turned out to be more profitable. The survey found a statistically significant relationship between diversity and innovation outcomes in all countries examined.

In fact, the more dimensions of diversity that were represented, the stronger the relationship between diversity and innovation. For example, companies with above-average total diversity, measured as the average of six dimensions of diversity (migration, industry, career path, gender, education, age), had 19% higher innovation revenues and nine percent higher EBIT margins, on average. As the study found, all six dimensions of diversity had statistically significant correlations with innovation, both individually and collectively, although industry, nation of

---

[14] Delivering Through Diversity, McKinsey & Company.

[15] Waiter, is that inclusion in my soup? A new recipe to improve business performance, Deloitte, May 2013, https://www2.deloitte.com/content/dam/Deloitte/au/Documents/human-capital/deloitte-au-hc-diversity-inclusion-soup-0513.pdf.

[16] Newman (2019).

[17] Korn (2019).

origin, and gender had slightly larger effects. The impacts of different dimensions of diversity were mostly additive, although educational background/age and career path/industry, were somewhat correlated. The conclusion was that a broad-based approach to diversity that values multiple aspects of diversity is most likely to benefit an organization's innovation outcomes.[18]

Link to talent pool access—Organizations that focus on diversity and have instituted gender-friendly policies and practices, leads to enhanced employee recruitment success and lower levels of employee turnover. Research has also shown evidence for the link between greater diversity and increased talent recruitment and retention. Studies show a correlation between the focus of an organization on diversity and their ability to recruit and retain talent.[19] Further, organizations that have more gender diversity and have also developed gender-friendly policies and practices are correlated to lower levels of employee turnover.[20]

Link to employee engagement and loyalty—Organizations that invest in initiatives that support the feeling of inclusion and lead to an inclusive climate have the benefit of higher employee satisfaction, more engagement, and higher employee commitment. Employee experiences of inclusion contribute to engagement and retention; indeed, 35% of an employee's emotional investment to their work and 20% of their desire to stay at their organization is linked to feelings of inclusion.[21] Organizations with strong "diversity climates" (i.e., inclusive work cultures characterized by appreciation of individual differences and the adoption of practices to advance underrepresented groups) are likely to **increase employees' job satisfaction and commitment to the company.**[22] Strong diversity climates are also associated with reduced instances of interpersonal aggression and discrimination. [23] Further, women experience less discrimination and sexual harassment in inclusive workplace cultures.[24]

Link to good decision-making—There is an increasing focus on women on boards in response to quotas and also because gender-diverse boards are shown to have better decision-making. Research shows that gender-diverse corporate boards are associated with more effective risk management practices, increased engagement among board members, fewer controversial business practices, and a higher

---

[18] Lorenzo and Reeves (2018).

[19] Juan M. Madera et al., Top Management Gender Diversity and Organizational Attraction: When and Why It Matters, *Archives of Scientific Psychology*, 7, no. 1, 90–101, http://dx.doi.org/10.1037/arc0000060

[20] Maurer and Qureshi (2021).

[21] Report: Getting Real About Inclusive Leadership, Catalyst, November 21, 2019, https://www.catalyst.org/research/inclusive-leadership-report/.

[22] McCallaghan et al. (2019).

[23] Perry and Li (2020).

[24] Yu and Lee (2020).

propensity to invest in higher-quality audits. For example, adding women to a board can improve investment efficiency and prevent risky overinvestment decisions.[25] Having women on the board reduced the incidence of fraud,[26] and earnings manipulation.[27] Organizations often aim to have a minimum of 30% women on boards and reaching gender parity on boards to provide the best chances to drive excellent board performance.

Whether by correlation or causation, these research findings indicate that there are links between diversity and better business performance. However, the traditional business case is not the only reason why organizations choose to pursue greater diversity—there are ethical and societal reasons, too.

3.　The Ethical Case for diversity

The ethical case for diversity is built on satisfying moral considerations, such as the responsibility to support the universal right of people to enjoy work and be fairly treated, without discrimination.

Fundamental human rights principles are universal—The ethical case is closely connected to the principle of universal human rights, which is a powerful business imperative. Since 2000, with the introduction of the UN Global Compact's ten principles[28] and especially since the introduction of the "Protect, Respect and Remedy" framework for business and human rights through the 2008 Ruggie Report,[29] there has been growing momentum for business to demonstrate responsible corporate citizenship and ethical business practices, including rights-based diversity and inclusion. In 2011, the UN Human Rights Council endorsed the UN Guiding Principles on Business and Human Rights (UNGPs) developed by John Ruggie, which set out 31 principles to prevent and address human rights risks arising from business activities.[30]

When discriminatory practices are challenged, the first recourse is often an ethical one founded on the universal principle of equal opportunity—for example a case setting out why each person should have the right to pursue work and be

---

[25] Shin et al. (2020).

[26] Wahid (2019).

[27] Fan et al. (2019).

[28] The Ten Principles of the UN Global Compact, https://www.unglobalcompact.org/what-is-gc/mission/principles, accessed March 20, 2021.

[29] Protect, Respect and Remedy: A Framework for Business and Human Rights, Report of the Special Representative of the Secretary General on the issue of human rights and transnational corporations and other business enterprises, John Ruggie, Human Rights Council, April 7, 2008, https://media.business-humanrights.org/media/documents/files/reports-and-materials/Ruggie-report-7-Apr-2008.pdf.

[30] https://en.wikipedia.org/wiki/United_Nations_Guiding_Principles_on_Business_and_Human_Rights.

treated fairly. This fundamental principle of non-discrimination as a human right is enshrined in the landmark Universal Declaration of Human Rights (UDHR), adopted by the United Nations in 1948, where the right to equal work conditions was accepted as a global principle.[31] The UDHR has since become the foundation for all anti-discrimination legislation, codes, and conventions.

Profile of a Courageous Leader

Eleanor Roosevelt

A champion of human rights, Eleanor Roosevelt played a pivotal role in establishing the Universal Declaration of Human Rights (UDHR) for which she received the UN General Assembly's first standing ovation for a single debate when the UDHR was passed in Paris on December 10, 1948 as a common standard of achievement for all peoples and all nations.[32, 33] It set out, for the first time, fundamental human rights to be universally protected.

Article 23 in the UDHR sets out the right of each human being to work, as follows[34]:

1. Everyone has the right to work, to free choice of employment, to just and favorable conditions of work and to protection against unemployment.
2. Everyone, without any discrimination, has the right to equal pay for equal work.
3. Everyone who works has the right to just and favorable remuneration ensuring for himself and his family an existence worthy of human dignity, and supplemented, if necessary, by other means of social protection.
4. Everyone has the right to form and to join trade unions for the protection of his interests.

It marked the first time the world had come together to agree on a set of fundamental freedoms for all people on earth. Today the UDHR is the most translated document in the world, available in 500 languages.[35] It is viewed as a moral guide for the UN and people around the world.

But when Eleanor Roosevelt entered the UN just a few years prior to this historic event, she was concerned that she wouldn't earn respect from her colleagues or be taken seriously as she didn't possess a college degree and was often the only woman

---

[31] United Nations, Universal Declaration of Human Rights, accessed December 17, 2020, https://www.un.org/en/universal-declaration-human-rights/#:~:text=Drafted%20by%20representatives%20with%20different,all%20peoples%20and%20all%20nations.

[32] United Nations, Universal Declaration of Human Rights.

[33] Gardner (1998).

[34] Article 23 of the Universal Declaration of Human Rights, accessed December 17, 2020, https://www.humanrights.com/course/lesson/articles-19-25/read-article-23.html.

[35] United Nations Foundation, "How One Woman Changed Human Rights History," December 10, 2018, https://medium.com/@unfoundation/how-one-woman-changed-human-rights-history-84fd8f67d54b.

in the room; in fact, she was the only woman in the U.S. delegation to the UN.[36] But as an outspoken activist for women's rights and social justice, Roosevelt was not daunted. She wielded her diplomatic skills as chair of the Human Rights Commission which developed the Declaration, resolving tensions among its members, and ensuring that the Commission represented a wide range of culture and beliefs.[37] Roosevelt has been called by UN Assistant Secretary-General for Human Rights Andrew Gilmour "the quintessential multilateralist, looking beyond her national interests and recognizing that certain values and interests transcend national agendas."[38]

In one of her last speeches, Roosevelt famously asked, "Where, after all, do universal human rights begin? In small places, close to home—so close and so small that they cannot be seen on any maps of the world. Yet they are the world of the individual person; the neighborhood he lives in; the school or college he attends; the factory, farm or office where he works. Such are the places where every man, woman and child seeks equal justice, equal opportunity, equal dignity without discrimination. Unless these rights have meaning there, they have little meaning anywhere. Without concerned citizen action to uphold them close to home, we shall look in vain for progress in the larger world."[39]

Actual human rights protections still vary—Three quarters of a century after the adoption of the UDHR, much work remains to be done to ensure these basic human rights. Many leaders assume outright discrimination in employment and other areas to be largely resolved—but that is not the case.

Multiple countries still either do not offer statutory protection against discrimination in work or offer only very limited discrimination protection. According to the 2019 World Bank report "Women, Busines and the Law," which measured gender discrimination in 187 countries, as little as a decade ago, no country gave women equal legal rights. By 2019, only Belgium, Denmark, France, Latvia, Luxembourg, and Sweden had enshrined gender equality in laws affecting work.[40]

Other countries protect against *direct discrimination* but not *indirect discrimination*, as defined below:

- **Direct discrimination** occurs when somebody is treated unfairly because of a protected attribute. For example, someone is not offered a promotion for being a woman and the job goes to a less qualified man.
- **Indirect discrimination** occurs when a policy of an employer or organization applies to everybody but results in people with certain protected characteristics

---

[36] United Nations Foundation, "How One Woman Changed Human Rights History.".

[37] United Nations Foundation, "How One Woman Changed Human Rights History."

[38] Chandler Green, "70 Years of Impact: Insights on the Universal Declaration of Human Rights," The United Nations Foundation, https://unfoundation.org/blog/post/70-years-of-impact-insights-on-the-universal-declaration-of-human-rights/.

[39] Madeline Branch (2015).

[40] https://openknowledge.worldbank.org/bitstream/handle/10986/35094/9781464816529.pdf.

(e.g., race or gender) being put at a disadvantage. For example, under the work contract the worker is required to travel internationally at short notice. This may prejudice working mothers from satisfying this job requirement in countries where a woman is considered to have primary responsibility for taking care of children.

LGBTQI+citizens in particular generally have limited or highly restrictive rights in much of the Middle East and face hostility in other parts of the globe. According to the 2020 report on state-sponsored homophobia from the International Lesbian, Gay, Bisexual, Trans, and Intersex Association (ILGA), there are six countries where the death penalty for homosexuality is legal (three of them in the Middle East): Brunei, Iran, Mauritania, Nigeria (12 northern states), Saudi Arabia, and Yemen.[41] There are an additional five countries where the death penalty may be imposed: Afghanistan, Pakistan, Qatar, Somalia, and the United Arab Emirates.[42]

Even Japan has yet to enact anti-discrimination legislation on the grounds of sexual orientation and gender identity, despite nearly 100 civic groups signing a letter in 2020 to then Prime Minister Shinzo Abe urging him to act.[43] As of the writing of the book, there is increasing pressure for Japan to do more to support gender advancement and mitigate ongoing systemic gender bias.

Voluntary responsible business practice—This wide global variation in human rights protection has a direct bearing on diversity and inclusion practices. It is one of the reasons why many multinational companies adopt "one entity" standards, i.e., universal policies and practices that apply wherever they do business. These are often founded upon recognized global standards and principles such as those embodied in the UDHR. Such principles may not be legally enshrined in the countries or markets where the firms operate, but they choose to go "beyond compliance" and implement them as part of a responsible business or "corporate social responsibility" approach. This is seen by many leaders as not only the "right" thing to do, but a prudent way to avoid reputational risk, playing into the business case. It is also closely linked to the fourth case, the societal case for diversity.

4.   The Societal Case for diversity

The societal case for diversity is built on the responsibility of organizations to support broader social cohesion and equality. For many organizations this is manifested in their support for the 2030 Agenda and the importance that inclusion and equality hold across the 17 SDGs.

---

[41] ILGA World Updates State-Sponsored Homophobia Report: "There's Progress in Times of Uncertainty," ILGA, December 15, 2020, https://ilga.org/ilga-world-releases-state-sponsored-homophobia-December-2020-update.

[42] ILGA World Updates State-Sponsored Homophobia Report, ILGA.

[43] "Japan: Introduce LGBT Non-Discrimination Law," Human Rights Watch, May 15, 2020, https://www.hrw.org/news/2020/05/15/japan-introduce-lgbt-non-discrimination-law.

Organizations are a reflection of their external environments and the broader systemic behaviors and belief systems that can result in discrimination and the perpetuation of inequality and inequity. In parallel with efforts to prove the business case for diversity, since the early 1990s there has been growing focus on how diversity is not only important for organizations and supporting anti-discrimination legislation, but a critical ingredient to a cohesive society. The World Summit for Social Development in Copenhagen in 1995 defined an inclusive society as:

> A 'society for all' in which every individual, each with rights and responsibilities, has an active role to play (United Nations, 1995, para 66). Such an inclusive society is equipped with mechanisms which accommodate diversity and facilitate/enable people's active participation in their political, economic and social lives. As such, it overrides differences of race, gender, class, generation, and geography, and ensures equal opportunities for all to achieve full potential in life, regardless of origin. Such a society fosters, at the same time, the wellbeing of each individual, mutual trust, sense of belonging and inter-connectedness.[44]

The societal case for diversity is closely connected to the ethical case but on a larger scale. It is deeply rooted in the concept of diversity being a feature of all societies, as reflected in the value of multiculturalism, for example, and that it should be embraced through the value of respect. The focus is on embracing societal diversity in order to release its potential to create richer, more cohesive, and diverse economies and communities that are characterized by less conflict and more sustainability as a whole. It is widely recognized that businesses and institutions as a whole cannot thrive in societies that fail,[45] so contributing to cohesion and societal wellbeing is also ultimately in the organization's enlightened self-interest. Leadership under the societal case becomes about going beyond compliance and toward excellence in all spheres—governance, environmental protection, stakeholder satisfaction, and the wellbeing of society as a whole.

The UN 2030 Agenda is a powerful example of how the societal case for diversity and inclusion can be translated into a core business agenda.

2   The Importance of a Multi-Case Approach for Diversity

While leaders today are more confident speaking about the business case for diversity, many still struggle to create a strong holistic narrative around the conditions for realizing Diversity Performance in their organizations and articulating the societal return from their diversity investments, as illustrated by the following excerpt from an interview with a leader being queried about the business case.

---

[44] Social Inclusion, United Nations Department of Economic and Social Affairs, accessed December 17, 2020, https://www.un.org/development/desa/socialperspectiveondevelopment/issues/social-integration.html.

[45] https://www.greenbiz.com/article/paul-polman-businesses-cannot-succeed-societies-fail

Extract from an Executive Interview Regarding Questions on the Business Case for Diversity:

What is the leading rationale for you pursuing diversity within your organization?

We pursue diversity because we are convinced that we are more successful with diversity than without diversity.

Could you explain which diversity benefits you obtain from diversity in your organization?

We believe that with more diversity we are more innovative, and that we have better decision-making in our leadership ranks. This allows us to be more competitive, while delivering on our growth objectives. This is good for business.

Have you been able to measure this uplift in innovation and better decision-making as a result of increased diversity? if so, how do you do this?

No, we rely on supporting research that other institutions are doing. We have not baselined this for ourselves. However, our sense is that we are having different types of discussion in the leadership ranks because of the presence of women.

If you sprinkle more gender and minority diversity within your organization, do you get a direct and additional uplift in performance from this additional diversity?

I can't answer that concretely. But I suspect that is the case.

Are there circumstances when the business case does not work for you? Namely, when you add more gender and minority diversity, without return or negative return to your performance?

I'm sure there must be situations where this is the case, but I am unable to reply concretely to this question.

Do you believe that the business case motivation for diversity in your organization is effective in obtaining buy-in and support for diversity?

I believe that the business case motivation is very helpful. It is not a soft measure; it is the language of our leaders and the language of our shareholders. Quite simply, it is easier to motivate the attention and focus and investment in something when there is a clear return on the investment formula.

Is there another case in point you could make that would drive attention and focus and ownership around diversity?

I guess that we could also say that diversity is the right thing to do, but I have learned that what gets people's attention is business performance. That's why we stress this case.

Yet increased diversity does not always translate into business performance. Does that mean that organizations should abandon it? The short answer is no. While a strong business case for diversity is vital, it is even stronger when combined with an ethical and societal rationale.

Diversity Performance is a function of five elements working in concert—selecting the right diversity characteristics to support the strategic narrative of diversity, creating the conditions for an inclusive environment, advancing equity to support the contribution of the full team, providing inclusive and involved leadership, and creating a unifying purpose that serves to direct team effort toward a common goal. Whether this can be captured as a business performance outcome depends on the timeframe over which performance outcomes are measured.

The reality is that a homogeneous team, comprised of members with the same educational background and specialization, may often be more efficient than a diverse team, in the *short term*. From a pure, short-term business case perspective, this could be a reason to avoid diversity. However, over the *long term*, a homogenous group defaults to patterns of thinking that stifle innovation because they are bound by groupthink. Katherine Phillips has led original scholarly primary research in this field (see Profile of a Courageous and Inclusive Leader, Chapter 8) and has found that homogeneous groups are more efficient but lead to groupthink, while heterogenous groups are less efficient but harder working.[46] As the Bank of Ireland case study in Chapter 4 shows, groupthink can be disastrous.

This is where developing a multi-case approach to diversity is useful. This approach tends to take a longer term, more holistic perspective on the many types of value that diversity brings to organizations and society as a whole. It has the benefit of capturing important drivers for diversity and inclusion that a traditional business case approach ignores, and this has led to criticism of the business case as a sole lens for why organizations should pursue diversity.

In one article "The business case for diversity is a sinking ship,"[47] the author writes:

> Under its flashy exterior, 'business case' rhetoric has resulted in an epidemic of misinformed leaders and D&I strategies that don't work. It has created organizations with good diversity optics but plagued with a revolving door of diverse talent and stagnant progress on important D&I issues. The cause: well-meaning advocates and leaders fundamentally misunderstand and misuse the business case for diversity. If we want to right the sinking ship that is the business case for diversity, we need to get over our infatuation with the buzzwords of the 'business case' and actually understand the mechanisms of how diversity actually brings benefits to organizations. We need to resist the pull of performative D&I work, even when it makes good money, and remember that D&I work is rooted in justice, not profit. And finally, we need to learn how to use the 'business case' tactically and sparingly, rather than as a miracle cure for every D&I-related context.[48]"

Another article, "Reframing the Business Case for Diversity: A Values and Virtues Perspective," suggests that focusing on the business case alone is actually associated with displacement of equal opportunities and is unethical:

> because the business case perspective ignores the historically rooted and today still persisting inequalities in society and organizations ... the business case perspective does not constitute an ethical approach to managing diversity.[49]

---

[46] Phillips (2014).

[47] Lily Zheng, "The Business Case for Diversity Is a Sinking Ship," Medium.com, https://medium.com/swlh/the-business-case-for-diversity-is-a-sinking-ship-d7a42d61f884.

[48] Lily Zheng, "The Business Case for Diversity Is a Sinking Ship.

[49] van Dijk et al. (2012).

Building a rationale for diversity that centers squarely on the traditional business case, with a focus on shareholder profit and value, also runs the risk that the diversity focus may be abandoned when performance outcomes are not immediately met. As a result, there has been a growing chorus of support for organizations to pursue more than one case for diversity—indeed to combine all four diversity cases presented in this chapter.

As early as the mid-1990s, researchers concluded that for the business case for diversity to be a powerful lever in supporting Diversity Performance, it was important to:

- move away from the simplistic business case for diversity and define the conditions that are required to capture the benefits of diversity;
- develop a case for diversity that is both business motivated *and* socially motivated; namely, by capturing the value of diversity to the greater society; and to
- improve the rigor in formulating and monitoring the achievement of the business case.[50]

Focusing solely on the business and compliance cases for diversity can actually undermine the very D&I performance that make organizations more competitive in the long run: because the traditional business case tends to be short term and shareholder-centric, it risks undervaluing non-financial success factors that create financial value over time. As discussed in Chapter 2, Millennials and Gen Z—tomorrow's investors, employees, and consumers—also expect organizations and their leaders to focus beyond shareholder profit on a wider purpose that includes supporting more equality, equity, and sustainability. For these stakeholders, diversity must be built on a case that is ethically and societally driven, too.

Ultimately it is when equity is raised collectively—and when organizations are driven with strong leadership and purpose—that diversity and inclusion can flourish and the business benefits of diversity are realized. Combining all cases for diversity helps to create the ground conditions for this to happen.

Next we explore how to construct a multi-case approach to diversity and which case for diversity is required at each stage of Diversity Performance.

3   How to Build the Case for Diversity in Practice

Depending on an organization's Diversity Performance maturity level, the Integrated Diversity Model sets out a range of evidence-based initiatives that can be implemented to build the necessary capabilities to establish a robust rationale for diversity, build the diversity case, allocate investments, and measure the impact of

---

[50]T. Kochan et al., "The Effects of Diversity on Business Performance: Report of the Diversity Research Network."

Table 1 Build Case Capability and Initiatives for Five Stages
Overview of initiatives to build the diversity case at each stage of diversity maturity.

	Stage 1	Stage 2	Stage 3	Stage 4	Stage 5
	Legal Compliance	Stakeholder Requirements	Organizational Performance	Reinvention	Societal Value
Focus	Legal case	Business case Legal case	Business case Legal case	Ethical case Business case Legal case	Societal case Ethical case Business case Legal case
Skills	Developing legal case	Developing business case	Effectiveness of initiatives Maintain case	Investment review effectiveness	Societal impact SDG contribution
Process	Build case Review	Build case Monitor	Assess effectiveness	Review strategic contribution	Societal impact assessment
Responsibilities	Legal	HR and legal; D&I lead	Senior leaders Diversity office	Top leadership	Partner leaders
Metrics	Legal incidents & costs	Stakeholder sanctions	Performance outcomes	Innovation, competitiveness	SDG impact
Technology	Case management	HR	Enterprise	Enterprise & niche	Partner enablement

the diversity case. The full range of initiatives to develop the organization's Build Case capability at every stage of maturity is summarized in Table 1.

4   Stage 1 Organizations: Legal Compliance

At Stage 1, the primary focus is on preventing discrimination lawsuits or legal fallout arising from discriminatory practices. The organization is also focused on satisfying and anticipating quotas and meeting affirmative action requirements (in countries where this is present). Stage 1 organizations tend to focus on the legal case for diversity, which is typically the responsibility of the Legal and Risk Management Office. Building the legal case requires an expert view on legal requirements and sanctions involved for non-compliance. As part of the legal case, it is necessary to quantify the risks and costs associated with non-compliance. Cost is usually evaluated as not only the legal sanction itself, but the cost of internal and external resources, the deflected attention from leadership, and the impact on stakeholders, including reduced customer loyalty, disengaged employees, loss of contracts, etc. Investments are targeted at those initiatives that specifically reduce the risk of discrimination occurring (such as compliance training) and satisfying affirmative action and quota requirements, for example, by recruiting and head-hunting support for specific roles.

5   Stage 2 Organizations: Stakeholder Requirements

At Stage 2, organizations have largely satisfied the capability for supporting zero-discrimination compliance and delivering on the legal case for diversity and now focus on satisfying the minimum expectations of their customers and employees. As a reminder, Stage 2 organizations prioritize satisfying customers' and employees' expectations and requirements by adopting a minimum set of diversity best practices and activities which might include, for example, support for Employee Resource Groups (ERGs). As a result, while the legal case focus remains, HR, Customer Relations, and Marketing will at this stage typically focus on identifying the top requirements of employees and customers in relation to diversity representation and inclusion activities. The business case in Stage 2 organizations incorporates the investments needed to satisfy these requirements; the consequence of not satisfying the requirements is also evaluated.

6   Stage 3 Organizations: Organizational Performance

At Stage 3, the focus shifts to building a business case for diversity forged on the conviction that diversity in the organization will impact performance outcomes. The organization identifies a number of strategic business goals, such as increased customer satisfaction and more satisfied employees and identifies the diversity initiatives that, together, will support this desired performance outcome. Stage 3 organizations are required to baseline the selected strategic business goals to reflect a baseline of current performance and measure the impact on the baseline of targeted investments. At a minimum, Stage 3 organizations are advised to define clear strategic performance outcomes, baseline their current performance, identify the milestones in improving the performance outcome, link initiatives directly to satisfying the performance outcome, and evaluate if the performance outcome and a return on its investment in initiatives have been achieved.

7   Stage 4 Organizations: Reinvention

At Stage 4, the objective is to expand on the performance case, with an additional focus on not only satisfying the performance objectives but evaluating whether the diversity initiatives are supporting the organization's need to transform with the market, to innovate and remain relevant to its consumers and to achieve the best decision-making to manage risk and harness opportunities. At this stage, the nature of the business case for diversity has evolved to a different level of richness and detail. It requires deliberate and systematic evaluation of whether the elements of performance characteristics, inclusive behaviors, advancement of equity, leadership, and purpose are optimally enabled, and whether the right capabilities and initiatives are in place. Usually, the business case is a multi-disciplinary effort, sometimes residing with the Diversity Office, but with a direct line to the financial, human resources, marketing, and innovation areas to prepare a robust case and obtain the necessary inputs and baselines. While the focus is on developing the business case, there is continued support of the legal case as well as a new focus on building the ethical case for Diversity Performance. The latter is a consequence of needing to advance equity within the organization to support the Diversity Performance requirements.

8   Stage 5 Organizations: Societal Value

At Stage 5, focus shifts from internal transformation of the organization to supporting diversity outcomes in the wider value chain and partner ecosystem, as well as making a direct contribution to society. The organization emphasizes a business case that embraces the societal case for diversity. Societal outcomes that are important to the organization are identified and Diversity Performance outcomes are directly linked to these societal objectives. Organizations at this stage may use the framework of the 2030 Agenda to define success. Many Stage 5 organizations are already linking their Diversity Performance outcomes to one or more of the SDGs, such as Goal 5: "Achieve gender equality and empower all women and girls" and its underlying targets—for example SDG 5.5: "ensure women's full and effective participation and equal opportunities for leadership at all levels of decision-making in political, economic and public life." Similarly, organizations can work toward contributing to Goal 8: "Promote inclusive and sustainable economic growth, employment and decent work for all," target 8.5: "by 2030, achieve full and productive employment and decent work for all women and men, including for young people and persons with disabilities, and equal pay for work of equal value."[51]

9   Evaluating the Diversity Case Focus

Leaders seeking an initial understanding of which diversity case they have in focus may find Table 2 valuable.

An analysis of Table 2 reveals the following:

- All organizations, from Stage 1: Legal Compliance to Stage 5: Societal Value, are required to support the ethical motivations for diversity as stated in the UN Human Rights Charter of 1948 and ensure there is zero tolerance for discrimination in their organization.
- All organizations, from Stage 1: Legal Compliance to Stage 5: Societal Value, are required to support legislation that prohibits discrimination—this should be incorporated in the case for all organizations.

---

[51] UN Sustainable Development Goals, https://www.un.org/sustainabledevelopment/economic-growth/, accessed March 14, 2021.

Table 2 **Typical Statements per Diversity Case**
Common assessment dimensions for constructing an integrated case for diversity.

Case/Stage	Typical statements per diversity case
Legal	We strive to be compliant to all current diversity regulation.
	We anticipate and ready ourselves to satisfy expected new diversity regulation.
	We suggest additional diversity legislation to be passed so as to promote diversity more broadly.
	We define internal (quota, representation) rules for ourselves, ahead of diversity legislation.
Business	We have identified the diversity characteristics that provide an uplift in performance for our context.
	We have identified the effectiveness of initiatives in supporting diversity performance.
Ethical	We ground our diversity focus in the right of every human being to partake in work in a safe and non-discriminatory environment.
	We link the practice of diversity to the values that are important to us such as equality, equity, respect and safety.
	We institute a zero-tolerance policy for any form of discrimination.
	We speak as leaders about our personal and ethical conviction about the importance of diversity and the ethical case for diversity.
Societal	We described how the diversity in our organization contributes to a better and more inclusive society.
	We have connected our diversity targets to one or more of the Sustainable Development Goals in UN Agenda 2030.
	We extend our rationale for the diversity case to our partners and unite our partners in contributing to the societal goal /Agenda 2030

- From Stage 2: Stakeholders Requirements onwards, organizations need to have a clear understanding of the drivers of performance through diversity, articulate this, measure these and connect them to diversity characteristics.
- From Stage 4: Reinvention, organizations need to have a keen view of how to frame the diversity case for business model transformation and resilience.
- From Stage 5: Societal Value, there needs to be a case for diversity that is also deeply anchored within the societal case for diversity and attached to societal objectives, such as the SDGs.

Anticipate Future Required Capabilities for Diversity Performance Through An Integrated Diversity Case

The strongest strategic diversity narratives will be built on an understanding of the legal, business, ethical, and societal rationales for diversity. Without clarity around the benefits of taking a holistic approach to diversity, it is difficult to appreciate the organization's strategic diversity drivers and the potential transformational opportunities of the diversity journey may be missed. While at the early stages of diversity maturity there may be good reasons to restrict the organization to a single, tightly focused case, this will ultimately make it difficult for the organization to evolve, compromising its diversity purpose.

Adopting an integrated case for diversity does not mean leaders should abandon the business case for diversity—on the contrary it is important for every organization to continue to work toward tangible business benefits through Diversity

Performance. But in light of changing stakeholder expectations, to futureproof the organization it is key to create a narrative around diversity that encompasses the ethical and societal cases for diversity, too. Organizations that anchor their focus, ambition, and narrative in all four cases will not only resonate deeply with stakeholders, but will benefit from the potency of a stronger case for diversity to build support, drive success, and sustain momentum.

When the case for diversity is multifaceted and reinforcing, it becomes stronger and more compelling. Moreover it delivers more benefits to more stakeholders, yielding business benefits and compliance outcomes while satisfying stakeholder expectations and contributing to much-needed societal change. Building a strong, multi-dimensional case for diversity also makes it easier for the leader to address and onboard all parts of the organization, using appropriate language and arguments and serves to remind the team why they should work together to ensure diversity "sticks." Setting out a convincing and inclusive case for diversity is a key foundation for embedding inclusive behaviors in the organization.

10   Concluding Remarks

This chapter outlines four primary cases, or reasons, for leading diversity within the organization—the business case, the legal case, the ethical case, and the societal case. Each case, or rationale, emphasizes distinct organizational diversity benefits and rather than applying only one, leaders are encouraged to advance a combination of all four cases for diversity. This creates the strongest foundation and ensures a more holistic, stakeholder-centered approach.

In Chapter 8 we explore another core capability—the importance of leadership and embedding inclusion in daily behaviors.

References

Dobbin, Frank, and Kalev, Alexandra. "Why Diversity Programs Fail." *Harvard Business Review*, July–August 2016, https://hbr.org/2016/07/why-diversity-programs-fail.

Fan, Yaoyao, Jiang, Yuxiang, Zhang, Xuezhi, and Zhou, Yue. "Women on Boards and Bank Earnings Management: From Zero to Hero." *Journal of Banking & Finance*, 107 (2019), 105607, ISSN 0378–4266. https://doi.org/10.1016/j.jbankfin.2019.105607

Hirsh, Elizabeth. "Do Lawsuits Improve Gender and Racial Equality at Work?" *Harvard Business Review*, November 14, 2019, https://hbr.org/2019/11/do-lawsuits-improve-gender-and-racial-equality-at-work/.

Korn, Morgan. "It's Time for Car Companies to Wake Up: Women Now the Focus of the Industry." ABC News, July 3, 2019. https://abcnews.go.com/Business/time-car-companies-wake-women-now-focus-industry/story?id=64087181.

Lorenzo, Rocio, and Reeves, Martin. "How and Where Diversity Drives Financial Performance," January 30, 2018. https://hbr.org/2018/01/how-and-where-diversity-drives-financial-performance.

Madeline Branch. "10 Inspiring Eleanor Roosevelt Quotes." The United Nations Foundation, November 6, 2015, https://unfoundation.org/blog/post/10-inspiring-eleanor-roosevelt-quotes/#:~:text=%E2%80%9CWhere%2C%20after%20all%2C%20do,or%20office%20where%20he%20work.

Maurer, Cara C., and Qureshi, Israr. "Not Just Good for Her: A Temporal Analysis of the Dynamic Relationship Between Representation of Women and Collective Employee Turnover." *Organization Studies*, 42, no. 1 (2021): 85–107. https://doi.org/10.1177/0170840619875480.

McCallaghan, Sean, Jackson, Leon T. B., and Heyns, Marita M. "Examining the Mediating Effect of Diversity Climate on the Relationship Between Destructive Leadership and Employee Attitudes." *Journal of Psychology in Africa*, 29 (6): 563–569. https://doi.org/10.1080/14330237.2019.1695078.

Newman, Jennifer. "It's True! Women Really Do Shop More …for Cars." Cars.com, May 3, 2019. https://www.cars.com/articles/its-true-women-really-do-shop-more-for-cars-403085/.

Perry, Elissa L., and Li, Aitong. "Diversity Climate in Organizations." *Oxford Research Encyclopedia of Business and Management* (Oxford University Press, 2020)

Phillips, Katherine W. "How Diversity Makes Us Smarter." *Scientific American*, October 1, 2014, https://www.scientificamerican.com/article/how-diversity-makes-us-smarter/.

Richard N. Gardner. "Eleanor Roosevelt's Legacy: Human Rights." *The New York Times*, December 19, 1988, https://www.nytimes.com/1988/12/10/opinion/eleanor-roosevelt-s-legacy-human-rights.html.

Shin, Y. Z., Chang, J. Y., and Jeon, K., et al. "Female Directors on the Board and Investment Efficiency: Evidence from Korea. *Asian Bus Manage* 19 (2020): 438–479. https://doi.org/10.1057/s41291-019-00066-2.

van Dijk, Hans, et al. "Reframing the Business Case for Diversity A Values and Virtues Perspective." *Article in Journal of Business Ethics*, 111, no. 1 (2012) (November): 73–84, ISSN 0167–4544. https://doi.org/10.1007/s10551-012-1434-z.

Yu, H. H., and Lee, D. Gender and Public Organization: A Quasi-Experimental Examination of Inclusion on Experiencing and Reporting Wrongful Behavior in the Workplace. *Public Personnel Management*, 49, no. 1 (2020): 3–28.https://doi.org/10.1177/0091026019836196.

Wahid, A. S. "The Effects and the Mechanisms of Board Gender Diversity: Evidence from Financial Manipulation." *J Bus Ethics* 159 (2019): 705–725. https://doi.org/10.1007/s10551-018-3785-6.

Embedding Inclusion in Daily Behaviors

8

There is no more impactful way to create an inclusive environment than through the behavior, practices, and actions of inclusive leaders. These leaders create a culture-in-motion and are emulated for being outstanding diversity and inclusion role models. Leadership directly impacts Diversity Performance, which is why it is one of the five critical elements in the Virtuous Circle. It can magnify Diversity Performance by contributing to greater engagement, creativity, wellness, and decision-making.

In organizations where leaders are inclusive and provide a safe environment in which people are respected and feel they can more easily collaborate, strong Diversity Performance can drive even more diversity. This in turn leads to more inclusion, advances in equity, and a stronger unifying purpose.

However, when leaders resist diversity, a key element of the Virtuous Circle is missing, and performance suffers as a result. Acquired diversity can become suppressed and stereotyped and individuals within the organization can be made to feel like an out-group. Where this is the case, teams that to all intents and purposes *appear* diverse will actually underperform more homogeneous teams. Worse still, it can create an unsafe or toxic environment, stifle inclusionary practices and inhibit equity, with the result that people become disengaged and may even leave the organization.

This chapter provides the leader with the understanding and the tools to embed inclusive behavior in the organization every day. Embed Behavior Capability is the third capability of the Integrated Diversity Model (Fig. 1).

The qualities of inclusive leaders are presented, along with the characteristics of an inclusive organization and how to realize the Embed Behavior capability. Four case studies illustrate pivotal moments on the path to inclusive leadership: for one organization, how to turn around a toxic environment and for another, how to nurture the behaviors required to achieve greater gender diversity. And the stories of two leaders—Grace and John—are told to exemplify the traits of inclusive

© Diversity and Performance BV 2021
K. Formanek, *Beyond D&I*, https://doi.org/10.1007/978-3-030-75336-8_8

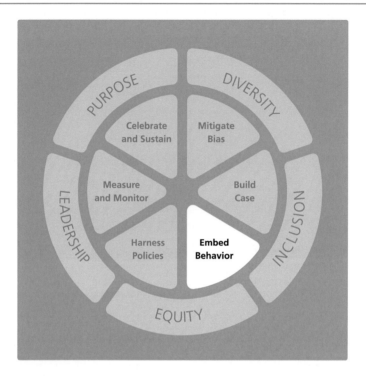

Fig. 1 **Embed Behavior**
Third Capability of the Integrated Diversity Model.

leadership. Leaders will gain key insights on why the Embed Behavior capability is so important to supporting Diversity Performance outcomes and closing diversity gaps in the organization.

1   Lack of Inclusive Leadership Is Costly

Many leaders have the misguided notion that by simply adding diversity characteristics to a team, one can deliver on the societal and business case for diversity. This is not the case. Without inclusive leadership, even the most well-resourced diversity programs are likely to fail. When teams are diverse *and* supported by inclusive leaders, they experience high levels of positive benefits, as a number of primary academic studies confirm.[1] In contrast, in organizations where diversity is simply window-dressing and managers suppress diversity, diverse teams actually perform worse compared to homogeneous teams.[2]

---

[1] Kochan et al. (2003).

[2] Kochan et al., "Effects of Diversity."

Non-inclusive leadership can be costly to organizations, not only financially but in terms of employees' wellbeing, according to recent business research. Disengaged workers have been shown to display 37% more absenteeism, and 60% more errors and defects. Further, in those organizations where employee engagement scored low, productivity dropped by 18%, profitability by 16%, job growth by 37%, and the share price declined 65% over time. In contrast, organizations where employees were highly engaged saw a 100% uptick in job applications.[3]

When workers are disengaged, they are less likely to feel loyal to the organization. Workplace stress, exacerbated by a non-inclusive environment, leads to an increase of almost 50% in voluntary turnover.[4] Disengagement can drive employees to look around for new jobs, turn down promotions or resign. Turnover costs associated with recruiting, training, lowered productivity, lost expertise can be significant.[5] Replacing a single employee can cost approximately 20% of that employee's salary, some studies show.[6]

But when a leader creates an environment of respect and support for diversity, honors workplace dignity and personally sponsors diversity initiatives, it is a different story. Such leaders are regarded as stewards of the values of diversity and inclusiveness. The following case study is illustrative of such a leader.

Case Study: Empowering People to "Grow like a flower in the Sun"

A leader of a fast-growing, successful organization in South Africa, Grace is consistently described by those who know her or have worked for her as a role model in inclusive leadership. She is recognized for providing a safe environment, fostering respect and fairness, personally sponsoring diversity and inclusion, and creating the conditions for collaboration and learning. When people leave the organization, they talk about the impact she has had on their lives: being seen and heard, having a voice, receiving support, and leaving with more confidence than when they joined.

She describes her approach to inclusive leadership as follows: "I would not call it a philosophy; I would call it my values." Grace grew up in South Africa as a person of color but had the privilege to attend a private school. Her mother worked as domestic help and her father as a gardener in the same large home in Sandton, an affluent part of Johannesburg. Since many children were separated from their parents through apartheid policies, Grace felt fortunate that both her parents were employed in the same home. The family who employed her parents saw that Grace was sharp

---

[3] Seppälä and Cameron (2015).

[4] Workplace Stress, the American Institute of Stress, https://www.stress.org/workplace-stress, accessed January 6, 2021.

[5] Seppälä and Cameron, "Proof that Positive Work Cultures Are More Productive."

[6] Boushey and Glynn (2012).

and alert and hungry for knowledge and offered to pay the fees for her to attend private school.

Her mother and father were proud of her but also a little fearful about her leaving the family circle. They worried that Grace might forget her roots and her friends, being immersed in a privileged environment. They gave her some advice: "Never stop seeing your brothers and your sisters in the streets." She interpreted their words to mean: "Never stop having the informal conversations, from your heart, to find out how someone is doing. You have been lucky to have an opportunity; don't forget those who feel they have no opportunities."

These words echoed in her ears during her school years. During lunch breaks, she would take her sandwich into the school gardens and have a friendly discussion with the gardeners. As she returned her plates to the canteen kitchen, she would ask the staff about their family or a sick aunt. She would speak with her fellow students at school, who were seemingly confident and "had it all," with compassion and curiosity and learned that "a person's outside face masks much internal pain."

These informal discussions became part of her life as she completed school and university and made her way into the organization where she now holds a leadership role. She sums up the values and beliefs she gained during her life as follows: "All people have value." From discussions on the playground, in the canteen and during her education, Grace says she learned that "all people have something to say. All people want to be seen. All people want to be heard. And if you take the time for the unique individual, they grow like a flower in the sun. And this is good for the person and also good for the organization."

Grace's perspective reflects a beautiful definition of diversity, sometimes referenced by educational institutions:

The concept of diversity encompasses acceptance and respect. It means understanding that each individual is unique and recognizing our individual differences. These can be along the dimensions of race, ethnicity, gender, sexual orientation, socio-economic status, age, physical abilities, religious beliefs, political beliefs, or other ideologies. It is the exploration of these differences in a safe, positive, and nurturing environment. It is about understanding each other and moving beyond simple tolerance to embracing and celebrating the rich dimensions of diversity contained within each individual.[7]

▶   **Key takeaway** Diversity for Grace was not an abstract term or a concept that was complex to explain. It came down to her values and beliefs that every person is deserving of respect and her curiosity about each person's unique story. This created an environment where people felt valued, safe, and that they were seen and heard.

---

[7] "Definition for Diversity," Queensborough Community College, accessed December 12, 2020, https://www.qcc.cuny.edu/diversity/definition.html.

2   The Traits of Inclusive Leaders

It is valuable for leaders to be clear on the question "*Who* is an inclusive leader?" This question requires a reflection on the individual qualities that support inclusive behaviors. Thinking about the traits of inclusive leadership, the South African phrase *ubuntu*, comes to mind, a Nguni Bantu term meaning "humanity." The phrase was used often by the late Nelson Mandela. *Ubuntu* is all about inclusion—about being warm, welcoming and generous, willing to share, which defines much of Mandela's legacy. But all leaders can aspire to *ubuntu*. It describes leaders with a deep personal commitment to diversity, who value diversity in their own lives, which makes them better able to navigate the journey of inclusiveness. In fact, leaders who have experienced exclusion in their personal life and during their career journey are often more inclusive. Those leaders have felt the emotion of being excluded, of not belonging, and this lived experience makes them more empathetic to others who are similarly excluded.

Research shows that the presence of inclusion within a team or organization depends significantly on leaders; in fact, what leaders say and do can make as much as a 70% difference to an individual's feeling of inclusion.[8] Through a 360-degree assessment of 400 leaders by almost 4,000 individuals rating their leaders, one business study found that a leader's awareness of personal and organization biases to be the number one factor that people cared the most about.[9]

Since leaders have such a significant impact on whether people feel included in an organization, it is valuable to understand those exceptional leadership traits that lead to a sense of inclusion. Research, combined with years of practical experience working with organizations, reveals a number of traits that are often reflected in the most inclusive diversity leaders:

- **Personal commitment to diversity**—Such leaders take the time to think deeply about why diversity is important to them and why the quest for diversity connects to their personal values. They carefully think about their journey in life and why diversity has been meaningful to them. They may have experienced what it is like to be excluded, and inclusion has become an important value for them. As a result, they are naturally motivated to support diversity because it is not an intellectual exercise but rather a personal and emotional process. It is authentic.
- **A conscious leader**—Inclusive leaders are humble; they are consciously aware that they may have unconscious biases or blind spots or a lack of cultural knowledge. They invite others to act as a mirror and play back what the leader does and says, and what one as an individual often does not see. This is a

---

[8] Bourke and Titus (2020).

[9] Bernadette Dillon and Juliet Bourke, "The six signature traits of inclusive leadership."

leader who is curious about people and their blindspots and knows that through understanding comes the possibility for change. Such a leader can take the balcony view: step back in the heat of the moment to see the dynamics of what is happening, with the ability and willingness to adjust one's behavior and inspire others to be mindful, too.

- **A deep listener**—They listen without seeking to confirm what they want to hear, but with the curiosity to challenge and expand their knowledge. They listen with their heart. This means that the listening is not only about themselves, but about the other person. It is listening with compassion and empathy. When one listens in this way, the other person feels seen, heard, and valued. They are genuinely interested in what people have to say and to expand their lens on the world. By listening deeply, they arrive at deeper insights and better solutions.
- **A natural collaborator at heart**—Such a leader creates the circumstances for team cohesion and has an appreciation for the dynamics of psychological safety. This leader is focused on empowering others and has a trust in the team and the experience and insights that they bring to a shared approach.
- **A courageous leader**—An inclusive leader knows that when team members are excluded and bias reigns, equity is not advanced. This leader has the courage of their convictions to step forward and say that something is important, and it must be addressed, even if it is uncomfortable. This leader is prepared to have frank discussions about what might be occurring in the organization and the courage to acknowledge one's own biases and ask others for their feedback. It is the courage to stand up and admit faults, in a spirit of humility and service to the organization.
- **An active driver of diversity**—The inclusive leader does the day-to-day heavy lifting to ensure team members are treated fairly. Such a leader is not passive but strives for continuous improvement, ensuring that they are precipitating actions, initiatives, and serving as sponsor and ally as required. This leader takes ultimate accountability but expects others to be partners in diversity, too.

In short, inclusive leaders realize that inclusion is a journey and not a destination and that the journey starts with themselves, as the *"Lived Experience"* case study in this chapter illustrates. It is only when a leader can deeply reflect on their own diversity and uniqueness that they provide the space for other members of their team and organization to do the same. Such an approach reflects American author Marianne Williamson's quote: "As we let our own light shine, we unconsciously give other people permission to do the same."[10] An inclusive leader is also inclusive to themselves. They dare to bring their whole self to work and by their example invite others to do the same.

---

[10]Williamson (1992).

3   The Bank Account of Trust

To understand the kind of fundamental change required to shift from a non-inclusive environment to an inclusive environment, it helps to lean on the concept of the "emotional bank account" as described in Stephen Covey's seminal leadership book *The Seven Habits of Highly Effective People*.[11] Covey uses the Emotional Bank Account as a metaphor for building relationships of trust. Covey described any relationship-enhancing behavior or action as a "deposit on a bank account" and any relationship-destroying action as a "withdrawal on a bank account."[12] As he wrote:

> We all know what a financial bank account is. We make deposits into it and build up a reserve from which we can make withdrawals when we need to. An Emotional Bank Account is a metaphor that describes the amount of trust that's been built up in a relationship. It's the feeling of safeness you have with another human being.
>
> If I make deposits into an Emotional Bank Account with you through courtesy, kindness, honesty, and keeping my commitments to you, I build up a reserve. Your trust toward me becomes higher, and I can call upon that trust many times if I need to. I can even make mistakes and that trust level, that emotional reserve, will compensate for it. My communication may not be clear, but you'll get my meaning anyway. You won't make me 'an offender for a word.' When the trust account is high, communication is easy, instant, and effective.
>
> But if I have a habit of showing discourtesy, disrespect, cutting you off, overreacting, ignoring you, becoming arbitrary, betraying your trust, threatening you, or playing little tin god in your life, eventually my Emotional Bank Account is overdrawn. The trust level gets very low. Then what flexibility do I have? None. I'm walking on mine fields.[13]

In a non-inclusive environment, many activities can destroy trust and lead to withdrawals from the Emotional Bank Account. At a certain point, the withdrawals lead to a negative balance on the Emotional Bank Account and the organization can no longer function effectively.

Case Study: Lived Experience Enriches the Embed Behavior Capability

As a successful businessman with a successful career profitably turning around businesses, John was for the most part a leader focused on outward actions to foster diversity and inclusion. This included making sure the organization possessed the right talent, setting out a strategic narrative emphasizing the need for diversity of thought, and establishing objectives with his leadership team to create an inclusive environment.

---

[11] Covey (2004).

[12] Covey, *The 7 Habits of Highly Effective People*.

[13] Covey, *The 7 Habits of Highly Effective People*.

However, employees did not truly get a sense of his personal journey and while he oversaw a diverse organization, people would not describe him as an inclusive leader. That all changed when his son was seriously injured in a traffic accident and became confined to a wheelchair. Through that family tragedy, he came to understand in his son's experience, as well as in his role as a father, what it means to be seen as "other" or "different." Diversity was no longer simply a strategic necessity: it had become critical for him personally.

He would tell this story to the organization many years later because the accident initiated the inward work. He began to explore the questions, "Who am I? Why is this important for me personally?" He became not just a good leader but a great leader. The outward and inward roles had converged and created authenticity, inspiration, and credibility.

▶   **Key takeaway** Empathy from lived experience is a powerful force for inclusive leadership.

4   Embedding Inclusive Behaviors Through Leadership

It is important for leaders to understand that when it comes to practicing inclusive behavior, they should set their sights high. Members of the organization are looking for consistency in leadership behavior and when it is consistent, they will emulate the behavior.

A leader cannot be considered inclusive when they are inclusive *on average*. To be rated as an inclusive leader by members of the organization requires day-to-day consistency in inclusive behavior. For example, on a five-point scale (from "strongly agree" to "strongly disagree"), an average rating of 4 out of 5 could mean that some team members assess the leader as inclusive and others do not. It is only when *everyone* agrees or strongly agrees that they are being treated fairly and with respect, are valued, and feel that they belong and are psychologically safe, that the leader can be evaluated as a truly inclusive leader.[14]

When leaders understand that inclusive leadership is not about averages but about consistently demonstrating excellent behaviors, day after day, this becomes a powerful enabler for the organization to sustain the Virtuous Circle of Diversity Performance.

If inclusiveness revolves around the leader's daily interactions with members of the organization and their stakeholders, it is also reflected in the interactions among its members. The feeling of belonging and being included for a member of an organization is the *sum of their personal interactions with others in the organization.* How this plays out in practice is revealed in the following case study of an organization that was struggling to embed inclusive behaviors.

---

[14] Bourke and Titus (2019).

Case Study: Turning Around a Non-inclusive Culture

The leadership team of an organization had focused aggressively on recruiting more ethnic diversity into their organization. Yet the organization was losing 40% of these candidates within three years of being hired. When the organization began to dig into the reasons for this revolving door, it became clear there was a non-inclusive culture and that grievances and concerns had been building up. The leaders considered how they could remedy this tide of negativity and an initial suggestion was to organize a community event where people could get together and enjoy themselves.

One event, of course, is unlikely to be sufficient to transform a non-inclusive culture into one that supports diversity. Instead, a rich tapestry of inclusive behaviors, uniting events, and interactions is necessary to turn the tide on past behaviors and initiate new behaviors. Such a process is demanding of an organization's leaders and its people. Trust needs to be restored, which takes time. Leaders who expect immediate improvements following one-off community events are likely to be disappointed.

Many leaders are prone to thinking that one deposit will result in a positive balance on the Emotional Bank Account—and this was certainly true for these leaders struggling with a non-inclusive culture. Their suggestion to hold a "fun community event" was in effect a symbolic deposit on the Emotional Bank Account.

It was insufficient for three reasons. Firstly, the emotional deposit of the community event may be more valuable to the leaders than the recipients. Secondly, the bank account may be overdrawn to such an extent that one deposit would not result in a positive emotional bank account, given that a cultural turnaround depends on a pattern of deposits that enhance trust. Thirdly, even if theoretically the community event brought the bank account back to zero, the Emotional Bank Account would quickly be depleted by negative withdrawals, given the current non-inclusive culture.

The leaders of this organization realized that the Emotional Bank Account with the minority groups in their organization was overdrawn and indeed negative. In a number of work sessions, the leaders identified behaviors and actions that constituted emotional withdrawals to the bank account of inclusiveness. This included occasions where biased behavior displayed in meetings remained uncorrected, when minority recruits had not been sponsored and were left to fend for themselves, when office events did not take into account religious public holidays, etc.

To correct this situation, the leaders identified the behaviors and actions that would support the building of inclusiveness, for example:

- Requesting feedback from their team on whether the leaders were inclusive to the team and for team members to provide feedback when this was not the case.
- Communicating why diversity is important to the leaders personally and for the leaders to correct themselves humbly when they made an unwitting and biased comment.
- Summoning the courage as leaders to discuss issues that were important to diversity (e.g., unwritten rules about who can be promoted) and demonstrating a willingness to re-evaluate whether such rules were systemically biased.

This process was repeated with the organization and its leaders in order to truly hear the members of their organization and to provide them with a voice. This created the first step in healing the culture and creating inclusion and respect and safety. Collectively, the organization committed to creating an environment where people were seen and heard and where leaders acknowledged that they were required to do much of the heavy lifting themselves and unearth their own biases and non-inclusive behavior.

Today the organization is steadily building trust and engagement has improved. Perhaps the most impactful feedback from a person in the group is captured in this sentence: "I don't feel like a minority. I feel like a unique individual."

▶   **Key takeaway** Leaders have a critical role in facilitating an environment of inclusiveness. They have a line of sight on the Emotional Bank Account. They can identify, sponsor, and reward actions and behaviors that lead to inclusiveness deposits to the bank account. They can also stop behaviors that deplete the Emotional Bank Account of inclusiveness and diversity.

5   The Voice of Employees

Building an inclusive culture requires deep understanding about what constitutes inclusion for the members of an organization. Employees are asked two connected questions: "When do you experience a sense of inclusion and what contributes to this feeling in the organization? Please provide examples."

Responses obtained over the past five years of work in more than 15 global organizations, with replies from over 3,000 employees, confirm the following list as comprising the most important criteria for members of an organization to feel included.

The most important criteria for members of an organization to feel included

- My voice counts and has meaning
- I feel safe and can bring my whole self to work
- I trust the leadership because they really care about diversity. They walk the talk.
- I feel empowered by access to resources and ability to collaborate
- My values and personal purpose have a home in the organization's purpose

---

1.   My voice counts and has meaning

I feel included when I have a voice. By this, I mean that I don't have to shout to be heard, but that there is room to speak and/or I am invited to share my opinion by the leader/team members. I can see that my voice counts, when the leader invites me to share my view in a dominant or extrovert group; and when the leader or team summarizes what I said or refer to our discussion later in the meeting.

Having a voice is not just being invited to speak but believing that one has been heard and has contributed meaningfully to the organizational outcome.

2.   I feel safe and can bring my whole self to work

> I feel included when I feel safe enough to be myself; when I don't have to hide parts of who I am, when I come to work; when I can be my authentic and unique self. I feel safe and am able to bring my whole self to my work when people ask me about me as a person outside of work: about my hobbies and my family; when the dress code is not overly prescriptive nor aligned only to the attire of the dominant group; when people are informed and respectful of my religion; when the leader is also authentic and open about what they do and who they are; when we start our meeting with a check-in; when people remember key events in my life, like becoming a mother, or nursing a sick parent.

Safety to be oneself is important for a sense of belonging.

3.   I trust the leadership because they really care about diversity. They walk the talk.

> I feel included when I value and trust the leadership of the organization; when leaders 'walk the talk' of what they communicate about the importance of diversity; when I get a sense that the leaders are personally vested in the outcome, because they genuinely and personally care about the outcome. I see this because the leaders share their personal story and explain why this matters to them. They are also humble in how they speak about themselves, as if we are all equal, as if we all matter. And they acknowledge that they are also biased and solicit feedback.

The role of leaders, both senior leaders and managers, is absolutely critical to a sense of inclusiveness and comes down to these day-to-day actions.

4.   I feel empowered by access to resources and ability to collaborate

> I feel included when I feel empowered to perform, without leaders second-guessing my outcome and controlling the outcome; when I am able to leverage resources; when I am able to reach out to fellow team members and collaborate, without feeling that I am not allowed to do this; when leaders are accessible to me.

Empowerment is not only about giving a person a clear objective. It is about creating the circumstances and values that support collaboration and the equitable access to resources, including people and expertise.

5.   My values and personal purpose have a home in the organization's purpose

> I feel included when I know how I contribute to our strategy and our purpose around diversity; when I feel that my values and my own purpose are aligned with the diversity values and the purpose of the organization.

Meaningful contribution to a purpose and the identification with that purpose are important to support inclusion.

6   Translating the Voice of Employees into Daily Leadership Actions

At the heart of employees' feedback is a desire to belong in the organization and have an environment that safeguards respectful collaboration—an environment where leaders engage in daily practices that create deposits in the bank account of inclusion, in other words.

According to Covey, there are six ways to make deposits (or reduce withdrawals)[15] and the employee feedback supports the important role of consistently respectful behaviors which demonstrate that leaders:

1. **Understand the individual**—by listening intently to what the other person is saying, showing empathy, caring for others, acting with understanding, kindness, and compassion.
2. **Keep commitments**—by honoring one's promises and delivering on one's commitments, always.
3. **Clarify expectations**—by making sure that there is alignment on mutual expectations.
4. **Attend to the little things**—by showing small kindnesses, a smile, a warm greeting, a genuine "how are you today," remembering the things that are important in the lives of others.
5. **Show personal integrity**—by acting each and every day with integrity, demonstrating the values of respect for others, and being consistent with what is set out for others to do.
6. **Apologize when a withdrawal occurred**—by extending sincere and immediate apologies for the mistakes that are made and humbly taking personal responsibility and setting the infringement right.

Leaders who embody such inclusive practices are a source of inspiration to their colleagues and people within an organization. An excellent example of such a leader is the late Kathryn W. Phillips (See Profile of a Courageous and Inclusive Leader), a pioneering researcher and professor in diversity whose insights were partly the result of her own personal experience as a Black woman who sought to embody the very qualities of inclusive leadership that she studied.

Profile of a Curious and Courageous Leader:

Kathryn W. Phillips

For the late Kathryn W. Phillips, a trailblazer in researching the benefits of diversity in the workplace, diversity was more than a score—it had to be threaded into an organization's culture, principles, and values. As a professor, most recently at

---

[15] Covey, *The 7 Habits of Highly Effective People*.

Columbia Business School, she studied the ways that companies and organizations can maximize the benefits of hiring employees with diverse backgrounds. In a 2014 essay in *Scientific American*, "How Diversity Makes Us Stronger" she wrote "The first thing to acknowledge about diversity is that it can be difficult."[16] She conducted groundbreaking empirical research showing that the tensions that can result from diversity—discomfort, conflict, or challenging interactions—can yield better outcomes.[17] Phillips grew up in a Black neighborhood of Chicago and in third grade was selected to attend a nearly all-white magnet school. As reported in *The New York Times*, she later recalled, "I was introduced at a young age to diversity, to difference, to ignorance."[18] She went on to become the first Black woman to receive tenure at both the Kellogg School of Management at Northwestern University and the Columbia Business School, where only 3.7% of tenured faculty are Black and only 6.2% are underrepresented minorities. She was a highly dedicated teacher, mentor, and collaborator, on a lifelong quest for insight into diversity built on personally experiencing ignorance and a lack of diversity as a young student.

These experiences prompted Phillips to study how and why diverse groups function differently than homogenous ones—a journey that was cut short too early when Phillips died of cancer at age 47.[19] In a speech she gave at Columbia in 2015, Phillips spoke of her background bridging social groups in Chicago and as a college track and field athlete. "My life in the middle led me to a question: What small change can we make as individuals to capture the benefits of diversity?" she said.[20] One of her colleagues, Columbia's Vice Provost for Faculty Advancement Dennis Mitchell, described Phillips as a dedicated teacher, mentor, and collaborator who worked tirelessly to create an inclusive community. "She embodied a rare combination of selflessness, humility, and grace while being a relentless advocate and guide for her students," Mitchell said in a statement.[21] He noted that Phillips spearheaded efforts upon arriving at Columbia to increase recruitment and career development of junior women at the Business School.[22] Professor Daniel Ames of Columbia Business School described Phillips as "one of the most important scholars of her generation in advancing how we, as social scientists, think about the value of diversity."[23]

In early 2017 *Scientific American* re-published her work under the title, "How Diversity Makes Us Smarter and Powers Science and Innovation." As Phillips wrote in that essay, "The fact is that if you want to build teams or organizations capable

---

[16] Phillips (2015).

[17] Cowley (2020).

[18] Cowley, "Katherine W. Phillips, 47, Dies."

[19] Cowley, "Katherine W. Phillips, 47, Dies."

[20] Phillips (2015).

[21] Sofia Kwon, "Katherine Phillips, Business School Professor, Leaves Lasting Legacy of Workplace Diversity." Columbia Spectator, last modified February 19, 2020, https://www.columbiaspectator.com/news/2020/02/20/katherine-phillips-business-school-professor-and-workplace-diversity-advocate-has-died/.

[22] Kwon, "Katherine Phillips Leaves Lasting Legacy."

[23] Kwon, "Katherine Phillips Leaves Lasting Legacy."

of innovating, you need diversity. Diversity enhances creativity. It encourages the search for novel information and perspectives, leading to better decision-making and problem-solving."[24] In short, as Phillips' research made clear, metrics count but the scorecard alone cannot be the goal. Meeting a quota is not the same as recognizing the business value of diversity. Kathryn Phillips' life work was dedicated to the idea that the organization must value individuals for their unique contributions, and that the more diverse and inclusive the organization, the more infinite its business potential. Through her life's work, she changed the way businesses thought about diversity, equity, and inclusion.

7   How to Embed Inclusive Behaviors in Practice

What can be done in practice to embed inclusive behavior? Depending on an organization's Diversity Performance maturity level, the Integrated Diversity Model sets out a range of evidence-based initiatives that can be implemented to embed inclusive behavior (Table 1).

8   Stage 1 Organizations: Legal Compliance

At Stage 1, the primary focus is to integrate members within the existing culture of the organization. This is typically done by incorporating into new hire orientation programs the culture of the organization and compliance with the norms and rituals that are part of the organization's "DNA." Stage 1 organizations tend to have limited inclusion activities and the focus is mostly on "admitting" new members into the organization to support legal requirements.

9   Stage 2 Organizations: Stakeholder Requirements

At Stage 2, the primary focus is not on imprinting the organization's own culture onto new members, but rather being more welcoming to new members and recognizing different cultures and communities. Leaders initiate Employee Resource Groups for specific communities such as women, LGBTQI+individuals, people with disabilities, or those from different cultural or ethnic backgrounds. Stage 2 organizations also invest in diversity events to stimulate a sense of belonging among all members and conduct surveys to understand the level of employee satisfaction.

---

[24] Phillips, "How Diversity Makes Us Smarter."

Table 1   Embed Behavior Capability and Initiatives for Five Stages
Overview of initiatives to embed behavior at each stage of diversity maturity.

	Stage 1 Legal Compliance	Stage 2 Stakeholder Requirements	Stage 3 Organizational Performance	Stage 4 Reinvention	Stage 5 Societal Value
Focus	Incorporate in own culture; admitted	Create sense of community; welcomed	Support seamless collaboration; valued	Support break-through thinking; embraced	Contribute to societal inclusiveness
Skills	Own culture	ERGs; Networks; Communities	Team effectiveness; Equality & respect	Psychological safety; Equity; fairness	Leave no one behind
Process	Orientation	ERG Setup events	High-performance teams	Culture-wide values & behavior	Partner values & behavior
Responsibilities	Limited	HR; D&I lead	All leaders diversity office	All members	Partners & organization
Metrics	Hiring & retention	Satisfaction index	Inclusive leader Index	Inclusiveness index	Partner inclusion index
Technology	Training systems	ERG support tools	Collaboration tools	Idea tools pulse surveys networking tools	Partner sharing tools

10   Stage 3 Organizations: Organizational Performance

At Stage 3, the primary focus is to create the cultural dynamics to facilitate high-performance teams and create the values and behaviors that allow for seamless and productive interactions. Many organizations that describe themselves as "meritocracies" are in Stage 3. Often, employees are provided with mentors, members receive resources for their development and there are clear protocols around showing respect and courtesy to other members of the team. At Stage 3, there is also an effort to value diversity rather than simply tolerating it. As a result, the organization will tend to hold cultural events where members can learn about colleagues from different cultures and backgrounds. Leaders are also increasingly evaluated on being inclusive leaders, for example by conducting 360-degree assessments where team members can evaluate whether leaders are demonstrably inclusive. An organization at this stage also conducts surveys to evaluate engagement, happiness, and sense of inclusion among all members.

11   Stage 4 Organizations: Reinvention

At Stage 4, the primary focus is to truly embrace diversity in all its forms. The focus is on creating a sense of safety which allows for respectful disagreement and ensuring that the conditions are in place to stimulate diversity of thinking. Whereas in Stage 3, mentors will be chosen or assigned, in Stage 4, emphasis is on assigning active sponsors who are able to assist in advancing equity and access to opportunity, resources, and networks. Employees are evaluated individually on their needs and how they can be supported in being successful in the organization. At Stage 4, organizations regard inclusion not as a set of activities and events, but rather a critical part of their culture. Indeed, many organizations at this stage talk about the principle of inclusiveness, namely the philosophy to strive for fairness and the advancement of equity and individualized support to create a flourishing environment for diversity. Measurement of inclusive behaviors is not confined to leaders, but all members are evaluated on the degree to which they support and nurture an inclusive, safe, and respectful environment. Finally, members of a Stage 4 organization usually cannot advance in their career without demonstrating that they are inclusive leaders.

12   Stage 5 Organizations: Societal Value

At Stage 5, the priority is to shift from creating an inclusive environment in the organization to supporting inclusiveness in the organization's wider value chain and partner ecosystem. Organizations at this stage are committed to contributing to societal inclusiveness within their supply chain, among industry partners and other stakeholders and the values and principles of equity, equality, and sustainability will often be promoted throughout their value chain. The intention is to assure that products and services delivered by the organization and its partners fully adhere to the principles of equity and inclusiveness.

13   Inclusive Leadership as a Core Capability

Stage 4 and 5 organizations attach so much value to an inclusive environment that many organizations elevate the Embed Behavior capability to a core capability. This capability is often referred to as the "Inclusive Leadership core capability."

A core capability defines what an organization does at its core:

> Core capabilities are 'built up over time,' 'cannot be easily imitated' and 'constitute a competitive advantage for a firm.' For example, this may include excellent customer service or ceaseless innovation.[25]

> Core capabilities are distinct from other types of capability and sufficiently superior to similar capabilities in competitor organizations so as to provide a 'sustainable competitive advantage.'[26]

By switching to the term "Inclusive Leadership core capability," it is with this definition in mind—namely, a capability that provides the organization with a competitive and differentiated ability to survive in a complex world while delivering on

---

[25] Leonard (1998).

[26] D. A. Leonard, *Wellsprings of Knowledge.*

its mandate. The Inclusive Leadership capability is a critical enabler of sustainable Diversity Performance for Stage 4 and 5 organizations.[27]

A core capability does not happen by accident, it is comprised of a clear strategy and intent, underpinned by processes, often enabled by technology, with clearly assigned roles and responsibilities and systematically measured and rewarded. The key components of the Inclusive Leadership core capability are as follows:

Strategy—Organizations need to set out why inclusive leadership has been elevated to a core capability by connecting inclusive leadership to the achievement of the business goals. Strategic integration of the Inclusive Leadership core capability includes the following elements:

- Recognizing inclusiveness as a key value in the organization.
- Defining inclusive leadership as a core capability for the organization.
- Embedding goals around realizing an inclusive leadership capability in the organization's mission, vision, and business strategy and reflecting it in its financial annual review.
- Assessing and measuring the organization's inclusive leadership capability and reporting on progress of goals set for its achievement.

Process—Organizations need to imprint inclusive diversity leadership into their processes. Every talent-touching process needs to support the inclusive leadership goal, enabled by technology where possible. This includes the following:

- Job and role specifications that include a section on inclusive leadership.
- Recruitment interviews which focus on inclusiveness by asking candidates to talk about what inclusiveness means to them. Candidates should also be presented with case studies of toxic situations and explain how they would handle them.
- Succession planning that requires an evaluation of the inclusiveness of leaders and whether they would support the advancement of inclusiveness within their new role.
- Performance management which includes assessment of leaders on the inclusiveness axis where the outcome impacts executive compensation.
- Training and development that includes training and coaching which assists leaders on becoming excellent inclusive leaders.

Technology—This is a great enabler of the inclusive leadership capability, allowing digitization of processes, data mining of metrics, and seamless process outcomes. Through webinars, webcasts, and instant messaging solutions, the organization is able to remove the traditional barrier of not being able to participate physically in the room to being able to join from any location. This can drive up feelings of inclusion for many who have been traditionally excluded from

---

[27] Argote (2013).

decision-making processes and updates on the organization. Not only are organizations able to include more people through the virtual environment but organizations can also increase inclusion by offering online training on allyship, behavior sensitivity training, and on learning more about different perspectives and diversity of background. Further, webcasts and webinars help to ensure that members feel connected and in tune with important strategy decisions and updates from the company.

With the global COVID-19 pandemic, the role of technology has become even more pronounced. While it can foster inclusion, it can also contribute to a lack of inclusion and to the inequality gap. Technology has enabled more people to work virtually, even in roles that had previously not been considered suitable for remote work, allowing them to retain their employment at a time of economic uncertainty. On the other hand, it has brought work into people's homes, contributing to a feeling of being always on-call. This has been experienced in particular by women who have the lion's share of childcare and household work in addition to their jobs, and as a result, many have left the workforce in order to prioritize their families. Another way in which technology does not necessarily enable inclusion is that in countries where a majority of the population lack digital access, the digital divide can perpetuate inequality gaps.

With more employees working virtually, leaders need to ensure that people are connected by the requisite technology[28] so that they can participate in equitable meetings and in an environment in which everyone is acknowledged as belonging and invited to contribute and share. With virtual communication being the prime means of communicating for many, ensuring the employee's experience is positive and reducing barriers to participation are critical. When handled thoughtfully, and always taking into consideration both its positive and potential negative impact on diversity, inclusion, and equity, technology can continue to be an important enabler of inclusiveness in the post-COVID landscape.

People—The actors and influencers responsible for realizing the core capability of inclusive leadership should be clearly identified. When organizations elevate inclusive leadership capability as a core and differentiated capability, the responsibility to be inclusive leaders is assigned to all people in the organization. This is not the domain of middle management and senior leadership alone. Every member of the organization is seen as an inclusive leader. That means the following elements need to be in place:

- The CEO or most senior leader is held accountable for realizing the inclusive leadership capability, including by the Chair of the Board.
- The directors on the board are held accountable for realizing the inclusive leadership capability within their area of responsibility.
- Every single person in the organization, no matter what level of responsibility they have, is required to "live" and support inclusive leadership in the organization.

---

[28] Tulshyan (2020).

Metrics—Organizations need to measure their inclusive leadership capability against clear goals, tied to metrics. This includes the following:

- Conducting capability assessments on the inclusive leadership capability in the organization and identifying the gaps.
- Taking a 360-degree assessment that includes an assessment of leaders as inclusive leaders.
- Tying remuneration to achievement of inclusive leadership objectives.
- Linking opportunities for promotion to a track record of inclusive leadership.

Case Study: Global Bank Realizes Its Inclusive Leadership Capability

A global banking institution was frustrated by a lack of progress on the diversity front. Like many financial institutions, it was hard-hit by the financial collapse in 2008. Many organizations at this time were evaluating the role of diversity in enhancing their ability to both predict and adequately respond to the next, inevitable financial waves in the market. The leaders of this bank believed in the benefits of diversity and felt that with greater diversity of thought, they would be able to innovate more rapidly for their stakeholders and be better placed to anticipate and respond to risks.

In 2012, four years into their diversity journey, the Board of Directors assessed that the organization had made some, but not sufficient, progress in attracting, retaining, and leveraging cognitive diversity (diversity of thought) in their organization. This is how one of the board members expressed it:

We find it difficult that we have not booked more progress on the diversity front, despite considerable efforts. Our Chair of the Board has been extremely vocal about the need for diversity. We have gathered a taskforce to guide and monitor the achievement of our diversity targets. We have hired an external recruitment agency to support our recruitment efforts. We have instituted diversity days and we have created a new leadership program on diversity. With all these efforts one would expect we would have a more flourishing pipeline. The issue is that we find people with the diversity of thought that we are looking for, we place these people within our organization, and we then lose these people at almost the same rate. So net, after four years, I fear that we are not really more cognitively diverse, and I fear we are losing stamina and the will to make this happen. And yet, we cannot afford to give up, given the lessons of 2008.

In fact, the organization was experiencing a blindspot in their approach to advancing diversity. It was so focused on the metric of "recruiting cognitively diverse people" that they had forgotten about what happens to cognitive diversity when it streams into the organization. The communication from the Chair and the CEO in public forums had created an expectation among talent that the organization was diversity friendly and inclusive. However, the inclusive practices were in fact very limited.

Over several months, the organization traced the experiences of 50 candidates who had been recruited for their cognitive diversity and had left within two years. Their feedback was collected from each juncture of their journey—from hiring and the time they read the job and role specification to their first interview, their orientation week, their first project, their experiences with other team members, and the process leading up to their decision to leave. The most common reasons these candidates cited for leaving the organization were "disappointment with leaders," "a feeling that I have been hired for my color and gender but not to be part of a team," and "a gap in expectations in relationship to the organization's diversity commitments."

Many of the candidates had been excited about the bank's messaging expressing commitment and genuine desire to attract diverse candidates to the organization. The candidates did not doubt the bank's publicly stated intent for cognitive diversity. However, once part of the organization, each candidate remarked on the gap between the desire for cognitive diversity and their actual experience of being there but not feeling welcomed, seen, or heard. In other words, they felt "asked to be part of the team" (diversity) but did not feel "they had the opportunity to play" (inclusion) and were left to sit on the bench. Further, it seemed "the team outcome did not apply to all" (belonging).

The candidates' feedback confirmed that the bank had an almost entirely absent inclusive leadership capability. Inclusiveness was talked about but rather superfluously. There were no inclusive leadership reference values. Leaders were not evaluated on being inclusive leaders. The members of the organization were not skilled in inclusiveness practices, and there were no monitored metrics on inclusiveness.

The bank found the analysis based on the candidates' feedback very helpful. The CEO spoke passionately about the need to develop a leading, differentiated, and highly valuable inclusive leadership core capability. This commitment was translated into an organizational intent. An intention alone can create the flame of activity and focus and, in this case, the realization of an inclusive leadership core capability.

From the moment the CEO stated the organization's intent, the bank was motivated to not only talk about inclusiveness but to have inclusive leadership as a core capability in their organization. Design sessions were held with the leadership and key stakeholders to create an Inclusive Leadership Capability Blueprint (Fig. 2). This was achieved through capability design sessions where the organization looked at each element of a core capability—strategy, process, people, process, and metrics—and identified what was required overall and the gap in focus and initiatives.

After designing the Inclusive Leadership Core Capability Blueprint, the CEO assigned responsibilities for a capability owner to have end-to-end overview of the capability. Clear milestones were put in place for realizing the capability blueprint. The most impactful action was upfront communication about the bank's intent to hold leaders and members of the organization accountable for creating an inclusive environment. This was supported by creating training and other enabling measures for leaders. For example, one leader began meetings with a 10-min check-in, asking three questions: "How are you feeling today, what are your hopes for this meeting, and are there any distractions that prevent you from being fully present in the meeting, so that we are aware of these and can plan around these?" This simple intervention allowed people to feel connected and bring their whole self to the meeting.

As the bank moved forward on its diversity journey, it made considerable advances. An inclusion index was introduced to measure whether employees felt included, a baseline inclusion index score was taken and thereafter interim inclusion index measurements were taken. Over two years, there was a 30% increase in the inclusion index. In addition, each leader received a 360-degree evaluation on their rating as an inclusive leader and the average score of all leaders on inclusive leadership moved from an average score of 3.5 (out of 5) to 4.2. Currently, there is an upward trend in the leadership inclusiveness score and the aim is to have all leaders meet a minimum level of 4.6. The bank also found increased loyalty among employees, including a marked increase among minority groups, as measured by their tenure with the bank.

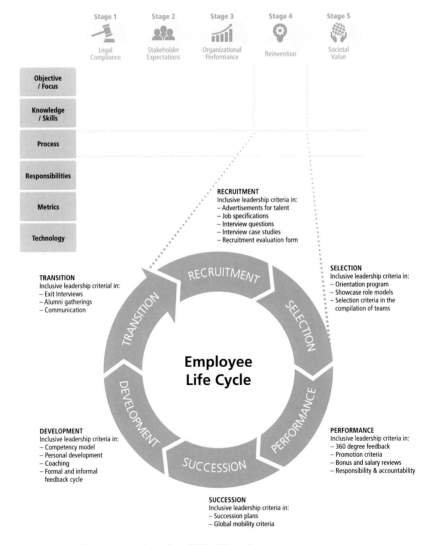

Fig. 2 Inclusive Leadership Core Capability Blueprint
The banking institution's blueprint outlines key process requirements for their inclusive leadership capability.

▶   **Key takeaway** Inclusive leadership was achieved not just by realizing the capability blueprint design but by creating a real and impactful capability. The results have been impressive and continue to trend upward. There is now a Virtuous Circle in place in the bank which is leading to increased Diversity Performance.

14   Measuring the Health of the Embed Behavior Capability

Organizations wishing to realize the Embed Behavior capability can obtain valuable feedback from the following three sources:

1. **Stakeholder feedback**—Feedback *from* stakeholders (including employees, contingent workers) on whether they feel included in the organization.
2. **Leader Evaluation**—Feedback *on* leaders and whether they practice inclusive leadership.
3. **Capability review**—The health of the capability, assessed by how extensively inclusiveness is embedded in the culture, processes, measurement, and responsibilities across the organization. A powerful strategy is to make it count for all team members in performance reviews.

Stakeholder feedback—There are various ways in which organizations receive feedback on employee satisfaction. Many of these instruments include questions aimed at capturing employees' feelings of inclusion, for example satisfaction surveys comprising 60 or more questions to obtain a measure of employees' satisfaction with the organization. Often such surveys include six typical statements which have been found to be directly connected to the feeling of employee inclusion (Table 2).

By inviting employees to evaluate these six critical inclusiveness statements on a five-point scale, the organization obtains a measure of the stage of inclusion in the organization. The inclusion score can then be mapped to the Virtuous Circle Five Stages Framework introduced in Chapter 3. This inclusion measurement allows the organization to immediately identify which aspects of inclusion are lacking for their stage of Diversity Performance and provides insight into whether the gap in inclusion is related to lack of belonging, lack of connection of self to the purpose of the organization, lack of equity advancement, and/or a lack of leadership.

Leadership evaluation—Inclusive leaders are identified as being inclusive by demonstrating a number of behaviors and practices on a daily practice. As previously set out, this includes the leader being personally committed to diversity, being conscious of their blindspots and biases, being a deep listener, creating circumstances to collaborate, being courageous in dealing with inequities, and being an active driver of diversity. Inclusive leadership behaviors are a good focal point for seeking feedback on leaders in the organization, by evaluating eight typical leadership statements (Table 2).

Table 2   **Assessing the Embed Behavior Capability**
By asking employees to evaluate select statements, organizations can gain a measure of the health of their inclusive leadership behaviors.

Source	Statement
1. Stakeholder Feedback	I feel like I belong in my organization.
	I feel like I can reveal/bring my whole self to the organization.
	I feel like my work/role contributes directly to the purpose of the organization.
	I feel safe to share my thoughts and feedback to my team.
	I feel that I have the same access to resources and opportunities as others do.
	I feel like I am supported by my leaders to be succesful.
2. Leadership Evaluation	The leader is personally committed to diversity and inclusiveness.
	The leader is aware of their own bias and mitigates own bias.
	The leader actively works to mitigate institutional bias by creating a fair and equitable environment.
	The leader creates conditions for team collaboration.
	The leader actively intervenes so as to allow all employee voices to be heard.
	The leader is culturally intelligent and confidently navigates different cultures.
	The leader is an ally and sponsor to me and those who require allyship.
	The leader is a role model of inclusive leadership.
3. Capability Evaluation	Inclusive leadership is defined as a core, differentiated capability for our organization.
	Inclusive leadership criteria included in all talent processes.
	Inclusive leadership goals set, metrics defined, measurement and reporting and review in place.
	Inclusive leadership responsibilities clarified for capability, and for processes and measurements.
	Technology is leveraged to provide insight and transparency on state of inclusiveness.

Capability evaluation—For those organizations at Stage 4 and 5 which have elevated the Embed Behavior capability to be a core capability, there are five additional questions that can be asked (Table 2). These questions are helpful to determine the extent to which Embed Behavior has been elevated to a core capability within the organization. At a minimum the organization has declared the Inclusive Leadership capability to be a core capability, leadership responsibility has been assigned for realizing the capability, it is regarded as critical for offering a differentiated positioning of the organization relative to other organizations and is fully supported by processes, policies, technology, metrics, and knowledge that promote deep inclusiveness within the organization.

15   Concluding Remarks

Embedding inclusive behavior into daily actions is indispensable for realizing the strategic diversity narrative for each organization. Regardless of the organization's desired stage, day-to-day behaviors, actions, and values of leaders and members of the organization are ultimately what shapes the diversity journey. The behaviors of leaders in particular serve as signals to others on what constitutes "acceptable" behavior. When leadership behavior is inclusive, there tends to be significant uptake and adoption of these evidenced behaviors by other members of the organization. When leadership behaviors are toxic, in contrast, this can lead to a chain reaction of similar behavior throughout the organization, undermining the diversity journey.

Recognizing this, organizations wishing to reach Stage 4 or 5 Diversity Performance elevate the Embed Behavior capability into a core capability, which may be referred to as the "Inclusive Leadership core capability." At these stages, inclusive behavior reminders, rewards, training, measurement, and support become engrained in all parts of the organization so that all members reflect inclusiveness in their daily practices.

Inclusive Leadership is about each individual "leading themselves" to be respectful team members—up and down the chain of command. That is when the real magic happens: when the entire organization recognizes inclusive leadership not just as a supporting capability, but as a core and differentiated capability. The organization is then better enabled to navigate a complex environment and the optimum conditions are created for diversity of thought to become an engine of transformation.

In Chapter 9 we will explore how to harness policies for strong Diversity Performance.

References

Argote, Linda. *Organizational learning* (Boston, MA: Springer, 2013). https://doi.org/10.1007/978-1-4614-5251-5.

Boushey, Heather, and Glynn, Sarah Jane. "There Are Significant Business Costs to Replacing Employees," Center for American Progress, November 16, 2012, https://www.americanprogress.org/issues/economy/reports/2012/11/16/44464/there-are-significant-business-costs-to-replacing-employees/.

Bourke, Juliet, and Titus, Andrea. "The Key to Inclusive Leadership." *Harvard Business Review*, March 6, 2020, https://hbr.org/2020/03/the-key-to-inclusive-leadership.

Bourke, Juliet, and Titus, Andrea. "Why Inclusive Leaders Are Good for Organizations, and How to Become One." *Harvard Business Review*, March 29, 2019. https://hbr.org/2019/03/why-inclusive-leaders-are-good-for-organizations-and-how-to-become-one.

Covey, Stephen R. *The 7 Habits of Highly Effective People: Powerful Lessons in Personal Change*, 25th anniversary edition (New York: Simon & Schuster, 2004).

Cowley, Stacy. "Katherine W. Phillips, 47, Dies; Taught the Value of Difference." *New York Times*, February 13, 2020. https://www.nytimes.com/2020/02/13/business/katherine-w-phillips-dead.html.

Kochan, Thomas et al. "The Effects of Diversity on Business Performance: Report of the Diversity Research Network." *Human Resource Management* 42, no. 1 (Spring 2003): 3–21. https://doi.org/10.1002/hrm.1006.

Leonard, D. A. *Wellsprings of Knowledge: Building and Sustaining Sources of Innovatio*In Paperback ed. Boston: Harvard Business School Press, 1998.

Phillips, Katherine W. "Why Diversity Matters," Talks at Columbia, YouTube, December 11, 2015, video, 16:00. https://www.youtube.com/watch?v=lHStHPQUzkE&ab_channel=Talk-satColumbia

Phillips, Katherine W. "How Diversity Makes Us Smarter." *Scientific American*, October 1, 2014. https://www.scientificamerican.com/article/how-diversity-makes-us-smarter/.

Seppälä, Emma, and Cameron, Kim. "Proof that Positive Work Cultures Are More Productive." *Harvard Business Review*, December 1, 2015. https://hbr.org/2015/12/proof-that-positive-work-cultures-are-more-productive. Workplace Stress, the American Institute of Stress, https://www.stress.org/workplace-stress, accessed January 6, 2021

Tulshyan, Ruchika. "How to Be an Inclusive Leader Through a Crisis." *Harvard Business Review*, April 10, 2020. https://hbr.org/2020/04/how-to-be-an-inclusive-leader-through-a-crisis.

Williamson, Marianne. *A Return to Love* (New York: HarperPerennial, 1992), 190–191.

Harnessing Policies to Realize Diversity Performance

9

On the Diversity Performance journey, an important tool that organizations can harness is making sure they have the right policies to support diversity in practice. Using the analogy of the sports team, if diversity is the selection of various skilled and talented players to the team, and inclusion results in diverse players being asked to join the game rather than sit on the bench, then policies are the rules of the game. Practices are how the rules of the game are applied and the players' recourse when the rules are broken. Policies need to be tuned and adapted to the required stage of Diversity Performance. Policy coherence ensures that the rules are clear, that the organization is working in sync and that every team has a shared understanding of how the game is played.

This chapter looks at the Harness Policies capability of the Integrated Diversity Model (Fig. 1).

This chapter explores why policies are such a vital ingredient in an organization's pursuit of Diversity Performance, and why the best policies are ones that are valued by members of the organization. Two case studies—a not-for-profit specializing in healthcare aimed at underserved populations and a technology company struggling to attract greater gender diversity—illustrate how policies can be successfully implemented in two very different types of organizations. The chapter also demonstrates how the Virtuous Circle Five Stages framework and the Integrated Diversity Model provide valuable direction in creating policies and practices that enhance Diversity Performance.

1 Policies: The Key to Accountability

Policies provide direction and ensure consistency in how to interpret guidelines and apply them in practice. They also establish accountability for actions and outcomes, provide efficiency in operations and give members clarity on how an organization operates. When team members understand that there are not only

© Diversity and Performance BV 2021
K. Formanek, *Beyond D&I*, https://doi.org/10.1007/978-3-030-75336-8_9

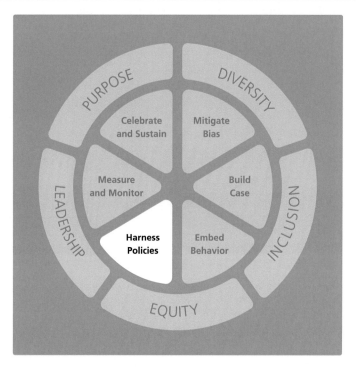

Fig. 1 Harness Policies
Fourth capability of the integrated diversity model.

generally accepted rules of engagement, but recourse when rules are broken, this provides a sense of safety and lowered stress for all members of the organization but particularly for those in minority groups. For example, an organization that has a zero tolerance policy on discrimination will ideally address any incidents of discrimination immediately and decisively, with a set of clearly defined consequences. When applied in practice, this kind of policy provides confidence to minorities that there are rules and remedies in place to secure a safe environment.

To be effective, however, discriminatory actions which violate the organization's non-discrimination policy, such as a racial slur, should result in immediate, identified sanctions. Lack of consequences following an incident is problematical: firstly, the rules of the game are undermined, as players are not sure if the rules actually apply. Secondly, ignoring an act of discrimination could prompt disengagement and cynicism as people observe that the organization does not really practice what it preaches. Finally, when there are incidents of discrimination and policies are not enforced, it can spark employee backlash: in the sports analogy, players may simply walk off the field and everyone loses. To be effective in guiding practices, policy implementation requires a consistent approach, and as policies are continuously evolving, this means regularly reinforcing the link between policies and practices.

2   Ten Barriers to Effective Diversity Policy

Insights gained through policy audits conducted at many client organizations, together with analysis of leading diversity policies reveal 10 key reasons why diversity policies can under-deliver.

1. **A perception gap in the value of the policy between leaders and target groups**

In one 2019 global survey by the Boston Consulting Group (BCG), 16,500 people representing women, racially or ethnically diverse employees, and people of the LGBTQI+ community were asked about the diversity issues that affect them versus what the leadership thinks, particularly where leadership was made up of mostly white middle-aged males.[1] The results revealed a striking perception gap between employees' and leaders' perceptions on diversity issues. Such gaps can lead to the adoption or perpetuation of policies that are not required or valued— or worse, leaders failing to put in place a policy that is sorely needed. The BCG research revealed the following[2]:

- Leaders said day-to-day experience and major decisions were free of bias, while 50% of employees surveyed stated that they see bias as part of their day-to-day experience at work.
- Leaders believed that the recruiting phase represented the biggest obstacle to minority candidates, particularly women and racial and ethnic minorities. In contrast, employees identified obstacles throughout the employee journey, from recruitment to advancement to leadership commitment.
- Leaders assumed that minority groups faced minor obstacles in their career progression, while members of these groups perceived the gaps in equity and opportunity as significant.

2. **An assumption that all diversity policies are equally valued by all minority groups**

Leaders often institute policies that apply to all members of the organization on the assumption that these policies are equally valued by all members. This is not the case in practice: for example, parental leave policies may be valued by parents but less so by employees without children. In the same way, policies may be applied generally to all minority groups, even though there are clear differences between them regarding which policies are most valuable and most likely to support equity and its advancement.[3] Later in this chapter, we explore which policies

---

[1] Krentz et al. (2019).

[2] Matt Krentz et al., "Fixing the Flawed Approach to Diversity."

[3] Matt Krentz et al., "Fixing the Flawed Approach to Diversity."

are considered most valuable for minority groups including women, LGBTQI+, people with disabilities, and ethnic/racial diversity.

3. **Minority employees not sufficiently consulted**

Perhaps surprisingly, the intended beneficiaries of policies are often left out of the loop when it comes to the development and application of diversity policies. This is particularly likely to occur when leaders' perceptions of what is valuable diverge from those at whom the policies are targeted. Employee resource groups (ERGs) are a great way to tap into employees' views on diversity policies and practices, but they are currently not leveraged enough. ERGs were first formed in the 1960s by employees who share a common characteristic—i.e., ethnicity, gender, generation, or religious affiliation, but the scope has since expanded to include interest-based groups, for example, individuals who support the environment or promote volunteerism. These groups are a great potential entry point for more effectively integrating diversity policies and practices within the organization. Among the benefits they bring are:

- Stronger engagement with minority groups which can lead to career advancement, leadership skill development and greater visibility, and access to senior executives.
- Insight into diverse cultural competency that can fuel better intelligence for the executive team on the concerns of minority group employees.
- Collaboration both internally and externally among different ERGs dedicated to a specific minority group, supporting diversity initiatives in their value chain and within society.
- Thought leadership from minority employees that can help cultivate business innovation and growth opportunities by offering a different lens on a complex environment.

To fulfill this valuable role for their members and the organization, ERGs need to be properly supported through deliberate sponsorship, a committed budget, and provision of digital resources, but many lack this support, being largely ad hoc and volunteer-led. While they may get support from specific leaders, incidental costs are often paid out-of-pocket and this work is typically done in addition to full-time roles, without extra compensation.[4] Where ERGs do receive support, they often transition from informal social networks into think-tank groups that directly impact the business. Empowered in this way, they can be instrumental in steering policies and ensuring that practices are tailored to the situation on the ground, helping to advance the strategic narrative of diversity in the organization.

---

[4] Bethea (2020).

4.   Policy effectiveness is overlooked

There is considerable scholarly and business research into what constitutes the most effective diversities policies and practices. One key finding is that while diversity policies can bolster workplace equity and business performance, poorly developed policies can prompt resistance and surface more difficulties for marginalized or underrepresented workers.[5,6]

One long-term study examining the effects of diversity policies at 816 U.S. workplaces over 30 years, reached the following conclusions regarding effective policies and practices[7]:

- Engaging managers in promoting diversity—e.g., through special recruitment and training programs—will increase diversity.
- Limiting managerial discretion in hiring and promotion—e.g., job tests, performance evaluations, and grievance procedures—will elicit resistance and produce adverse effects.[8,9]
- Increasing transparency for job seekers and hiring managers through job postings and job ladders will have positive effects. Transparency not only promotes more diversity by informing job seekers of the openings[10] but managers are more likely to censor their own biases when they expect others to review their decision.[11,12]
- Establishing monitoring of diversity efforts through internal professionals or external auditors positively catalyzes the effects of formal diversity programs.[13]
- Supporting external accountability to regulators will increase diversity effects.
- Primarily focusing on applying sanctions will cause fear and anxiety and limit the benefits of diversity initiatives.[14]

Policy evaluation can help to determine whether the right mix of proven policies is in place to deliver the envisaged results.

5.   A disconnect between policies and diversity protections

Policies are valuable when there is consistently applied recourse and when individuals are confident they will not be harassed or penalized by seeking recourse.

---

[5] Dobbin et al. (2015).

[6] Lambouths, Scarborough, and Holbrook, "Who Supports Diversity Policies?"

[7] Dobbin and Kalev (2016).

[8] Gouldner (1954).

[9] Hodson (1996).

[10] Castilla (2015).

[11] Kalev et al. (2006).

[12] Tetlock (1985).

[13] Kalev, Kelly, and Dobbin, "Best Guesses?"

[14] Dobbin and Kalev (2015).

Yet incidences of retaliation are rising and not adequately satisfied in the policy. Retaliation charges accounted for more than half (53.8%) of all charges in a review of the Equal Employment Opportunity Commission's litigation in 2019.[15] Together with policies that prohibit discrimination and harassment through a clearly stated zero tolerance for retaliation, leaders and team members can be educated about the prerequisites for creating a safe and respectful environment for those claiming discrimination.

6.   **Policies are not pruned**

Many organizations have too many diversity policies which are not integrated, and thus difficult to apply in practice. It is like having partial rules for the game applied by many different coaches. For instance, Human Resources, Risk Management, or the D&I function may all have responsibility for different diversity-related policies. Compartmentalizing policies in this way can lead to a plethora of policies each tackling one aspect of Diversity Performance without considering potential synergies or crossovers. In such a scenario, there is no overall diversity policy playbook to support the organization's strategic diversity narrative. The remedy is to review and prune the policies to weed out those that are not serving the organization because they are unnecessary or ineffective and focus instead on those policies which are impactful.

Policies should be guided by the strategic narrative of why diversity matters to the organization and focused on closing diversity gaps. For example, if the strategic narrative requires greater gender representation in the organization, a key priority is to ensure that the policies and practices instituted are valued by women and are well developed to meet their needs. In addition, policies that are highly valued as they impact all minority group members, such as zero tolerance for discrimination, need to be well anchored and consistently practiced right across the organization.

The first step is to conduct an inventory of all diversity policies and practices to ensure that there is no duplication and to address any gaps. An audit of the organization's full policy set can then be carried out to ensure that these are not working against its diversity and inclusion objectives. This will help to ensure policy coherence across the entire organization. Those policies that carry the greatest value for minority groups need to be well communicated across the organization, and ERGs can provide a good avenue for disseminating that information.

7.   **Failure to harness technology for engagement**

Technology can play a critical role in helping to engage the organization around policies and practices. Software solutions can support ERGs to provide policy input, deliver education, give sign-off as well as reaching new members and augmenting employees' voices.

---

[15] Taylor (2020).

Employee engagement digital platforms can help organizations in a number of ways, not least with real-time onsite and remote engagement. Sophisticated metrics and real-time data make it easier to track ERG activities and measure engagement for a clear view of ROI. Such platforms facilitate mentorship programs, increase employee referrals, improve employee orientation, and segment groups to promote richer employee self-identification and deeper inclusion. Sharing resources, educational opportunities, upcoming events, and inclusive stories with the broader company in real time becomes easier through technology. Not least, pulse surveys are also easier to facilitate for gathering information on what is important to employees, which policies they value and the organization's inclusive leadership performance.

8.   Legalistic language that does not inspire

To bring diversity practices to life, policies need to stir the conscience and stimulate desired behaviors among all members of the organization. To do this, policies need to be translated or communicated to the organization in a way that is not only understandable but resonates with individuals' values. This means avoiding technical jargon where possible and instead harnessing familiar language and imagery that aligns with the organization's culture and purpose.

9.   Governance of policies is lacking

Like a handbook for the rules of a game, good governance around policies needs to be clear, transparent, and consistently applied. A frequent problem is that governance of diversity policy becomes too distributed within an organization and there is no oversight on policy implementation. Once policies have been inventoried and linked to key diversity outcomes, it is important to establish clear oversight. For Stage 1 organizations, the policy governance overview may sit with risk management and/or HR. Once organizations evolve to a higher maturity levels, governance may be concentrated within one function of the organization—such as the Diversity and Inclusion Office—with operationalization distributed across various functions, such as HR.

10.   Linkage of policies to diversity narrative and goals

To ensure relevance and effectiveness, policies need to collectively and individually support the strategic narrative for Diversity Performance and the organization's strategic diversity goals. Policies are often developed bottom-up, with reference to best practices and as a response to legal requirements. While this is a good source of innovation, it needs to be done with a clear view of the diversity outcomes being sought and a clear sense of how these will be operationally supported.

To create policy alignment, some organizations develop a policy hierarchy map that links each policy into a "family of policies" that, together, contribute to key strategic outcomes that in turn link into the organization's strategic diversity narrative. For example, if the strategic narrative is about better reflecting the culture of their customers, and this entails increasing the representation of women of color in customer-facing roles, then the organization will need to think carefully about which policies will support this outcome. Policies around zero tolerance for racist behavior, policies around balanced recruiting slates, and policies to mitigate stereotypes and bias around race in the recruiting interviews would all be helpful in achieving this outcome. With a clear hierarchy of targeted and strategic policies in place, it is easier to collectively monitor progress toward key diversity outcomes.

An example of a robust, zero tolerance discrimination policy that overcomes these barriers is provided in the following case study.

Case Study: Creating Trust and Collaborative Commitment

A global not-for-profit organization that provides healthcare services for underserved populations was seeking to establish a zero tolerance discrimination policy. With local teams spread throughout the world, its worldwide organization spanned many races, ethnicities, religions, and cultures. The organization wanted to demonstrate that it acted in accordance with the same values reflected in its work highlighting the rights of underserved communities. The organization was committed to all aspects of diversity and had already established a discrimination policy that is shared with new employees at orientation and frequently referred to.

Their goal was to craft a policy that would engage and inspire, rather than one steeped in dry, legal language that would be off-putting and undigestible for employees. The aim was for all members to understand their part in personally mitigating discrimination through daily actions.

The organization collectively captured their commitment and rationale for diversity in the following statement: "We believe that diversity allows all of us individually to flourish as we flourish collectively with our organization. We believe that our diversity allows our organization to be better positioned now and in the future to deliver on our commitments to our stakeholders in an ethical, sustainable and agile way."

The organization then set out an overall diversity policy statement: "We celebrate our diversity each day by deliberately drawing in the diversity for it is a source of great richness to us collectively. We listen with curiosity and kindness and seek to understand so that diverse thoughts are liberated, connected, and translated for impact. We speak with respect so as to invite a rich dialogue occurring where thoughts can merge and extend. We raise our hand each time, in courage, when we see an injustice being done, with the aim not to admonish but to educate and enter into the courageous discussions that extend our own learning and that of the group.

We are continually on the lookout for biases so that we can advance equity throughout our organization and ensure that no one feels unseen or unheard. We lead by example each and every moment of the day in order to create an inclusive environment where people feel safe and can flourish."

Each statement in the overall diversity policy was supported with additional policies on zero tolerance of discrimination and harassment, a flexible work environment, parental leave for all parents, and advancement of allyship, for example. The organization's policies were endowed with certain qualities to make them effective and engaging:

- An avoidance of legal jargon, so it reads as a document that is meant to be inclusive and understandable—a "living" document.
- Use of the word "we" to invite inclusion.
- Clarity on definitions (e.g. what constitutes discrimination in everyday language).
- Examples of everyday situations employees may face.
- Guidance on the steps for recourse or sanctions, including an opportunity for internal learning after an infringement to become more aware and inclusive.

The organization's zero tolerance discrimination and harassment policy stated as follows:

"We commit to an environment where there is zero tolerance for discrimination and harassment and where all members of our organization have a responsibility to facilitate the attainment of this goal.

Discrimination includes and is not limited to:

- providing a preferential advantage to some over others, whether during the recruitment process or development process or promotion process and all processes that lead to the advancement and development of our people;
- causing a member of our organization to feel isolated through hostile behavior, whether by an individual or a group;
- supporting discrepancies in benefits, compensation, and growth opportunities for similar work and roles; and
- failing to accommodate physical and mental (dis)abilities etc.

Harassment includes and is not limited to:

- perpetuating stereotypes;
- undermining comments; and
- all actions that lead to the intimidation of one of more of our people and their sense of exclusion.

We all carry responsibility for identifying discrimination and harassment and never condoning it. When we witness discrimination, we have a duty to report the discrimination through a clear process. All cases of discrimination and/or harassment follow a transparent, independent review process. Discrimination and harassment findings are coupled with sanctions, up to and including the termination of employment. At the same time, any discrimination and harassment situation will result not only in dialogue with the affected parties, but will also be assessed for internal learning such that the organization can learn from the infringement and ensure that we incorporate this learning within our processes, our communication and our development."

▶ **Key takeaway** A key strength of this organization's policy is how it created trust in the collective commitment by leaders and members alike that zero tolerance for discrimination was an enshrined value and not only about legal compliance. This requires internal learning and reflection when infringements occur. It is important to define discrimination simply and clearly so that people know the full scope of its meaning. Namely, that all discrimination and harassment cases will be reviewed and if found to be present will lead to action, up to and including termination of employment.

3 How to Make Policies Work

Understanding which diversity policies are most valued by employees is a good starting point for leaders. This can be achieved by identifying all diversity policies in place in the organization and asking employees to rank the ones they consider to be of most value. In the 2019 BCG research noted above, employees from a group of 16,500 people across 14 countries: Australia, Brazil, China, Denmark, Finland, France, Germany, Japan, India, Italy, Norway, Spain, the UK, and the US were surveyed about the effectiveness of 31 diversity initiatives.[16] This type of primary research is very helpful, especially when it enables organizations to identify the perceived value of policies per minority group. In this case, BCG identified feedback for three minority categories: gender, LGBTQI+, and race. This was supplemented by scholarly research and diversity policy audits to reflect the leading policies for each minority group (Table 1).

4 Policies Highly Valued by Women

According to primary business research, women rank anti-discrimination policies as most important to them. This is followed by flexible work arrangements and advancement programs, including mentorship, allyship, and sponsorship programs.[17]

Flexible work arrangements and parental leave—The double burden of working and carrying a greater share of household and childcare is common for women in many countries across the world. American working women put in longer hours on the job, spent more time caring for their children, and did more work around the house than they did a year earlier, according to a 2019 U.S. Labor Department survey.[18] In the EU, 93% of women aged 25 to 49 who had children under 18 took

---

[16] Krentz et al., "Fixing the Flawed Approach."

[17] Krentz et al., "Fixing the Flawed Approach."

[18] Fuhrmans (2019).

Table 1 Policies Valued Highly per Minority Group

Research has found the following policies to be particularly highly valued by women, LGBTQI+ people, racial and ethnic minorities, and people with disabilities.

Women/Gender Equality	Race/Ethnic Group
Anti-discrimination policies	Zero tolerance for racism
Flexible work arrangements and parental leave	The presence of ethnic minority role models
Advancement policies and mentorship and support from both men and women within the organization	Policies aimed at retaining racial and ethnic minorities

LGBTQI+	People with Disabilities
Addressing zero tolerance for discrimination	A strategic commitment from leadership for supporting people with disabilities
Inclusive healthcare coverage	Policies regarding emergency preparedness
Parental leave with no exceptions	Flexibility of working from home
Non-gendered bathrooms	Access to digital content for the blind or visually impaired

Adapted from BCG "Fixing the Flawed Approach to Diversity", 2019

care of their children on a daily basis, compared to 69% of men.[19] Women in Asia and the Pacific worked the longest hours in the world: 7.7 hours daily, of which only 3.3 hours are paid, with the rest dedicated to unpaid care work.[20] China is a case in point: some 61% of women participate in China's labor force—higher than OECD member countries at 52%—but the meantime of unpaid work for women in China is 27.3 hours per week, markedly higher than men's 10.6 hours.[21]

Flexible work arrangements and workplace flexibility are therefore extremely important and require interventions for women to manage both work and home responsibilities. Increasingly, fathers among the younger generations are also seeking flexibility to play a caring role within their families. Flexibility doesn't look the same for every individual; for one employee it might be leaving early to pick up children from daycare or school, and for another the ability to work remotely on some days. A flexible work culture avoids a one-size-fits-all approach as dictating exactly how these policies may be used can make them less effective.[22] Clarifying and aligning expectations around what employees and the organization can expect from the other builds trust and increases the likelihood that flexible working arrangements will be successful and mutually beneficial.

---

[19] "The Life of Women and Men in Europe: A Statistical Portrait," Eurostat, European Union, last modified July 2020, https://ec.europa.eu/eurostat/cache/infographs/womenmen/bloc-3d.html-1?lang=en.

[20] "Unpaid Work in Asia and the Pacific," Social Development Policy Papers, United Nations Economic and Social Commission for Asia and the Pacific, December 19, 2019, https://www.unescap.org/sites/default/files/PP_2019-02_Unpaid%20Work.pdf.

[21] Feng (2019).

[22] "Give Employees Flexible Options for Flexible Work," *Harvard Business Review,* last modified May 22, 2019, https://hbr.org/tip/2019/05/give-employees-flexible-options-for-flexible-work.

Flexibility became even more of a priority with the outbreak of COVID-19. Almost overnight, organizations implemented a range of policies and initiatives that women (and other minority groups) appreciate—and have campaigned for—including expanded remote and flexible work, increased paid/or unpaid time off, additional flexibility to move from a full-time to a part-time schedule, expanded policies for how to use existing paid and unpaid leave and shorter workweeks.[23]

Advancement and mentorship policies—There is a clear discrepancy between the opportunities afforded to men and women on the career ladder. While 48% of men said they had received detailed information on career paths to jobs which had profit and loss (P&L) responsibility in the past 24 months, just 15% of women reported the same, according to the Working Mother Research Institute; and while 54% of men had a career discussion with a mentor or sponsor in the past 24 months, only 39% of women did.[24] Further, 71% of executives have protégés whose gender and race match their own, according to the Center for Talent Innovation.[25]

White male leaders tend to think that women most value support during the recruitment process, but for women a key priority is having visible female role models in the leadership team to demonstrate that advancement is possible. Such role models are more likely to understand the challenge of balancing work and home life in the face of societal expectations for women. Yet women also acknowledge not receiving sufficient support from other senior women leaders.[26] Women at higher levels may feel the need to build and display more male-specific emotional intelligence, or EQ competencies, which can undermine the interpersonal relationships and empathy so important to cultivate supporting relationships with junior women, according to some business research.[27] Other research has found that limited spots for women in a heavily male-dominated environment create competition and thus support of other women takes a backseat to winning the coveted spot. Yet another view is that a systemic bias has resulted in the need to keep "a dead-even balance" between women through the generations. When there is a promotion for some, this balance gets disturbed, resulting in behavior that tries to restore the balance, which can undermine rather than build up successful women.

---

[23] Diverse employees are struggling the most during COVID-19—here's how companies can respond, McKinsey & Company, November 2020, https://www.mckinsey.com/~/media/McKinsey/Featured%20Insights/Diversity%20and%20Inclusion/Diverse%20employees%20are%20struggling%20the%20most%20during%20COVID%2019%20heres%20how%20companies%20can%20respond/Diverse-employees-are-struggling-the-most-during-COVID-19-heres-how-companies-can-respond-vF.pdf?shouldIndex=false.

[24] "The Gender Gap at the Top," Working Mother Research Institute, 2020, https://www.workingmother.com/sites/workingmother.com/files/attachments/2019/06/women_at_the_top_correct_size.pdf.

[25] "Key Findings: The Sponsor Dividend," Center for Talent Innovation, 2019, https://coqual.org/reports/the-sponsor-dividend/.

[26] Andrews (2020).

[27] Heim et al. (2015).

Whatever the reasons, women supporting other women is a critical requirement for gender diversity, and the right conditions should be created to support this. Policies setting out the expectation of mutual support are a helpful way of accomplishing this goal: namely, by advocating the importance of being an inclusive ally and creating opportunities to self-assess and receive assessments on the allyship displayed by leaders to others in the organization. Other effective practices include opening up promotion slots for women and creating networking opportunities between senior women and women at earlier stages of their careers.

While women need to be allies for other women, the role of male leaders cannot be overlooked. Since men occupy the majority of leadership roles in organizations, with access to the information, budget, and influence afforded by such roles, they are pivotal to supporting and sponsoring women to advance their careers. Policies should ensure that men feel invited to contribute and play their role in this regard. Some business analysis shows that a third of men feel excluded from the diversity and inclusion journey.[28]

5 Policies That Support Ethnic and Racial Diversity

Interventions to reduce systemic and personal bias and promote ethnic and racial diversity within the organization are very important, according to primary business research. This includes policies that mitigate personal and systemic bias. Formal employee training to mitigate biases, increasing cultural competency, blind screening, removing bias from evaluations and promotion decisions, diverse interview panels, and bias-free day-to-day experience top the list of most valued diversity policies by people of color. This deep value placed on bias-free talent processes is in response to the systemic bias that results in unequal treatment in the workplace.[29]

Zero tolerance for racism policy—A policy on zero tolerance for racism is ranked as the most important policy for people of color, coupled with ongoing communication that a culture of tolerance and respect is among the organization's core values.

For organizations to demonstrate seriousness, such policies need to be established, if they don't already exist, and communicated widely. The organization should encourage open and honest dialog about what can be done, individually and collectively, to address racism.

Efforts to demonstrate zero tolerance for racism through policies and practices will fall flat if people of color or ethnic minorities believe that the statements of

---

[28] Donnelly (2017).

[29] Krentz et al., "Fixing the Flawed Approach."

support are simply marketing messages—a phenomenon known as "woke washing" in which commitments do not align with a brand's purpose, values, and practices.[30]

Underpinned with genuine commitment, a zero tolerance policy for racism and discrimination can be a call to action for every individual to take responsibility to create a safe, respectful environment and work diligently to vanquish systemic bias that contributes to inequity.

Ethnic diversity role models policy—A policy promoting greater visibility of role models who represent diversity in leadership is highly valued by people of color, given the absence of such role models. The scarcity of role models in leadership positions can perpetuate stereotypes that people unconsciously employ as they make talent leadership decisions.

Despite the importance of role models, few organizations place sufficient focus on the recruitment of minority role models, whether from the perspective of race, ethnicity, sexual orientation, disability, culture, or religion. In the UK, for example, over a third of the largest listed companies in the FTSE 100 are likely to miss the target established by the government-sponsored Parker Review to have at least one director from an ethnic minority by 2021.[31]

Among Fortune 500 boards of directors, progress has also been slow, according to the Alliance for Board Diversity. Some 80% of 1033 board seats in 2018 were filled by Caucasian/white directors, some 59% of them by Caucasian/white men. Women and minorities represented 34% of the seats. Between 2004 and 2016, minority men gained only one percent of seats. Minority women showed slight gains, up from three percent of board seats in 2004 to 5.8% in 2018. In 2018, just 19.5% of board seats in the Fortune 100 were held by African American/Blacks, Asian/Pacific Islanders, Hispanic/Latinos, and other minority groups, even though they made up 40% of the U.S. population.[32]

To address these gaps, organizations can set a policy that includes a goal to have ethnic minorities as role models, along with guidelines for how this will be accomplished and metrics to monitor progress. Taking a long-term view to filling the leadership pipeline, sponsoring and advancing role models and providing specific networking opportunities and career development are also critical.

Retention policy for people of color—Overall, attrition rates are higher for people of color, with the most pronounced losses occurring early in the pipeline. For example business research shows that, at entry level, a Black person is 1.4 times

---

[30] Vredenburg et al. (2020).

[31] Parker et al. (2020).

[32] "Missing Pieces Report: The 2018 Board Diversity Census of Women and Minorities on Fortune 500 Boards," Deloitte, https://www2.deloitte.com/us/en/pages/center-for-board-effectiveness/articles/missing-pieces-fortune-500-board-diversity-study-2018.html, accessed December 31, 2020.

more likely than a white person to leave a financial services firm,[33] in part due to feeling "alone" and "different." In the same survey, 75% of Black employees above entry level who were found to be in the minority and "alone," consistently reported higher levels of perceived discrimination than those who were not.[34] The sense of being alone diminishes with the presence of a role model, creating a sense of connection at the highest level.

Another policy that reduces the sense of being alone relates to allyship. Allyship is about empathy and acknowledging that Black and ethnically diverse colleagues face different issues than others, yet that everyone in the organization can be an ally to stand up and support change. This entails research and education to understand the issues facing Black and ethnically diverse colleagues, and to be continually open to learning new information in order to be an effective and trusted ally for minorities.

6   Policies That Deliver Value and Benefits for LGBTQI+

The four policies explored below have growing importance for the LGBTQI+ community.

Zero tolerance for sexual orientation, gender identity, and transgender discrimination—While there has been progress in some countries, fear still prevents LGBTQI+ employees from bringing their whole selves to work; in the U.S. almost half (46%) of this population of workers report being closeted in the workplace.[35] This situation is exacerbated when two thirds of non-LGBTQI+ employees believe it is "unprofessional" to discuss sexual orientation or gender identity in the workplace.[36]

As a result, individuals in this minority group often cover up or downplay aspects of their authentic selves (e.g. by hiding personal relationships or changing the way they dress or speak) in order to avoid discrimination.[37] Individuals can feel exhausted from spending time and energy concealing their sexual orientation and gender identity—an option that is not available to transgender employees who want to begin transitioning, unless they leave their current employers.[38] Some 35% of LGBTQI+ and slightly more than half (51%) of transgender employees in the UK disguised their identity at work for fear of discrimination.[39]

---

[33] Racial equity in financial services, McKinsey & Co, September 10, 2020, https://www.mckinsey.com/industries/financial-services/our-insights/racial-equity-in-financial-services.

[34] Racial equity in financial services, McKinsey & Co.

[35] Fidas and Cooper (2019).

[36] Fidas and Cooper, "A Workplace Divided."

[37] Catalyst, "What Is Covering?" Catalyst, December 11, 2014, https://www.catalyst.org/research/infographic-what-is-covering/.

[38] Rudin et al. (2020).

[39] Bachmann and Gooch (2018).

A zero tolerance anti-discrimination policy for LGTBQI+ is the most valued policy for this group. Participation in external events (such as Pride activities) was also important for signaling that the company is an LGBTQI+-friendly organization that values its employees.[40] Progress is being made in this area: 91% of Fortune 500 companies have gender identity protections enumerated in their non-discrimination policies and 98% of all businesses targeted by the Human Rights Foundation's Corporate Equality Index (CEI) 2020 offer explicit gender identity non-discrimination protections.[41]

Inclusive healthcare coverage without exception—Appropriate healthcare coverage is also ranked highly in the LGTBQI+ group, including equivalent-partner or spousal benefits as part of the employee's healthcare plan, life insurance, relocation assistance, adoption assistance, and transgender-inclusive healthcare coverage.[42] There is still a gap in transgender-inclusive healthcare coverage, however, with the 2020 CEI report finding that 65% of the Fortune 500 and 89% of the CEI universe of total targeted businesses offer transgender-inclusive healthcare coverage.[43]

One of the outcomes from the COVID-19 pandemic has been a number of policy changes adopted by organizations to support employees, including increased healthcare coverage. Since mental health is a particularly critical issue for LGBTQI+ individuals, policy steps could include the provision of healthcare services and counseling support as well as awareness of how mental health is affected by increased workload or availability of office connectivity and ensuring appropriate measures to address this.[44]

Parental leave with no exceptions—Parental leave policies tend to favor the "traditional" family stereotype of a two-parent family with a heterosexual mother and father, where the mother assumes the role of caring of the children. Yet the reality is quite different. There is a growing percentage of single-parent households, with 23% of children in the U.S. and 15% of children in Canada living in such households.[45] Same-sex marriage is now recognized in 29 countries,[46] with same-sex

---

[40] Krentz et al., "Fixing the Flawed Approach."

[41] Human Rights Campaign Foundation, "Corporate Equality Index 2020."

[42] Krentz et al., "Fixing the Flawed Approach."

[43] Human Rights Campaign Foundation, "Corporate Equality Index 2020."

[44] Diverse employees are struggling the most during COVID-19—here's how companies can respond, McKinsey & Company, November 2020, https://www.mckinsey.com/~/media/McKinsey/Featured%20Insights/Diversity%20and%20Inclusion/Diverse%20employees%20are%20struggling%20the%20most%20during%20COVID%2019%20heres%20how%20companies%20can%20respond/Diverse-employees-are-struggling-the-most-during-COVID-19-heres-how-companies-can-respond-vF.pdf?shouldIndex=false.

[45] Kramer (2019).

[46] Marriage Equality Around the World, Human Rights Campaign, https://www.hrc.org/resources/marriage-equality-around-the-world, accessed February 11, 2021.

couples raising families. Children are also being raised by parents located in two different countries or by grandparents or step-parents. Whatever the construct, the parent—defined as someone caring for a child—looks to their country and employer to recognize their "caring" role and have this role supported through parental benefits.

The requirements to accommodate different types of family units will only grow in view of declining marriage rates, increased rates of cohabitation outside of marriage, and greater likelihood of children being born to unmarried couples. In fact, a whole range of different family units make up an increasing percentage of all families but are often not recognized by law in many jurisdictions and thus risk losing critical parental benefits. Despite a growing percentage of same-sex couples, there remain barriers in many countries for this minority group.[47] In Japan, about 8.9% of the population identifies as LGBTQI+,[48] but same-sex marriages are not allowed and parental benefits are not given.[49] This is despite a growing percentage of citizens supporting this type of protection and research confirming that the wellness of same-sex couples and their children is enhanced through recognition and legislation that supports benefits.[50,51]

Non-gendered bathroom policies—It is hard to identify the actual percentage of the world population that is transgender because the analysis is incomplete. In the U.S., it is estimated that approximately 0.58% of the adult population identifies as being transgender, with the District of Columbia having the highest percentage at 2.77%.[52] While these percentages seem small, this translates into millions of transgender people in the U.S. Yet many organizations only have gendered bathrooms which can make transgender employees feel uncomfortable in that their full person is not being recognized. It may be interpreted as forcing people to make a choice that doesn't necessarily align with their gender and thereby creates an "environment that is not affirming to anyone [who] identifies as transgender, genderqueer, gender neutral or non-binary and only affirms those [who] identify on the gender binary, particularly cisgender people,"[53] as one analysis has pointed out.

---

[47] "Table 1: Household Characteristics of Opposite-Sex and Same-Sex Couple Households: 2018 American Community Survey," US Census Bureau, 2019.

[48] "Dentsu Diversity Lab Conducts LGBT Survey 2018," Dentsu, January 10, 2019, https://www.dentsu.co.jp/news/release/2019/0110-009728.html.

[49] Glauert (2019).

[50] "Resolution on Sexual Orientation and Marriage," American Psychological Association, archived May 11, 2011, https://web.archive.org/web/20110511190536/http://www.apa.org/about/governance/council/policy/gay-marriage.pdf.

[51] Pawelski et al. (2006).

[52] "What Percentage of the Population is Transgender 2020," World Population Review, https://worldpopulationreview.com/state-rankings/transgender-population-by-state, accessed December 26, 2020.

[53] Lobell (2019).

A workplace that provides gender-neutral bathrooms fosters an inclusive environment and shows that the company cares about diversity. It also demonstrates that a company doesn't just tolerate workers' differences but affirms them. It "sends a clear message that the organization does not just talk about diversity and inclusion; it acts on it. It sends the message that the organization respects and values every person for who they are and what they contribute, not by what sex they were assigned at birth or their gender identity,"[54] according to the Society for Human Resource Management.

7 Policies That Deliver Value and Benefits for Persons with Disabilities

Of the estimated one billion—or 15%—of the world population with disabilities, 80% are of working age. The right of people with disabilities to decent work, however, is frequently denied. People with disabilities, particularly women, face enormous attitudinal, physical, and informational barriers to equal work opportunities.[55]

Often, awareness and confidence about how to foster inclusion of persons with disabilities in the workplace is lacking. This can lead to inaccessible work tools, inadequate workplace adjustments, insufficient support to help persons with disabilities keep their employment and a lack of targeted support for Small and Medium-Sized Enterprises (SMEs) regarding the employment of persons with disabilities.[56]

In addition, there is concern about the cost of accommodating persons with disabilities. In fact, making such accommodations generally entails minimal cost and is typically a fruitful investment: as much as 59% of accommodations cost absolutely nothing to make, while the rest typically cost only $500 per employee with a disability, according to one study.[57]

Progress is being made in this area, as these figures show:

- The Disability Equality Index (DEI) 2020 which benchmarks the Fortune 1000 and America's top 200 revenue-grossing law firms (Am Law 200) on disability workplace inclusion, showed that 75% of multinational companies had disability inclusive standards of workplace non-discrimination that apply to all employees, compared to 69% in 2019.

---

[54] Lobell, "Gender Neutral Bathrooms."

[55] Disability at work, the International Labour Organisation, https://www.ilo.org/global/topics/disability-and-work/lang--en/index.htm, accessed January 7, 2021.

[56] Fundación ONCE and ILO Global Business and Disability Network, *Making the Future of Work Inclusive of People with Disabilities,* 2019, http://www.businessanddisability.org/wp-content/uploads/2019/11/PDF_acc_FoW_PwD.pdf, 10.

[57] "Benefits and Costs of Accommodation," Job Accommodation Network, last modified October 21, 2020, https://askjan.org/topics/costs.cfm.

- Some 42% of multinational companies reported that their non-U.S. operations had established disability-focused ERGs or affinity group chapters.
- A total of 85% of businesses with a company-wide written statement of a commitment to diversity and inclusion specifically named "disability."
- Some 70% of businesses had an accessibility expert to resolve accessibility and compatibility issues necessary for people with disabilities to use technology systems.[58]

Stakeholders are increasingly demanding more focus on people with disabilities. For example, a global investor coalition, representing more than $2.8 trillion in combined assets, has called on companies in which they invest to become more disability inclusive, through a "Joint Investor Statement on Disability Inclusion."[59]

The Disability Equality Index assesses the extent to which the strategic narrative commitment is entrenched in all facets of the organization.[60] Drawing on the DEI evaluation, the following policies and practices are considered important to people with disabilities:

A strategic leadership commitment to people with disabilities—Policy initiatives include a written D&I statement of commitment that specifically mentions disability and is posted internally and externally, including in the annual diversity report and/or company report. In addition, the organization officially recognizes a Disability Employee Resource Group (ERG)/Affinity Group with executive sponsorship and sets organization-wide, numeric goals for employment and tenure of persons with disabilities.

Additional priority policies include surveys assessing the engagement of people who self-identify as a person with disability, assessed against overall engagement and within business units, geographic regions, and levels, and a diversity council with a mission statement specifically including commitment to persons with disability group. Having people with disabilities in senior roles is also important, such as serving on the board of directors and other senior executive leadership roles. Leaders of organizations can also participate on the boards of directors of disability-focused organizations. Another valuable practice is for senior executives to serve as allies, sponsors, and mentors to people with disabilities and be evaluated for this as part of their performance evaluation.

Emergency preparedness policies catering for persons with disabilities—It is incumbent on organizations to create a safe work environment at all times and certainly in emergencies. Policies in this area need to reflect a number of aspects,

---

[58] Disability:IN, "Disability Equality Index."

[59] "CEO Letter on Disability Inclusion," Disability:IN, October 29, 2020, https://disabilityin.org/in-the-news/ceo-letter-on-disability-inclusion/.

[60] "Disability Equality Index," Disability:IN, https://disabilityin.org/what-we-do/disability-equality-index/, accessed December 24, 2020.

such as emergency preparedness procedure(s), business continuity plans catering for people with disabilities, along with buddy systems and designated teams of volunteers to provide assistance to people with disabilities where needed. Further measures include visual and audible fire alarm system components, stair-descent devices, automatic accessible Intranet messages, designated safe places to wait for assistance, and a confidential accessible system for submitting and tracking emergency evacuation assistance needs.

Supporting flexibility to work from home—Flexible work arrangements are highly valued by people with disabilities so organizations should ensure that digital support (e.g. work-from-home productivity tools) are accessible and that there is a process to transition work accommodations and adjustments to an alternate environment (e.g. bringing assistive technology or ergonomic equipment home).

Access to digital content—More than 200 million people are blind or visually impaired and this has a huge impact on their quality of life and employability. Less than 50% of people who are blind or visually impaired are employed. Even with high educational attainment, the variation between the wages of people with visual impairments and those with no disability who have a bachelor's degree or higher is $14,727—the largest earnings difference among workers at all educational levels. In Europe there are an estimated 30 million blind and partially sighted persons.[61] Catering to this large group of potential employees and consumers through more progressive and inclusive disability policies should be a priority for diversity-driven organizations.

The first step in creating robust policies is to assess the level of digital accessibility and whether it is meeting the needs of this population. Digital content should be tested for accessibility, including social media postings, blog posts, multi-media, and newsletters. It is important to ensure that digital products such as apps, products, services, and experiences including training, presentations, documents, and social media are accessible and usable by individuals with disabilities.

Disability-Focused Suppliers—Finally, another policy measure that organizations can take is to demonstrate supplier diversity practices, or social procurement, that fully include or preference disability-owned, veteran-disability-owned, and service-disabled veteran-owned businesses.

8   How to Harness Policies in Practice

Depending on an organization's Diversity Performance maturity level, the Integrated Diversity Model sets out a range of evidence-based initiatives that can be implemented to harness policies effectively (Table 2).

---

[61] Bourne et al. (2017).

Table 2   Harness Policies Capability and Initiatives for Five Stages
Overview of initiatives to harness policies at each stage of diversity maturity.

	Stage 1 Legal Compliance	Stage 2 Stakeholder Requirements	Stage 3 Organizational Performance	Stage 4 Reinvention	Stage 5 Societal Value
Focus	Zero discrimination	Representation Talent processes	Team practices Rewarding Leadership role	Equity Needs-based Valued	Partners Value chain Reinforcement
Skills	Compliance training	HR requirements ERG interaction	Evidence in practice	Pre-requisite for advancement	Partner alignment
Process	Compliance rules	Develop policies Apply best practices	Evaluate Apply	Co-craft with ERG Pilot & pioneer Prune	Reinforce with partners
Responsibilities	Legal	HR	Leaders Diversity office	Leaders ERG	Partner diversity council
Metrics	Drive compliance	Incorporated by HR	Applied by teams	Valued by beneficiaries	Supporting partners
Technology	Compliance management	Policy management	Policy management	Policy management ERG platform	Partner policy enablement

9   Stage 1 Organizations: Legal Compliance

At Stage 1, the primary focus is to satisfy legal requirements that outlaw discrimination and advocate quotas and affirmative action in certain communities. Stage 1 organizations put in place clear non-discrimination policies, where sanctions for discrimination, such as termination of contract, are clearly laid out. This is coupled with policies requiring employees to attend mandatory compliance training, in which the rules of engagement are communicated.

10   Stage 2 Organizations: Stakeholder Requirements

At Stage 2, policies are focused on ensuring the targeted representation of people in the organization (usually specified for women, race/ethnic group, LGBTQI+, and people with disabilities). Stage 2 organizations will tend to have clear policies around advertisement of positions, and recruitment, assessment, salary, and benefit processes, with the aim of supporting representation targets. For example, the organization can specify that in any recruiting slate, there need to be at least 25%candidates of color or women. Stage 2 organizations make use of ERGs to help communicate policies throughout the organization, and obtain feedback and/ or sign off on policies.

11   Stage 3 Organizations: Organizational Performance

At Stage 3, policies are focused on the advancement of earmarked talent, including policies around the appointment of mentors, and respectful and inclusive conduct. There are also policies that set out the evaluation of performance. Often a Policy Management system is in place to support the policy process from design and sign off to distribution, and finally revision.

12   Stage 4 Organizations: Reinvention

At Stage 4, organizations are focused on developing diversity policies that drive engagement and loyalty and are regarded as effective and valuable by employees. Policies are a method to stimulate engagement and loyalty and advance a sense of belonging and of being valued.

13   Stage 5 Organizations: Societal Value

At Stage 5, the emphasis shifts from having a blueprint of diversity policies inside the organization to evaluating policies that support and leverage diversity guidelines within the supply chain, where applicable. In addition, there is a focus on evaluating policies for the contribution they make to society. For example, providing equal parental leave to both parents is regarded by organizations as also supporting gender equality within society.

To illustrate the process of arriving at an "ideal" diversity policy, the following case study examines a technology organization that had set a priority to expand gender diversity.

Case Study: Supporting More Women in STEM

The leader of a diversity-minded technology company knew that to increase the number of women in the organization, the right set of policies, practices, and processes was just as important as vision and aspiration. Their goal was to have 30% women at leadership level (up from 17%) and 40% female workforce representation overall (up from 21%). As identified in their strategic narrative, this leader was convinced that with greater diversity they could better meet their customers' needs, spur innovation and contribute to the societal goal of developing and advancing women in STEM.

To realize this admirable aspiration, the leader recognized that diversity infrastructure needed to be implemented—the scaffolding that would hold up the vision and steadily advance it until it became part and parcel of how the organization operated on a day-to-day basis. To achieve that meant understanding how to embed diversity policies within talent processes and ensure that these were the right policies.

Table 3 Confirming Policies Valued as Important by Women in the Organization

Policies ranked highly by women	Priority Ranking
Zero tolerance for discrimination with firm action for transgressions	1
Flexibility policy, including part-time work and working from home	2
Parental leave policy, for both parents	3
Formal training policy to mitigate biases especially in mid-manager promotion process	4
Bias-free day-to-day experience policy, including bias awareness workshops for all leaders	5
Structural intervention policies (such as lactation rooms)	6
Balanced candidate slates policies	7

Adapted from BCG "Fixing the Flawed Approach to Diversity", 2019

Crafting a robust diversity policy is not a matter of simply putting out a statement and disseminating it around the organization. Policymaking is complex: one challenge is maintaining the delicate balance between instituting global talent policies while acknowledging and accommodating labor laws in specific countries where the organization operates. For instance, in many Asian countries, including China and India, there were strict labor laws that mandate maximum permissible working hours in a week. In India, for example, female employees were prohibited from working beyond certain evening hours in factories and commercial establishments[62] as well as having caps on overtime hours in a day/week and companies were obliged to provide transportation for women in the event of longer working hours. Another issue to grapple with in devising policies was the different philosophies between countries with regards to hiring and firing—in the U.S., for example, boom-and-bust periods were often characterized by a hiring-firing seesaw, while in Asia companies must show evidence that the downsizing or layoffs were warranted.

The technology organization acknowledged the complexity of the task but was determined to create robust diversity and global talent policies to drive the diversity focus throughout their organization.

For this purpose, the organization decided to survey women in the organization to ask them which policies were most important to them. Through this they identified seven policies regarded as most critical to women. They also segmented the responses to reflect different ranking of policies, depending on role and seniority. Feedback was received through a process of surveying all women in the organization and inviting women to workshops entitled "deep listening policy sessions." At these workshops, women were invited to share the challenges they face in their daily work and the policies that would make a difference to them and support advancement of gender diversity in the organization. The results are reflected in Table 3.

Having received clear direction from their women colleagues, the organization performed a review of their current policies, pruned those policies that were not regarded as adding value, and focused on designing policies that supported the requirements of women and were regarded as valuable.

---

[62] "About Women Labour," Government of India Ministry of Labour & Employment, https://labour.gov.in/womenlabour/about-women-labour, accessed January 6, 2021.

▶   **Key takeaway** Today, the technology company is regarded as a pioneer in
      advancing gender diversity and known for being a leader in advancing new
      and innovative policies in the industry. The deep listening policy sessions
      have become a standard within the organization to propose and vet policies.
      The organization has grown its representation of women in STEM and has
      reached 38% women in STEM in its senior ranks, now ranking as a sector
      leader on gender representation. This company continues to innovate and re-
      gards their policy capability as critical to their success.

14   Concluding Remarks

The Harness Policy capability is a critical enabler of Diversity Performance. It
provides clarity on the rules of engagement for the diversity journey. When policies are developed to provide value to the members of the organization and when
they are applied consistently and fairly, they become a powerful enabler of diversity. However, for this to occur, organizations need to avoid and preempt multiple barriers that hinder diversity. With a policy architecture of clear governance,
where policies are collaboratively developed, consistently applied, transgressions
are sanctioned, and the needs of employee groups are identified and satisfied,
organizations will be well-prepared to reach their desired stage of Diversity Performance.

In Chapter 10 we examine the importance of the Measure and Monitor capability for Diversity Performance.

References

Andrews, Shawn. "Why Women Don't Always Support Other Women." Forbes. Last Modified
     January 21, 2020. https://www.forbes.com/sites/forbescoachescouncil/2020/01/21/why-wom-
     en-dont-always-support-other-women/.
Bachmann, Chaka L., and Becca Gooch. "LGBT in Britain – Work Report." Stonewall, April 25,
     2018. https://www.stonewall.org.uk/lgbt-britain-work-report.
Bethea, Aiko. "What Black Employee Resource Groups Need Right Now/." *Harvard Business
     Review*, June 29, 2020. https://hbr.org/2020/06/what-black-employee-resource-groups-need-
     right-now.
Bourne, Rupert R. A. et al. "Magnitude, Temporal Trends, and Projections of the Global Prev-
     alence of Blindness and Distance and Near Vision Impairment: A Systematic Review and
     Meta-Analysis." *The Lancet* 5, no. 9 (2017): 888–897. https://doi.org/10.1016/S2214-
     109X(17)30293-0.
Castilla, Emilio J. "Accounting for the Gap: A Firm Study Manipulating Organizational Account-
     ability and Transparency in Pay Decisions." *Organization Science* 26, no. 2 (March–April
     2015): 311–631. https://doi-org.ezp.sub.su.se/10.1287/orsc.2014.0950.
Dobbin, Frank, and Alexandra Kalev. "Why Diversity Management Backfires (And How Firms
     Can Make it Work)." Harvard University Edmond J. Safra Center for Ethics, February 26,
     2015.   https://ethics.harvard.edu/blog/why-diversity-management-backfires-and-how-firms-
     can-make-it-work.

Dobbin, Frank, and Alexandra Kalev. "Why Diversity Programs Fail." *Harvard Business Review*, July–August 2016. https://hbr.org/2016/07/why-diversity-programs-fail.

Dobbin, Frank, Daniel Schrage, and Alexandra Kalev, "Race Against the Iron Cage: The Varied Effects of Bureaucratic Personnel Reforms on Diversity." *American Sociological Review* 80, no. 5 (2015): 1014–1044.

Donnelly, Grace. "Survey Confirms What Diversity Professionals Have Long Suspected: People Think Inclusion in the Workplace Hurts White Men." Fortune, September 28, 2017. https://fortune.com/2017/09/28/survey-diversity-hurts-white-men/.

Feng, Xue. "Women in East Asia Job Market: How Hard It Is to Make a Work–Family Balance?" Women in Business, Smart Week. Last Modified June 3, 2019. https://www.smartweek.it/women-in-east-asia-job-market-how-hard-it-is-to-make-a-work-family-balance/.

Fidas, Deena, and Liz Cooper. "A Workplace Divided: Understanding the Climate for LGBTQ Workers Nationwide." Human Rights Campaign Foundation, 2019, p. 7.

Fuhrmans, Vanessa. "Female Factor: Women Drive the Labor-Force Comeback." *The Wall Street Journal,* March 1, 2019. https://www.wsj.com/articles/female-factor-women-drive-the-labor-force-comeback-11551436214?mod=article_inline.

Glauert, Rik. "Nine Percent of Japan's Population Is LGBT, Research Finds." *Gay Star News*, January 11, 2019. https://www.gaystarnews.com/article/nine-percent-of-japans-population-is-lgbt-research-finds/.

Gouldner, Alvin W. *Patterns of Industrial Bureaucracy: A Case Study of Modern Factory Administration* (New York: The Free Press, 1954).

Heim, Pat., Tammy Hughes, and Susan K. Golant, *Hardball for Women: Winning at the Game of Business* (New York: Penguin, 2015).

Hodson, Randy. "Dignity in the Workplace Under Participative Management: Alienation and Freedom Revisited." *American Sociological Review* 61, no. 5 (October 1996): 719–738.

Kalev, Alexandra, Erin Kelly, and Frank Dobbin. "Best Practices or Best Guesses? Assessing the Efficacy of Corporate Affirmative Action and Diversity Policies." *American Sociological Review* 71, no. 4 (August 2006): 589–617. https://www.jstor.org/stable/30039011.

Kramer, Stephanie. "U.S. Has World's Highest Rate of Children Living in Single-Parent Households." Pew Research Center, December 12, 2019. https://www.pewresearch.org/fact-tank/2019/12/12/u-s-children-more-likely-than-children-in-other-countries-to-live-with-just-one-parent/.

Krentz, Matt et al. "Fixing the Flawed Approach to Diversity." BCG, January 17, 2019. https://www.bcg.com/publications/2019/fixing-the-flawed-approach-to-diversity.

Lobell, Kylie Ora. "The Benefits of Offering Gender Neutral Bathrooms in the Workplace." *SHRM* (December 6, 2019). https://www.shrm.org/resourcesandtools/legal-and-compliance/employment-law/pages/gender-neutral-bathrooms-in-the-workplace.aspx.

Parker, John et al. "Ethnic Diversity Enriching Business Leadership." *The Parker Review* (February 5, 2020). https://assets.ey.com/content/dam/ey-sites/ey-com/en_uk/news/2020/02/ey-parker-review-2020-report-final.pdf.

Pawelski, James G. et al. "The Effects of Marriage, Civil Union, and Domestic Partnership Laws on the Health and Well-Being of Children." *Pediatrics* 118, no. 1 (July 2006): 349–364. https://doi.org/10.1542/peds.2006-1279.

Rudin, Joel et al. "Bigenderism at Work? Organizational Responses to Trans Men and Trans Women Employees." *Organizational Management Journal* 17, no. 2 (April 2020): 63–81. https://doi.org/10.1108/OMJ-02-2018-0507.

Tetlock, Philip E. "Accountability: A Social Check on the Fundamental Attribution Error." *Social Psychology Quarterly* 48, no. 3 (September 1985): 227–236, https://doi-org.ezp.sub.su.se/10.2307/3033683.

Taylor, Robin Banck. "EEOC FY 2019 Statistics Released: Charges of Discrimination are at an All-Time Low But the Percentage of Retaliation Charges Continues to Rise." JD Supra, February 6, 2020. https://www.jdsupra.com/legalnews/eeoc-fy-2019-statistics-released-64606/.

Vredenburg, Jessica et al. "Brands Taking a Stand: Authentic Brand Activism or Woke Washing?." *Journal of Public Policy and Marketing* (August 14, 2020). https://doi.org/10.1177/0743915620947359.

Measuring and Monitoring the Vital Signs of Diversity

10

When a doctor conducts a wellness check on a patient, the first step is to evaluate the vital signs of essential body functions such as heartbeat, breathing rate, temperature, and blood pressure. While not conclusive for diagnosing illness, these signs can help assess a person's general physical health and give clues about the possible disease. When vital signs fall within normal ranges, it indicates that the body is operating as it should. But ranges falling outside of what is typical for the patient's age can be a sign of a medical problem; a low body temperature, for example, may signal that the body is in distress. Using the patient's medical history, a physician can determine whether there is cause for concern, or if the condition can be eliminated through a standard treatment option. If there is cause for concern, the physician may initiate further tests and treatments.

The protocol is the same for diversity in organizations—and this chapter looks closely at the Measure and Monitor Diversity capability of the Integrated Diversity Model (Fig. 1).

Measuring the vital signs of Diversity Performance is critical for understanding whether an organization is 'healthy' or 'sick.' If the vital signs of diversity are out of balance, the first recourse is to look at recent history, and if no cause is found, to investigate further. Because they are so vital to the healthy functioning of Diversity Performance, metrics to measure diversity should be on the scoreboard of every CEO and senior leader who cares about diversity and shared in real time for immediate attention. An uptick in discrimination, harassment, retaliation lawsuits and grievances, or a drop in inclusive leadership performance are all signals that the organization may be 'sick' and that diversity efforts are at risk.

© Diversity and Performance BV 2021
K. Formanek, *Beyond D&I*, https://doi.org/10.1007/978-3-030-75336-8_10

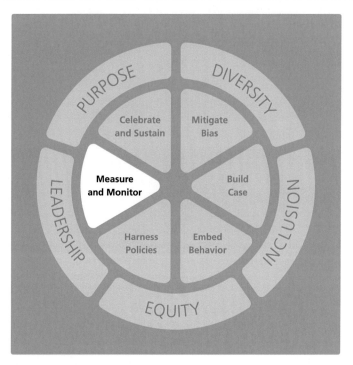

Fig. 1 **Measure and Monitor**
Fifth capability of the integrated diversity model.

1   Defining the Vital Signs of Diversity

A common vital sign set by organizations is that the percentage of women in leadership positions is growing versus stagnating, with reference to say a target of 50%. Consider a scenario in which the percentage of women in senior leadership in an organization unexpectedly falls to 48%—an indication that the organization may 'have caught a cold.' The leader would first consult the dossier, to pinpoint the causes leading to that two percent decline, in order to get back on track. That dossier might show that two women in leadership roles in the U.S. had resigned without warning. This should be of key concern to the leader, who then initiates a more comprehensive health review to better understand why this happened. Through a thorough review, a number of lagging key performance indicators measuring outputs, past developments and effects, and leading indicators measuring inputs, expected future developments and causes, will be examined to identify what is happening in practice so comprehensive action can be taken to get the organization's diversity "bill of health" back on track.

The following list includes other vital signs of diversity and how they manifest:

- **A negative trend in employee engagement pulse surveys**—Decrease in overall engagement, satisfaction and inclusion figures, where possible compared to engagement in minority groups.
- **Unstable rates of retention**—Lower retention rates for minorities relative to the overall population.
- **Job offer declines**—Fewer recruitment offers accepted, particularly by minorities.
- **Benefit gaps**—Bigger salary and benefits gaps for minorities versus the rest of the population.
- **Grievances**—Allegations of unconscious bias or systemic bias emerge more frequently in the organization's grievance channels.
- **Leadership rating decline**—Negative trend in inclusive leadership pulse surveys.
- **Shrinking minority representation**—Decreased or static levels in percentages of minority representation per level, location and business unit, revealing gaps.
- **Negative feedback from customers and suppliers**—Feedback on diversity issues in pulse surveys revealing problems.
- **Promotion gaps**—Minorities not being promoted or advanced at the same rate as the overall population.
- **Distribution of line versus staff and specialized versus general roles**—Imbalance in minority representation in positions holding more responsibility, authority, and higher compensation.

2 Selecting the Right Measures

Acting on the vital signs of diversity in a timely manner means deploying a holistic and integrated set of metrics to lead the diversity journey and realize Diversity Performance. The challenge is how to do that. A holistic measurement framework for diversity indicates when an organization's diversity health is in trouble. To make that diagnosis, the leader is able to leverage the tools that have been presented so far—the Virtuous Circle and the Integrated Diversity Model, complemented with relevant Key Performance Indicators (KPIs).

Well-designed KPIs provide a focus for strategic and operational improvement, create an analytical basis for decision-making and help focus attention on what matters most. Returning to the health analogy, an individual's weight is a lagging KPI, as it represents the outcome of a number of input indicators such as calories consumed or amount of daily exercise. Similarly, shifting the gender balance on a senior leadership team depends on the outcome of specific, measurable actions such as recruiting women or promoting them to management roles. While the gender balance on the senior leadership team is the ultimate indicator that needs to be tracked (a lagging indicator), it is affected by specific actions that have already occurred and which are expected to lead to the desired outcome (a leading indicator) such as the composition of the recruiting panel and the amount of unconscious bias training it has received.

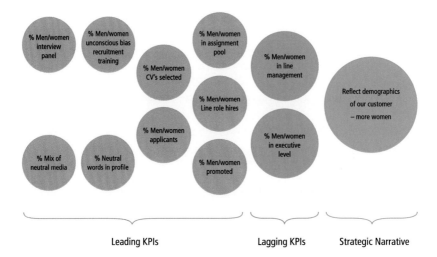

Leading KPIs   Lagging KPIs   Strategic Narrative

Fig. 2 Leading and Lagging KPIs for Gender Representation
A "leading" KPI, like the percentage of women on the interview panel, acts as an input, or essential stepping-stone, for the "lagging indicator" of percentage of women in line management (the outcome). Both sets of KPIs contribute, in this example, to the ultimate objective of increasing the gender balance at the executive level, in order to satisfy the organization's strategic narrative of better reflecting its customer demographics.

The chart below describes how leading and lagging KPIs in a hypothetical organization together contribute to the overall aim of increasing gender balance at the executive level, in line with the organization's strategic narrative of better reflecting the demographics of its customers. In this example, indicators that could influence hiring decisions include the gender balance within the list of candidates recently promoted, the gender balance of line role hires (which is a way to enhance the talent pipeline), and the gender balance in the assignment pool (or expatriate pool, since international experience is often part of the career track for senior leadership roles). If the aim is gender balance of the line role hires, it is necessary to look more closely at the process, such as gender balance in the recruitment funnel, including applicants and CVs selected. A gender-balanced candidate pipeline is often a function of bias and this means holding bias workshops and tracking attendance at unconscious bias workshops for people involved in recruitment. This could include requiring that the interview panel is comprised of a 50:50 gender-balanced team.

To finetune an organization's diversity KPIs, it is helpful to define the leading and lagging indicators for the organization and identify one or two input factors that will most positively impact a lagging KPI (Fig. 2).

3 Key Diversity Outcomes to Measure

The leadership adage "what gets measured gets done" is particularly relevant for realizing the strategic narrative for diversity within the organization. Without complete, clear, and robust measures underpinning all aspects of the diversity journey, the leader lacks the ability to guide the journey and to hold members of the organization accountable for their contribution.

The Virtuous Circle and Integrated Diversity Model are underpinned by an integrated system of metrics including the following: closure of the Diversity Performance gap, progress of the strategic roadmap per milestone and outcomes, achievement of business goals linked to the diversity cases, and the health of the Virtuous Circle within the organization, given the evolving external environment and company mandate.

Answering the following questions is a valuable exercise, as part of a comprehensive diversity framework, in identifying the right metrics to support the organization's response.

1. Is the Virtuous Circle at the required level for the organization?
2. What is the health of each element of the Virtuous Circle?

   a. Do we reflect the diversity characteristics that we need for Diversity Performance at all levels of the organization?
   b. Do we embody the level of inclusion that is required?
   c. Have we closed the equity gaps?
   d. Is the purpose of and rationale for diversity clear and embraced by all?
   e. Do we have leadership support and involvement for Diversity Performance?

3. What is the health of the Integrated Diversity Model?

   a. Are we mitigating bias in our organization?
   b. Are we delivering on our case(s) for diversity?
   c. Do we have an inclusive environment and inclusive leaders to support our Diversity Performance requirements? Has there been a behavior shift?
   d. Are the right policies in place to guide practices and are they valued by their beneficiaries?
   e. Are all aspects of our Diversity Performance being measured and is there clarity on ownership of the metrics?
   f. Are we celebrating and sustaining our diversity journey continuously and dynamically?

4. Has the Strategic Diversity Roadmap been realized, per plan, per budget, per expected outcome?

   a. Are the diversity initiatives identified and being delivered with the results and outcomes (e.g. return on investment) required?
   b. Do we have the right diversity investments in place and are we optimizing the benefits?

4   Common Barriers to Measurement

Organizations frequently encounter barriers which first need to be addressed in order to measure progress successfully. Some of the most common are described below:

- **Data privacy restrictions**—An inability to collect data about individuals based on minority status due to existing legislation in many countries.
- **Incomplete measurement of all five elements of the Virtuous Circle**—Focusing mostly on diversity demographic metrics to the exclusion of other metrics such as inclusion, equity, leadership, and how to realize the case for diversity, gives the organization only a partial measurement of performance.
- **Lack of global diversity measurement standards**—The lack of global, universal standards that allow benchmarking and comparing of apples-with-apples is a serious hindrance to measuring Diversity Performance.
- **Failure to contextualize the metrics**—A reliance on copy-and-paste diversity metrics that does not take context into account. Each organization and context is unique, with varying degrees of privacy laws, all of which must be taken into account for a full picture of Diversity Performance.
- **Faulty interpretation of metrics**—When any single metric is viewed in isolation it can be misleading and lead to erroneous conclusions that can hinder progress.
- **Lack of holistic measurement**—Each element of a holistic measurement system for diversity must be included to get a complete picture of the organization's vital signs and achieve "wellness" through prevention.
- **Unclear accountability and responsibility for managing and delivering on metrics**—A lack of clear responsibility for metrics. Poor clarity and communication around who is responsible for delivering on metrics and tracking progress can be a major obstacle.

Each of these barriers is examined here in depth to understand how they have developed over time and what can be done to address them to gain a full picture of diversity health.

Data privacy restrictions

A key barrier that many organizations encounter in tracking the progress of Diversity Performance is balancing the need for disaggregated data with satisfying privacy legislation and requirements. Many countries do not allow measurement per minority group. For example, regulations may prohibit identification by race and ethnicity, which can make tracking board ethnic and racial representation more difficult. The processing of data revealing racial or ethnic origin may raise sensitive privacy questions. Two aspects of the right to privacy are especially in focus in this respect: protecting personal data and respecting individual self-determination and here, regional differences are notable. While personal data protection norms in Europe are often viewed as prohibiting data collection on racial and ethnic origin, the U.S. has long collected such data and data availability is not typically a topic of debate. Indeed the 2030 Agenda specifically calls for the collection of disaggregated data in order to better support those vulnerable groups that are commonly left behind.[1]

In principle, EU law forbids the processing of "sensitive data," which includes data revealing racial or ethnic origin. Many European states share a widespread attitude that collection of data on racial and ethnic affiliation by public or private entities presents major privacy issues. There is also concern that such data could be abused by state authorities. This must be seen in light of traumatic historical events such as the Holocaust, where data systems, including population registers, played a significant role in the persecution of the Jews and Roma people.[2]

There are exceptions to the EU prohibition on data collection if it is needed to address racial or ethnic discrimination, however, and if there is explicit and informed consent from the persons concerned. Personal data protection norms are intended to safeguard the rights of people whose data is being processed. For instance, the purpose for which the data is being compiled must be clearly stated and only strictly necessary data should be collected.[3]

With the 1997 Treaty of Amsterdam, the EU acquired the right to take action to combat discrimination based not only on sex, but on racial or ethnic origin, religion or belief, disability, age, and sexual orientation. Yet many EU countries remain reluctant to collect data on racial or ethnic origin. The most common objection is that processing such data would infringe on the right to privacy, and the EU has adopted far-reaching legislation restricting the treatment of such data.[4]

There are distinct differences between European countries in how data collection is handled. Ireland and The Netherlands are an exception to the norm in terms of collecting statistics relating to race and ethnicity. In Ireland, these statistics are broken down by self-declared ethnic affiliation, as part of their anti-discrimination scheme. The Netherlands gathers statistics on ethnic minorities or so-called *allochtons*, under a classification system that uses indirect criteria such as country of birth. France, on the other hand, is a country with deeply embedded opposition, as part of its political culture, to identifying people based on their ethnic origin. As sociologist Didier Fassin puts it, the idea of establishing "racial statistics" is in France a "national taboo." Still, there is an emerging public debate on introducing mechanisms for measuring discrimination and monitoring equality programs.[5]

In the U.S, by contrast, the adoption of civil rights legislation in the 1960s led to extensive anti-discrimination programs that included sophisticated systems of statistical monitoring and processing of data relating to race or ethnicity. Racial

---

[1] Bizikova (2017).

[2] Ringelheim (2009).

[3] Ringelheim, Collecting Racial or Ethnic Data.

[4] Ringelheim, Collecting Racial or Ethnic Data.

[5] Ringelheim, Collecting Racial or Ethnic Data.

classifications, for instance, have always been represented in laws and institutions. The term "race" first appeared on the census form in 1990 and the Equal Employment Opportunity (EEO-1) form was updated in 2005 to better take into account individuals' feeling of identity.[6] This form is required by the U.S. Department of Labor from employers with at least 100 employees, and federal contractors with at least 50 employees, and includes information about employees' job categories, ethnicity, race, and gender.[7] In the U.S., there is a strong affinity for self-identification as the preferred method for collecting data on race and ethnicity.

For organizations collecting such data on minority groups, using it can present dilemmas. For instance, while some organizations in the U.S. have begun to explicitly ask employees if they want to identify as LGBTQI+to ensure benefits or programs meet their needs, some experts raise concerns about their ability to retain confidentiality or anonymity, potentially leading to adverse actions against those employees. Other organizations may be reluctant to collect such data, fearing possible data breaches, or will restrict questions about sexual orientation to those countries where such status is legal.[8]

While there are regional variations, it is vital for leaders to take into consideration these legal and ethical requirements around collecting and storing sensitive and private information. To ensure an organization stays within legal requirements, voluntary surveys to obtain information about diversity must be stored with the utmost confidentiality.

Incomplete measurement of all five elements of the Virtuous Circle. Diversity Performance is a function of the five elements of the Virtuous Circle: diversity, inclusion, equity, purpose, and leadership. Yet most organizations focus on measuring one or more of these elements and reporting on standalone outcomes instead of bringing them together through the Virtuous Circle and the Integrated Diversity Model. Issues around measuring the five elements are discussed below.

Diversity—Minority representation on its own is not sufficient. Many organizations use diversity representation metrics on the basis of demographics (such as gender or ethnicity) as their proxy for diversity. Reflecting demographic representation, while critical in fulfilling the ethical, legal, business, and societal cases for diversity, is not the only metric and does not by itself result in Diversity Performance.

While minority representation is not a complete indicator of diversity, it is a necessary step to set a baseline, yet many organizations either do not collect or

---

[6] Ringelheim, Collecting Racial or Ethnic Data.

[7] "Legal Requirements, U.S. Equal Employment Opportunity Commission," https://www.eeoc.gov/employers/small-business/legal-requirements#:~:text=Employers%20who%20have%20at%20least,Department%20of%20Labor%20every%20year, accessed February 13, 2021.

[8] Moody (2016).

do not report such data. As noted above, this is in part due to legal restrictions in some countries on the sharing of minority representation data. However, even where measurement of representation in categories for race or ethnicity is allowed, this is rarely done.

Of the dozen Fortune 500 companies on the 2019 50 Best Workplaces for Diversity list, none had fully disclosed their Equal Employment Opportunity (EEO-1) data as mandated by law—data which includes employment by race/ethnicity and gender. Some 400 companies did not share any data about their employees' gender or ethnicity. Only one in five provided information demonstrating that they are measuring progress. A scant 3.2% of the companies released complete data for employees' race and gender in each job category.[9]

The tech sector dominates the list of companies in the 2019 Fortune 500 that do report full diversity numbers—that is, both gender and racial diversity data. This follows a 2011 investigation by *CNN Money* which lodged Freedom of Information Act requests for workforce diversity data from 20 of the most influential U.S. tech companies. The investigation revealed little insight into diversity data and a general lack of transparency.[10] Three years later, Google was the first tech company to release a diversity report voluntarily,[11] followed by other leading firms like Alphabet, Apple, Facebook, Microsoft, and Twitter. But while tech companies state that they value diversity, their annual diversity reports show little change in the last six years, according to data published in 2020.[12]

In light of the Black Lives Matter Movement, there has been increased pressure for companies in the U.S. to report on racial diversity. The 2021 Fortune 500 list has announced it will include companies' self-reported diversity, equity, and inclusion data, which users will be able to sort and rank.[13] In the EU, the non-financial reporting directive requires large public interest companies with over 500 employees (circa 6,000 large companies and groups) to include non-financial statements in their annual reports, yet data is only required for the diversity of company boards (including age and gender).

Tracking demographic characteristics such as race and gender, where this is allowed, is often seen as low-hanging fruit with respect to metrics, as this can be done easily and with a high degree of accuracy. Even if companies do not make demographic information publicly available, organizations should, where allowed, at a minimum track these diversity characteristics internally to monitor progress.

---

[9] Donnelly (2017).

[10] Pepitone (2013).

[11] Fairchild (2014).

[12] Rooney and Khorran (2020).

[13] "Fortune and Refinitiv Encourage Unprecedented Corporate Diversity Disclosure and Accountability Through New Measure Up Partnership," *PR Newswire*, October 26, 2020, https://www.prnewswire.com/news-releases/fortune-and-refinitiv-encourage-unprecedented-corporate-diversity-disclosure-and-accountability-through-new-measure-up-partnership-301159688.html.

Inclusion—Frequently not measured, or if so, incorrectly. While 85% of D&I leaders cited organizational inclusion as the most important talent outcome of their D&I efforts, in one 2019 business research survey,[14] only 57% of organizations actually deploy that metric to monitor D&I progress, and many of them lack confidence in its viability as a metric.[15]

Organizations assess how inclusive the environment is by applying various methods. This may be as simple as asking five questions on a pulse survey or having a comprehensive inclusion index or instrument. The questions are most critical to ask to relate to the factors that contribute to an employee's sense of what it means to be included. This can be part of a regular employee engagement survey or incorporated into a specific inclusion survey or index. Employees are typically asked to rank whether they are valued for their differences and unique contributions, can be open about their views without fear of retaliation or rejection, are rewarded fairly based on job performance and achievements, and feel confident about the organization's grievance mechanisms. This qualitative data is an important companion to "harder" quantitative metrics such as attrition rates, pay gaps, tenure of employees, and number of incidences of discriminatory or biased behavior.

Equity—Hampered by global measurement standards. This has meant that organizations have developed their own metrics for equity. A number of best practices for measuring equity used by organizations include:

- Feedback from employee focus groups, where an independent and external facilitator obtains feedback from minority groups on their sense of fairness in the system and processes and whether equity is advanced.
- Feedback on the question, via a pulse or within an engagement survey or inclusion survey on a question such as: "I believe that all people have a fair chance of being promoted, regardless of their gender, ethnicity, race, sexual orientation, etc."
- Minimum percentage of contracts, consultants, and vendors led by individuals from underrepresented minority populations.
- Score on systemic bias audits.
- Distribution of people who are initiating grievance procedures, discrimination, harassment, or retaliation suits.

Leadership—Critical to employees' perception of diversity. Tracking inclusive leadership is a critical metric. Teams with inclusive leaders are 17% more likely to report that they are high-performing, 20% more likely to say they make

---

[14] "Gartner Says Diversity and Inclusion Are the No. 1 Talent Management Priority for CEOs; Most D&I Initiatives Ineffective," Press Release, *Gartner*, October 30, 2019, https://www.gartner.com/en/newsroom/press-releases/2019-10-30-gartner-says-diversity-and-inclusion-are-the-no--1-ta.

[15] Gartner, "Diversity and Inclusion Are the No. 1 Talent Management Priority."

high-quality decisions, and 29% more likely to report behaving collaboratively."[16] Typically, organizations measure inclusive leadership on a scale of 0 to 5 where participants are asked to rate their leaders on the following statement: "I am treated fairly and respectfully, am valued, and my leader provides me with a sense of belonging and I feel safe to disagree."[17] Some organizations conclude that the leader is inclusive if the average of the participant scores is high. Research confirms that this is not the case: an inclusive leader is one who is rated every time by each reviewer as inclusive. So the leader who receives an average of 4 out of 5 on the basis of a score of 3/5, 3/5, 5/5, and 5/5 may be considered on average an inclusive leader, but actually the true indicator is to score 5/5 each time. This is a higher level of expectation and becomes important in setting goals for the measurement of inclusive leadership.

Purpose—The degree to which the diversity purpose or strategic narrative for diversity resonates with the organization. For a compelling diversity purpose, people must identify with its intention and feel committed to that intention. This can be measured in a number of ways:

- Feedback from employee focus groups, where an independent and external facilitator obtains feedback from the group on why diversity is important to the organization.
- Frequency in communication from the CEO and the leaders, on the rationale for diversity both publicly and within the organizations.
- Review of specific references to the rationale for diversity in public statements, annual reports, corporate websites, and other channels.
- Pulse surveys or similar asking employees to provide their understanding for the rationale for diversity within the organization.

Lack of global diversity measurement standards

Leaders often struggle due to the absence of global diversity measurement standards that can be adopted by organizations to measure and report diversity in a way that allows for transparency and benchmarking between organizations and nations. One effort to address this gap is the Gender and Diversity KPI Alliance (GDKA), which supports the adoption and use of KPIs to measure gender and diversity in member companies and organizations.[18] By signing on to GDKA, signatory companies commit to using or working to implement three key performance indicators to evaluate diversity in their organization:

1. Percentage of representation on an organization's board.
2. Percentage of representation by employee category, in territories where this is allowed.

---

[16] Bourke and Titus, "Inclusive Leaders."

[17] Bourke and Titus (2019).

[18] Gender & Diversity KPI Alliance, date accessed December 28, 2020, https://www.gdka.org/.

3. Pay equality: the ratio of compensation by employee category (e.g., equal pay for equal work).

These KPIs were chosen because they highlight the progress of minorities through an organization's structure and represent a starting point to analyze and monitor diversity within an organization, tracking progress over time. Companies are encouraged to disaggregate the data by underrepresented groups wherever feasible. Another recommendation is to select employment categories that are meaningful, keep them consistent over time and include total compensation when calculating pay ratios. While not mandated to publish their KPIs, participating organizations are encouraged to do this.[19]

Having diverse voices on an organization's board of directors is seen not only as a business imperative but an ethical obligation and part of an organization's fiduciary requirements. A bare minimum metric is having at least one minority (woman or person of color) on each board. A stretch goal is to have at least three underrepresented voices present in the boardroom. A more advanced metric for board minority representation is to distinguish representation of minorities not only in board seats, but also by percentage of board committee leads and chairs of boards. While a board of directors consists of people elected by the company shareholders to represent and advance their interests, a management committee consists of people elected by an organization's members to represent and advance their interests. Committees have limited authority, power and responsibilities, and typically operate under their own charter. The board holds ultimate responsibility for any actions made by the committee.

There are different ways in which to approach greater representation. Norway, for example, was the first country to legislate a gender quota law. A voluntary gender quota of at least 40% of each sex was first implemented in 2003 and went into force in 2008.[20] This has had significant implications for the composition of Norwegian boards, where in 2020 women accounted for 43% of board chairs.[21] So if the metric of improved representation is adherence to a legally mandated quota, this must be taken into account and benchmarked by organizations.

Bringing this together in metrics for board diversity, the following KPIs are often used:

---

[19] KPI Position Statement, Gender & Diversity KPI Alliance, https://www.gdka.org/kpis/position-statement/, accessed January 7, 2021.

[20] Aagoth Storvik, Women on Boards–Experience from the Norwegian Quota Reform, CESifo DICE Report 1/2011, https://core.ac.uk/download/pdf/6662323.pdf.

[21] 2020 Global Board Diversity Tracker, Egon Zehnder, 2020, https://www.egonzehnder.com/global-board-diversity-tracker/tracker-highlights.

Board Representation Metrics[22]

Minority board representation percent = Number minority board members/total number board members × 100, broken down for each diversity group that is defined in a strategic narrative (e.g. women, people of color or people with disability).
Minority committee leader representation percent = Number committee leads/total number committee leads × 100, broken down for each underrepresented group that is defined in a strategic narrative (e.g. women, people of color, people with disability).

---

5 Percentage of Representation by Employee Category in Pipeline

A second KPI that has been identified as critical is the percentage of minority representation in the organization's talent pipeline by employee category. Organizations have tended to measure and share percentage representation for the whole organization or split into leadership/non-leadership representation splits. It is less common to measure and report representation along the entire talent pipeline from initial hiring to promotion to manager or leader or senior leader, and to do this for different categories of employees and per geography.

Why is this so essential? Because when organizations focus exclusively on measuring the percentage of women in leadership roles to the exclusion of the measurement of women at other stages of career progress, the organization may falsely conclude that they are in good shape when this is not the case. In many organizations, women remain significantly outnumbered at the managerial level, often referred to as "the missing rung," which is why it is so critical to measure representation by employee category along the entire pipeline of talent advancement.[23]

Pipeline Representation Metrics Per Employee Category[24]

Minority representation percent along talent promotion pipeline = Number of minority members/total number of members × 100, at first promotion level, second promotion level, third promotion level, up to final promotion level.
Minority representation percent along talent event pipeline = Number of minority members/total number of members × 100, at recruitment, at promotion (see above), in succession planning, in the strategic assignment, at departure/exit et al.

---

[22] Gender & Diversity KPI Alliance.

[23] "Women in the Workplace 2020," McKinsey & Company, last modified September 30, 2020, https://www.mckinsey.com/featured-insights/diversity-and-inclusion/women-in-the-workplace#.

[24] Gender & Diversity KPI Alliance.

6   Pay Equality: The Ratio of Compensation by Employee Category

A third KPI that has been identified as critical to measure is the ratio of compensation by employee category. Pay equality is a crucial KPI in the realm of diversity, not only for representation at the board level and within the talent pipeline but also to ensure that people are paid the same for equal work. Historically, there has been very limited transparency on the gender variances on the level of the total compensation package, including benefits, shares, and bonuses. When evaluating this KPI, compensation is not just salary but should include base salary, incentives, and stock/options and ratios should be evaluated for similarly situated employees based on their level/category, and role/job type in the organization.

Historically, there has been very limited transparency on the gender variances on the level of the total compensation package, including benefits, shares, and bonuses. One of GDKA's aims is to create more transparency on this aspect. They stress that when evaluating this KPI, compensation is not just salary but should include base salary, incentives, and stock/options and ratios should be evaluated for similarly situated employees based on their level/category and role/job type in the organization.

Pay equality = (the average total compensation of the underrepresented group / the average total compensation for the majority group) x 100[25]

Apply formulae for each employee category.

For example, if you used "upper management" as a category and were looking at gender, it would be:

(the average total compensation for women in upper management / the average total compensation for men in upper management) x 100.

To determine whether employees are compensated on an equal pay for equal workbasis, it is helpful to evaluate ratios for similarly situated employees based on their level/category and role/job type in the organization.

Failure to contextualize metrics

As the case studies in this book demonstrate, each organization has its own diversity journey to navigate and obstacles to overcome. This underscores how important it is for metrics to take into account the specific organization, its national context and privacy laws. There is no one-size-fits-all set of diversity metrics that can be copied from one organization to another. Each organization must carefully identify the metrics most essential to advancing diversity within its unique context, as these examples show:

---

[25] Gender & Diversity KPI Alliance.

- A software organization, for example, was in the process of integrating four companies and needed to cultivate its talent pipeline to achieve better customer alignment and innovation, including i-cloud specialization, younger talent and a footprint within Asia. In its case, it requires metrics that focus on achieving required diversity characteristics in these identified areas. The organization will need to put in place metrics that determine recruitment targets for salespeople in Asia, the required iCloud specialized resources to be recruited per software development location, and the number of younger sales managers to be hired for their sales team.
- A hospitality organization, on the other hand, needs to institute metrics that will immediately identify pay gaps (salary and benefits) and close them, monitor and record grievances for immediate resolution, monitor attendance at unconscious bias training of all resources and assess the use of budget in developing and rolling out a comprehensive allyship capability.
- The Vice President of a life sciences company needs to dismantle leadership stereotypes through a combination of initiatives including instituting role models, increasing awareness of unconscious biases and talent blindspots, and setting metrics for equal selection of men and women on leadership programs, among other initiatives. All of these items will need to be measured for the completion and advancement of gender diversity.

These three examples demonstrate the importance for organizations to identify their unique diversity aspirations and challenges and focus on the specific metrics that will provide them with early warning signals and an indication of progress against key milestones and outcomes.

While metrics need to be normalized and adapted to context, the ability to benchmark and get a sense of trends within an industry requires a common set of metrics. After technology companies were pressured to publicly share their employee diversity statistics, many now publish annual diversity reports which provide a degree of comparison within the sector.[26]

Faulty interpretation of metrics

Metrics viewed in isolation can skew conclusions. For example, an organization with a gender diversity target of 50% of all employees might be gratified when this metric is achieved. One could conclude that the organization is on track, however, on closer scrutiny, it is revealed that 70% of staff roles are occupied by women, yet there is an absence of women in leadership roles, specialized roles, and decision-making roles. Moreover, it is apparent that 50% of the staff roles will be made redundant as they are being automated. The single gender representation metric does not tell the whole story.

---

[26] https://money.cnn.com/2013/03/17/technology/diversity-silicon-valley/index.html "How Diverse Is Silicon Valley?" Most tech companies really, really don't want you to know, and the U.S. government isn't helping shed any light on the issue.

Reporting a specific metric can also hide a key issue. This often occurs with retention. Many organizations monitor the tenure of minority employees against the tenure of employees for the dominant group. Assuming the tenure is identical, the conclusion might be that minorities are satisfied and are not leaving the organization at a higher rate. In this case, the data did not reflect whether employment was ended voluntarily or involuntarily. A closer look at the data shows that 35% of the minority employees (versus 20% of the other employees) who left their employment had their employment terminated. On the surface, the metric indicates a favorable and healthy situation, but when the data is cut in another way, a problem is revealed.

Lumping groups together when measuring demographics can also be problematic. For example in the UK, minority representation is often measured using BAME (Black, Asian, and Minority Ethnic), a common abbreviation that is widely used by government departments, public bodies, media, and others when referring to ethnic minority groups (similar to BME, or Black and Minority Ethnic). However, this can obscure gaps in representation. For example, in higher education, it might look like BAME representation is strong, when actually higher representation of Asian students is masking the fact that there is severe underrepresentation of Black students.

Lack of holistic measurement

Metrics often run year-to-date or annually, reflecting the state of diversity at a point in time. This is helpful for identifying whether the annual diversity goals were met, but, in the nature of lag indicators, it gives a sense of looking over one's shoulder into the past instead of looking forward.

Few organizations have instituted metrics that are forward-looking and focus on progress along the diversity journey. Such metrics identify whether the business goals of the organization have been advanced by diversity and whether diversity initiatives and investments have delivered a return on investment (in time, resources, and budget). When the strategic narrative for diversity has been captured and the business case for diversity is clear, organizations are better able to measure progress against their strategic diversity intent and their required business case outcomes.

Unclear accountability and responsibility for managing and delivering on diversity metrics

Often accountability and responsibility for management and delivery of metrics is distributed across different functions within organizations, which can contribute to a lack of clarity and direction. It is important to clearly establish responsibility and ensure engagement at all levels of management; that is, to establish an appropriate accountability infrastructure. For example, if a list of maximum five criteria for experience for a job role sits with the line manager and recruitment partner, this could be tracked by the HR Lead on a quarterly basis as part of the standard operations review meeting. A strong D&I governance structure can be extremely helpful in this regard.

Leaders play a decisive role in spearheading diversity and measuring progress, but every member of the organization should also feel a sense of personal accountability. With clear accountability and responsibility, best practices and interventions can more easily be identified and shared across the organization with a common approach to interpreting and applying the findings. Linking inclusive leadership behaviors to performance reviews can play an important role in this regard.

7   The Organization's Diversity Wellness Check

Returning to the healthcare analogy, it is useful to understand other distress signals in diversity health. For instance, sometimes a doctor may want to augment the data provided from the patient's vital signs with additional metrics. One example is the Biomass Index that collates a range of indicators to determine a healthy weight. It is not a perfect measure, but the higher the BMI, the higher the risk of developing a number of serious conditions. This test provides some future perspective on health and high potential health risks.

An organization's diversity and inclusion metrics should serve three purposes: diagnose risk areas and opportunities, track the progress of initiatives, and calculate the return on investment. An organization can evaluate the gap in its Measure and Monitor Diversity capability by using the Virtuous Circle Five Stages framework (Table 1).

8   Technology as Enabler of Diversity Measurement

Having a data-driven approach to diversity metrics can help focus efforts in the right areas, and this is enhanced by the smart use of technology. A company's data is often based on "complex reward and compensation structures with over a thousand different elements of pay," as experts in technology software geared to inclusion have noted.[27] Using Artificial Intelligence (AI) and machine learning technology makes it possible to comb through data from multiple sources, which for some clients could be as many as 16 data sources to integrate and provide accurate insight into an organization's compensation and benefit patterns. That makes it easier to pinpoint gaps without the risk of human error. For example, one approach involves performing regression analysis to account for pay differentials based on legitimate factors, such as experience, education, and training, and then identifying outliers based on gender, race, and age. Regression analysis can be described as a distinct group of statistical processes which capture the relationship between a dependent variable (or 'outcome variable') and one or more

---

[27] Abrar (2019).

Table 1   Measure and Monitor Capability and Initiatives for the Five Stages
Overview of initiatives to measure and monitor diversity at each stage of diversity maturity.

	Stage 1 Legal Compliance	Stage 2 Stakeholder Requirements	Stage 3 Organizational Performance	Stage 4 Reinvention	Stage 5 Societal Value
Focus	Compliance outcomes	Representation Stakeholder satisfaction	Performance outcomes	Transformation outcomes	Societal impact
Skills	Definitions	Measurement protocol	Correlation diversity & performance	Correlation diversity & innovation	Applicability to partners SDGs
Process	Set targets Monitor	Evaluate satisfaction	Measure performance	Analyze contribution	Align with partners
Responsibilities	Legal	HR	CFO diversity office	CEO diversity office	Leaders diversity council
Metrics	Representation of inherent diversity traits	Representation of inherent & acquired diversity traits	Diversity & Inclusion Performance outcomes	Equity Strategic goals Roadmap Gap closures	Societal impact
Technology	Compliance	HR	Performance management system	Enterprise performance	Partner enablement

independent variables ('predictors', 'covariates', or 'features').[28] The complexity of this exercise makes it labor intensive and prone to mistakes, which makes technology helpful in supporting this process.

Technology can be used to support diversity dashboards, including tracking and monitoring the effectiveness of diversity and inclusion initiatives. Other technical solutions can illuminate existing gender gaps and generate suggestions relating to hiring, wages, performance and promotions as well as predictions, and analysis of monetary outcomes. Finally, technology can help to increase transparency, enable more regular reporting and facilitate pulse surveys. There is considerable value in using technology to bolster diversity metric systems.

9   How to Build the Case for Diversity in Practice

What can be done in practice to create a comprehensive measurement capability? Depending on an organization's Diversity Performance maturity level, the Integrated Diversity Model sets out the focus, responsibilities, process and technology enablement that need to be present for comprehensive measurement and monitoring of Diversity Performance at each stage (Table 1).

---

[28] "Regression Analysis," Wikipedia, date accessed December 28, 2020, https://en.wikipedia.org/wiki/Regression_analysis.

10   Stage 1 Organizations: Legal Compliance

At Stage 1, the primary focus is on measuring legal compliance and, as a result, the organization will put measures in place to monitor and report on compliance outcomes. For example, the number of discrimination complaints made, number of discrimination complaints settled, cost of discrimination cases, tracking of discrimination cases within the history, the trend of discrimination complaints, etc. For measurement to occur, the definition of discrimination complaints will need to be carefully defined and needs to be consistent with the definition of discrimination in employee policies. The legal and HR functions will be heavily involved in the measurement process. Those organizations that must satisfy quota and affirmative action requirements require detailed representation measurements, according to the definitions set out in the regulations. Finally, the organization will proactively monitor regulatory developments in the various countries where it operates in order to anticipate new developments and respond to new regulations. The measurement process is enabled by legal and compliance solutions.

11   Stage 2 Organizations: Stakeholder Requirements

At Stage 2, organizations have largely satisfied the capability for supporting zero-discrimination compliance and delivering on the legal case for diversity, and focus instead on satisfying minimum expectations of customers and employees. As a result, measurement is focused on tabulating actual diversity outcomes and initiatives against the expectations of their stakeholders. Usually, the Diversity Performance KPIs are measured against employee satisfaction and customer satisfaction for these diversity specific outcomes. For example, employees may require that the organization invests in Affinity Networks or Employee Resource Groups, that these are active and funded in order to support community events, and this needs to be measured and reported. Guests may require that the hospitality staff of an international hotel chain are educated on cultural norms and traditions of the primary customers and guests. In this case, employee attendance at multicultural training may be one metric, as well as the number of customer complaints relating to service considered to be "insensitive" to the norms, values, and rituals of the customer group. Typical measurement instruments could consist of customer satisfaction surveys and customer complaint monitoring.

12   Stage 3 Organizations: Organizational Performance

At Stage 3, the focus shifts to measuring the relationship between increased diversity (inherent and acquired characteristics as defined) and identified performance outcomes (such as increased innovation revenues, decreased employee sickness and increased employee engagement). These performance outcomes will most likely have been included in one or more of the cases for diversity. Stage 3 organizations are required to set a baseline for the selected strategic business goals within the Build Case capability and report against this baseline. Measurement will also focus on evaluating the return of investment on the various diversity initiatives. Stage 3 organizations are deliberate and complete in the measurement of Diversity Performance. Progress on these metrics is often reported directly to the most senior financial leader of the organization, such as the CEO or CFO. Furthermore, the diversity measurement will be included in a review of the organization's core strategy and will often leverage the processes of a Diversity Council.

13   Stage 4 Organizations: Reinvention

At Stage 4, the objective is to expand on the performance case, with additional focus on not only satisfying performance objectives but evaluating whether the diversity initiatives are supporting the organization's need to transform with the market, to innovate and remain relevant to its consumers and achieve the best decision-making to manage risk and harness opportunities. Within the Build Case capability, the strategic business goals related to the Reinvention Stage have been defined. For example, the ability of the organization to win market share through the launch of a pioneering service, or driving growth through a new business unit, or picking up lost revenues from an aging product by new innovations. Some strategic goals for an educational institution could be creating a new educational program and increasing the percentage of international students. The challenge at this stage is to identify the leading and lagging KPIs that will enable measurement of diversity investments and outcomes for these strategic goals.

14   Stage 5 Organizations: Societal Value

At Stage 5, focus shifts from internal transformation of the organization to supporting diversity outcomes in the wider value chain and partner ecosystem as well as having a direct contribution to society. This means not only making reference to the SDGs in strategy but also setting metrics and measuring real impact. Measurement is supported by linking diversity investments and outcomes to clear societal goals, namely the underlying targets of the 17 UN Sustainable Development Goals. Many Stage 5 organizations are already linking their Diversity Performance outcomes to one or more of the SDGs, such as Goal 5: "Achieve gender equality and empower all women and girls" and Goal 8: "Promote inclusive and sustainable economic growth, employment and decent work for all."[29] To support societal

---

[29] UN Sustainable Development Goals, https://www.un.org/sustainabledevelopment/economic-growth/, accessed March 14, 2021.

impact some organizations have developed SDG frameworks that score companies on their contribution to the SDGs. The SDG Compass developed by the Global Reporting Initiative, UN Global Compact, and World Business Council for Sustainable Development provides guidance for companies on how to align their strategies with the goals, set priorities, and measure and monitor their contribution to the realization of the SDGs, presenting five steps companies can take to maximize their contribution to the Global Goals.[30]

A 2018 analysis by Ethical Corporation found that 69% of corporate brands stated that their business is integrating the SDGs into the business strategy, up from nine percent the previous year. However, over half of the respondents (56%) stated that their company was not measuring its contribution to the SDGs. North American respondents stated the lowest level of measured targets against the SDGs (36%), followed by Asia/Pacific (46%) and Europe (47%). Fewer than 10% had targets to measure their contribution to the SDGs.[31] There is a growing group of corporate sustainability leaders that have set robust metrics around the goals and are tying these to corporate performance. As more investors adopt the SDGs as a lens for impact investment, measuring and monitoring performance against the goals is likely to accelerate.

15   Concluding Remarks

A robust set of metrics is essential to measure Diversity Performance. Measuring diversity should be a strategic focus area that combines several different measurements over and above basic representation of minority groups. A holistic and integrated measurement approach is the best way to overcome common hurdles to effective evaluation of diversity progress.

Good metrics can help to identify and manage bias blind spots, identify risks, prioritize initiatives, set targets and program goals, define accountability, and measure impact and return on investment from initiatives. When metrics demonstrate a financial return on the diversity investment, it can help to engage stakeholders, boost leadership commitment, make the case for additional resources and provide a strong basis on which to push for further change. Not least, if metrics can demonstrate sustained commitment to equality and fairness, this enhances employee trust, customer satisfaction and improves brand image.

Equipped with hard data, the organization can confirm the health of its Virtuous Circle and the maturity of its IDM capabilities and strengthen its strategic narrative. Knowing how well the organization is performing in its diversity

---

[30] SDG Compass, https://sdgcompass.org/, accessed March 15, 2021.

[31] The Ethical Corporation Global Responsible Business Benchmark Report 2018, http://1.ethicalcorp.com/LP=20716.

aims enables the team to take stock of progress, share results, learn lessons and acknowledge improvements, creating an important opportunity to recalibrate and revitalize the diversity journey.

In Chapter 11 we focus on the Celebrate and Sustain capability.

References

Abrar, Fatima. "29 D&I Measurement Tools and Technologies." *Crescendo*. Last Modified February 27, 2019. https://crescendowork.com/guide-start-diversity-inclusion-strategy/2019/2/27/diversity-inclusion-measurement-tools-technologies.

Bizikova, Livia. "Disaggregated Data is Essential to Leave No One Behind." *International Institute for Sustainable Development*, October 12, 2017. https://www.iisd.org/articles/disaggregated-data-essential-leave-no-one-behind.

Bourke, Juliet, and Andrea Titus. "Why Inclusive Leaders Are Good for Organizations, and How to Become One." *Harvard Business Review*. Last Modified March 29, 2019. https://hbr.org/2019/03/why-inclusive-leaders-are-good-for-organizations-and-how-to-become-one.

Donnelly. Grace. "Only 3% of Fortune 500 Companies Share Full Diversity Data." *Fortune,* June 7, 2017. https://fortune.com/2017/06/07/fortune-500-diversity/.

Fairchild, Caroline. "Why Google Voluntarily Released Dismal Diversity Numbers." *Fortune*, May 29, 2014. https://fortune.com/2014/05/29/why-google-voluntarily-released-dismal-diversity-numbers/.

Moody, Kathryn. "Why Some Employers Are Asking About Employees' LGBT Status." *HR Dive*, March 15, 2016. https://www.hrdive.com/news/why-some-employers-are-asking-about-employees-lgbt-status/415596/.

Pepitone, Julianne. "Black, Female and a Silicon Valley 'Trade Secret,'" *CNN Business*, March 18, 2013. https://money.cnn.com/2013/03/17/technology/diversity-silicon-valley/index.html.

Ringelheim, Julie. "Collecting Racial or Ethnic Data for Antidiscrimination Policies: A US-Europe Comparison." *Rutgers Race and the Law Review*, 10, no. 1 (2009): 39–142. http://hdl.handle.net/2078.1/118449.

Rooney, Kate, and Yasmin Khorran. "Tech Companies Say They Value Diversity, But Reports Show Little Change in Last Six Years." June 12, 2020, *CNBC*. https://www.cnbc.com/2020/06/12/six-years-into-diversity-reports-big-tech-has-made-little-progress.html.

Celebrating and Sustaining Diversity

11

A diversity journey is at its heart a change journey. There will be periods of effort and investment, moments of great satisfaction when progress is made, but also setbacks and disappointments. That is normal and to be expected. What is important is to harness the energy of the organization to make the diversity journey a sustainable one. Each diversity journey is unique but there are shared ways to sustain it and create an abundance of energy which the organization can draw from to keep diversity in a state of constant renewal. The journey needs to be tended like a fire: it relies on the guardian of the fire to put the logs on at the right time, to ensure that not too many logs are put on at the same time, so there is enough oxygen for the fire to burn long and brightly.

This chapter explores the many ways in which organizations can celebrate and sustain diversity and the importance of doing so. The Celebrate and Sustain Capability is the sixth and last capability of the Integrated Diversity Model (Fig. 1).

If a diversity journey is not sustained, its flame will flicker and die and all the effort that has gone into working toward the vision of a diverse, equitable, and inclusive organization can fizzle out.

There are proven ways in which a leader can tend to and sustain the diversity journey and we explore each of these in this chapter. They include:

- Celebrate and create communities
- Nurture grassroots support
- Make accountable and reward
- Pilot and test interventions and share best practice
- Provide continuous feedback on progress.

Diversity journeys take stamina—not least because they are evolving, and the external environment is never static. They seldom follow a linear journey; there are peaks and troughs, just as there are in other change journeys. Creating a

© Diversity and Performance BV 2021
K. Formanek, *Beyond D&I*, https://doi.org/10.1007/978-3-030-75336-8_11

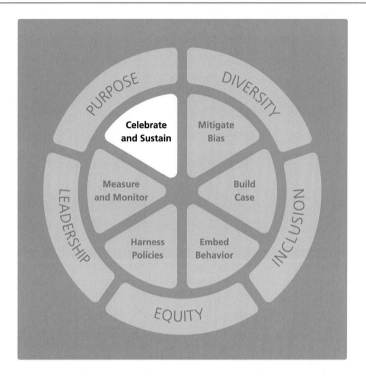

Fig. 1 **Celebrate and Sustain**
Sixth Capability of the Integrated Diversity Model.

diverse organization is not easy, but it is always enriching. By tending to all the logs on the fire, the chances of success are greater, as the case studies in this chapter illustrate.

1   Celebrate Achievements and Milestones

When starting a diversity journey, leaders often make use of townhalls and kickoff events to mark the start of an important endeavor. Over time, however, this communication and dialog can taper off. This should not be the case. The organization and its stakeholders are eager for regular updates and reminders of the desired stage of Diversity Performance and how the organization is progressing toward key milestones and performance outcomes. This is where diversity celebration days can play a role.

Organizations celebrate diversity in different ways, marking both the smaller achievements and the larger milestones. While the celebration of diversity, inclusion, and equity is a 365-day commitment, it is meaningful to honor specific diversity days that have been set out in either the organization's calendar or are celebrated nationally or globally. Certain events are particularly meaningful for specific minority groups and should have a place on the organization's diversity calendar. This includes, but is not limited to acknowledging, women and their allies on March 8 (International Women's Day),[1] and employees with disabilities on December 3 (International Day of Disabled Persons).[2] While still largely a U.S. phenomenon, "Juneteenth," celebrated on June 19th is significant as the commemoration of the ending of slavery in the U.S., a tradition now spreading beyond the U.S. to a broader observation of African American Emancipation Day.[3]

Celebrating important religious holidays or events is also important. Marking the unique cultural attributes that enrich the organization can help employees find common ground, deepen appreciation for one another's culture and create a depth of learning about one another.

For LGBTQI+ employees, it is important for the organization to recognize Pride Day as well as National Coming Out Day[4] on October 11. These events are part of LGBTQI+ persons' identities and about bringing their whole selves to work. According to the Human Rights Campaign Foundation, 46% of LGBTQI+ individuals are closeted at work, and 28% are totally closeted and not open about their own LGBTQI+ status to anyone in their lives.[5] Coming out takes courage and is an ongoing process; organizations supporting events on these dates can help by underscoring their support for the LGBTQI+ community. On Spirit Day,[6] in October, millions wear purple in a stand against bullying and to show their support for lesbian, gay, bisexual, and transgender youth. An organization's participation in external events (such as Pride festivals and gay pride parades) is important, as it sends a strong signal that the company is an LGBTQI+ -friendly organization that values its employees.

As well as commemorating these events internally, it also matters how the organization reflects its values around diversity to the outside world. The organization profiled below puts that philosophy into practice by engaging employees, customers, and suppliers in the celebration of diversity.

---

[1] International Women's Day, accessed December 30, 2020, https://www.internationalwomens-day.com/.

[2] "International Day of Persons with Disabilities, 3 December," United Nations, accessed December 30, 2020, https://www.un.org/en/observances/day-of-persons-with-disabilities.

[3] History of Juneteenth, Juneteenth.com, https://www.juneteenth.com/history.htm, accessed February 13, 2021.

[4] "Celebrate National Coming Out Day with HRC!" Human Rights Campaign, accessed December 30, 2020, https://www.hrc.org/resources/national-coming-out-day.

[5] A Workplace Divided, The Human Rights Campaign, 2018, https://assets2.hrc.org/files/assets/resources/AWorkplaceDivided-2018.pdf?_ga=2.91243613.678613926.1613266656-1596224117.1613098303.

[6] Spirit Day, accessed December 30, 2020, https://www.glaad.org/spiritday.

Case Study: Celebration of Diversity Infusing Daily Life

The approach an organization takes to celebrate and sustain diversity can be genuinely inspiring. At a research organization in Belgium, the celebration of diversity is on display for all to see. The walls of the lobby at their head office are adorned with full-color, framed pictures of people representing every color of the rainbow: old and young, people of color, and many in different cultural dress. The overall impression is one of abundance, summed up by a sign on the wall that reads, "We Serve: Our People. Our Stakeholders. Our Society."

This acknowledgment of the importance of diversity does not stop at the lobby. Along a corridor leading to the conference room, the walls are covered with brown paper with different colored papers taped to it, connected with arrows. Employees, customers, and suppliers know this as the Diversity Wall, and they all played a part in creating it. Each of the colored papers reflects a different initiative that supports the shared diversity purpose. A traffic light legend indicates whether the diversity initiative is up and running and delivering results.

Beyond this constant daily reminder of what diversity means to the organization, employees look forward to the annual Diversity Day and regular celebrations of specific national cultural days, when the canteen prepares food and displays decorations distinctive to that country.

While these acts of celebration are important and valued, it is what they reflect that is truly remarkable. This is an organization where everyone acknowledges the beauty in their differences. Employees feel a sense of belonging, the safety to be completely themselves, and the comradeship with their colleagues who come from a wide range of backgrounds and experiences. Everyone harnesses their life experiences in a positive way and it infuses the work environment with a particular energy.

This is a thriving and profitable organization that has perfected an approach to keeping diversity relevant and alive. Its employees often talk about the deep emotion they feel in the way diversity is celebrated, a coming-together in perfect harmony, creating connections, and fostering collaboration.

▶ **Key takeaway** In this organization, diversity initiatives are not driven top-down; everyone feels a sense of ownership—employees, suppliers, and customers alike. As a result, diversity initiatives are connected and re-enforcing and there is a palpable sense of pride among everyone in the organization that they have created this diversity outcome together.

2   Global Diversity Week

Where diversity days may be focused on specific communities, a Global Diversity Week is an excellent way to create widespread awareness about the importance of diversity, with a blend of initiatives led by the headquarters, along with local events that support the week's themes. Diversity week initiatives create connections and stimulate courageous discussions that can encourage more people to embrace and advocate for inclusion. The ultimate purpose of a Global Diversity

Week is to gain commitment for diversity through personal actions that can become an ongoing source of support.

Global Diversity Weeks often focus on a core theme—such as welcoming an individual's whole self to the organization, moving from bias to listening and from talk to action, and understanding what it means to be inclusive. It is a good opportunity to introduce tools that enable team members to build their skills, create awareness and support ongoing discussions around diversity, with a focus on sparking long-term engagement and involvement. For instance, the organization might consider a virtual commitment wall where people could sign up. Or it could offer creative ways for people to explore different topics around diversity, such as a myth-buster quiz, virtual reality unconscious bias experiences, developing skills to intervene when discrimination is shown, and inclusion nudges (tips and behaviors to be more inclusive).

Celebrating diversity should be fun and enjoyable, an opportunity to forge connections between people and spark dialog and engagement. Because diversity can quickly become a loaded subject—policy- and metrics-driven and mired in legal compliance issues—it is important to acknowledge that diversity is about more than policies and guidelines; first and foremost it is about bringing people together, to express their whole selves and unique backgrounds in a way that is inspiring and inclusive. Everybody loves a celebration, and when events are pleasurable and everyone enjoys participating, diversity no longer feels like "hard work"—it becomes the very fabric of the organization, which indeed it should be. An organization that has really captured the fun in diversity is the business school INSEAD.

Case Study: INSEAD Champions Grassroots Celebration of Diversity Throughout the Year

Celebration of diversity sums up pretty well the business school INSEAD, which attracts a global student body and calls itself the Business School of the World. INSEAD differentiates itself on its diversity, stating "We bring together people, cultures and ideas to develop responsible leaders who transform business and society."[7]

INSEAD does this at scale. Its 145 professors represent some 40 nationalities, its MBA programs have 38% women and its Executive programs span participants from more than 2,000 companies and 130 nationalities.[8]

---

[7] "Who We Are," INSEAD, accessed December 30, 2020, https://www.insead.edu/about/who-we-are.

[8] "INSEAD at a Glance," INSEAD, January 2017, https://www.insead.edu/sites/default/files/assets/dept/news/docs/INSEAD-at-a-glance_english-jan-2017.pdf.

Encouraging a grassroots approach, INSEAD makes the celebration of diversity a constant feature of the institution with frequent spontaneous student celebrations of diversity. National Cultural Weeks take place every second week, and the atmosphere has been described as follows in a blog by one MBA student:

One of the best things about INSEAD is the diversity of its students. And to encourage cross-cultural exchanges within its eclectic student body, INSEAD National Weeks were born, where students from one nationality put together a week of activities to showcase their country's culture, food, and music, etc. This past week was Lebanon Week and it was a huge success! The whole school was transformed: colorful decorations indoors, shisha outdoors, everyone wearing navy blue Lebanese Week T-shirts and we even received name plates with our names in Arabic. There were activities every day… a belly dancing class, introduction to Lebanese cooking, film night, traditional dinner, chicken shawarma lunch, a Lebanese party and more! Luckily for us, National Weeks take place every other week so the next one's just around the corner![9]

▶   **Key takeaway** Bringing fun and community-building to the acknowledgment of diversity makes it something to look forward to and appreciate.

3   Fostering Grassroots Community

Many people contribute to the diversity journey, including senior leaders and line managers who take specific responsibility for diversity outcomes. But every employee has a role to play in supporting diversity, for example, by taking part in unconscious bias training or other initiatives such as allyship involvement.

Diversity champions are an important enabler for ensuring that the diversity journey is sustainable. These are individuals who are passionate, convinced, and energetic change agents who walk the talk of diversity and inspire others.

Diversity champions are typically spread right throughout the organization and in every geographic region, making it easier to reach the grassroots. They become the "face" of diversity in the organization, giving employees an accessible and approachable touchpoint and the opportunity to acknowledge day-to-day wins. They are attentive in bringing to managers' attention key accomplishments from around the organization, particularly by those who may be less visible or marginalized. They are also helpful in reviewing policies or other workplace culture messaging to ensure that such communication is reflective of everyone in the organization and strikes the right tone.

Such champions or change agents are comfortable about starting open discussions around diversity in the workplace, educating their colleagues about relevant topics, and gathering important insights about how safe and secure employees feel

---

[9]Li (2010).

at work. For this reason, they should be tapped as a key resource to help leaders in their efforts to make the workplace more inclusive. These champions will also most likely be the ones who are behind the celebrations and events.

Sometimes diversity champions are members of the Employee Resource Groups, or employee networks. They may represent specific minority groups, but in general the intention is to encourage anyone who shares an enthusiasm for the diversity journey to become a diversity champion. There will always be members of an organization who are naturally impassioned and excited about the change. It is important to start with that coalition of the willing. They are prepared to test their own preconceptions and recruit others to join them. The special power of diversity champions lies in forging community. Community is about shared purpose, about connections, and being united around a common goal. Thanks to the way in which they rally the community, diversity champions are often the glue that binds the organization's diversity, equity, and inclusion journey together.

For a diversity journey to gain traction, it is often on the ground that the most powerful persuasion takes place: through the conversations held in office breakrooms, canteens, and staff meetings. People need to feel ownership of diversity goals and in this regard, the Employee Resource Groups that represent specific minority groups can be valuable allies. Because these champions are so important to the diversity journey, sustaining their spark is vital. This can be done by ensuring that they are involved in the evaluation of the diversity journey and have the means to support grassroots events. Successful diversity organizations allocate investments to sustain the journey and ensure diversity champions are properly resourced to build broader team support.

As discussed below, it is also vital to recognize, acknowledge and reward the contribution of diversity champions as a means to retain focus and goodwill.

4   Rewarding Those Who Support the Journey

Public recognition has an important role to play in demonstrating that championing and promoting diversity is valued by the organization. Some do this by instituting a Diversity, Equity and Inclusion Champion Award, recognizing individuals who have helped the organization make great strides on the journey. Another important form of recognition can be a Diversity Leadership Award or Inclusive Leader Award, for someone who has been consistently rated by their colleagues as embodying the behaviors and norms that make people feel psychologically safe, seen, and heard.

Similarly, a Sponsor of the Year Award recognizes those leaders who play an active role in supporting the shared diversity purpose and facilitating connections between diversity ambassadors. Sponsorship is particularly critical in the area of equity because it goes beyond making oneself available as a mentor, to address the specific needs of individuals. Sponsors become active advocates and champions for diversity. As sponsors, senior people use their personal clout to advocate for others who may be more junior or less visible in some way, but who deserve to be recognized. For this reason, sponsorship has become a valuable tool for increasing diversity in an organization's senior ranks. Sponsors not only give feedback and advice; they also use their influence with other senior executives to advocate for an individual's advancement in the organization and to ensure that they are visible to key decision-makers. This makes sponsorship a potent tool for actively promoting individuals from underrepresented groups into positions that are more senior, or into assignments that are higher status or mission critical. They willingly expend their political capital on a protégé because they believe in them and have formed a special connection.

For organizations at Stage 4 and 5 Diversity Performance, other accolades and means of recognizing diversity and inclusion role models include the opportunity to offer preferred supplier status or instigate diversity awards for partners in the broader value chain, such as Inclusive Supplier Awards.

Financial benefits are also a powerful way to recognize diversity leadership. At both Microsoft and Intel, for example, diversity is included among the strategic performance goals that determine half of executives' yearly cash incentives—and at Intel some seven percent of employee bonuses are tied to meeting hiring and retention goals.[10] Connecting diversity and inclusion outcomes to the salary and performance of team members in this manner makes it clear that the organization takes diversity seriously.

5   Make Everyone Accountable

An important way to sustain diversity is to hold everyone accountable for the diversity journey, especially the most senior executive and other top leaders. No matter the type of organization, the diversity journey needs to be anchored with the leaders who have ultimate accountability for the Diversity Performance outcome.

To ensure accountability for Diversity Performance outcomes, there needs to be clarity around which entities are responsible for the delivery of diversity projects and programs. At Stage 4 and 5 organizations, this is formalized through a number of executive steering committees such as a Diversity Executive Steering Committee or Global Diversity Board that guides critical decisions, allocates sufficient resources, and holds people accountable for results. This high-level committee should include several senior leaders, as well as the highest-ranking leader in the organization such as the CEO.

It is also essential to cascade ownership for diversity to every individual in the organization. As described in Chapter 9, policies need to guide behavior and metrics need to be measured and reported, as explained in Chapter 10. Together, policies and metrics create clarity on the importance of advancing diversity, equity, and inclusiveness. At the heart of a successful diversity journey is that everyone is able to describe what "good" looks like. For example, intervening when

---

[10] https://www.payscale.com/compensation-today/2019/03/tie-bonuses-to-diversity-goals.

discrimination occurs, piggybacking and building on ideas, listening fully to input, and "being the change that we want to see." Everyone in the organization should understand the inclusive behaviors that pertain to their role. Some organizations go further by factoring an individual's diversity and inclusion work into individual performance ratings, whereby exceptional or very strong rankings are not given unless certain requirements for inclusive behavior are met. Together, these approaches help to ensure that diversity and inclusion become everybody's business and that the organization works together as a whole.

6   Sharing Best Practice and Providing Feedback

Sharing successes and interventions that have worked in practice is an important facet of celebrating and sustaining the diversity journey. This is achieved by piloting and testing different interventions and scaling the most effective ones. Through a Diversity Council, for example, regions and/or sectors within an organization can be invited to adopt a best practice, pilot it, evaluate it, and report back to the Diversity Council on its effectiveness. The pilot regions are also asked to recommend enhancements for the initiative and to share their experience. By inviting parts of the organization to become involved in testing out diversity initiatives, leadership is able to expand involvement around diversity. This also enables other parts of the organization to piggyback on the progress that has been made and focus their efforts on localizing and further enriching the initiative. This practice of piloting and testing and sharing out interventions and best practices is a great way to support innovation and forge collaboration and advancement of diversity capability throughout the organization.

Providing feedback on how the journey is progressing is also crucial, detailing how gaps are being closed, how everyone is contributing and sharing obstacles being faced or overcome, for example through a town hall. Ideally, this process will involve two-way feedback:

1. The leader reports out to the organization on progress of the strategic roadmap and how well goals are being met, and
2. The organization provides feedback, perhaps through regular pulse surveys or sharing experiences about the diversity journey on the company intranet.

Diversity champions including Employee Resource Groups are a valuable conduit for feedback, both from within the organization and by bringing in external perspectives from customers or partners. They highlight when the journey is going well and provide encouragement when there are bumps in the road. Some organizations host diversity, equity, and inclusion "lunch n' learns" where employees are invited to share their stories, or an aspect of the organization's diversity journey is openly discussed.

In short, continuous feedback on the progress of the journey is another important log on the fire of Diversity Performance.

7   How Leaders Keep the Flame Burning

Leaders who take the time to thank their organization for the role they have played in enabling diversity re-energize the organization. Gratitude is also a way of reaffirming their personal commitment to the diversity journey and why it is important to their purpose, and sustaining focus and commitment.

Useful lessons can be learned from the experience of leaders who are recognized as impactful and inspiring in taking their organization on a successful diversity journey. These leaders share authenticity and personal conviction in their quest for diversity. They connect diversity to a greater societal goal, see it as a journey, pay tribute to everyone who makes that journey possible, and reaffirm that it is an ongoing process, with a North Star that guides the organization forward.

In the case study below, the story of a leader from a life sciences organization provides a good example of the kind of personal connection to diversity that sustains, inspires, and re-energizes others on the journey.

Case Study: When Diversity Becomes an Occasion for Celebration and Renewal

"I grew up with a sick sibling, who was dependent on a cure that was not available. She was stoic and strong and not willing to give up, yet she was chronically ill and there was no cure to help her live a rich life. That experience planted my passion for the life sciences industry, as an industry that has the capability to protect life, restore health, and change people's lives. Today I am CEO of a world-wide organization that is committed to developing cures for many of the world's chronically ill.

My early life shaped me to passionately believe that everyone deserves a treatment and that life science organizations have an enormous responsibility to society. Patients look to us to put our best foot forward and to maximally innovate and create breakthrough treatments for them.

The question that occupied me as I moved from being a postdoctoral research student, to working in the laboratories of our great organization to leading one of our therapeutic areas and now standing as CEO before you, is "What is required to create breakthrough treatments in a fast changing world?"

It starts in my mind with understanding the experience of a patient living with a specific disease or condition. Understanding all the touch points that they experience during their journey and creating solutions with empathy and a desire to meet their needs. Quite simply we need to have a deeper understanding of our patients and also their caretakers.

We also need to be more inclusive in our clinical trials, increasing participation with members of the demographic groups that will receive the treatments.

To be able to do these things, there is in my mind no more important requirement to reflect the diversity of our patients and to gather the diversity required to support breakthrough innovations. "In understanding, we can serve." The long and short of it is, our organization cannot deliver on the hopes of patients and their families without tapping fully into the diversity of thought and leadership."

This is where our journey on diversity is anchored. Our organization has the purpose to protect lives. And we have the responsibility to remove all barriers that prevent therapeutic solutions to fly. Therein lies our purpose.

This is where each and every one of you, present today, play such an important role. For you are the diversity of thought that we need to liberate. You are the ones that we depend on to create a respectful and collaborative environment so that all voices are heard and we can piggyback on new ideas. You are the ones that create the conditions for diversity to flourish."

▶ **Key takeaway** By drawing a powerful connection between personal lived experience and the core purpose of the organization, this CEO leveraged empathy to re-energize and revitalize the team's inclusion journey.

8   Sustaining the Virtuous Circle for Diversity Performance

Diversity is not a project or program. It is quite simply a journey and leaders need to ensure that the organization is still heading in the right direction. A leader takes the time to review progress that has been made, check in with stakeholders to ensure that the stage of Diversity Performance is still relevant and adjust the diversity journey as required.

Using the Virtuous Circle, the organization is continually monitoring whether the elements of diversity, inclusiveness, equity, purpose, and leadership remain aligned with the expectations of their stakeholders and are sufficiently vibrant to support the organization's transformation. This means checking in with stakeholders regularly to re-evaluate their needs and expectations and identify new requirements that may be emerging.

With this fresh stakeholder insight, leaders can assess whether the organization's strategic diversity narrative needs to be adapted, whether a shift from one stage of Diversity Performance to another is needed, and where gaps remain against the Virtuous Circle Five Stages framework (5VC) that need to be filled. This process usually results in updating the Strategic Diversity Roadmap to reflect new diversity capabilities that are required and new initiatives that need to be actioned.

Case Study: Sustaining the Virtuous Circle

Many organizations have had to evaluate the strength of their Virtuous Circle and their strategic diversity narrative during the pandemic. As explored in Chapter 2, COVID-19 has widened equity gaps everywhere, and its repercussions have been felt by organizations around the world. What does it mean to keep one's eye on diversity during times of acute change and how is the Virtuous Circle able to support that journey? Some executive search companies have leveraged the turbulent time of

COVID-19 to reinvent their business model and reinvent the way they have tapped into diversity of talent and thought for their clients and for their own transformation.

One of the major global executive search firms saw the direct impact of the pandemic on their employees, evidenced by increased stress, loneliness, and anxiety and their client organizations were reporting the same impacts.

This situation particularly affected women, who were experiencing a higher degree of mental health issues from having to juggle remote work and childcare.

At the same time, the shift to virtual work meant the organization had to change how it serviced its clients' recruitment processes. Jobseekers expected organizations to move from working solely at an office to a hybrid work environment, providing the flexibility to work from either home or office. Employees also expected organizations to take more responsibility for equity and help them deal with the impacts of the pandemic.

New qualities were also in demand among leaders for the post-COVID era. This included candor (honesty without ambiguity), fact-based communication, operating with empathy, having the ability to manage hybrid teams, being flexible and adaptable, humility (about uncertainty in a changing environment), and being active listeners.[11] Organizations were looking for a new breed of leaders who could communicate at ease with their employees and who created opportunities for dialog and connection with others.

Since many of these trends, including remote work, appeared to be a more permanent part of post-pandemic work life, the organization recognized it needed to revisit its strategic narrative for diversity. It abandoned the traditional model of matching the client specification to its candidate database to evaluate prospects, instead, fundamentally transforming its approach. It launched a digitally supported process, created a virtual meeting environment as well as an in-person experience for meetings between candidates and hiring organizations. It advised clients on new expectations for key roles (including inclusive leadership) and put emphasis on diversity teams rather than isolated diversity candidates. In its new strategic narrative, its aim was not only to help clients find diversity leaders, but to emulate the same approach within the organization to "walk the diversity talk."

▶   **Key takeaway** This organization understood that to be more inclusive to the needs of clients it needed to be more inclusive itself. It recognized that with remote working as the new normal, inclusive leadership capability was a differentiator, for itself and its clients. This meant pivoting the business model from specialists competing against one another to win client revenue to a collaborative model where diverse team solutions for clients could be found. As well as being a new differentiator, this changes the organization's purpose and diversity characteristics. By identifying long-term ingredients for agility, diversity of thought, and connection to customers, the organization positioned itself to emerge even stronger in the post-COVID-19 era.

---

[11] Brownlee (2020).

9   How to Celebrate and Sustain the Journey in Practice

What can be done in practice to revitalize and re-energize an organization's diversity journey? Depending on its Diversity Performance maturity level, the Integrated Diversity Model sets out a range of evidence-based initiatives that the organization can implement to reinvigorate its journey (Table 1).

10   Stage 1 Organizations: Legal Compliance

At Stage 1, the emphasis is on sustaining legal compliance. At this stage, the focus is not so much on celebrating diversity but on admitting or recruiting a certain level of diversity, incorporating diversity into the organization's own culture and satisfying various regulations. Sustaining activities will be triggered when new regulatory developments occur, and if new requirements need to be met.

11   Stage 2 Organizations: Stakeholder Requirements

At Stage 2, the primary focus moves from imprinting the organization's own culture onto new members, to being more welcoming to new members and recognizing different cultures and communities. At this stage, there are more celebratory

Table 1   Celebrate and Sustain Capability and Initiatives for the Five Stages
Overview of initiatives to highlight successes and build ongoing support at each stage of diversity maturity.

	Stage 1 Legal Compliance	Stage 2 Stakeholder Requirements	Stage 3 Organizational Performance	Stage 4 Reinvention	Stage 5 Societal Value
Focus	Meet legal obligations	Sharing with stakeholders Community building	Recognizing diversity accomplishments	Sustaining diversity journey Culture	Energizing further contribution to society
Skills	Legal reporting requirements	Stakeholder celebration events	Diversity events Cultural insights	Organization Celebrations	Partner gatherings
Process	Legal process	Stakeholder process	Performance process	Strategic process	Partner process
Responsibilities	Legal	HR Marketing	Diversity office D&I champions	All	Partner leaders Diversity council
Metrics	Legally reported	Stakeholder events Community events	Diversity celebrations	Culture celebration Values day	Societal days of celebration
Technology	Compliance	HR CRM	Event management	ERG platforms	Partner enablement

events around communities, acknowledging cultural heritage, celebrating International Women's Day, participating in Gay Pride, and providing a budget for ERGs to create community events. When ERGs are in place and well-established, they tend to play an important role in co-ordinating activities and organizing celebratory events. Sustaining activities are triggered around new requirements coming from stakeholders, mainly employees and customers.

12   Stage 3 Organizations: Organizational Performance

At Stage 3, the primary focus is to create the cultural dynamics to facilitate high-performance teams and create the values and behaviors that allow for seamless and productive interactions. Celebrations build on Stage 2 by creating celebratory events at the team level, often associated with the achievement of Diversity Performance outcomes by the team. D&I Champions are a critical part of sustaining the journey at this stage and may be appointed in each unit of the organization or even in each team. Sustaining activities are aligned to the strategic review process of the organization where business objectives are set. This triggers an assessment to evaluate how strategic performance goals affect team objectives and which diversity actions need to be supported.

13   Stage 4 Organizations: Reinvention

At Stage 4, the primary focus is to truly embrace diversity in all its forms. The organization seeks to recognize each member as a unique individual and creates celebratory events where employees develop more insight into and appreciation of others. This might involve holding lunches where members are invited to educate their colleagues by describing their cultural heritage or their unique specialization and/or congregating a community around important diversity themes. The organization celebrates events where the teams have contributed to key breakthroughs and where diversity is described and celebrated as a critical input. The Diversity Office, working with ERGs and D&I Champions, ensures continued focus on celebratory events. Sustaining activities for diversity are frequent and connected to strategic review processes, with the overall aim of supporting those diversity requirements that allow the organization to respond to its environment and continuously reinvent itself.

14   Stage 5 Organizations: Societal Value

At Stage 5, the priority is to shift from celebrating diversity internally to creating bridges to external partners and celebrating joint diversity successes within its value chain or sphere of influence. Here the organization makes use of Partner

Awards to recognize partners for exceptional diversity contributions. Sustaining activities are carried out with partners, usually through a Diversity Partner Council.

15   Concluding Remarks

As organizations work with the Virtuous Circle of diversity, inclusion, equity, purpose, and leadership, they recognize it as a reflection of the constantly changing environment around them. Sustaining the journey is about injecting adequate energy and resources and adjusting as needed in response to this external environment and evolving stakeholder requirements.

Through celebration, an organization acknowledges all the dedication, commitment, resources, and contributions that have brought them to this place, and that the outcomes achieved would not have been possible without these efforts. Celebration rekindles its own flame—renewing more energy for the next stage of the journey.

Sustaining the Virtuous Circle keeps leaders alert and continually attentive to their strategic narrative for diversity and how this needs to change and evolve over time. By keeping their vision firmly on sustaining the journey, there is a greater chance of success in delivering on diversity goals. This leads to more confidence which feeds Virtuous Circle and inspires the next successes that keep the flame burning for the diversity journey.

References

Brownlee, Dana, "7 Leadership Traits for the Post COVID-19 Workplace," *Forbes*, May 7, 2020, https://www.forbes.com/sites/danabrownlee/2020/05/07/7-leadership-traits-for-the-post-covid-19-workplace/?sh=1db5ecc22d4d.

Li, Wendi, "Cultural Diversity at Insead," *Financial Times*, October 4, 2010, https://www.ft.com/content/6a2f8ecd-a079-3666-84c4-e92aefe18f03.

Part IV
SYNTHESIS of the WHY, the WHAT and the HOW

SYNTHESIS of the WHY, the WHAT and the HOW

Understand Stakeholder Expectations

What do my stakeholders expect of me?

Understand Diversity Performance

What are the key elements and stages of Diversity Performance?

Measure the Diversity Performance Gap

3 steps to improve Diversity Performance

Map the Performance Gap

Close my Diversity Performance Capability Gaps

Which initiatives do I need to put in place to achieve my desired future level of Diversity Perfomance?

Craft my Future Diversity Narrative

What is my desired future level of Diversity Performance?

Capture my Current Diversity Narrative

What is my organization's existing level of Diversity Performance?

PERFORMANCE AND CAPABILITY ROADMAP

Build the 6 Key Diversity Capabilities

- Mitigate Bias
- Build Case
- Embed Behaviors
- Harness Policies
- Measure and Monitor
- Celebrate and Sustain

Compare my Diversity Narratives

What is the gap between my current and desired Diversity Performance?

Close the Capability Gap

Develop my Strategic Roadmap to close the gaps

Where are my biggest Capability Gaps?

Understand my Current Diversity Capabilities

Which capabilities do I currently have in place?

Understand my Future Diversity Capability Needs

Which capabilities do I need to achieve my chosen future level of Diversity Performance?

Measure the Diversity Capability Gap

3 steps to improve Diversity Capability

Conclusion: Transformation Through Perseverance

12

The story of the Springboks is a chronicle of courageous leadership, transformation, and perseverance. It marks an intergenerational shift, set in motion by Nelson Mandela that is still underway today (Fig. 1).

Whether it is a national rugby team or a global organization, diversity is about being asked to be part of the team, but it does not end there. Inclusion is about having the opportunity to play, versus sitting on the bench. Equity is the recognition that players have had historically uneven access to training and resources and providing access to these resources to liberate talent. Leadership is setting out the unifying intent, promoting healing, and creating the bridges that build trust with the team. And the purpose is the rousing call to action that connects the team with its stakeholders and unifies them all around a higher goal.

The Springboks' 1995 World Cup—captured in the film "Invictus"—and the transformation that has followed mirrors the Diversity Performance approach presented in this book. Yet the story of the Springboks should not be seen as a fairytale. There was no magic wand and a "happy ever after." Their story exemplifies the journey of diversity in an organization and its broader societal context. It is an ongoing journey that requires stamina. It involves taking steps forward and then a step back, while keeping eyes trained on the all-important end-goal of inclusivity. At the outset is a courageous leader who personally believes in and is committed to diversity and harnesses this energy to inspire action. On every journey, there will be cynics and diversity capability gaps, and the approach will need to be adapted and re-designed to take into account changing contexts and new requirements.

The Springbok win in 2007 was another critical milestone and celebration on this road. But 2006 brought consternation when, between June and August, the Springboks lost four internationals in a row, including a 0–49 loss against Australia. This marked only the second time in South Africa's proud 100-year rugby history that its Test side has been left scoreless and was its second biggest loss

© Diversity and Performance BV 2021
K. Formanek, *Beyond D&I*, https://doi.org/10.1007/978-3-030-75336-8_12

Fig. 1   Transformation through Perseverance
The Transformation of the Springbok Team.

ever: their performance was described as "bumbling and ill-disciplined" as they
made a "litany of elementary errors."[1] When summoned to account for this poor
performance, the reason given by the coach was "because of transformation"—a
reference to the organization's goals to address the lack of Black South African
player representation on the squad.

It would have been easy at this point to abandon the path to diversity, but that is
not what happened. In 2015 there was further criticism and dismay. The Springbok
line-up had been 18% Black South African players in 2014 but in 2015 diversity
dipped once again. Chester Williams, who had made history in 2004 as the first
Black South African player, stated "They give a Black player a chance but then
they don't give him another chance to get better. At this stage they give a Black
player one opportunity and if he doesn't make it he doesn't play again. Clearly

---

[1] "Wallabies thrash Springboks 49-0," *The Sydney Morning Herald*, July 16, 2006, https://www.
smh.com.au/sport/wallabies-thrash-springboks-49-0-20060716-gdnz12.html.

we can't only have two Black players in the Springbok team. It's unacceptable."[2] COSATU (Congress of South African Trade Unions), an influential ally of the late Mandela's governing African National Congress (ANC), warned that Springbok shirts would be burned in protest if "the government allows the old rugby mafia to control a national sport for their own interest."[3]

A 2015–2019 transformation plan was therefore put in place with the aim of non-whites making up half of all domestic and national teams by 2019. It was acknowledged by the Rugby body that change had to take place from the ground up, starting at school and club level, with particular attention to the questions of equity, equality, excellence, access, organizational culture, and good corporate governance. With this additional focus and clear KPIs and targets, some key transformational goals were met, and in 2019, for the first time, a Black South African Captain led a squad with 40% Black South African players to victory.

Yet the Springboks journey is still not complete. A recent assessment of the 2015 to 2019 Transformation Plan acknowledged that, while much has been done, there still is much to be done at grassroots, including improving access to assets. Now a new Transformation Plan to 2030 has been adopted, renewing and extending the code's commitment to develop a sustainable pipeline of talent from school level upwards.

So a quarter of a century after that great symbolic victory back in 1995, when Mandela took the first crucial steps toward unity, the Springboks now have a clear diversity and inclusion pathway to 2030. There are powerful lessons we can take from this journey to guide the diversity leader on their own journey.

1   Understanding Expectations

Mandela had a dream of uniting a nation. The way to ensure prosperity and cohesion in South Africa was to embrace the power in diversity of a rainbow nation. In his speech as the first Black president of South Africa he declared: "The time for the healing of wounds has come, the time to bridge the chasms that divide us has come, and the time to build is upon us."[4] He knew that this was what South Africans needed—and what the world wanted—and he realized this could be kickstarted through sport.

Traditionally an Afrikaner sport, rugby in South Africa had been segregated and was a stark symbol of racial division that had seen "Black people cheering

---

[2] Smith (2015).

[3] Smith, David. "Lack of black players in South Africa team puts race under spotlight before World Cup".

[4] Inaugural Speech, Pretoria [Mandela]—5/10/94, University of Pennsylvania African Studies Center, May 11, 1994. https://www.africa.upenn.edu/Articles_Gen/Inaugural_Speech_17984.html.

for the opposition."[5] There was a clear opportunity to unite team, spectators, and the nation under the slogan "one team, one country." There was the opportunity to "make real and substantial changes and to change the sport which had largely been the standard-bearer of apartheid into the standard-bearer of the new democracy."[6]

When the Springboks won the final against New Zealand and celebrations broke out across South Africa, an entire people stormed onto the streets to celebrate. All appreciated the historic significance of the moment which set in motion a legacy that is still alive today.

> Leaders set out a vision that unifies all members of the organization and its stakeholders.

2   Setting the Desired Level of Performance

A national team should reflect the nation. For South African rugby to become a nationally representative sport, the line-up and very identity of the Springboks had to radically change. This was not something that could be achieved overnight. It would be a multi-year effort and it would require a deliberate and carefully monitored strategy, with clear milestones, and an eye on future performance. In the SA Rugby Strategic Transformation Development Plan 2030 (STDP2030) this future vision is set out and the future state is defined as one of equality of opportunity. A Strategic Roadmap is defined and targets key pillars, including providing equitable access to structured and organized rugby participation at school and club level; creating prospects for provincial and national representation; and developing and improving skill and capability. This Roadmap is underpinned by demographic representation, including 60% generic Black (black African, Coloured and Indian representation) with the ultimate goal of creating "a sport demographic profile in line with the national population demographic."[7]

> "Transformation is about the soul of the nation," the plan states, "correctly defined and utilized [it] is a powerful tool not only to correct injustices of the past but also to establish a sustainable competitive advantage."[8]

---

[5] Smith (2013).

[6] Heagney (2020).

[7] Strategic Transformation Development Plan 2030, South Africa Rugby Union. https://www.sarugby.co.za/media/q03hxfmw/strategic-transformation-development-plan-2030-cycle-1.pdf.

[8] Strategic Transformation Development Plan 2030, South Africa Rugby Union. https://www.sarugby.co.za/media/q03hxfmw/strategic-transformation-development-plan-2030-cycle-1.pdf.

> Leaders support their future vision with a strategic narrative that defines Diversity Performance objectives, sets out clear strategic goals and a roadmap to deliver on them.

3   Understanding the Current State

In 1995, only one person of color, Chester Williams, was in the team that played in the final against New Zealand. Later, he would reveal that he felt an outsider and was uncomfortable with his own commodification as a poster-boy for black South Africans, seeing his image promoted as the change that still had a long way to go in substance. "All I wanted," he told *The Economist* in 2019, "was an opportunity so that I can prove to the world that Black people can also play rugby."[9]

SA Rugby has come a long way since then. In 2014, the Springboks averaged just 18% Black South African player representation: by 2018 this had risen to 39%.[10] After 127 years of whites captaining the green and gold, Siya Kolisi became the first Black South African Test skipper in 2018 and it was a team fielding six Black South African players that claimed victory in the 2019 World Cup in Japan.

Yet the diversity journey is far from over. Representation, both on and off the field of play, continues to be a problem area for National and Provincial Male teams and Boards, where SA Rugby acknowledges it is still "far away" from its 2019 Strategic Transformation Plan targets.[11] As a result, following an "as-is" analysis, its STDP2030 sets out a "catch-up strategy" for under-developed areas—including, for example, equitable resource distribution, elimination of inequalities, increased access to participation opportunities and skills, and capability development.

> Leaders capture the current state of diversity and set baselines to enable existing performance to be benchmarked against the future diversity vision.

4   Closing the Performance Gap

When it comes to diversity transformation, deep change takes time. It makes sense to start with the development and focus area that will raise diversity the most. Closing the performance gap cannot be opportunistic and needs to be deliberate and additive, otherwise entropy sets in.

---

[9] Linde (2021).

[10] Strategic Transformation Development Plan 2030, South Africa Rugby Union. https://www.sarugby.co.za/media/q03hxfmw/strategic-transformation-development-plan-2030-cycle-1.pdf.

[11] Strategic Transformation Development Plan 2030, South Africa Rugby Union. https://www.sarugby.co.za/media/q03hxfmw/strategic-transformation-development-plan-2030-cycle-1.pdf.

For example, STDP2030 sets out six key focus areas where SA Rugby intends to close the Diversity Performance gap: Access to the game; Skills and Capacity Development; Demographic Representation; Performance; Community Development and Social Responsibility; and Corporate Governance. Each focus area is underpinned by Key Performance Indicators (KPIs), such as "increasing accessibility amongst women and designed groups to become referees," and this has been paired with clear outputs—for example, "launch a campaign to recruit women referees; focus recruitment on designated groups; and establish educator and coaching systems in every referee society."

With a clear understanding of the gap to be closed between the current baseline and the future vision, the leader can set about building the key diversity capabilities needed to close the performance gap.

> From their current baseline, leaders develop a strategic roadmap to address their biggest performance gaps, underpinning each outcome area with meaningful KPIs.

5   Building Key Diversity Capabilities

The six diversity capabilities of the Integrated Diversity Model support and enable the diversity journey.

1. **Mitigate Bias**—Tackling bias is at its essence about rewiring mindsets and beliefs and the Springboks emblem is a dramatic example of what happens when bias is overcome.

Prior to 1995, rugby had been a game played predominantly by Afrikaners—it was their pride. Black South Africans preferred football, in fact, there was a communicated hatred for rugby: rugby was a "white sport" and would not be supported by the nation. Following the 1994 election, there was intense debate about the right of the Springboks to exist alongside democracy. When efforts were made to drop the Springboks name, emblem, and colors after he came to power, Mandela intervened. He argued that taking away things that were dear to Afrikaners' hearts would only increase their insecurity and come in the way of building a rainbow nation. He convinced those opposed to the Springbok emblem that it had a place in the future of the country and could hold for the new generation of South Africans a different meaning.

Saving the Springbok symbol became about transforming its meaning and this transformation occurred when the Springboks won and Mandela strode out, attired in the team colors and cap, to present the trophy to Pienaar. That day the Springboks stopped being the property of Afrikaners and became South Africa's pride.[12]

---

[12] Maghavan (2019).

The next bias that needed to be overturned was the default thinking that to play rugby well, you needed to be a typical white player. This was challenged when Diversity Performance proved it wrong—namely the 2019 win under the captainship of Siya Kolisi with a multiracial squad.

> Leaders acknowledge the presence of mindsets, bias and beliefs and, where helpful, rewire and repurpose these so they do not stand in the way of Diversity Performance.

2. **Build the case for diversity**—The diversity leader creates a unifying call to action and makes a strong case. Mandela advocated two key diversity cases: the societal case (enabling healing, unifying the country) and a performance case (the intention to win). These connected cases allowed Mandela to navigate important and challenging topics. His strategic goal was to unite a nation with a difficult and fractured past behind a common team, to promote healing. An additional and connected goal was for the Springboks to perform and win. The better the performance, likely the better the healing—and as it happened, this was indeed the case.

These same societal and performance cases continue to drive modification and improvement of the team today. As the STDP2030 states: "Transformation, correctly defined and utilized, is a powerful tool not only to correct injustices of the past but also to establish a sustainable competitive advantage targeted at enhancing overall competitiveness internationally."[13]

> Leaders set out a clear case for diversity, connected to strategic goals and the wider imperatives of the organization and its stakeholders.

3. **Embed Behaviors**—Leaders walk the talk by demonstrating inclusive behaviors. The trust between Mandela and Pienaar, between Pienaar and the players, was made possible by values-based actions. As Pienaar said, the life lesson he learnt from Mandela is that "good leadership is based on good values."[14] After his meeting with Mandela, prior to the 1995 final, Pienaar

---

[13] Strategic Transformation Development Plan 2030, South Africa Rugby Union. https://www.sarugby.co.za/media/q03hxfmw/strategic-transformation-development-plan-2030-cycle-1.pdf.

[14] Smith, "Francois Pienaar."

admitted: "I was so nervous before I went into his office and when I left, I sat in my car and just felt that I had been in the presence of a very wise and caring man and I felt safe."

Diversity leaders check up on their team. During their final pre-World Cup training session at a sports field in Cape Town, Mandela visited the Springboks to wish the awestruck young men well. Not only did he set out his intent and engage "his captain," he also busied himself with the preparation, morale, and performance of the team.

Mandela's values and behavior were a source of inspiration to the team. After their surprise win over Australia, they visited Robben Island. "I was very emotional when I walked into Mr Mandela's cell," Francois Pienaar admitted, "I was the last to walk in when we visited Robben Island. And you realize how incredible it is. That place is so small and he was there for 17 years. Yet he comes out and he has forgiveness in his heart, he has compassion and selflessness. He gave so much. But I would say 'genuine' is the one word I would use. He's real. There is no act."[15]

> Leaders drive the diversity change they aspire to and are an authentic and inclusive voice for transformation.

---

4. **Harness Policies**—The diversity leader puts in motion policies and actions to "operationalize" diversity. The appointment of former Springbok rugby captain Morné du Plessis, for example, as manager on the eve of the 1995 World Cup, was symbolic for the new Springboks. One of the few apartheid-era players sensitive to the inequity of the system, he had voiced his understanding of the rationale behind the sporting boycott and his appointment was important in enhancing the image of SA rugby. Together with the Springboks Captain, Francois Pienaar, who was friendly, accessible, articulate, and enjoyed a good relationship with President Mandela, this was important for building bridges.

At the national level, the Broad-Based Black Economic Empowerment (B-BBEE) Amendment Act of 2014 sought to promote the achievement of the right to equality, increase broad-based and effective participation of Black South African people in the economy and promote equal opportunity and equal access. Being B-BBEE compliant is not only a regulatory requirement, but is now also a requirement for sponsors and industry bodies who wish to do business with SA Rugby.[16]

---

[15] Smit (2019).

[16] Strategic Transformation Development Plan 2030, South Africa Rugby Union. https://www.sarugby.co.za/media/q03hxfmw/strategic-transformation-development-plan-2030-cycle-1.pdf.

Rather than a multitude of policies and initiatives, effective performance depends on having the right, targeted policies and initiatives, with a regular review process to ensure they are delivering.

> Leaders carefully select the right policies to operationalize the diversity change they want to see.

5. **Measure and Monitor**—As stated in SA Rugby's STDP2030, "if you can't measure something, and know the results, you can't possibly get better at it."[17] The organization had a clear objective of increasing representation in rugby over the period 2015 to 2019 and to drive this, incremental targets were set for team demographics from 30% generic black in 2015, rising by five percent each year to reach 50% by 2019.

The strategic transformation plan (2015–2019) was assessed to monitor progress and evaluate whether the diversity transformation journey was on course. Detailed performance metrics are collected for all levels of rugby, including the Springboks, against these targets. The composition of Presidents of Unions, Board Members, pipelines, coaches, referees, medical and scientific specialists is also reported, right down to school rugby participation. This data is made available internally via a "Footprint and E-Filing system" that provides a real-time dashboard for the Strategic Performance Management department to monitor achievement against its targets.

When measurement is strategic, integrated, comprehensive, and relevant, it allows the organization to keep a close eye on progress and correct course when needed.

> Leaders have clear strategic goals that are cascaded through supporting measures and KPIs that enable the organization to know if it is achieving its diversity objectives.

6. **Celebrate and Sustain**—Diversity journeys have to be energized and revitalized to make important statements and maintain momentum, and rituals and celebrations have an important part to play in this.

In the lead up to the 1994 World Cup, the Springboks needed to demonstrate that they were humble, excited, and proud of their new democracy. To mark the occasion, they all learned the words of the "new" part of the national anthem, "*Nkosi Sikeleli: Africa*," in addition to the "old" "*Die Stem*" part that they already knew, which many South Africans associated with the apartheid order. It was a strong symbolic gesture of unity.

---

[17] Strategic Transformation Development Plan 2030, South Africa Rugby Union. https://www.sarugby.co.za/media/q03hxfmw/strategic-transformation-development-plan-2030-cycle-1.pdf.

A diversity leader gives thanks and celebrates what has been achieved to sustain success. As Mandela walked onto the field to present the trophy to the South African captain, Francois Pienaar, the two men exchanged a warm smile. Almost in unison they spoke exactly the same words: "Francois, thank you for what you've done for this country"—"Mr. President, thank you for what you've done for this country."

Diversity journeys require energy and stamina that comes from celebrating successes, sharing progress, and tapping into grassroots support.

> Leaders take the time to acknowledge important moments and milestones on the diversity journey and empower those around them to keep the flame alive.

6 The Final Step: Empowering Successors

Nelson Mandela, Francois Pienaar, and Siya Kolisi are all examples of courageous and transformational leaders united by the bigger goal of unifying the diverse people of a nation. Successful diversity and inclusion is a journey that has to be planned, managed, and resourced. It requires capable and inspirational leaders with vision and determination who in turn inspire other champions to continue to drive progress toward shared and cherished diversity goals.

The journey of diversity leadership is a never-ending one. As SA Rugby's STDP2030 affirms, "The bar of excellence rises inexorably. We need to be more effective and creative in developing strategies, practices, processes, talent, and skills that will make us winners in a hyper-competitive world."[18] Ultimately this is a journey that is not about a single organization—and the transformation of South African rugby is part of the wider "longer term transformational goal of an accessible, equitable, sustainable, competitive and demographically representative sport system."[19]

As the Springboks story shows, when teams are united through diversity, everyone wins. Wherever the organization is on its diversity journey, there is real value to be found in approaching diversity and inclusion strategically. The models in this book set out a pathway that every leader can follow to achieve this. With the vision, the commitment and the right capabilities, every organization can be a diversity leader.

* * *

---

[18] Strategic Transformation Development Plan 2030, South Africa Rugby Union. https://www.sarugby.co.za/media/q03hxfmw/strategic-transformation-development-plan-2030-cycle-1.pdf.

[19] Strategic Transformation Development Plan 2030, South Africa Rugby Union. https://www.sarugby.co.za/media/q03hxfmw/strategic-transformation-development-plan-2030-cycle-1.pdf.

References

Smith, David. "Lack of black players in South Africa team puts race under spotlight before World Cup," *The Guardian*, August 13, 2015. https://www.theguardian.com/sport/blog/2015/aug/13/south-africa-racism-rugby-world-cup-heyneke-meyer.

Smith, David. "Francois Pienaar: 'When the whistle blew, South Africa changed forever'," *The Guardian*, Dec 8, 2013. https://www.theguardian.com/world/2013/dec/08/nelson-mandela-francois-pienaar-rugby-world-cup.

Heagney, Liam. "The uncomfortable truth about the Springboks 1995 RWC win, told by the man who ushered in racial quotas," *RugbyPass*, May 24, 2020. https://www.rugbypass.com/news/it-was-a-when-they-shot-kennedy-moment-most-south-africans-will-remember-what-they-were-doing-griffiths-springboks/.

Linde, Daniel. "Chester Williams: pioneer of excellence," *Africa Is a Country*, accessed September 10, 2021. https://africasacountry.com/2019/11/a-pioneer-of-excellence.

Maghavan, N. "Invictus: how Nelson Mandela Used Rugby to unite South Africa," *The Hindu BusinessLine*, November 3, 2019. https://www.thehindubusinessline.com/news/sports/invictus-how-nelson-mandela-used-rugby-to-unite-south-africa/article29870024.ece

Smith, Andrew. "Interview: Francois Pienaar on his debt to Mandela, winning the World Cup and sport's ability to transform lives," *The Scotsman*, October 11, 2019. https://www.scotsman.com/sport/interview-francois-pienaar-his-debt-mandela-winning-world-cup-and-sports-ability-transform-lives-1405399

Afterword

Looking Forward—Beyond D&I

There is no more important ingredient for the wellbeing of our world, its organizations, and its people than embracing our diversity.

Diversity in its full sense is not the sum of a person's characteristics, an organization's metrics, or a society's social justice commitments. Diversity constitutes the web of life, on land and in the ocean. It is the lifeblood of healthy ecosystems. Just as biodiversity boosts ecosystem productivity, so does human diversity enhance the performance of organizations. In the same way that rich biodiversity supports sustainability and interdependence among all forms of life, diversity results in greater agility, future-readiness, and resilience of organizations. Healthy ecosystems can better withstand and recover from a variety of disasters, and diversity in organizations facilitates recovery from shocks such as global pandemics or financial collapse. The rich biodiversity of our planet is mirrored by the astonishing diversity of talent and perspective in society, of different colors, creeds, ages, preferences, identities and abilities, each and every individual truly unique. Embraced by organizations, this diversity can unleash performance such as creativity, wellness, and productivity.

To thrive, ecosystems and biodiversity require balance. When an ecosystem bears the onslaught of pollution, overfishing, or neglect, this balance is threatened and requires intervention and restoration. Diversity in organizations also requires the caring hand of leaders to stay in balance and flourish as an integral part of the organization's culture. This balance arises when leaders are committed, when they understand the strategic benefit of diversity on performance and when they put in place the conditions for diversity to thrive.

It is through the everyday words, actions, and gestures between people, in organizations, that diversity is nurtured. When we nurture it consciously in our organizations, society as a whole becomes better. The systemic inequalities and inequities that persist—racism, discrimination, denial of the right to use one's talents or of access to jobs and opportunities—are collectively diminished when organizations confront these head-on. When every organization does this, soci-

© Diversity and Performance BV 2021
K. Formanek, *Beyond D&I*, https://doi.org/10.1007/978-3-030-75336-8

ety as a whole changes. Leaders have the power and the opportunity to steer this change, and they need to resolve to stay the course to ensure diversity gains are not reversed.

Crisis as a Catalyst for Change

COVID-19 has been a systemic shock that threatens to undermine diversity investments diligently built up over many years. It is minority groups that are being hit the worst. Beyond being a public health crisis, the pandemic has had a devastating impact on poverty levels and inequality. As so often occurs, it is women, the poor, the elderly, the disabled, LGBTQI+ communities, and migrant populations who have borne the brunt of the fallout from the pandemic—at work and elsewhere. As we recover, this is the moment for every organization, regardless of the stage of its diversity journey, to recognize that we all share the ethical and societal case for diversity. A global crisis is a collective challenge to our societal ecosystem which calls for a collective answer.

In considering the impact of COVID-19 on diversity progress there are important lessons we can learn from past challenges. Chief among these is that organizations that use this period of turmoil to invest in their talent pool will be better placed to weather future storms. In 2008–2009, at the heart of one of the most significant global financial crises, organizations scrambled to survive. Often at these moments, strategic, long-term priorities suffer. Yet when leaders were asked to evaluate the organizational dimensions most critical to emerging from the crisis, the majority named leadership and talent as critical enablers for recovery.

Organizations that ramp up their focus and invest strategically to support Diversity Performance today, will benefit from strong talent and leadership tomorrow. Looking to the future, a number of change waves are rapidly approaching that will require organizations to be healthy, resilient and agile in navigating the inevitable disruptions ahead.

Six Reasons to Invest in Diversity for Greater Resilience

Strengthening Diversity Performance for greater business resilience should now be on every leader's radar. There are six compelling reasons for investing in diversity as we emerge from the pandemic:

1. **Leveraging the new-normal of remote working**—Pandemic lockdowns saw teams working digitally from home as never before. While for some the ability to work virtually has brought the benefits of flexibility and greater work-life balance, for others—particularly some minority groups—it has accentuated overload, mental health issues, and a sense of isolation. Leaders will need to critically evaluate and design how work is executed in a way that enables diversity and inclusion in a virtual environment, while supporting those unfairly or disproportionately impacted due to parental or other responsibilities.

2. **Many more #MeToo's**—The pandemic has heightened the global gap between the richest and the poorest, while digital connectivity and societal outrage over longstanding inequalities have strengthened. Societal movements for greater equity and equality are here to stay, with their accompanying manifestations of social protest and upheaval. Organizations will need to anticipate how they respond to such movements and consider how they can reflect evolving stakeholder expectations in their own strategic diversity narratives. Given continued bias against people with disabilities, a #metoo movement for this demographic is long overdue.

3. **A magnifying glass on discrimination**—Recent years have seen a rash of headlines about prominent people from every sector of society being forced to apologize or resign from high-level positions after exhibiting sexist, racist, or other biased behavior. Leaders must become attuned to what may be construed on the global stage as highly biased statements or behaviors, reflect on their own biases and consider carefully how they communicate. In an environment where the leader's voice is easily captured and amplified to a global audience by social media, biased statements can spell disaster not only for the leader, but the organization.

4. **The pervasive role of Artificial Intelligence (AI)**—With Internet search prediction, digital voice assistants, online banking, traffic monitoring, and more, AI will increasingly allow organizations to manage customer relationships, predict consumer preferences, simplify hiring and talent management and make processes more efficient. But if this AI is founded on biased thinking and discriminatory algorithms, it will reinforce and increase inequities. Simply automating biased processes and replicating biased decision-making will not advance diversity of thought or yield better business results. To minimize this risk, organizations must deliberately de-bias processes and prevent bias from being designed into AI tools and decision-making.

5. **Mass automation of jobs**—Those who are already vulnerable—women, LGBTQI+ people, those with disabilities and people of color—are the same people who tend to predominate in jobs most at risk of being automated. Organizations need to take a long-term perspective and conduct scenario analysis to understand how diversity of talent will be impacted by automation and proactively support the reskilling of minority groups.

6. **Linking organizational goals to Agenda 2030**—The UN Sustainable Development Goals are an open invitation for organizations to contribute to solving the world's greatest global challenges—including the pursuit of diversity, equity, and inclusion. These goals offer an opportunity to gain a richer understanding of how to create value for all stakeholders. As the decade of action on the SDGs accelerates, organizations from businesses to non-profits and local and national governments will increasingly be measured by the contribution they make to the SDGs. Already, some are incorporating the goals into their diversity charter commitments, and the call for organizations to demonstrate how they contribute will only increase.

Leading Diversity with Confidence and Courage

Leading diversity can be incredibly rewarding. By harnessing the five elements of diversity, inclusion, equity, leadership and purpose, the organization has the key ingredients for Diversity Performance and the lens to ensure that it remains in tune with the issues stakeholders increasingly place value on.

The potential is enormous when the five elements augment performance in a virtuous and sustainable way. This is good for the leader, good for the organization, and good for society.

There is no one-size-fits-all approach to diversity. Yet a universal truth is that we are all part of society—our human ecosystem—and when this comes into balance, we all benefit.

It is my hope that this book supports all leaders on the diversity journey and that the tools and insights it shares give you the courage, confidence, and strength of purpose to realize your diversity vision.

Glossary

Acquired diversity: Involves traits that an individual gains from life experience, work experience, specialization, and cultural appreciation.

Ageism: Stereotyping and discrimination against individuals or groups on the basis of their age.

Business case: This case for diversity is built on identifying and satisfying the diversity requirements (inherent and/or acquired characteristics) that are linked directly or indirectly to organizational performance such as enhanced financial performance, innovation, engagement, supply of scarce talent, customer satisfaction, etc.

Cognitive diversity: Diversity of thought leading to different styles of problem-solving and often leading to unique perspectives and breakthrough thinking arising from multifaceted views being applied. The opposite of "groupthink."

Core capability: A capability that provides an organization with a competitive and differentiated ability to survive in a complex world while delivering on its mandate.

Cultural entropy: The amount of energy consumed in doing unproductive or unnecessary work, as a result of dysfunction (friction and frustration) in an organization that is generated by self-serving or fear-based actions of leaders.

Customer congruence: When what is provided, promised to, and received by the customer matches what the customer sees to be their desired or actual self.

Disability: Can include long-term physical, mental, intellectual, or sensory impairments which, in interaction with various attitudinal and environmental barriers, hinders their full and effective participation in society on an equal basis with others.

Diversity: The sum of the traits and characteristics, inherent and acquired, that make a person unique relative to their fellow individuals/others.

Diversity performance: Organizational performance and outcomes that are directly linked to the presence of the five Elements of diversity represented in the Virtuous Circle: diversity (inherent and acquired characteristics), inclusion, equity, leadership, and purpose (strategic narrative and rationale for diversity).

Diversity performance gap: The gap between the current and aspirational strategic narrative as defined in terms of current and desired Diversity Performance.

Diversity performance stage: The third evolutionary stage of Diversity Performance where the primary focus is on supporting organizational outcomes such as increased financial performance, innovation, engagement of employees, customer congruence and loyalty, etc.

Effectiveness: The extent to which an intervention works when applied to the real world.

Efficacy: The extent to which an intervention can work under ideal circumstances.

Embed behavior capability: One of six diversity capabilities required to support Diversity Performance. For organizations at Stage 4 and 5, who elevate the Embed Behavior capability into a core capability, it is then referred to by the industry name "Inclusive Leadership core capability." At this level, Inclusive Leadership is regarded as a differentiating capability for the organization, leading to more competitiveness and greater agility.

Entropy: Organizational entropy is a measure of the level of disorder or uncertainty in a closed system or process. The higher the level of disorder, the greater the degree of organizational inefficiency.

Equity: The recognition that individuals have had unequal access to resources through societal, institutional, and personal bias practices that have limited their full participation. Equity enables their full access to resources by acknowledging the specific needs of historically prejudiced groups/individuals.

Ethical case: This case for diversity is built on satisfying moral considerations, such the responsibility to support the universal right of people to enjoy work and be fairly treated, without discrimination.

Explicit bias: The attitudes and beliefs that we have about a person or group on a *conscious* level and evidenced in discriminatory practices such as deliberate racial slurs, hate speech, and intentionally treating people differently.

Five stages: The five evolutionary stages of Diversity Performance in an organization: Legal Compliance, Stakeholder Requirements, Organizational Performance, Reinvention, and Societal Value.

Hidden disability: Disability that may not be immediately obvious such as autism, diabetes, Chronic Fatigue Syndrome, or mental health conditions, etc.

Heterogeneous: Diverse in character or content.

Heterogeneous teams: Sometimes called mixed or diverse teams, comprised of a variety of inherent and acquired diversity characteristics, as required for the stage of Diversity Performance set out in as strategic narrative.

Homogeneous: Of the same kind, similar or alike.

Homogeneous teams: A team where the group members have similar traits, characteristics and norms often leading to a less diverse orientation or "groupthink."

Implicit bias: Occurs when our social behavior is influenced by *unconscious* associations and judgements and affects understanding, actions, and decisions in an unconscious way, making them difficult to control. This may lead to certain characteristics and qualities being attributed to all members of a group, e.g., "stereotyping."

Inclusion: The actions, norms, practices, and behaviors that create an organizational environment where each unique individual is able to contribute fully to the organization's purpose, through the presence of a safe environment where individuals are treated fairly and respectfully, with recognition of their specific needs.

Inclusive leadership core capability: The industry name for the Embed Behavior capability once it has been elevated into a core capability and differentiating factor leading to more competitiveness and greater agility for an organization— usually those who are at Stage 4 and 5. It is one of six diversity capabilities required to support Diversity Performance.

Inclusiveness: Within organizations, inclusiveness refers to a desired culture and philosophy that encompasses the hallmarks of equity and the practices of inclusion. Inclusiveness results from a combination of values, behaviors and practices.

Inherited diversity: Involves characteristics an individual is born with, such as gender, ethnicity, physical disabilities or sexual orientation.

Intersectionality: Overlapping social categorizations, such as gender, race, class, often leading to a multiplicity of discrimination or disadvantage.

Intersecting identities: When an individual's identity consists of multiple, intersecting factors such as gender, race, ethnicity, class, etc.

Lagging indicator: A lagging indicator is an output measurement, for example, the percentage of women in executive roles.

Leadership: The values, behaviors, practices, and actions of the most senior members of an organization in gathering the diversity characteristics required to deliver on its purpose and goals and create a safe, inclusive, and equitable environment where all people are engaged to support the purpose.

Leading indicator: A leading indicator is a predictive measurement, for example, the balance of women and men on a recruiting slate influencing how many women will be invited to have a recruitment interview.

Legal case: This diversity case is built on satisfying legal diversity requirements, such as quotas, affirmative action, minimum representation, etc., such that there are no legal compliance issues and penalties that would result in a financial sanction.

Legal compliance stage: The first evolutionary stage of Diversity Performance where the primary focus of diversity is to satisfy legal requirements such as quotas, and avoid legal sanctions.

LGBTQI+: Individuals who identify as lesbian, gay, bisexual, transgender, queer, intersex, and other.

Minority: A culturally, or demographically distinct group that coexists with, but is subordinate to, a more dominant group.

Out-group: A social group with which an individual does not identify. People may for example not identify with a specific cultural or ethnic group or a group of people in an organization who share similarities that are different to the dominant group in the organization.

Personal bias: The bias that we have individually, which can be either explicit or implicit.

Purpose: The motivating force that inspires and connects stakeholders to deliver a shared vision for diversity. How diversity intersects with the organization's reason for being and why it exists.

Racism: A belief that one group is superior to others because of the color of their skin or ethnicity.

Reinvention stage: The fourth evolutionary stage of Diversity Performance where the primary focus is on creating the capability of the organization to continually transform in response to the changing environment and evolving stakeholder requirements. The Reinvention Stage seeks to gather diversity traits and characteristics that together allow for innovation and agility and resilience of the organization.

Societal case: This diversity case is built on the responsibility of organizations to support broader social cohesion and equality. Many organizations build this case on their ability to support the achievement of the UN's 2030 Agenda by connecting diversity to one or more SDGs.

Societal value: The fifth and the last evolutionary stage of Diversity Performance. Here the organization is focused on leveraging their Diversity Performance to support societal goals and create stakeholder value, e.g.,by contributing to the achievement of the SDGs.

Stakeholder requirement stage: The second evolutionary stage of Diversity Performance where the primary focus of diversity is to satisfy the expectations of key stakeholders, The second evolutionary stage of Diversity Performance where the primary focus of diversity is to satisfy the expectations of key stakeholders, specifically employees and customers, and avoid stakeholder penalties like boycotts, absenteeism, or brand damage.

Stereotyping: Making generalizations about personal characteristics of a group of people or ascribing collective characteristics associated with a particular group to every member of that group, discounting individual attributes.

Stereotype threat: Concerns about confirming negative stereotypes in the workplace.

Strategic (Diversity) Narrative—Current: Captures the current rationale for diversity within an organization and describes the existing state of each Diversity Performance element: performance, inclusion, equity, leadership, and purpose.

Strategic (Diversity) Narrative—Future: The vision and rationale for where diversity fits within the organization's transformation and value creation journey. It reminds all stakeholders why the desired state of diversity is critical to the longevity and sustainability of the organization. It crystallizes the diversity characteristics, inclusion, equity, leadership, and purpose that are the right fit for the organization within its context. And it serves as an anchor for the organization's diversity mandate, unifying the organization around a shared statement of intent for Diversity Performance.

Strategic narrative: An organization's rationale for diversity, that sets the future aspiration for Diversity Performance.

Systemic bias: The inherent tendency of a system and its processes, policies, and protocols to support a particular outcome. This can be in society or within organizations or institutions. In society, we see systemic bias when societal processes support an advantage for a specific group and disadvantage another group.

Virtuous Circle: The first core model in *Beyond D&I*, comprising the five elements of Diversity Performance: diversity, inclusion, equity, leadership, and purpose. The Circle is virtuous because the elements reinforce each other through a positive feedback loop, yielding Diversity Performance.

Virtuous Circle Five Stage Framework: The five elements of the Virtuous Circle each described for the five evolutionary stages of Diversity Performance. Also 5VC.

Index

© Diversity and Performance BV 2021
K. Formanek, *Beyond D&I*, https://doi.org/10.1007/978-3-030-75336-8